PSYCHO-POLITICAL ASPECTS OF SUICIDE WARRIORS, TERRORISM AND MARTYRDOM

Publication Number 1111

AMERICAN SERIES
IN
BEHAVIORAL SCIENCE AND LAW

Edited by

RALPH SLOVENKO, B.E., LL.B., M.A., Ph.D.

Professor of Law and Psychiatry
Wayne State University
Law School
Detroit, Michigan

PSYCHO-POLITICAL ASPECTS OF SUICIDE WARRIORS, TERRORISM AND MARTYRDOM

A Critical View from "Both Sides" in Regard to Cause and Cure

Edited by

JAMSHID A. MARVASTI, M.D.

CHARLES C THOMAS • PUBLISHER, LTD.
Springfield • Illinois • U.S.A.

Published and Distributed Throughout the World by

CHARLES C THOMAS • PUBLISHER, LTD.
2600 South First Street
Springfield, Illinois 62704

© 2008 by CHARLES C THOMAS • PUBLISHER, LTD.

ISBN 978-0-398-07802-7 (hard)
ISBN 978-0-398-07803-4 (paper)

Library of Congress Catalog Card Number: 2007047138

With THOMAS BOOKS *careful attention is given to all details of manufacturing
and design. It is the Publisher's desire to present books that are satisfactory as to their
physical qualities and artistic possibilities and appropriate for their particular use.*
THOMAS BOOKS *will be true to those laws of quality that assure a good name
and good will.*

*Printed in the United States of America
LAH-R-3*

Library of Congress Cataloging-in-Publication Data

Psycho-political aspects of suicide warriors, terrorism, and martyrdom : a crit-
ical view from "both sides" in regard to cause and cure / edited by Jamshid A.
Marvasti.
    p. cm. -- (American series in behavioral science and law ; 1111)
    ISBN 978-0-398-07802-7 (hard) -- ISBN 978-0-398-07803-4 (pbk.)
    1. Terrorism--History. 2. Suicide bombers. 3. Suicide bombings. I. Marvasti,
Jamshid A.
    HV6431.P796 2008
    363.325--dc22
                                                        2007047138

This book is dedicated:

To the thousands of American children who on 9/11 learned that one or both of their parents were dead or missing;

To those Afghani children, who even during family celebrations were not safe and were mutilated in an air raid; to the British children who were bombed on their way to school;

To children in Pakistani villages and Iraqi cities who were victims of "collateral damage" and "map changing" policies of superpowers;

To those Israeli children who constantly live in dreadful fear and shock and Palestinians who die while throwing rocks;

To the memory of all children of the world who have suffered from war and violence.

CONTRIBUTORS

Kenneth M. Cunningham, L.C.S.W. is a licensed clinical social worker and a doctoral student at the University of Connecticut, School of Social Work. As a clinical social worker, he has practice experience in the fields of child welfare, mental health and substance abuse treatment, and emergency psychiatric evaluations. He has conducted research in prisons to assess the impact of the correctional environment on the learning outcomes of incarcerated adult learners and in charter schools to identify the developing role of school social workers. His current research interests include mental health recovery, neurobiology, stigma associated with mental illness, and models of psychiatric and substance abuse assessment.

Gagan Dhaliwal, M.D. is an Assistant Clinical Professor, University of Alabama, Birmingham, School of Medicine, Huntsville, Alabama, and also maintains a clinical and forensic psychiatry practice in Huntsville. Doctor Dhaliwal received his medical degree from Dayanand Medical College, Ludhiana, India, and completed his medical internship and psychiatric residency at Eastern Virginia Medical School, Norfolk, Virginia. He subsequently completed a fellowship in Child and Adolescent Psychiatry from the University of California, San Diego, and a fellowship in Forensic Psychiatry from New York University. Doctor Dhaliwal's primary research interests are in legal and psychiatric aspects of violence and forensic aspects of neuropsychiatry and psychopharmacology.

Valerie L. Dripchak, Ph.D., L.C.S.W. is an associate professor in the graduate school of social work at Southern Connecticut State University in New Haven, Connecticut. She received her doctorate degree from Fordham University in New York. Doctor Dripchak is a licensed clinician and has provided psychotherapeutic services to traumatized children and families for the past thirty years. She has developed graduate and post master's curricula for practitioners to become better skilled in the treatment of trauma and has presented more than thirty workshops on the topic of trauma at national and regional conferences. Doctor Dripchak has gone on to author more than a dozen publications. She recently has been given the Judith Mishne Commemoration Award by the *Clinical Social Work Journal* for her writings and excellence in clinical practice with children and adolescents.

Jess Ghannam, Ph.D. is Chief of Medical Psychology, Clinical Professor of Psychiatry and faculty in the Global Health Sciences Program at the University of California, San Francisco. He has been working in Palestine for over fifteen years teaching, conducting research on post-traumatic stress disorder, and developing community health centers and micro-clinics throughout Gaza and the West Bank. Doctor Ghannam writes and presents frequently on the Middle East.

Justine McCabe, Ph.D. received doctorates in cultural anthropology (Duke University) and psychology (California School of Professional Psychology). She has lived in Iran and conducted field research in Lebanon and northern California. Doctor McCabe is a former staff research associate at the University of California, Davis and fellow at the Henry A. Murray Research Center, Radcliffe Institute for Advanced Study, Harvard University. Since the mid-1990s, she has traveled regularly to Israel and the Occupied Palestinian Territories where she has conducted respite workshops for humanitarian workers and seminars on human attachment under conditions of political violence. Doctor McCabe practices psychology in New Milford, Connecticut where she is writing a book, *Suffering in America: Transformations in the Context of Culture.* She is also Co-Chair of the International Committee, Green Party of the United States.

Claire Chantal Olivier received her Bachelor Degree in Anthropology from Connecticut College. She later worked in San Francisco for several years on homelessness, environmental issues, and human rights with a local and international focus. Her additional interests include conflict resolution and peace studies. Currently she is living in Guatemala, studying Spanish and volunteering with various humanitarian organizations.

Susan Phillips Plese is a Professor Emeritus of Journalism at Manchester Community College in Connecticut, as well as an adjunct professor with twenty-seven years experience as reporter, editor and columnist. She is a member of the Society of Professional Journalists; a member of Soroptomist International, working for the welfare of women and children throughout the world; and a volunteer tutor of ESL students in the Manchester Public Schools. She holds a B.A. from Upsala College and an M.A. from the University of Connecticut. She is involved in several groups addressing homelessness, mental illness, and fetal and infant mortality.

FOREWORD

Why the "clash of civilizations"? The main theme of this extraordinary book written and edited by Jamshid A. Marvasti, M.D., is that violence breeds violence. In this book, *Psycho-Political Aspects of Suicide Warriors, Terrorism and Martyrdom*, that theme is explored in all of its dimensions.

An important question is whether jihadist violence is primarily a product of religious ideology or of geopolitical grievance. Many Muslims perceive the United States and Israel as the biggest threat to Islam since the Crusades. Osama bin Laden has articulated the argument that Islam is under attack by the United States and its allies. Bin Laden and his followers believe that they are doing God's work, and nothing will deter them from their mission, as evidenced by suicide bombers, and their belief that they will be rewarded in the afterlife.

Terrorism is sustained by three elements: (1) grievances, (2) a conspiratorial interpretation of the grievances, and (3) a license to act, which may be given by religious authority. Mohamed Atta, the Egyptian who piloted the plane that struck the North Tower of the World Trade Center, was convinced that the Jews were striving for world domination and considered New York City the center of world Jewry, which was, in his opinion, Enemy No. 1. In the "Letter to the American People" of November 2002, bin Laden warns: "The Jews have taken control of your media, and now control all aspects of your life making you their servants and achieving their aims at your expense." He goes on: "Your law is the law of rich and wealthy people. . . . Behind them stand the Jews who control your policies, media and economy."

President Mahmoud Ahmadinejad of Iran belittles Israel as a "filthy Zionest entity" and seeks to wipe it off the map. Islamist Hamas is ardently dedicated to the destruction of Israel. The perplexing question arises: What is the appropriate response? President George Bush saw Saddam Hussein as threatening and invaded Iraq.

A look back in history. In the 1930s, to no avail, the Soviet Union urged England and France to join together to prevent Hitler from overtaking Czechoslovakia. Hitler exploited popular resentment over Germany's perceived illegitimate defeat in World War I ("the stab in the back" by communists and Jews) and the unjust "peace" imposed at Versailles. In an article in a popular American magazine (*Harper's*, Sept. 1933), Trotsky warned that the war of 1914–called the "war of democracy"–is leading to "the war for liberation" from the results of World War I.

Bin Laden pointed to revenge as prompting the 9/11 attacks. He declared, "The people of Islam have suffered from aggravation, inequity, and injustice imposed upon them by Zionists, Crusaders alliance." He also protested the occupation by the United States of the holiest places of Islam, the Arabian Peninsula. He says that the United States has plundered Arabian riches, dictated to its rulers, and humiliated its people. In his words, "What America tastes now is something insignificant compared to what we have tasted for scores of years."

At the end of World War II, after centuries of domination by Ottoman Turks and European imperialists, Arabs believed that an Arab renaissance was forthcoming, but it was not to be. The victorious Western powers in World War I carved up the Ottoman Empire and installed rulers who would assure the flow of oil. The founding of the State of Israel following World War II was taken as a grievous calamity, and the defeats in the wars against Israel were humiliating. Yet, well before there was a Jewish state there was over a century of Arabs killing Jews through massacres and pogroms.

Assuredly, terrorism is not unique to today's clash of civilizations. It is as timeless as human conflict. The word "terrorism" derives from the Latin *terrere*, which means to frighten, and the first recorded use of the term as it is currently understood derives from the eighteenth-century "Reign of Terror" associated with the French Revolution. Stalin's regime was marked by terror. Bin Laden in 1997 condemned the United States government as hypocritical for not calling the bombing of Hiroshima terrorism. The Allied carpet bombing of Dresden killed thousands of civilians to "demoralize the German government," as Winston Churchill put it. Doctor Marvasti uses the term "suicide warriors" because he wants to be neutral and non-judgmental. A "warrior" is a label for someone who takes part in or is experienced in warfare. Similarly, an Israeli psychiatrist at a recent conference of the American College of Forensic Psychiatry used the term suicide "missionaries" rather than "bombers" because she, too, wished to remain neutral. The desire to be neutral, however, may result in moral relativism.

Doctor Marvasti maintains that the key motivation of many suicide bombers is the invasion and occupation of their land or holy place. Their rage, humiliation, or feelings of injustice combined with their perception that the only appropriate way to address their grievances is through further violence. Women become martyrs when their social structure is threatened, such as after the loss of a husband or male relative. They are not prompted by the reward of 72 virgins in Paradise.

To what extent, if any, does belief in an afterlife affect the way one lives in this life? The suicide bomber believes that his enemy will go to hell and he will go to paradise. So many Muslims are eager to turn themselves into bombs–the Koran makes this activity seem like a career activity. In the Koran, God says, "Those who are slain in the cause of God, he will not allow their works to perish. He will vouchsafe them guidance and ennoble their state. He will admit them to the Paradise."

The public view tends to be that the suicide bomber must be insane, but in fact they are not suffering from psychopathology in the traditonal sense. They do not qualify for any *DSM* diagnostic category. Indeed, individuals with significant mental illness are excluded from terrorist groups or acts because they are unable to tolerate the rigors of training, preparation, planning, or teamwork required for terror activity. Bin Laden is not clinically mad–he provides reasons for his actions that, while morally outrageous and religiously irresponsible, could be accepted by otherwise logical people who share his premises.

The psychiatric literature has indicated that terrorists exhibit two ego defense mechanisms: (1) paradoxical narcissism, and (2) projective identification. In paradoxical narcissism the individual appoints himself or herself as judge, jury, and executioner of his cause. The terrorist feels the world must conform to his or her needs, and if it does not, someone must pay the price to make it fit. However, Doctor Marvasti maintains this narcissism does not explain how the same person will then sacrifice his life for the welfare of others, as many suicide activists perceive that they do. The other criticism of this theory is that these qualities are not exclusively seen in terrorists. In projective identification, the individuals is splitting off the bad part of themselves, projecting it onto others, and then trying to destroy it.

In this book of 17 chapters, the reader will find the following discussions: (1) controversy in definitions of suicide bombers/warriors, terrorism and martyrdom; (2) proliferation of suicide bombers: why "ordinary people" participate in war and terrorism; (3) what motivates the suicide bomber; (4) trauma of terrorism and political violence on civilians: diagnosis and treatment; (5) homegrown "worrier" and "warrior": Muslims in Europe and the United States; (6) psychological autopsy of the suicide bomber; (7) suicide and self-destructive behaviors: learning from clinical population; (8) counterterrorism: violence breeds violence and increases terrorism and discontent; (9) the failure of counterterrorism: the need for a psychosocial and nonmilitary solution; (10) Western leaders and terrorism: psycho-political impact and interactions; (11) sowing seeds of war: Israeli and Palestinian child deaths in the context of September 11; (12) Palestine: a nation traumatized; (13) trauma of terrorism: pharmacotherapy in acute trauma and PTSD; (14) female suicide warriors/bombers; (15) understanding the mothers of suicide bombers and martyrs; (16) neurobiopsychosocial aspects of violence; and (17) history of war crimes, martyrdom, and suicide bombers/warriors. To cover these topics, seven contributors join with Doctor Marvasti.

Doctor Marvasti was born and raised in Iran and thus provides an out-of-the-ordinary perspective of the "clash of civilizations." He received his M.D. degree from Jondi Shapoor University (Ahwaz, Iran) and completed his psychiatric training at the Rhode Island Medical Center and the Institute of Living (Hartford, Connecticut). For the last 30 years he has practiced adult and child psychiatry at the Manchester Memorial Hospital in Manchester, Connecticut. He was previously an Associate Clinical Professor of Psychiatry at the University of Connecticut.

This book is Doctor Marvasti's third in the American Series in Behavioral Science and Law, the others being *Psychiatric Treatment of Victims and Survivors of Sexual Trauma* and *Psychiatric Treatment of Sexual Offenders*. He also edited the book *Child Suffering in the World: Child Maltreatment by Parents, Cultures and Governments in Different Countries and Cultures*, as well as a number of articles and chapters in books on the subject of psychic trauma and psychotherapy. He has presented scientific papers at international psychiatric meetings in the Middle East, Europe, Canada, and the United States.

Doctor Marvasti here gives us another wise book–thoroughly en-gaging in its discussion of the most pressing issue of our time.

Ralph Slovenko, Editor
American Series in Behavioral Science and Law

PREFACE

In this book there is no intention to praise or to condemn suicide bombers. Instead, the text endeavors to present from all points of view the history, prejudice, double standards and distortions regarding this important subject in both Western and Eastern news media and governments. The failure of current counterterrorism policies and the issue of "killing breeding more killing" indicate a need for deeper understanding of these bombers/warriors.

Following the proverbial statement "It takes a village to raise a child," I would like to make an amendment: "It takes two villages to raise a terrorist." What are the two villages in this metaphor? How do they create and raise suicide bombers? Although one is the village of the "offender/terrorist" and the other is the village of the "victim/target," what is surprising is that they both may contribute to the development of suicide bombers. One village's method is military and economic dominance, which to some extent involves invading/occupying, humiliating, and colonizing. The other village, the one that is perceived to be invaded, raises suicide bombers by transforming their "perceived victims" into "victimizers" often by supplying arms, training, religious/spiritual support, and honoring them as "martyrs." Unfortunately, most of the Western governments and their major media are focusing their counterterrorism efforts on this village, identified as "terrorist." Meanwhile, the other village continues the policies of occupation/invasion, the practice of double standards, and alienation of civilians through its military domination and corporate exploitation. The Western governments and the major media seem to have ignored that some terrorism may have evolved as a reaction to such events. Terrorism could be a message from those who sense that no one listens to their "perceived injustices" except when they become "suicide bombers."

In this book I have tried to explore and analyze the news/comments/opinions from both sides of the globe. At times I have focused on the "other side's" interpretation of events to present a different perspective than that normally found in our major news media.

The "other side" is comprised of Middle Eastern people and also of those

Americans/Westerners who believe that certain Western policies may have promoted hostility/resentment against the West. One such American is a former U.S. Air Force lieutenant colonel who flew many bombing missions in Vietnam before becoming a Catholic priest. As he astutely stated, "We are not hated because we practice democracy, value freedom, or uphold human rights. We are hated because our government denies these things to people in Third World countries whose resources are coveted by our multinational corporations."

In this book, I also have reviewed literature from "both sides," and I have attempted to point out that possibly the most common motivational factor for many of these bombers/terrorists is the element of "occupation/invasion" of their land or holy places. On the basis of this explanation, I speculate that after the "occupier/invader" leaves their land, hostility may cease. This opinion is contrary to what many Western government officials claim in regard to the present war in the Middle East. In fact, what they assert is not too different from what many American officials claimed in the Vietnam war: "If we don't stop them in Saigon, we will have to fight them in Seattle." History has proven otherwise.

I bring up the negative aspect of war and violence as a psychological trauma and discuss the concept of "soft power" or nonmilitary and psycho-social strategies and procedures to decrease hostility and terrorism. Although I believe that war usually is only judiciously analyzed in retrospect, it must be fought in the present. However, an "unjust" war (which feeds terrorism), is just too harmful to wait to be understood, and needs scrutiny from the beginning. I should add that my opinion is that any war (with any label) is harmful to humanity and needs to be avoided.

Throughout the chapters for which I have been a contributor, I have attempted to remain neutral in regard to the interchangeable terms of suicide warriors/terrorists/bombers/activists on both sides of the current conflicts. One such term, "suicide missionaries," I learned from an Israeli psychiatrist during her presentation at an American College of Forensic Psychiatry conference in April, 2006, as she used this word instead of "bomber" to respect neutrality. Unfortunately, I was not successful in including a chapter on the victimization of Israeli children and civilians by Middle East terrorists. A few potential writers from both the United States and Israel were originally interested, but at the last moment were not able to complete the task. However in the fourth chapter, I added a few research summaries on the subject of traumatization of Israeli children and adolescents by Palestinian violence.

Chapter 1

> *Because I do it with one small ship, I am called a terrorist. You do it with a whole fleet and are called an emperor.*
>
> A pirate, from St. Augustine's City of God

Doctor Marvasti and Doctor Dripchak explore the controversy regarding the definitions of "suicide bombers/warriors," "terrorism" and "martyrdom." The two explain that these definitions are frequently in the eyes of the beholders, and that political/religious orientation and loyalties to "one's tribe" color what someone sees or perceives. For example, if a person carries his bomb in his hand, he is called a terrorist, but if someone carries it in an F-16 and still bombs civilians, he may be labeled a war hero or freedom fighter. The chapter further notes that "one man's trash is another's treasure," and that the words "terrorist," "freedom fighter" and "martyr" become interchangeable depending on who is reporting the events and who is publishing the report.

In this chapter, Marvasti and Dripchak also review the "other side" literature and report that the words "Jewish terrorist" and "Christian terrorist" are used in non-Western countries as frequently as Westerners use "Muslim terrorist." Western news media have avoided attaching the label of "Christian" or "Jewish" to terrorists even though such terrorists intone religion to support their activities, such as a "Christian" terrorist blowing up an abortion clinic or a "Jewish" terrorist assassinating the Prime Minister of Israel because he gave land back to the Palestinians and, from his point of view, this was contrary to The Bible. The authors point out double standards, discrepancies in both Western and Eastern news media, and eventually declare that although history is written by both the victor and the loser, the victor's media has more influence and dominance. A quote from Noam Chomsky suggests that Western regimes also commit terrorist activities, but they refer to these activities as "counterterrorism."

The authors further explore the definition of "terrorism" from the point of view of the U.S. government and United Nations through the concepts of "state-sponsored terrorism" and "state-caused" terrorism. The conclusion in this chapter is that there is no universal consensus about how to define such controversial and emotionally charged words as "terrorism," "war crime," "martyrdom" and "suicide bomber." The Talmud states, "We don't see things as they are; we see things as we are."

Chapter 2

> *An army of principles can penetrate where an army of soldiers cannot.*
>
> Thomas Paine

In this chapter, Doctor Marvasti, a trauma specialist, discusses the question of "why war?" from a psychological/anthropological point of view. He refers to psychoanalytic literature to explain that human beings react to being defeated in war by creating new wars rather than mourning and grieving the trauma of the "lost war."

Doctor Marvasti presents and examines psychoanalytic writings of Vamik Volkan, Abigail Golomb and David Lotto. Discussed also is the concept of the "Vietnam Syndrome" which deems "grieving the loss" of the Vietnam War to be a more painful process than that of creating a new war (with the hope of reversing the previous defeat). Marvasti also analyzes the process of "dehumanization" of the enemy as a procedure to decrease the natural human inclination toward empathy and to bypass the inhibition against killing.

The chapter explores whether or not "ordinary people" can become suicide bombers. Also considered are the dichotomies of "us" versus "them" and "myth" versus "historical" fact. Abigail Golomb's examples of the "cowboy and Indian" in the U.S. are mentioned: Western culture considers the cowboy as "hero" and the Indian as "wicked" as if it were the Indian who had come from another place and stolen the land from the cowboys. This perspective parallels the example of the Israelis and Palestinians in their conflict.

Chapter 2 concludes that war/violence has been a major part of human experience and that aggression is not solely the character of soldiers, since ordinary people under certain circumstances also may exhibit these behaviors. People are not born warriors or terrorists but can develop into them.

Chapter 3

> *You will never end terrorism by terrorizing others.*
>
> Martin Luther King, Jr.

In this section, Doctor Marvasti utilizes psychological/sociological tools to consider the factors that motivate suicide bombers. In the review of literature from "both sides," the author concludes that the element of occupation/invasion of homeland/holy places of suicide warriors is the most frequent/consistent variable reported.

This chapter discusses the motivational elements of (1) nationalism, (2) rage and revenge, (3) psychic trauma and dissociation, (4) religion, (5) group process, (6) poverty, (7) perceived injustice, humiliation, shame and despair, (8) cultural support, and (9) remuneration. The author concludes that these motivational factors are varied and complex yet can be divided into "internal" and "external" experiences (e.g., psychic trauma and humiliation are internal experiences which may be triggered/caused by what is occurring in the external environment such as occupation and invasion). Suicide bombers/warriors probably will continue to exist as long as there are life situations in which people feel that this type of violence is the only way to change their world and to improve their nation/tribe's status quo.

Chapter 4

A whole life can be shaped by an old trauma, remembered or not.

Lenore Terr

In this chapter Doctors Marvasti and Dripchak consider terrorism as a trauma and examine the psychological responses following catastrophic events among adults and children. The impact of terror is partially connected to society's response to the "terrorist" act. The authors note that more dysfunctional behaviors probably are created by the response than by the actual event. Significant information on the impact on children on both sides of recent military conflicts is presented. The authors discuss the psychological impact of terrorism and atrocities on victimized Israeli children and adolescents. The authors further explore the intergenerational transmission of trauma. Finally this chapter discusses crisis intervention and psychotherapy. Models appropriate for the treatment of trauma such as Eye Movement Desensitization, Dialectical Behavioral Therapy, Cognitive Behavioral Therapy and Play Therapy are applied to victims of "terrorist trauma."

Chapter 5

When slavery was a custom, every right-minded person supported it. Nothing is as powerful a legitimizer as social custom, even more powerful than law.

Thomas Szasz

Doctor Marvasti introduces the concept of homegrown "worrier" and "warrior" by referring to Muslims residing in Europe and the United States. He focuses on possible similarities and differences between U.S. Muslims and European ones. Marvasti finds that more radicalization appears evident in European Muslims than among those in the U.S. Also explored are the situational elements in Europe which possibly foster an environment of armed violence by these homegrown "warriors." In considering the 7/7 attacks in Great Britain the author reviews specific profiles of terrorists: Mohammad Sidique Khan, Shehzad Tanweer, Abdullah Jamal and Hasib Hussain.

Marvasti discusses racial discrimination and stereotyping of the Muslim population by certain Western groups and the elements of resentment, alienation and distortion by some of the Western news media. "Other side" literature reveals that the Western attitude toward Israel has become a source of resentment and rage in some young Muslims in the West. However, in this chapter, the author indicates historical evidence of collaboration and co-existence between Jews and Muslims.

Research by the Pakistani-American Public Affairs Committee on Muslims living in the U.S. is used to explore the issue of integration of Muslims into Western culture, their attitude toward U.S. government policies, and their feeling of discrimination and commitment to their own religion/culture.

Also discussed is a similar but smaller investigation conducted on Iranian-American Muslims. In summary, it seems that most respondents are fond of Americans but resentful of the Western news media and wanted to "correct" the misconception that the nineteen terrorists of 9/11 do not represent the 1.3 billion Muslims in the world.

Chapter 6

Our children are not born to hate, they are raised to hate.
Thomas della Peruta

Doctors Marvasti and Dripchak provide a psychological autopsy of the suicide bomber. In an extensive review of literature, they dissect this type of fighter by examining the bomber's family structure, socioeconomic status, education, religion, ideology and other demographic details. The authors conclude that there is no single profile that can be created to identify these suicide attackers as they are a heterogeneous group. The purported psychopathology of terrorists and two specific ego defense mechanisms, paradoxical narcissism and projective identification, are examined. As the issues of justification and rationalization are explored, it becomes evident that the one major commonality among these bombers is the perceived injustice of the occupation/invasion of their homelands. From that point of view, the authors speculate that anyone, given a particular set of internal and external circumstances, could become a bomber/warrior.

Chapter 7

Suicide is a permanent solution to a temporary problem.
Phil Donahue

In this section Doctor Dripchak, a clinician who has evaluated and treated many suicidal patients, presents up-to-date, "state-of-the-art" information in regard to suicide in the clinical patient population. Her goal is to explore whether what we learn from this population can help augment our understanding of the suicide bombers and their motivation.

In this chapter, the author explores the historical, legal, and religious aspects of suicide. She compares suicide notes of the clinical population with those of suicide bombers/warriors. She also explores the similarities and differences between suicide bombers and suicidal patients.

Chapter 8

We can bomb the world to pieces, but we can't bomb it into peace.
An anti-war slogan

This chapter focuses on counterterrorism. Dr. Marvasti discusses that "violence breeds violence" and increases terrorism and discontent. He attempts to demonstrate "what doesn't work" in counterterrorism by reviewing literature from "both sides" and by concluding that "killing leads to more killing." Included is a quote by Sir Peter Ustinov who stated that "terrorism is the war of the poor and war is the terrorism of the rich." Identified are elements within counterterrorism which may have contributed to terrorism. Considered also are the "wounds" of the Middle East population in regard to the Israeli/Palestinian conflict as documented in "other side" literature.

Doctor Marvasti presents a hypothetical question: If Palestinians could use the techniques of Mahatma Gandhi, Nelson Mandela or Martin L. King, Jr. in responding to Israel, would it be possible to "disarm" the Israeli extremists (without using any arms) and attract the sympathy of Jewish citizens to see them as "victims" rather than "offenders"? The author notes that as history indicates, violence breeds violence and extremism leads to the development of "other side" extremists.

State-sponsored terrorism, "state-caused terrorism," and the limiting of civil liberties (as a side effect of counterterrorism) are explored. The failure of the Western counterterrorism techniques which rely solely on "killing" the suspected terrorist (while disregarding the many innocent civilians also killed in the process) increases the resentment/discontent in "both sides" of the conflict. This result is probably what terrorists wish for. Military invasions may kill some terrorists, but such actions fertilize the ground for more.

Chapter 9

Madness answered with madness simply deepens, it never dispels.
Mahatma Gandhi

Doctor Marvasti discusses the failure of counterterrorism and points out the need for a psychosocial and nonmilitary solution. He reviews the "other side" news media/opinion and tries to find an explanation for the negative view in various countries toward the U.S. and British governments. This chapter attempts to explore "what may work" in countering terrorism. The suggestion is that if some U.S. policies have had a negative impact, they can be corrected by America itself. As one of the previous Presidents mentioned, "There is nothing wrong with America that can not be cured with what is right in America."

The subjects discussed in psychiatric literature in regard to "what may work" are alleviating psychic trauma, listening to the "oppressed" group and their perceived injustice, decreasing humiliation, acknowledging stereotyping/prejudicial thinking/writing toward an "oppressed" population and decreasing the level of hatred. Supporting the "moderate" population and instituting moderate government policies are also beneficial. Doctor Marvasti discusses the "concept of nonviolence" and the psychology of "soft power" which utilizes nonmilitary strategies to shape international relations/behavior. He refers to the writings of Joseph Nye and also of Ben Franklin who wrote, "There never was a good war or bad peace."

In this chapter, Doctor Marvasti briefly refers to the great Persian poet and clergyman, Mevlana Rumi (of 13th century); although he lived in an era of terrorism and genocide, no words or stories of revenge or retribution occur in his thousands of verses. Instead this Islamic clergyman chose to focus on commonality of humanity and love, even for one's enemy: "From love, thorns become flowers."

Historical evidence presented in this chapter confirms that whenever Western governments have supported a dictator/tyrant in Third World countries, the populations of those countries have developed resentment/hostility toward the West, and conversely, whenever these governments have opposed a dictator and brutal regime, people of those countries have developed a positive attitude toward the West. Doctor Marvasti refers to the CIA-sponsored coup d'état of Iran in 1953, which overthrew the democratic government of Doctor Mosaddeq. Although at that time it may have been considered a victory for the U.S., the hostility and resentment created toward the West eventually culminated in the Islamic revolution of 1979.

Chapter 10

> *The shepherd has always tried to persuade the sheep that their interests and his own are the same.*
>
> Marie Beyle

This chapter discusses the impact of terrorism as a trauma on Western political leaders, and the ways in which these two entities may interact with each other (e.g., some Western leaders may exploit terrorism/ nationalism/religion to accomplish their own agenda). The author notes Sinclair Lewis' words from 80 years ago, "When fascism comes to America, it will be wrapped in the flag, carrying a cross."

This section also discusses leaders as human beings who are subject to developing Post Traumatic Stress Disorder (PTSD), acute stress disorder, excessive anger, narcissistic insult and urges for retaliation after experiencing the trauma of terrorism. Dr. Marvasti questions whether or not leaders also demonstrate an "identification with the aggressor" or a "compulsion to repeat the trauma" when they are exposed to the trauma of terrorists. These topics, as well as leaders' public reactions, internal struggles, transformations of defeat into victory, and references to the terrorists as "cowards," are subsections of this chapter. In addition, the subject of leaders' communication with God is explored. Doctor Marvasti speculates that this phenomenon may reflect genuine and honest feelings of leaders which others may misunderstand.

The author also focuses on the opportunistic type of leader: such a person may exploit terrorism to create fear in his nation, thus uniting citizens to back his/her policies. The statement of Martin Luther King, Jr., "We have guided missiles and misguided men" reinforces this.

Extensively reviewed and quoted in this regard are the writings of Doctor John Mueller (professor of political science at Ohio State University). The psychological subject of "fear of death," its impact on "war-oriented" leaders, and increased support by their traumatized nations also are discussed.

In the final section of the chapter, the author provides examples of peaceful reactions of some leaders in response to terrorism, aggression, and other combative gestures by their enemies. Doctor Marvasti concludes that a leader is a human being with frailties common to all, and therefore should not be idolized as a superhuman figure. Leaders are also "working through" their own childhood issues and possible traumas, and their reaction to terrorism may reflect how successful they have been in this endeavor.

Chapter 11

> *Is it any comfort to know that the tanks murdering in my name are digging*
> *a grave for my people as well?*
>
> Aharon Shabtai

This chapter is authored by Justine McCabe, Ph.D., a psychologist and cultural anthropologist who has worked in Lebanon and Iran, and traveled frequently to Israel and the Occupied Palestinian Territories where she has volunteered and done respite training with relief workers. Doctor McCabe considers the losses felt by Palestinians and Israelis by comparing the deaths of their children in the first and second Intifada to the deaths experienced by Americans in the September 11, 2001 attacks.

Doctor McCabe's comparative statistics reveal that between 2000 and 2007, 118 Israeli children died. This rate of Israeli child deaths would be the equivalent of 129 children's deaths in the Palestinian population. However, there were actually 930 Palestinian child deaths during this time. She uses these figures to comprehend the gravity of these deaths in terms of the American population: 118 Israeli child deaths over 6.5 years would be the equivalent of 4,355 American child deaths, while 930 Palestinian child deaths would be the equivalent of 31,638 American child deaths. Doctor McCabe then translates these child deaths in terms of the 2,973 Americans who died in the September 11 attacks, finding that 118 Israeli child deaths are equivalent to two September 11 attacks for Israelis, while 930 Palestinian child deaths are the equivalent of twenty-five September 11 attacks for Palestinians. She explains that the killing of children in particular creates a distinctive emotional context that evokes the most intense, primitive feelings (hatred, hostility and revenge) among Palestinians and Israelis. These in turn, lead to more child deaths, thereby contributing to the perpetuation of the conflict. Her data also highlight the gross asymmetry and inequality that have defined the relationship between Palestinians and Israelis since 1948, highly relevant in understanding the perpetuation or resolution of the conflict.

Doctor McCabe indicates that the effect of the deaths of these innocent children, Israeli and Palestinian, can be likened to the "loss of innocence" that Americans felt after the September 11 attacks. Noting the decisive role that their government plays in resolving the Israeli-Palestinian conflict, she suggests that perhaps by empathizing with the loss of Israeli and Palestinian children, Americans would be moved to pressure their government to restore the equality between these two peoples that is essential for an enduring peace. Concomitantly, world leaders must firmly enforce international laws prohibiting the killing of civilians–especially children–whether by states or individuals.

Chapter 12

> *Violence, even well intentioned, always rebounds upon oneself.*
> Lao Tzu

In this chapter, Doctor Jess Ghannam focuses on the subject of "Palestine-A Nation Traumatized." This chapter is particularly revealing as it presents the feelings and perceptions of a conflict from the "other side." This vantage point allows the reader to compare it with reports/news media from the West and discover the significant differences/discrepancies in reporting.

Doctor Ghannam initially explains that according to the Geneva Convention, the "occupier army is responsible for the health/wellness of the inhabitants under occupation." He reviews documentation from neutral sources (such as the UN and human rights groups) that indicate that the physical/mental health conditions of Palestinians in the occupied territories are devastating. Doctor Ghannam refers to the international laws of health care to point out the ways in which the implements of occupation: segregation, closure, curfew, blockades, military checkpoints and frequent invasions by the Israeli Army were detrimental to the health and hygiene of civilians.

Doctor Ghannam presents research on 229 adolescents in the Gaza Strip who were exposed regularly to the trauma of Israeli's army attacks. The results of these studies reveal the widespread presence of PTSD and depression; yet, Doctor Ghannam also acknowledges the resilience of Palestinian children despite their continued exposure to devastating traumas.

Chapter 13

> . . . stress can set off a ripple of hormonal changes that permanently wire a child's brain to cope with a malevolent world. Through this chain of events, violence and abuse pass from generation to generation as well as from one society to the next.
>
> Martin Teicher

In this section, Doctor Marvasti and Kenneth M. Cunningham discuss current aspects of pharmacotherapy in treatment for trauma of terrorism. The definitions of trauma, its short and long- term negative impacts, and psychic trauma are explained in biochemical and anatomical terms. The authors note that emotional trauma/stress may cause biochemical and anatomical changes in the brain. In the past, it was assumed that "something emotional," no matter how devastating it could be, would have impact only on the "software" of the brain's "computer." But as the writers explain, scientific literature now points toward damage and changes in the anatomy of the brain (hardware) as well as alteration of biochemical/hormonal pathways. Also discussed is medication for treatment of PTSD and for the possible prevention of the negative impact of psychic trauma.

Chapter 14

> I have to tell the world that if they do not defend us, then we have to defend ourselves with the only thing we have, our bodies. Our bodies are the only fighting means at our disposal.
>
> Hiba, female suicide bomber trainee

In this chapter Doctor Marvasti and Susan Phillips Plese review the literature on female warriors from an historical point of view. They focus their attention on the recent phenomenon of female suicide warriors/bombers.

The authors review literature which analyzes the motivation of female suicide activists and criticize the bias in the findings/conclusions. According to

Marvasti and Plese, these analysts have focused on the "personal motivators" of the female fighters such as losses, sexual affairs, divorce, gender conflict, and infertility. They have ignored the more political factors of nationalism, ideology and the urge to fight against the perceived invader/occupier, as if a female could not have idealistic/activist views. The authors explain that nationalism and the desire to resist the enemy of their state touches the hearts of both women and men as does cultural humiliation, desperation, injustice and rage.

President Arafat addressed 1000 Palestinian women in 2002 and referred to his female fighters with this famous statement, "You are my army of roses which will crush Israeli tanks." However, historical facts reveal that Sri-Lankan and Chechen fighters have utilized proportionately many more female suicide bombers/warriors than Palestinians.

Chapter 15

> We will not learn how to live together in peace by killing each other's children.
>
> Jimmy Carter

In this chapter the hardship of being a mother of a suicide bomber is explored. Doctor Marvasti and Claire Olivier have reviewed the literature on Palestinian mothers and challenge the allegation that these mothers encourage or pressure their children to become "martyrs." The authors explain that what encourages/proliferates terrorism/suicide bombers in a culture are not the mothers, but the perceived sense of injustice, humiliation and the devastating impact of occupation/invasion of their homeland. These are the core motivating factors.

The authors frequently refer to the writings of Doctor Eyad Sarraj, a prominent psychiatrist in Gaza, who has had many professional contacts with mothers of past and probable future "martyrs" while practicing psychiatry in a culture which is known to have suicide "missionaries."

The authors, through their literature review, have speculated that there are two different reactions of these mothers: the one expressed in public and the other experienced in private, which reflect their cultural context and rituals. In public these mothers may contain their tears (if they can) and express strength, nationalism and support for the "resistance movement," but in their hearts, they are bleeding, grieving and suffering. One should not be deceived by the public expressions of pride, honor and stoicism nor take them to be indicators of a lack of pain and loss.

A New York University graduate student from Jerusalem interviewed sixteen "mothers of martyrs" from the West Bank and reported that these mothers cared deeply for their "martyred" sons and were not able to prevent them from entering into the military conflict. The authors conclude that mothers living in war zones or occupied territories face unique challenges not experienced by many other mothers, even those whose children become soldiers.

Chapter 16

> *Though this be madness, yet there is method in't.*
> William Shakespeare

In this section, Gagan Dhaliwal, M.D., a child psychiatrist, reviews the "Neuro-bio-psycho-social aspects of violence." He explains that violence and war have always been a part of human civilization and are a complex and multidimensional phenomenon. Although some individuals may suffer from mental illness that increases their potential for violence, mental illness does not necessarily create a violent attitude. Factors that may increase the risk of violence include growing up in poverty, exposure to family/neighborhood violence, and certain medical disorders. Scientific literature indicates that violence is a heterogeneous phenomenon in nature, and possibly no single factor or gene can explain it.

Chapter 17

> *It is only a generation after a war that the ordinary people begin to admit that it was a futile, foolish, and unnecessary one- which is something the prophets, poets, and philosophers were nearly stoned for saying as it began.*
> Sydney Harris

In this chapter Doctors Marvasti and Dripchak review the history of war crimes, martyrdom, and suicide bombers/warriors. The two explore the historical definition of war crimes and refer to cases possibly unknown to many Westerners.

In the history section on martyrdom in Islam, Marvasti and Dripchak introduce the Shia concept of martyrdom by referring to the epic of Imam Hussein and his seventy-two soldiers in Karbala, Iraq who were massacred by a much larger army. Imam Hussein and his small force knew that they would be killed and yet did not submit; so, in this way they might be considered suicide missionaries. Also, the Iranian suicide battalion (Intehari) in the Iran-Iraq war was motivated by Imam Hussein's martyrdom.

The authors explain that the history of political violence and suicide attacks against powerful enemies dates back to ancient times, even in The Bible when the story of Samson could be considered a suicide mission. What is different in contemporary times is the extent of the lethality of the weapons and the speed in conveying the events to the world in "high definition color" through TV and the Internet. Also, the extent of disinformation, justification, double standards, and war propaganda has increased.

These authors point out that since most of the time history is written primarily by the victor of a conflict, no longer may history be considered totally factual and free of personal judgment. Therefore, the quest to achieve objectivity may be only an elusive goal, even if information from both sides is revealed. As Gary Wills stated: *"Only the winners decide what were war crimes."*

J.A.M.

ACKNOWLEDGMENTS

I am thankful to many dedicated professionals and friends who encouraged, helped and gave ideas so this book would materialize. I thank Professor Ralph Slovenko, the Editor of the American Series in Behavioral Science and Law, who has always been an inspiration for me. I would like to thank all the authors of each of the chapters as well as my contacts around the world that provided ideas and stimuli.

I could not have accomplished this project without technical and editorial help from many sources. I received tremendous editorial assistance from Susan Roche, Mana Zarinejad, and Susan Plese. In this project Mary Ellen Procko and Claire C. Olivier were my research assistants as well as my right and left hands. Whenever I couldn't write anymore, they energized me. Alexandra Cieza, Kathy Ouellette and Laila Marvasti helped with typing, organizing and creating references. Jamie Roche and Mo Vafadar were the computer brains and did all my technical work. Thanks to Shahla Zarinejad, a Librarian who helped to obtain many books and references for me.

Finally my deepest gratitude to Manchester Memorial Hospital Library Staff: Jeanine Cyr Gluck, Kimberly Person, and Ellen Francoline who obtained many articles and books for me from as far away as Europe.

CONTENTS

PSYCHO-POLITICAL ASPECTS OF SUICIDE WARRIORS, TERRORISM AND MARTYRDOM

Chapter 1

CONTROVERSY IN DEFINITIONS OF SUICIDE BOMBERS/WARRIORS, TERRORISM AND MARTYRDOM

Jamshid A. Marvasti and Valerie L. Dripchak

If the existing government of Afghanistan had declared war on the United States at 8 A.M. EST, September 11, the attacks on New York and Washington would have been air raids.

Anonymous, European Union representative[1]

We do not see things as they are. We see them as we are.

Talmud

INTRODUCTION

The definition of terrorism is in the eye of the beholder (viewer). This makes for a conundrum that is much like the story of the four blind men who were touching an elephant and explaining what the elephant was like. All four were right (as they explained what they sensed), and all four were wrong (because each explained only a part of the elephant and not the elephant itself). In regard to terrorism, the elements of desires, subjectivity, prejudice, and political or religious affiliation also interfere with what "blind men" perceive. As a result, two mistakes occur: first, only one part of the terrorism is identified or explained; and second, this single part is distorted because the subjectivity of the examiner creates the double-blind effect.

DEFINITION OF THE TERM TERRORISM

The term terrorism has its origins in the Latin verb *terrere* which means to frighten (*Wikipedia Encyclopedia*: Terrorism). *The Merriam Webster Dictionary* (2000) defines terrorism as a systematic use of a state of intense fear as a means to induce coercion. Because acts of terrorism have become more prevalent throughout the world in the post-September 11 era, the definition has expanded to "a strategy of using political violence, social threats or coordinated attacks closely associated with unconventional warfare in manner of conduct and operation" (*Wikipedia Encyclopedia*: Terrorism). The National Research Council has used the term to refer to an illegal use of violence by groups with political or ideological motives whose primary goal is to force governments into some action by inducing fear in their people (Smelser & Mitchell, 2002).

One of the problems with defining terrorism is that the label of a terrorist is not static. Salman Akhtar, a psychoanalyst, has defined it as being, "time-bound. As political loyalties shift, today's terrorist becomes tomorrow's hero" (Hough, 2004, p. 814). A freedom fighter can become a terrorist, or a terrorist can become a peacemaker. It is a gray area to define exactly when that role changes. Bin Laden was originally recognized as a freedom fighter when he and the Taliban militants were committing atrocities towards the (pro-Soviet Union) Afghanistan government. Later, he became a terrorist when he and the Taliban changed the directions of their guns to point toward western interests.

Yasser Arafat, on the other hand, was originally labeled a terrorist and a "child murderer." However, after he agreed to sit at the peace table his image in the western news media became more "civilized," and he became a candidate for the Nobel Peace Prize.

Saddam Hussein was not always considered to be the enemy. The Reagan administration supported Saddam Hussein throughout the 1980s and looked the other way as he used chemical weapons against his Kurdish population (Herman, 2002). The United State supplied him with weapons of mass destruction (WMD) and financial loans. This was until he disobeyed the U.S. by marching into Kuwait in 1990 and then lost its friendly support (Herman, 2002).

Similarly, up until 1942, the Jewish underground fighters in Palestine were terrorists. Western sympathy began to spread in 1942 as more people heard of the Holocaust, and "by 1944, the terrorists of Palestine, who were Zionists, suddenly began being described as freedom fighters" (Ahmad, 2001, p. 11).

Some of the definitions regarding terrorism are further influenced by political or ideological perspectives, or both. For example, Marjorie Cohn (2002), an associate professor of law, divided terrorism into several political categories and explained that one needs to distinguish among the following terms: individual terrorism, such as the September 11, 2001, attacks; state/government terrorism, such as Israel's occupation and aggression against the Palestinian population; international state terrorism, such as the bombings in Afghanistan by the government of the United States and the United Kingdom; and state-sponsored and supported terrorism, such as the United States government's financial and military support for Israel, and a national liberation struggle, such as Palestinian movement.

Joseph Sobran questioned whether terrorism should be defined in an ideological way. He raised such questions as: Can the end justify the means? Is it possible to be a terrorist and a freedom fighter at the same time? Is it possible to use bad methods for good purposes? (Kemp, 1986, p. 135).

At times the methods that one uses to fight determine whether one is defined as a terrorist or not. The label of terrorism has been used based on who is the attacker and who is killed. If you kill someone that we like, it may be called terrorism by our news media. If you kill someone that we do not like, we may rationalize the action by suggesting that it just helps to keep the peace or is a kind of self-defense, or is collateral damage. From another point of view, as Marvasti stated, "If you carry your bomb in your hand, you're a terrorist. If you carry your bomb in an F-16, you are a freedom fighter—a war hero" (Bates, 2003).

Western news media and governments consider terrorists to be those who do not belong to any organized or official armed forces. They represent no recognized government and therefore their people or movements have no "seat" in the United Nations. For example, the massacre of the American Marines in Beirut in 1983 by a suicide bomber was considered terrorism, but if that same act were performed by an Egyptian or a Jordanian soldier, it would be labeled an act of war rather than terrorism.

Heskin (1980, p. 74) stated that terrorism is an emotionally charged topic. He referred to the bombings in Birmingham public houses in November of 1974 by the Provisional Irish Republic Army (IRA), in which a dozen people were killed or injured. These actions were universally condemned as terrorism. However, he asserted that such atrocious behavior is not a sufficient definition of terrorism. For example, the British bombing of Dresden, the American bombing of Hiroshima, or the German bombing of London are not considered acts of terrorism, although they too resulted in deliberate massacre of innocent civilians. Heskin added that, "the behavior of the perpetrators (governments) was, numerically at least, more atrocious than the Birmingham pub bombings, and its effects more calculated and cold-blooded." The citizens of the countries that were bombed were inhabitants of a land that was at war with the perpetrators. Yet the Provisional IRA also claimed it was at war with Britain. Is there a difference? Does war then justify the deliberate killing of civilians?

ONE MAN'S TRASH IS ANOTHER'S TREASURE

Herzog (2002), in an article about the mind of the terrorists, explained that one person's terrorist is another person's savior or freedom fighter. He presented the examples of Abdullah Ocalan and Abimael Guzman Reymoso. The first one, Ocalan, is a hero in the Kurdistan Workers Party to many homeless and countryless Kurds but a terrorist and an anarchist in the eyes of the Turkish government. Reymoso is a hero and liberator to many of Peru's poor and impoverished masses, but to the Peruvian regime, he is a dangerous terrorist (Herzog, 2002). Hezbollah's leader, Nasrallah, is considered a terrorist by the Israeli and U.S. governments. However, after thirty-four days of fighting with the Israeli army during August of 2006, several U.S. media sources (Jervis & Stone, 2006) reported that in the Arab world, he is now at the level of an epic "folk hero," and poets are writing poems about him.

Another example of this discrepancy is evident in examining the organization of Lohamei Herut Israel (Lehi). Lehi was formulated as a freedom fighter movement with plans to expel the British from Palestine and to establish the Israeli nation. At the time of its creation, this organization was described as terrorists by the British.[2] At the present time, however, most historians (including the British) are reluctant to look back and label this group as terrorists, even if there appear to be similarities between what Lehi did half a century ago and what the Palestine Liberation Organization (PLO) is doing now. The goal of both movements is to take back their lands (or what they perceive to belong to them) through armed struggle against the occupying army.

THE CONTROVERSY IN DEFINING THE TERM

Who is the slayer, who is the victim? Speak.

Sophocles

Chomsky (2001) has suggested that western governments also participate in terrorist activity, but they call it counterterrorism. It is surprising that this title has not been challenged more by mainstream news media in the West. From a psychological perspective, the knowledge we have produces our judgments, which therefore dictate our actions. If the news media control the type of information we receive, then the news media are able to shape our judgment and eventually our actions and behaviors. Consequently, if a government or political group influences the news media, then it is able to influence the world.[3]

As psychoanalyst Salman Akhtar (2003, cited in Hough, 2004) has pointed out, terrorism was first used to describe the tyranny of a government that condoned policies which oppressed its nation's people. This was termed "terrorism from above" and referred to people such as Stalin and Hitler. What we currently have as the definition of terrorism, Akhtar has stated, is "terrorism from below," which refers to violent groups whose actions are against oppressive governments. Defining any group's protests as terrorism weakens or invalidates the group's actions. Why, Akhtar has wondered, "should we, who know that there are these two types of terrorism, restrict ourselves to considering only one?" (Hough, 2004). In doing this, it suggests that governments, regardless of their activities, are more innocent than the smaller terrorist groups.

In addition, Akhtar (cited in Hough, 2004) has explained that there is a possible overlap among terrorist groups and others, such as street gangs and spiritual cults. Common elements may include the psychodynamics of idealization, devaluation of others, and an outwardly narcissistic striving that covers up an unconscious masochistic agenda.[4] Akhtar also added that violent ethnopolitical acts that are perpetrated by "loners" are generally described by the news media as just crazy, rather than as terrorism (cited in Hough, 2004).

No single definition of terrorism is universally accepted, and this term has often been used negatively in one conflict but considered self-defense or liberation and freedom fighting in similar events elsewhere. For example, the occupation of France by Hitler's army and the subsequent armed French resistance movement under the leadership of then Colonel Charles de Gaulle was not called terrorism but a liberation movement (although Hitler denounced it as terrorism). The same situation is seen in the invasion of Lebanon (by Israel) and in Iraq (by the U.S. Coalition); usually resistance against the occupiers has been labeled terrorism, but the partisans would consider it fighting for freedom of their country.

A discussion of the use of terrorist as an identifying word was presented at the 44th Congress of the International Psychoanalysis Association. It was advised that because the term is so laden with political connections, it should no longer be considered an appropriate term for use in psychoanalysis (Siassi & Akhtar, 2006).

UNITED NATIONS' DEFINITION

Although there is no consensus from the United Nations organization, its Office for Drug Control and Crime Prevention has a short, succinct definition of an act of terrorism: "peacetime equivalent of a war crime" (*BBC News*, 2005). The implications that are inherent in the usage of the term terrorism are that the violence that is employed by a terrorist group is "immoral" or "unjustified" and that it tends to be executed without regard to innocent lives. However, to provide any global definition regarding the use of this term is not without debate. For example, U.N. Secretary General Kofi Annan called for a statement of "moral clarity" after the bomb attacks in London and Egypt in 2005 that would include the fact that the maiming and killing of civilians is unacceptable. The proposed definition of terrorism has been stalled in committee since 1996. The stalemate stems from the Palestinian–Israeli conflict. According to Arab League Secretary General Amr Moussa, there is a distinction between aggressive acts of violence and a nation that resists occupation from foreign invaders (*BBC News*, 2005).

The United Nations was not able to arrive at a unified definition of terrorism due to the components of the various definition proposals such as "cause political or governmental change," "threaten the nation, to create fear to punish a nation for what their government has done to the other" and so on (BBC News, 2005). Chomsky (2001) reported that the United States and Israel possibly sabotaged the creation of a consensus in definition of terrorism in the United Nations. Formal acceptance of a clear definition of terrorism by the United Nations continues to remain illusive at the time of this writing.

For the purpose of objectivity, we would wish that the focus of research on suicide warriors and political violence could be on, for example, Sri Lanka's conflict. From the western viewpoint, Sri Lanka is not a country with "emotionally charged" issues as is Israel, Palestine or Iraq. Otherwise, any assessment or analysis of the Arab-Israeli conflict may be colored by subjectivity, disinformation, bias, war propaganda, and the political or religious affiliation of the writer and reporter. That is why some news reports about a violent episode between Israelis and Arabs are reported differently in the different U.S. networks. Viewers of these media develop confusion in regard to who is the victim and who is the aggressor.[5]

UNITED STATES' DEFINITION OF TERRORISM

Sire, we have little defense against the opinion of a monarch, and even the most innocent man who ever lived will begin to be guilty if the King thinks him so.

Pierre Corneille

The U.S. government defines terrorism on an international level as those activities that involve violent or dangerous acts that are in violation of U.S. criminal laws. These acts are committed in order to intimidate or coerce civilians, influence government policy, or affect the conduct of a government. These activities may occur outside the United States or take place within its borders (*Wikipedia Encyclopedia*: Terrorism).

One of the first contemporary terrorist organizations in the United States could be considered the Ku Klux Klan. However, the members usually have not been identified as terrorists, "just racists." Plemmons reported that when victims of violence are in relatively lower power or socioeconomic class of society, acts of aggression against them are not usually labeled as terrorism. As an example, she refers to the 4700 lynching of blacks by whites that are documented in U.S. history (Bates, 2003).

DEFINITION OF SUICIDE BOMBER/ WARRIOR AND SUICIDE ACTIVIST

We are defining suicide bombers or warriors as people who must die first in order to harm or kill their enemies. Suicide bombers/warriors use their bodies to carry the weapons to achieve this end. This is different from other combatants who, when they attack the enemy, know that they may get hurt, but their weapon is not their body. In spite of the imminent danger to them, if there is the possibility that the attack can be carried out without the attacker's dying, it is not considered a suicide attack. The primary objective of both fighters is that the enemy will be killed or injured.

A suicide activist is a variation of the suicide warrior definition; in this case there is no other casualty except the suicide activist. This definition includes political suicides such as the German prison suicides in the 1970s, the Irish hunger strikes in the Maze prison in 1980s, and the monks who burned themselves during the Vietnam conflict to protest the U.S. government's policies. Another example is the Iranian "suicide battalion" (intehari,) which comprised foot soldiers who, during eight years of Iran-Iraq war, raced over mine fields. These people were blown up, but the platoon behind them was then able to progress through the now safe route. An elderly Iranian woman wrote a letter to an Iranian newspaper and suggested that she and other elderly individuals (who had lived their lives) should be invited to walk over the mine fields rather than young people.[6]

DEFINITION OF STATE-SPONSORED TERRORISM AND "STATE-CAUSED TERRORISM"

What do the nationalists say about killers punishing murderers and thieves sentencing looters?

Khalil Gibran

Liberty is the slogan of a party or sect that seeks to enslave some other party or sect.

Elbert Hubbard

It is very difficult to define and label what state-sponsored terrorism is. Most definitions of terrorism do not include legitimate government acts unless acting secretly in the absence of a state of war. Acts of war such as the atomic bombings of Nagasaki and Hiroshima, war crimes, crimes against humanity (e.g., the Holocaust), and government repression of its civilians are all differentiated from terrorism by some sources (*Wikipedia Encyclopedia*: Terrorism).

State-sponsored terrorism is defined as when a government or state sponsors, supports, directs, or organizes terrorist activity against its own citizens [7] or on another country (e.g., the U.S. support for the "Contras" in Nicaragua) (Chamorro, 1986; Herman, 2002). We want to distinguish this concept from state-caused terrorism. We have created this second term to define an activity in which a state or government indirectly encourages and promotes terrorism, although the government or state labels its activity as counterterrorism (e.g., "War on Terror"). This is a kind of side effect and an unintentional result of war policies, although some critics may claim it to be deliberate acts to create enemies in order to justify present or future wars. For example, a recent U.S. intelligence report disclosed that invasion of Iraq increased the risk of terrorism and the number of terrorists (*projo.com*, 2006). Looking at a videotape of Khan, a suicide bomber in London in 2005, revealed that he was directly connecting his action to the war in Iraq (Rai, 2006).

Chomsky (2001), a professor at Massachusetts Institute of Technology, described the controversial perception of the United States as a "leading terrorist state." He referred to "low intensity warfare" as a kind of terrorism because there are similarities within both actions. Atran also thought there was no difference between terrorism as defined by the U.S. Congress and counterinsurgency as defined in the U.S. Armed Forces manual. Atran (2003) reported that the International Court of Justice used the United States' own definition of terrorism during the 1980s to try to end the U.S. support for the terrorism of the Nicaraguan Contras. Variable definitions of terrorism have permitted selective applications to ever-changing U.S. priorities.

Post (2002) proposed a "spectrum of political terrorism" that can be further separated into "substate terrorism, state-supported terrorism and state or regime terrorism." Post explained that substate terrorism was the most diverse, and examples included leftist revolutionary groups (Peru), rightist groups (Nicaragua Contras), national separatist groups (Spain, Ire-land), religious extremists (Aum Shinri Kyo), as well as individual issues such as antiabortionists.

CLARIFYING DEFINITIONS

Political language is designed to make lies sound truthful and murder respectable, and to give an appearance of solidity to pure wind.

George Orwell

There are several controversial subjects that have not been universally clarified. For example, if during the war, noncombatant civilians are indirectly killed, what label should be used? If noncombatant civilians are deliberately killed, is this terrorism, a war crime, an atrocity, genocide or collateral damage? Looking at the references, collateral damage is defined in the *Encarta World English Dictionary* as "unintended damage to civilian life or property during a military operation" (Soukhanov, 1999), but what about the word unintended? If a criminal is hiding among children in a house, and by bombing that house, the children will be killed; is it unintended? Or from the beginning of the event is it understood that the children are going to die and are sentenced to death?[8]

Marsella (2003), in an enlightening chapter, defined terrorism as "a violent act against an existing legal government," although he acknowledged that without a specific historical and cultural context, all definitions are subject to debate. The questions that must be answered include what if an existing legal government has been established by force and is oppressive? What if the government stands against one's religious and political beliefs and does not provide for democratic change? Is resistance, civil disobedience or terrorism warranted? These questions are at the root of the controversy in understanding the definitions of terrorism, war, and freedom fighting (Marsella, 2003).

One might think that just by looking at the physical acts of violence themselves, one could determine if all of humanity would agree that they were atrocious inhuman acts. However, this is often not the case. As Ken Heskin pointed out, people still look back at the activities of the French Resistance in World War II as glamorous and admirable events. Yet, these acts were completely cruel. He continued, "It is, in fact, difficult to escape Clutterbuck's argument that the distinction ultimately boils down to a question of 'good guys' and 'bad guys' given the inescapable conclusion that atrocious behavior is the norm in conflict situations, whoever it involves" (Heskin, 1980, p. 76).[9]

CONCLUSION

As we have indicated in this chapter, the term terrorism is controversial, political, and subjective. There is no universal consensus of how to define terrorism. To resolve this issue we suggest, contrary to many professional ideas, that the definition of terrorism should not be connected to causing "political change." The term has been too muddled with one-sided posturing. We would prefer to use a different word when this event occurs (such as violence, war, aggression, or attacks rather than terrorism). We would like to raise the issue of using the term terrorism, only for violence that has no political, religious, or ideological undertones. As a consequence, examples of true acts of terrorism may be used to describe such actions as those of Theodore John "Ted" Kaczynski a.k.a. the "Unabomber" (a nickname given to him by the FBI and an acronym for university and airline bomber), who terrorized people from 1978 until his arrest in 1996. Another example of true terrorist acts was committed by two men, also known as the "Beltway Sniper Attacks," in the Washington, D.C. area in 2002. These attacks were indiscriminate shootings of people who were not known to either of the men.

NOTES

1. From R. Harre (2003). The social construction of terrorism. In F. M. Moghaddam & A. J. Marsella (Eds.), *Understanding Terrorism* (p. 91). Washington, D.C.: American Psychological Association.
2. For more information, *see* "Jewish terrorism" at www.wikipedia.com. *See also* Kinghoffer, J. A. (July 8, 2002). Jewish terrorism [On-line]. Available: http://hnn.us/articles/832.html. Judith Apter Klinghoffer is a senior associate scholar at the Political Science Department at Rutgers University, Camden, New Jersey.
3. In addition in war time, a country's media may justify disinformation (lies) on the basis of being at war, therefore legitimizing war propaganda. Although war propaganda is often used to deceive the enemy, it has also been used to deceive a nation's own citizens. Sadly, history has shown the veracity of the well-known proverb: the first casualty of war is the truth.
4. In reviewing multiple psychiatric sources, idealization refers to a defense mechanism in which a particular object is overvalued in order to protect it, possibly from fear of persecution or ambivalence. More simplistically, idealization is an

exaggeration of one's virtues and a minimization of one's faults. Devaluation, on the other hand, is the opposite of idealization. It is when one exaggerates the faults of others and minimizes their virtues. The word narcissism comes from the Greek legend of a boy called Narcissus. He fell in love with his mirrored image and was transformed into a flower with his name. Narcissism refers to a valuation of ones' own bodily attributes and by extension, one's deeds and personal qualities.

5. *See* Chapter 14 "Female Suicide Warriors/Bombers," which indicates how political affiliations and ideologies of writers may have an impact on their judgments and conclusions.

6. For more information *see* http://en.wikipedia.org/wiki/Hossein_Fahmideh.

7. State-sponsored terrorism is well-documented throughout global history. For example, SAVAK, the Secret Service of the Shah of Iran, was well-known to terrorize whoever opposed the dictatorship of the Shah whether they were within the country or abroad.

8. Coalition forces bombed a house in a Pakistani village based on information that a suspected terrorist might be inside. However, these forces also knew that this house contained several women, children, and other civilians. The villagers denied that this home was harboring a terrorist and mourned for the loss of these dozen civilians. In contrast, there have been reports of a number of conscientious Israeli soldiers and pilots who refused the orders of their commanders to shoot at a house filled with civilians because they knew that "unintended innocents" would be killed. For more information, *see* R. Chacham (2003). *Breaking Ranks: Refusing to Serve in the West Bank and Gaza Strip.* New York: Other Press; and C. McGreal, We are air force pilots, not mafia [On-line]. Available: http://fromoccupiedpalestine.org/node.php?id=1023.

9. Some antiwar literature has claimed that a potentially more appropriate term for the United States' "War on Terror" would be a "War on terrorist groups the U.S. does not support."

REFERENCES

Ahmad, E. (2001). *Terrorism: Theirs & ours.* New York: Seven Stories Press.

Akhtar, S. (2003, June 22). Terrorism Panel discussion held at the Spring Meeting of the American Psychoanalytic Association, Boston, MA. Quoted in G. Hough (2004). Does psychoanalysis have anything to offer an understanding of terrorism? *Journal of American Psychoanalysis Association, 52*(3) pp. 813–828.

Atran, S. (2003). Genesis of suicide terrorism. *Social Science, 299,* pp. 1534–1539.

Bates, B. (2003, June). Knowledge dismal on terrorism. *Clinical Psychiatry News,* p. 28

BBC News (2005, July 26). UN seeks definition of terrorism [On-line]. Retrieved May 15, 2006. Available: http://news.bbc.co.uk/2hi/americas/4716957.stm

Chamorro, E. (1986). US-sponsored contras are terrorists. In B. Szumski (Ed.), *Opposing Viewpoints Terrorism* (pp. 137–141). St. Paul, MN: Greenhaven Press.

Chomsky, N. (2001, October). The new war against terror. *Chomsky.Info* [On-line]. Retrieved February 12, 2007. Available: www.chomsky.info/talks/20011018.htm

Cohn, M. (2002). Understanding, responding to and preventing terrorism. *Arab Studies Quarterly* [On-line]. Retrieved October 24, 2006. Available: http://www.questia.com

Herman, E. S. (2002, July/August). The world confronts U.S. wars of terrorism. *Z Magazine* [On-line]. *15*(7). Retrieved March 14, 2007. Available: http://www.zmag.org/ZMag/articles/ julaug02herman.html

Herzog, A. (2002). The Mind of a terrorist [essay]. *Connecticut Medicine, 66*(4), pp. 237–239.

Heskin, K. (1980). *Northern Ireland: A psychological analysis.* New York: Columbia University Press.

Hough, G. (2004). Does psychoanalysis have anything to offer an understanding of terrorism? *Journal of American Psychoanalytic Association, 52*(3), pp. 814–828

Jervis, R., & Stone, A. (2006, August 17). From the dust of war, a more potent Hezbollah? *USA Today*, p. 1A.

Kemp, G. (1986). US support of terrorists is necessary. In B. Szumski (Ed.), *Opposing viewpoints terrorism* (pp. 133–136). St. Paul, MN: Greenhaven Press.

Marsella, A. J. (2003). Reflections on international terrorism: Issues, concepts, and directions. In F. M. Moghaddam & A. J. Marsella (Eds.), *Understanding Terrorism* (pp. 11–47). Washington, D. C.: American Psychological Association.

Merriam-Webster's Collegiate Dictionary (2003), 11th Edition. Springfield, MA: Merriam-Webster, Incorporated.

Post, J. M. (2002). Differentiating the threat of chemical and biological terrorism: motivations and constraints. *Journal of Peace Psychology, 8*(3), 187–200.

Projo.com (2006, October 1). Intelligence test [On-line]. Retrieved September 30, 2006. Available: http://www.projo.com/cgi-bin/bi/gold_print.cgi

Rai, M. (2006). 7/7 *The London bombings, Islam & The Iraq War.* London: Pluto Press.

Siassi, S., & Akhtar, S. (2006). Identity, destiny and terrorism: The effect of social terror on identity formation. *International Journal of Psychoanalysis, 87*, pp. 1709–1711.

Smelser, N. J., & Mitchell, F. (2002). *Terrorism: Perspectives from the behavioral and social sciences.* Washington, D.C.: The National Academies Press.

Soukhanove, A. (1999). *Encarta World English Dictionary.* New York: St. Martin's Press.

Wikipedia Encyclopedia: Terrorism [On-line]. Retrieved May 15, 2006. Available: http:// en.wikipedia.org/wiki/Terrorism

Chapter 2

PROLIFERATION OF SUICIDE BOMBERS: WHY ORDINARY PEOPLE PARTICIPATE IN WAR AND TERRORISM

Jamshid A. Marvasti

"WHY WAR?"

War does not determine who is right, only who is left.

Bertrand Russell

Why should you take by force from us that which you can obtain by love? Why should you destroy us who have provided you with food? What can you get by war?

King Wahunsonacook (Powhatan [Native American])

Storr (1978) has contended that although animals, along with humans, express aggression, cruelty seems to be one attribute held primarily by humans. Many theories exist to explain the existence of wars, aggression, and hatred of enemies. For example, Doctor Vamik Volkan, a prominent psychoanalyst, has suggested that human beings have a "need for enemies" to be external stabilizers of their sense of identity and support their perception of inner control (Volkan, 1988). As another example, Lloyd deMause has maintained that it is not greed or aggressiveness but fear that is the cause of war (deMause, 2006, p. 205). Further, Shermer (2003, p. 40) has offered a plausible evolutionary hypothesis that suggests that "limited resources led to the selection for within-group cooperation and between-group competition in humans, resulting in within-group amity and between-group enmity." Certainly, reflection on the history of the world gives the negative impression that war in and of itself engenders more war; as Lotto has explained, "a country responds to losing the war by starting another war rather than grieving the loss" (Lotto, 2006, p. 291).[1] In the USA, this phenomenon has been labeled the "Vietnam Syndrome"; in this case, "grieving the loss" seems a more painful process than that of creating a new war.[2]

Some of the greatest minds of modern civilization have contemplated this subject of deadly human aggression. For example, Einstein once asked Sigmund Freud: "Why War?" Freud responded with a treatise summarizing his belief that war serves as a great catharsis for the hostility that develops from the "constraints of civilization" (Persaud, 2004).[3] Doctor Abigail Golomb, a psychoanalyst, has pointed to childhood roots of such violence. She has specifically identified the effects of growing up in dictatorial cultures where ideologies are transmitted to the next generation very early (Siassi & Akhtar, 2006). Through this transmission of ideology, children develop an aversion to all strangeness, all difference. Therefore, in response to terrorists' acts, such children either identify with the aggressor or assume a victim's role in an attempt to categorize and understand this senseless situation. Thus, the child develops immunity to the fear of violence and instead uses violence not only to solve problems but also to protect the psychological self. As a result, aggression is integrated into the child's personality with little room to heal in the culture of hatred that has been created (Siassi & Akhtar, 2006).

A multitude of examples exist that illustrate peoples' motivations for war. In Abraham Lincoln's famous "Gettysburg Address," he spoke of having dedication for their cause of freedom. Lincoln was trying to inspire the discouraged Northern soldiers when he said, "From these honored dead we take increased devotion to that cause for which they gave the last full measure of devotion . . . that we, here, resolve that these dead shall not have died in vain." Another revered American patriot, Nathan Hale, also provided stirring words after his conviction for spying during the American Revolution: "I regret that I have but one life to give for my country." Similarly, McCauley (*ABC News*, 2005) has theorized that suicide bombers view themselves as sacrificing their lives for the greater good and regret that they only have one life to give for their cause. Another professional has even called them "perfect soldiers" (McDermott, 2005): "They saw themselves as pilgrims, soldiers of God." They carried the "power of belief to remake ordinary man."

THE PROCESS OF DEHUMANIZATION

One may also become motivated toward violence through the process of dehumanization, making someone less human. In general, the dehumanizing of enemy soldiers and civilians is a well-known war tactic. Soldiers are "brainwashed" so they will consider the enemy as inhuman and dangerous to humanity. As a result, such soldiers feel that they have a "license to kill." The action of dehumanizing was divided by Salman Akhtar (2003), a psychoanalyst, into five types (cited in Hough, 2004). The first type is evident in situations in which exposure to humanity is limited, such as in undomesticated children raised in the wild. The second and third types are evident in psychiatric disorders such as defect-based conditions seen in autism and regression-based disorders that are present in schizophrenia. The fourth type, noted in serial killers, is the result of catastrophically hostile introjections.[4] The fifth type is the result of a sociopolitical method used in oppressive times to create terrorists when other weapons are not available. This type of dehumanization "is directed against the natural human inclination toward empathy and remorse" (homicidal tendency) and "is also directed against self concern" (suicidal tendency) (Hough, 2004). Once dehumanized, certain "human" characteristics that might inhibit a person from committing violence no longer remain.

Humans, otherwise, can have a natural tendency to avoid killing someone if not provoked. As Persaud (2004) has pointed out, during the Korean Conflict in the 1950s, several American soldiers did not fire their guns at Koreans because the soldiers were resistant to killing. However, this tendency can be overcome with directed military training. Many normal, nonviolent people can be influenced into violence under the right circumstances (Persaud, 2004). For instance, during the military training for the Vietnam Conflict, recruits were conditioned by repeatedly shooting at enemy facsimiles in order to bypass their natural inhibitions against killing (Persaud, 2004).

CAN ORDINARY PEOPLE BECOME SUICIDE BOMBERS?

The definition of "ordinary people" can differ in various countries. The news media and international observers have documented that in the occupied territory of Palestine most, if not all, ordinary citizens have been exposed to the trauma of violence. One must acknowledge this difference in comparing ordinary citizens of Palestine to ordinary citizens of Switzerland, Canada, or other western countries.

Milgram (1974), a professor at Yale, has conducted a study using college-educated volunteers at Yale University for a research experiment. He divided the volunteers into two groups: the instructors and the subjects. These two groups were kept in separate rooms with a fake electrical shock system attached to each participant. Milgram's findings revealed that most instructors complied with orders to give potentially lethal shocks to their subjects when they failed a given task, even though the subjects (just acting) screamed in pain. Thus, ordinary people in this study were able to become "unordinary" and inflict pain upon innocent people. Although many analysts refer to Milgram's research to explain why young suicide bombers brutalize innocent citizens, we suggest that there are four other key elements that must still be considered:

1. Certain children, such as those in Palestine, Afghanistan, and Iraq, are being raised in total surroundings of war: it is what they see; it is what they breathe. This war around them informs the games they play with each other– one child, the suicide bomber, another, the weeping mother who cries for her dead son. There is no commander needed, as in Milgram's research, to push these people to become suicide bombers who kill civilians, because violence has already been absorbed into their way of seeing the world since childhood. A *USA Today* article by Zoroya in 2002 entitled "Curfew, Occupation Push Generation toward Radicalism" speaks of the anger, fear, and humiliation that is ever present in young Palestinian children as a result of army occupation. As Zoroya has expressed, "Israeli officials acknowledge the problem but see no alternative as long as Palestinian attacks continue" (2002). It is the many years of war and occupation that are breeding the radicalism that will produce a generation more creative and radical in carrying out their revenge and retaliation (Zoroya, 2002). One can wonder how many Palestinian children who grew up throwing rocks at Israelis have now become teenagers willing to use suicide bombing as a way to act on their feelings.

2. There is a justification or rationalization of choosing between bad and worse. Killing foreign innocent civilians is bad, but it may be worse if one's own people are killed. Perhaps this was the dilemma that President Truman and his entire cabinet dealt with when deciding whether or not to drop the bomb on Hiroshima. The bombing of innocent Japanese citizens would be bad, but perhaps the alternative of American soldiers being killed was considered to be worse (Marvasti, 2007a, b; MacNeil, 2007).

3. The third element, as explained by Volkan, deals with "cracks" in personal identity. Volkan has explored this component through his observations at a Palestinian orphanage (1997). As he has explained, in September 1982 the "Christian Phalangist militia" attacked two Palestinian refugee camps, killing civilians. In 1990, Volkan met with five child survivors who had been infants during the attack and who were now living in an orphanage. Upon observing the children, Volkan noticed their tendency to always stay together in a group, yet as such they played like normal children. When Volkan attempted to interview each child separately, he or she became abnormal. Their behavior, when separated, included hallucinating and destroying the room. In addition, he has noted that these children regressed to a "psychotic level" (Volkan, 2003 as cited in Hough, 2004). Volkan has concluded that this discrepancy of behavior was a result of a change, or replacement, of their

personal identity with a group identity. As Volkan (1997, p. 146) has pointed out, "an anxious or regressed group clings more stubbornly than usual to its ethnicity . . . these connections provide a netlike support that protects the group from deeper regression or disintegration" (1997, p. 146). Volkan also witnessed similar behavior, although less severe, in the rest of the children housed at that orphanage in 1991. Many of the orphanage's caregivers had been traumatized themselves and in caring for these children had passed on their "Palestinianism" which filled in the cracks of the children's identity (Volkan, n.d.). Moreover, Volkan has pointed out that these children were given the surname of "Arafat" (Volkan, 2003 as cited in Hough, 2004).

Speckhard and Akhmedova have also pointed out that when a person goes through an emotional overload due to severe trauma, "a psychological boundary is passed inside the individual in which he becomes in a sense already psychologically deadened and . . . becomes extremely vulnerable to those who would encourage him to make terrorist acts" (2005, p. 130).

Volkan (n.d.) has made the point that any person who has cracks in his or her personal identity is susceptible to having these cracks filled in by an outside source. One such source could be a "teacher" looking for people to train as suicide bombers. The next basic step in creating such bombers, as Volkan has explained, would be to use a teaching technique that would impose the large-group identity (ethnic and religious) into the "'cracks' of the person's damaged individual identity." Once this had occurred, rules that would normally govern a person's individual psychology would not apply. Then, "killing one's self (and one's personal identity) and 'others' (enemies) does not matter" (Volkan, n.d.).

Therefore, an ordinary Palestinian, Afghani, or Iraqi youth with multiple emotional traumas or losses may become a suicide warrior when his personal identity is melded into a group identity. Additionally, any cracks left in his personality may be filled by a mentor with nationalist slogans and ideas of devotion and self-sacrifice.

4. The fourth issue revolves around the definition of "innocent" civilians, those who are killed by bombers without any apparent reservation and those subjects in Dr. Milgram's study who were tortured by ordinary American students. Innocence is a term that one may not expect to need clarification. Often this term is connected with civilians (and not with soldiers) and can be thought to be indisputable when describing them.[5]

Are civilians always innocent? We maintain that although there can be "innocent" civilians, unfortunately, innocence is also in the eye of the beholder. After the N.Y. towers came down in 9/11, there was an outrage because so many innocent civilians were killed. Although Americans and people around the world would certainly agree with this statement, one wonders if bin Laden would. Critics have asked whether there is a difference between

U.S. civilians and the Japanese civilians who were bombed in Hiroshima and Nagasaki? In addition, terrorists have claimed that although U.S. civilians are not the ones with the guns, they do elect their leaders, and the taxes they pay do support the military and weapon production. Can citizens who live in a "democracy" be considered innocent regardless of the military action committed by their government? At least one suicide bomber might say no. Mohammad Sidique Khan was one of the bombers in the 7/7 attacks in Britain. He left behind a video with several statements, one of which was regarding the motivation for his attack, "Your democratically-elected governments continuously perpetuate atrocities against my people all over the world. And your support of them makes you directly responsible, just as I am directly responsible for protecting and avenging my Muslim brothers and sisters" (Rai, 2006, p. 131). However, we challenge two aspects of his statement. To begin with, we would suggest that his statements are potentially hypocritical because he and his fellow suicide bombers were British citizens whose democratic government was supporting the Iraq war, and their tax money supported this system. Furthermore, we would like to acknowledge the situation of the U.S. Presidential election of 2000. The majority of Americans voted for another candidate who was not apparently "war oriented," yet he did not win the overall election because of the Electoral College.[6] Americans do exist who believe that their tax money should be spent in other ways and generally reject the way the U.S. government is handling its international affairs. In addition, there are many Americans who are very much opposed to U.S. policies regarding the Middle East and are demonstrating in the thousands against the military activity of the United States and Israel. Despite the diversity of ideology within America, Khan and other terrorists have clearly put Americans and other westerners into one uniform group.

Palestinian suicide bombers have also been criticized for killing innocent Israeli civilians by many people, including fellow Muslims. Kimmerling (2003) however has raised the question, "But exactly who are civilians?" As he has noted, Israel has promoted itself as a "nation in arms." Israeli men and women are called in times of danger to don their military uniforms, thus becoming soldiers. When the danger has passed, they change back into civilians. Kimmerling has noted that critics have questioned how one can tell who is a solider and who is a civilian. This problematic case of civilian identity only increases in the cases of settlers in Israeli occupied territories. These settlers (whether they moved there on their own accord or were placed there by their government) are still on someone else's territory, according to Kimmerling. He has thus wondered if they are still civilian, because this is really an extension of the military's occupation (2003). From our point of view, however, Kimmerling's argument does not address the issue of the innocent Israeli children who are being killed.

WHY ARE SUICIDE BOMBERS PROLIFERATING?

I will return and be millions.
Eva Peron

From every drop of our blood, another revolutionary will be created.
Saeed Mohsen (statement before execution)[7]

It seems that suicide bombers feed upon one another and when one dies more appear. This violent act is a complex and multifaceted phenomenon with various motivating factors that will be explained in further depth in the next chapter. Here we would like to present certain psychological elements that have contributed to the proliferation and motivations of suicide bombers:

1. Survival guilt as part of posttraumatic stress disorder (PTSD) (e.g., Palestinian suicide fighters). Many Palestinians in occupied territories are suffering from PTSD after years of trauma created by homelessness, displacement, humiliation, and loss of family and friends in conflict with the occupying army. One of the signs of PTSD is the well-known phenomenon of survival guilt. When one member of a tribe is killed, jailed, or tortured, survivors wonder why they were spared while a comrade suffered. To cope with this guilt, the survivors may involve themselves with "martyrdom operations," increasing the number of young volunteers who are willing to give up their lives by using their bodies as weapons.

2. Identification with the martyr. As the number of suicide bombers increases and the culture glorifies such individuals, other young activists may identify with the martyrs and follow their path. There has been evidence of this type of identification in Palestine and Chechen.

3. Body is the source of pain. Many suicide bombers and activists have been injured physically in their past militant activities (which go back to their childhood). So, their bodies are sources of pain (rather than pleasure), and by destroying their bodies they possibly alleviate the source of pain. Any activity leading to arrest may cause additional pain because torture may be a routine interrogation procedure. Therefore, the potential bomber may choose suicide rather than another option (nonsuicidal) because his body already has produced pain, and suicide simply removes it.

A related issue involves the possibility that suicide may be a way to "escape from the self" (McNamara, 2004). From a psychological point of view, the self, like the body, tries to maximize pleasure and avoid pain. Clinical literature has revealed that at times suicide may be the result of a person's feeling that the self cannot maximize esteem or create pleasure. Instead this self becomes a source of psychic pain from which a person uses suicide to escape (McNamara, 2004). Although this speculation may have merit in clinical population cases, literature has indicated that suicide bombers/warriors are not part of the clinical population and that their suicidal actions possibly are not of psychiatric origin.

Freud also has written about the pleasure versus pain principle and maintained that it is human nature to run toward pleasure and away from pain. In referencing this theory, how do we define the actions of a suicide bomber? In clinical suicide cases we know that the pain of life is more severe than the possible pain of death (if there is any pain in death). Therefore, a depressed person may choose suicide as a way to escape the pain of life by seeking the numbness (or pleasure due to an absence of pain) of death. In addition, people have been interviewed who were depressed and suicidal and had certain religious convictions. Several of them held a belief that they may go to "hell" if they committed suicide. Yet, they considered their life to be more painful than any perception they had of hell. In relating Freud's theory to suicide bombers, the pain that they may feel can be caused by a variety of factors. Some of them may feel humiliated, invaded, traumatized, assaulted, or tortured or are suffering from a death of loved one by an "enemy." For them there may be pleasure to be gained through revenge or by ending perceived injustice.

4. No other way left. Feelings of helplessness, hopelessness, and frustration due to perceived injustice that remain unnoticed or unexpressed may contribute to suicide. Helplessness and hopelessness are not in themselves catalysts, but suicide is a reaction to the reasoning that "in no way can I defeat the enemy or inform the world of the injustice that is done to me and my nation. No one will listen."

THE ISSUE OF "US" VERSUS "THEM"–MYTH VERSUS HISTORICAL FACT

We must live together as brothers, or perish together as fools.
Martin Luther King, Jr.

The question has been raised in our minds as to why a great number of Saudi Arabians admire and support bin Laden as if he were the hero and innocent civilians killed on 9/11 were the sinful enemy. Psychoanalytical literature and professionals, including Abigail Golomb (Siassi & Akhtar, 2006), have explained how cultures may create a myth and ingrain images on individuals (especially children) without any historical facts. The issue of "us" and "them" may also play a role, as in anything we do (or my tribe did) is right and just, and all bad things are done only by them, the enemy. The myth of cowboys and Indians in the early U.S. West is an appropriate example. Indians were cast as wicked (as though they were the ones who stole the land), and cowboys were heroes who killed the bad guys. In fact, cowboys invaded and occupied the Native Americans' land and killed many of the tribes' men, women, and children. Yet it has been suggested that this path of genocide has its historical roots in the time of Christopher Columbus whose arrival in the New World was actually an invasion resulting in the enslavement of the people who were already living there. Even today there is a similar situation in Palestine. In the western news media, Palestinians are pictured as the offenders, as if they had come from other countries and had thrown out the Israelis and interned them in refuge camps. The suicide aggression and terrorism may continue to proliferate, as long as historical truth is distorted by prejudice.

When people divide the world into us and them, and good and evil, they miss the opportunity to understand the ways in which their actions might be influencing others' behavior for example, the ways in which the actions of the West could be causing certain reactions in the Middle East and vice versa. Ronald Pies (2001) a professor of psychiatry, has presented a viewpoint that we would like to challenge. In his article, Pies has stated that terrorism has nothing to do with western government actions. He has suggested that even if the United States ended world poverty or "stopped our arrogant ways," terrorism would still exist, and the United States would still be an object of hatred (2001). He has said that terrorism will continue as long as people exist who want the world to conform to their own wishes and that such individuals will accept any human cost for this (Pies, 2001). In his argument, Pies may be suggesting that the United States, (us) is good and terrorists (they) are evil, as are their actions. However, one may run into trouble with this type of black and white categorizing when the actions of the "good" group, begin to resemble those of the "evil" group.[8]

By reading Herman (2002), one may wonder what happens when the U.S. government's actions become similar to those that Pies has attributed to terrorists. As Herman has pointed out, "the Bush administration has announced its intention to project superior U.S. power across the globe, unilaterally and with a readiness to use force, to achieve its own ends and shape the world as it desires." Pies has adamantly suggested that terrorism will only end "when terrorists change the way they think" (2001). In addition, Pies' statements have given the impression that no cause and effect relationship exists between military invasion and occupation and counterreactions.[9]

Generally any culture that is involved in the dichotomy of us and them may ignore the fact that all people (friends and enemies) are human beings, even if they are different in color, dress, ritual, or religion. Saadi Shirazi, a Persian poet of 600 years ago, acknowledged this commonality in his poem:[10]

All human beings are in truth a kin;
All in creation share one origin. . .
When fate allots a member pangs and pains,
No ease for other members then remains. . .
If, unperturbed, another's grief canst scan
Thou are not worthy of the name of human.

CONCLUSION

It is clear that, regardless of the reason, war is and has been a major part of the human experience. Its impact is far and withstanding and is excluded from few, if any, nations. The human ability to be violent and aggressive may be experienced not only by soldiers but also by "ordinary people." It has been suggested that each person begins life as ordinary. Soldiers are created to be such; they are not born that way. As Milgram illustrated in his study, ordinary people who may never have considered themselves to be violent or aggressive may exhibit these behaviors under certain circumstances. Therefore, since all humans have the potential to participate in violence and war, perhaps the distinction between ordinary people and terrorists is a smaller gap than previously perceived. In addition, as we have indicated, there are various psychological factors that may help explain the proliferation of suicide bombers.

NOTES

1. War historians have cited that there was only a brief 100-year period of world peace, from 100 to 200 A.D., which was due to "the Roman empire's having everyone, fleetingly, in a thrall" (from N. Angier (2003.) Is war our biological destiny?" *New York Times*, November 11, p. D-1).
2. Chomsky commented about the speculation that the United States (or by proxy Israel) may attack Iran. He referred to the "wounded-beast phenomenon" by saying that it is conceivable that the catastrophes created by the current U.S. administration (wounded-beast) might precipitate a desperation attack against Iran in an attempt to reverse the failures in the Middle East. (From N. Chomsky, & G. Achcar,(2007). *Perilous power: The Middle East and U.S. foreign policy*; Boulder, CO: Paradigm Publishers, p. 231.)
3. In this book, we refer to professionals and researchers who have concluded that "occupation/invasion" of militants' land has been the most significant motivation for suicide bombers' actions. In regard to suicide bombers/warriors, one may modify the Freudian words "constraints of civilization" to "constraints of frustration and humiliation" due to the perceived occupation of their land.

Their actions can possibly be seen as a release from the constraints of occupation or invasion.

4. Psychoanalytical literature defines introjections as the process that occurs when one absorbs and incorporates the attitude of others as his or her own.

5. In addition, we believe that soldiers also may be considered "innocent", because it is the politicians who actually create war, not the eighteen- or nineteen-year-olds who have joined the army. A letter by one of the soldiers who was killed in Iraq to his wife is enlightening. This letter arrived a few days after he was killed. In it he wrote of his love for his wife and stated that if he had met her a little sooner, he would not have joined the army.

6. There are critics who consider the U.S. election process less than perfect. The Electoral College, television, and wealth have been identified as three contributing factors. It has been suggested that the American system of election is flawed. It has been suggested that one element of the system that has contributed to a flawed election system is the Electoral College. A candidate may win the election through the Electoral College even while losing the popular vote. Furthermore, because of the two-party system of nomination, voters may find themselves deciding between two unacceptable people: bad and worse. Television has played a major role in a candidate's success since 1959. For example, televised debates between Richard Nixon and John F. Kennedy were widely credited with Kennedy's marginal victory. Americans generally are capable of recognizing a good leader (sometimes in retrospect), especially in comparison to others considered weak or ineffectual. The real question is how Americans can identify inner qualities of a true leader, placing less importance on superficial aspects such as appearance, demeanor, race or gender. A more difficult goal is to remove the power of money from the process. Wealth is a significant factor in determining who can even attempt to reach a political position. The richest candidate may win despite inferior qualities, whereas a candidate who cannot raise millions of dollars has virtually no chance.

7. Saeed Mohsen was one of several organizers of the Mojahedin Khalgh Organization (MKO), founded in 1965. All of the founding members were middle-class students or recent graduates of Tehran University. The organization's goal was to oppose the Iranian regime which they felt was corrupt and oppressive. Before they could do anything substantial against the Shah's regime, they were all arrested and tortured by SAVAK (secret police). Most of them were also executed. Saeed Mohsen's statement was somewhat prophetic, because more militants entered the struggle against the Shah until the regime was overthrown in 1979.

8. Doctor Hamid Dabashi, an Iranian scholar and Columbia University professor, explained in his recent book how nations in the Middle East "live with deadly, spiraling cycle of violence, trapped between terrorism and the war on terrorism, which ultimately amounts to the same thing" (p. 6). He explained that whether one believes in the heads of western governments or in bin Laden "make(s) no difference when a bullet pierces your skull, or a suicide bomber blows himself or herself, and everything in sight to smithereens" (p. 7) (from H. Dabashi

(2007). *Iran: A people interrupted,* New York: The New Press).

9. It seems that Ronald Pies could be unaware of what terrorists (including bin Laden) have said in regard to their motivation, and also that he has not seen the videotapes/last messages of suicide bombers.

10. Saadi Shirazi was an Iranian poet and philosopher (1200–1292). After the Mongol Holocaust he wandered through the Middle East and developed an esoteric philosophy of a combination of Islam and Sufism. When he settled down in Shiraz to write, he showed a deep awareness of the absurdity of the human experience and often illustrated it with the contrast between practicality and spirituality. He used humor, cynicism and wisdom to challenge the continual subservience people needed to show to the whims of royalty. He remains the master of Persian love poetry to this day. (*See* http://www.iranchamber.com/literature/saadi/saadi.php)

REFERENCES

ABC News (2005, August 6). Experts: Suicide bombers not crazy [On-line]. Retrieved August 26, 2006. Available: http://abcnews.go.com/Nightline/print?id=1004809

Akhtar, S. (2003, June 22). Terrorism Panel discussion held at the Spring Meeting of the American Psychoanalytic Association, Boston, MA. Quoted in G. Hough (2004). Does psychoanalysis have anything to offer an understanding of terrorism? *Journal of American Psychoanalysis Association, 52*(3) pp. 813–828.

deMause, L. (2006,Winter). The Childhood Origins of the Holocaust. *The Journal of Psychohistory, 33*(3), pp. 204–231.

Herman, E. S. (2002, July/August). The world confronts U.S. wars of terrorism. *Z Magazine* [On-line]*, 15*(7). Retrieved March 14, 2007. Available: http://www.zmag.org/ZMag/articles/julaug02herman.html

Hough, G. (2004). Does Psychoanalysis have anything to offer an understanding of terrorism? *Journal of American Psychoanalysis Association, 52*(3) pp. 813–828.

Kimmerling, B. (2003, December 15). Sacred rage. *The Nation, 277*(20), pp. 23–30.

Lotto, D. (2006, Winter). Book reviews. *The Journal of Psychohistory, 33*(3), pp. 290–299.

MacNeil, J.S. (2007, July). Suicide bombers don't fit psychological profile. *Clinical Psychiatry News, 35*, 7, p. 35.

Marvasti, J. A. (2007a, April 26) *Psychological Autopsy of a suicide bomber.* Paper presented at the 25th annual symposium in forensic psychiatry of the American College of Forensic Psychiatry, Santa Fe, NM.

Marvasti, J.A. (2007b, August). Physicians as killers? *Clinical Psychiatry News, 35*, 8, p. 14.

McDermott, T. (2005). *Perfect soldiers.* New York: Harper Collins Publishers.

McNamara, D. (2004, July). Suicide for some is an escape from "the self." *Clinical Psychiatry News* [On-line]. Retrieved September 15, 2005. Available: http://www.clinicalpsychiatrynews.com/article/PIIS0270664404700399/fulltext.

Milgram, S. (1974). *Obedience to authority.* New York: Harper & Row.

Persaud, R. (2004, September). Inside the mind of a terrorist. *BBC News* [On-line]. Retrieved February 10, 2007. Available: http://news.bbc.co.uk/go/pr/fr/-/2/hi/uk_news/magazine/3699826.stm

Pies, R. (2001, October). Special forum: 9/11 and everyday life-a simple way to end terrorism. *Journal of Mundane Behavior* [On-line] *2*(3). Retrieved July 20, 2006 Available: http://mundanebehavior.org/issues/v2n3/9-11/pies.htm

Rai, M. (2006). *7/7 The London bombings, Islam & the Iraq war*. London: Pluto Press.

Shermer, M. (2003, September). "The domesticated savage." *Scientific American*, p. 40

Siassi, S. & Akhtar, S. (2006). Identity, destiny and terrorism: The effect of social terror on identity formation. *International Journal of Psychoanalysis, 87*, 1709–1711.

Speckhard, A., & Akhmedova K. (2005 Fall). Talking to terrorists. *The Journal of Psychohistory, 33*(2), 125–156.

Storr, A. (1978) Sadism and paranoia in M. H. Livingston (Ed.). *International terrorism in the contemporary world*. London: Greenwood Press. pp. 231–239.

Volkan, V. (1988). *The need to have enemies & allies: From clinical practice to international relationships*. Northvale, NJ: Jason Aronson, Inc.

Volkan, V. (1997). *Blood Lines: From ethnic pride to ethnic terrorism*. Boulder, Colorado: Westview Press.

Volkan, V. (2003, June 22). Terrorism Panel discussion held at the Spring Meeting of the American Psychoanalytic Association, Boston, MA. Quoted in G. Hough (2004). Does psychoanalysis have anything to offer an understanding of terrorism? *Journal of American Psychoanalysis Association, 52*(3) pp. 813–828.

Volkan, V. (n.d.). *Suicide bombers*. Retrieved June 4, 2007. Available: http://www.google.com/search?hl=en&q=volkan%2C+suicide+bombers%2C+biet+atfal+al-sommoud

Zoroya, G. (2002, August 6). Fear, rage fester inside for West Bank children: Curfew, occupation push generation toward radicalism. *USA Today*, p. 1A.

Chapter 3

WHAT MOTIVATES THE SUICIDE BOMBER?

Jamshid A. Marvasti

When the horrors of life outweigh the horrors of death, humans commit suicide.

Arthur Schopenhauer

Even dying (for the ideology or the cult) is then deemed the better alternative than being forced to live and work through one's own inner terrors: helplessness, dependency, inadequacy, separation, loss, death.

Juhani Ihanus[1]

INTRODUCTION

To continue our examination, we look within the wide spectrum of war and violence to examine those specific circumstances that could transform an ordinary person into a suicide bomber. What motivates a suicide bomber? What elements contribute to the creation of such bombers? What causes these aggressive acts? Is terrorism a way of communicating? As psychiatrist Jerrold Post has suggested, terrorists "give their lives to be understood, and . . . violence is their medium of communication" (Hough, 2004). To prevent terrorism, one must know the motivations for it. Prevention will occur from understanding the roots of terrorism; its etiology rather than its resulting branches.

We have reviewed extensive case histories of suicide bombers/warriors and analyzed their messages and families' statements, their environment, and their perceived sense of injustice and emotional pain. As Robert Lifton, a distinguished American psychiatrist, has maintained, no single factor on its own creates terrorism, and terrorism does not have a single relationship with

any specific society (Lifton, 2003). On the basis of our work, we have hypothesized that several elements have motivated these young warriors to take
their own lives and those of innocent civilians. Most of these elements have
also been explored by other professionals (Atran, 2003; Marsella and Moghaddam, 2005; Merari, 2005; Pape, 2005a, b; Rai, 2006; Roy, 2003; Sohail,
2006).

Overall these acts of violence and suicide bombings are aimed at changing policy, rather than enforcing one's way of life or causing religious conversion. Jackson (2005) has explained that in the case of some terrorists,
there is a sense of hopelessness about the future and a personal belief that
this type of violence is the only option left for them in terms of forcing political change. This belief is a result of their personal life circumstances, such as
living under foreign occupation and experiencing poverty, unemployment,
and exclusion from the political system (Jackson, 2005).

We also feel that the importance given to certain motivations may be relative to the motivations of the particular speakers or reporters. Some pro-
West writers may not indicate that the occupation or invasion of Palestine,
Iraq and Lebanon and unconditional support from western governments
could be factors that would motivate aggression against Israel and the United
States. They may instead focus on religion, recruiting organizations, financial
rewards for the suicide bomber's family, and fanaticism as the cardinal elements of motivation. Middle Eastern news media, on the other hand, would
potentially claim occupation, invasion, humiliation and injustice as the major
motivating factors. In addition, intellectuals, politicians, and civilians may all
view different factors as motivations for suicide bombers due to their own
circumstances and self-interests.

What follows is our effort to understand, from as many perspectives as
possible, why some people have chosen this path of violence. In our study,
we have included examples from various countries and time periods to illustrate that suicide bombing has a history and is not exclusive to any one society. In addition, the motivations for becoming a suicide bomber can be divided into external and internal factors, although these two groups are interconnected. Motivations such as military occupation, religion, poverty, group
bonding, cultural support and remuneration are external, yet they inform
and are affected by internal factors such as trauma, perceived injustice, and
humiliation. In a metaphoric sense, these motivational factors, one by one
are similar to trees. Standing alone, each may not create a large presence, but
when many are together, they create a jungle. Therefore, it is difficult to be
accurate in isolating any one specific factor as the only "true" cause of suicide bombing, and we encourage the reader to see the overlap of motivations, to see the grey area among the black and white.

MOTIVATIONAL FACTORS

The Element of Occupation/Invasion of Homeland

We shall defend our island, whatever the cost may be, we shall fight on the beaches, . . . we shall fight in the fields and in the streets, we shall fight in the hills; we shall never surrender.

Sir Winston Churchill

We know our lands have now become more valuable. The white people think we do not know their value; but we know that land is everlasting, and the few goods we receive for it are soon worn out and gone.

Canassatego (Native American)

Literature has revealed that the key motivation of many suicide bombers has been the invasion and subsequent occupation of their land, home, or "holy place." Pape (2005a), for example, writes that the ultimate goal of suicide bombers is to force the invading or occupying powers out of their country. Since 1980, the primary targets of such bombers have not been domestic opponents but rather military operations or foreign governments who oppose this withdrawal (Pape, 2005a). However, the generalization by Pape is not without exception. For example, bin Laden assassinated his domestic rival (Ahmed Shah Massoud) a few days before 9/11 by using two suicide activists who posed as TV reporters.[2]

More in keeping with Pape's theory, however, is the larger issue regarding bin Laden: his relationship with the United States turned from ally to enemy in response to a perceived invasion of his homeland. In 1990, the United States went into Saudi Arabia with a military force, in theory to help Saudi Arabia defend itself against Iraq's Saddam Hussein. Although Saddam was defeated, the U.S. military force remained (Ahmad, 2001). Eqbal Ahmad, who had met with bin Laden before his own death in 1999, has noted (long before the tragedy of 9/11) that, "bin Laden wrote letter after letter [to the U.S.] saying, 'Why are you here? Get out! You came to help but you have stayed on.' Finally he started a jihad against the other occupiers" (p. 23). Ahmad has further explained that despite all of his wealth, bin Laden is a tribal person, and as such, he has two codes he lives by: loyalty and revenge. He will be loyal as long as his ally is loyal, but if that changes, then he will seek revenge, as he has done with the United States (Ahmad, 2001).[3]

Pape (2005a) has explained that, in this sense, the 9/11 attacks by Al-Qaeda are similar to the previous example, in that both are reactions to occupation. Al-Qaeda targeted U.S. financial, military, and government bases because it believed that the United States had been exploiting the Arab nation. It has been questioned why the United States has even been "supporting" Saudi Arabia, because they have a government that promotes practices the United States would condemn, such as a fanatical dictatorial regime with no freedom of speech and limited, if any, women's rights (such as being able to drive or work outside of the home). The possible reason for this support is that it has enabled the United States to secure its oil supply. In Saudi Arabia there is little debate over the Al-Qaeda objection to American forces in the region. In fact, more than 95 percent of Saudis agree with bin Laden on this matter (Pape, 2005a). This outside governmental control could be termed neocolonialism (the creation of a puppet government) as compared to colonialism. As a microcosmic example of how neocolonialism has played out, let us examine their baseball team: a Little League baseball team that represented Saudi Arabia in the 2006 World Series was comprised of eleven Americans and one British citizen. On the international scale, if Saudi Arabia is only defined by its Arab-American oil company ARAMCO and is represented to the world by a baseball team without one Saudi citizen, one may wonder what has happened to its Arab citizenry and culture. The anger that has developed from societal changes such as these has often been directed toward perceived western exploitations and occupation.

Pape (2005b) surveyed 315 suicide attacks from around the world between 1980 and 2003. From this study he has concluded that terrorist campaigns had a secular and strategic goal in common: "to compel democracies to withdraw military forces from the terrorists' national homeland" (Pape, 2005b, p. 38). France, the United States, Israel, India, Sri Lanka, Turkey, and Russia were all such examples of democratic systems of governments that suicide campaigns targeted. Furthermore, Pape has stated that democratic governments are targeted more than authoritarian governments are for three reasons: (1) democracies are thought to be more influenced by forced punishment; (2) suicide attacks are techniques of the weak. The people they are attacking are almost always able to retaliate with far more strength. Therefore, attackers must have great interests at stake and must believe their target state will use some restraint. Democracies fit this description as they are believed to be less likely to kill civilians; and (3) it is harder to organize a suicide attack in authoritarian states (Pape, 2005b).

We however, would like to critique Pape's argument. Yes, most of the countries he has mentioned had democratic governments when attacked, but would it not be feasible to believe that even if these countries did not, they would still be attacked for occupying another's land? It seems that even if Israel were a dictatorship, Palestinians would still be attacking them because they are believed to be in Palestinian territory. In addition, these so-called democratic regimes have also killed many civilians, and one might be hard pressed to find universal agreement that some of these governments have used "restraint" (e.g., bombing of Hiroshima by the United States, and carpet bombing of Dresden by the British government). We wonder if Pape would argue that if the United States and Britain were not democratic governments then the events of 9/11 and 7/7 would not have happened. One should remember that one of the most hated regimes in Europe was a republic and elected Hitler as a leader.

Reuter (2002) has delineated the very real grievances of suicide bombers. He has noted that the Tamil Tigers (Sri Lanka) and the Kurdistan Worker Party (PPK) (Turkey) are persecuted minorities; whereas Palestinians and Chechen rebels and Iraqi resistance fighters are fighting for the independence of their land from occupying armies. Reuter has argued how groups experiencing unresolved conflicts, such as the Palestinians and the Chechens, can grow into Al-Qaeda-like organizations, that derive sustenance from genuine and often legitimate local anger and rage (Reuter, 2002).

Merari (2005), an Israeli researcher, has also supported the importance of this element of motivation in referencing data on Palestinians. His research has illustrated that 56 percent of Palestinian suicide bombers lived in refugee camps in occupied territories and had experienced personal trauma there. It is not only personal trauma that people living in occupied territories experience, however. According to reports by the Health Development Information and Policy Institute in Ramallah, during the first two years of the second Intifada, Palestinian health systems were hindered by Israel's closure policy, disrupting vaccination and early detection programs and dental examinations, affecting more than 500,000 children; upper respiratory infections increased by 20 percent, and more than half of the children in Gaza suffered parasitic infections; Palestinian children experienced symptoms of trauma, sleep disorders, thoughts of death, and feelings of hopelessness; thirty-six women in labor were stopped at military checkpoints and were denied access to medical facilities; and out of the fourteen women who gave birth at the checkpoints, eight babies died as newborn infants (Khouri, 2006). Many critics claim that these issues are the side effect of occupation and the struggle against it by the people of occupied land.[4]

Literature also has offered insight into activists who become "suicide killers." Dr. Sarraj, a prominent psychiatrist in the Gaza Strip, has written an article entitled "Understanding Palestinian Terror" explaining the frustration and emotional turmoil that Palestinians endure under Israeli occupation:

> We simply became the slaves of our enemies. We are building their homes on our villages. You learn how to watch in silence, pretending not to see the torture of your friends and humiliation of your father. You know what it means for a child to see his father spat on and beaten before his eyes by an Israeli. For seven long years our children were throwing stones and being killed daily. Nearly all our young men were arrested; the majority was tortured. All had to confess; we were exhausted, tormented and brutalized. Now do you understand why we have turned into suicide killers?[5]

Jackson (2005) has examined occupation as a motivation for suicide bombing from a slightly different angle. He is one of a few writers who have considered some of the suicide bombers to have been inspired by a warped sense of altruism, in that they are ultimately giving of themselves (their life) for their families and the good of their community. In addition, Jackson has noted that the primary motivation of suicide bombers is rarely their hatred toward their victims. They have more selfless aims, believing their fight is the good fight, and they are fighting for their comrades and society. They are "normal" their psychological profile being indistinguishable from the average person (Jackson, 2005). There are, however, critics who doubt that suicide bombers could have such an altruistic and selfless goal as ending the occupation or invasion of their land while justifying death of innocent civilians. Yet from the literature presented in this section, it is clear that occupation does play a role in creating suicide bombers.

The Element of Nationalism

And they searched his chest
But could only find his heart
And they searched his heart
And could only find his people.
Mahmud Darwish[6]

East or West? Home is best.
Proverb

Pape (2005a) has identified nationalism as the primary motivation for suicide bombers, rather than religion, despair, or the promise of an afterlife. Most suicide bombers, he has written, are motivated primarily by a desire to form their own country and oust foreign invaders from land they claim as their own. When they are viewed this way, suicide missionaries appear not to be irrational fanatics but rather, careful thinkers who have concluded that suicide attacks are the best way to coerce their enemies into conceding territory or granting nationhood. Actually, the difference between terrorists and more moderate leaders usually concerns the level of violence each party is willing to use to achieve the desired results. Pape has concluded that terrorists usually include only a few members of society, but they are the ones who are the most optimistic about the efficacy of violence in achieving the goals that their community supports (Pape, 2005 a).

The formation of a strong sense of nationalism can begin at a very early age. Volkan (1997) has examined orphaned children in Palestine whose strong group bonds extended beyond their orphanage. These children would involuntarily mimic the throwing of stones while watching children of the

Intifada on the television throw stones at the Israeli soldiers. These orphans clearly could identify with others living in an occupied territory and illustrated the group bonding process that encourages nationalistic ties. As defined by Hans Kohn (1944), "Nationalism—our identification with the life and aspirations of uncounted millions whom we shall never know" This identification, he continues, "is qualitatively different from the love of a family or of home surroundings. It is qualitatively akin to the love of humanity or of the whole earth" (Volkan, 1997, p. 150). It is in these repressed societies where group identity is stronger than personal identity that one can grow attached to a national leader who symbolizes the group identity. These leaders can wield great influence about the portrayal of an enemy group and the actions that should be taken towards them (Volkan, 1997, p. 146). In one example of the strength of nationalism, Volkan (2003 as cited in Hough, 2004) has described how during the occupation of Gaza, Palestinians would carry stones painted the colors of their national flag in their pockets. Touching these stones would reduce their anxiety, because they would feel connected to their larger community.

The IRA warriors, considered terrorists by western countries, serve as another example of a strongly nationalistic group. As Heskin has mentioned, in Ireland a historical legitimacy exists to "taking up arms in the defense of one's heritage and, explicitly in the Republican tradition, a cultural exaltation of armed conflict of the guerilla type" (1980, p. 85). The IRA has struggled for years against British occupation, and to many of the Irish, it was not out of the ordinary to think of joining the IRA, a group sympathetic to the nationalistic effort of many of the Irish (Heskin, 1980).

The last words of a suicide bomber, Mahir Abu-Surur, reinforce these warriors' focus on strong national ties, "it is the day of meeting the Lord of the World . . . make our blood cheap for the sake of Allah and out of love for this homeland and for the sake of the freedom and honor of this people . . . and Palestine be liberated" (Oliver & Steinberg, 2005, p. 120).[7]

The Elements of Rage and Revenge

It is men's nature to hate when they believe they have been wronged.

Plutarch

Humiliated children become children of vengeance.

Juhani Ihanus

Others may hate you. Those who hate you do not win unless you hate them. Then you destroy yourself.

Richard Nixon

Another key factor associated with suicide attacks and insurgency involves the feelings of rage and the subsequent desire for revenge. Psychiatric literature has revealed that revenge is a psychological defense against shame, loss, and humiliation. Karen Horney, for example, has considered revenge to be a defensive function whose purpose is to externalize self-hatred and guilt, thus preventing these feelings from turning inward (Horney, 1948 as cited in Lotto, 2006, p. 48). She has emphasized that another function of revenge is to restore injured pride and to undo the pain of shame and humiliation. Along these same lines, Searles (1956) has focused on the function of revenge as a protective factor for grief over a loss. Similarly, Jackson (2005) has stated that the desire for revenge may be a result of experiencing the trauma of losing someone. For example, he has mentioned that many Palestinian bombers and Chechen black widows (female suicide bombers) are known to have had family or friends killed by enemy security forces. Others, such as Volkan (1997), have pointed out that revenge may be used by individuals to avoid or decrease the painful aspects of the mourning process. In addition, several clinicians have recognized that revenge and vengeful wishes actually can be extremely pleasurable. In fact, Horney has labeled revenge as a kind of "vindictive triumph" (Horney, 1948, as cited in Lotto, 2006).

Connecting with a group can provide an outlet for someone who is suffering with feelings of rage and revenge. Literature has noted (Silke, 2003a, b) that someone who joins a militant group is first motivated by his support of the goals and grievances of the group. In addition, a person usually has experienced some form of injustice, and the group represents an opportunity for vengeance. As Marvasti has reported, political militants have been instructed to get in touch with their rage in order to sustain themselves while being tortured (1993, p. 489).

Cota-McKinley, Woody, and Bell (2001) have stated that revenge can fulfill a number of purposes, including righting the perceived injustice, returning the self-worth of the individual who seeks vengeance, and deterring future injustices. The decision to give one's life for revenge is not determined in an instant but is considered over a period of time that may include months or even years. This decision is one that may even be foretold from childhood. In the case history of the suicide bomber/martyr Muhammad al-Hindi, his brother has written about his birth: "That day he was born for revenge . . . revenge for me and my country and my people and the honor of my ummah [Islamic nation]. Revenge for Majdal [the name of the Arab town where the Israeli city of Ashkelon now stands] from which my parents were forced to flee . . . despite their huge love for its soil" (Oliver & Steinberg, 2005, p. 148). It is important to note, however, that some Islamic scholars have declared that in Islam, sacrifice should only be for God (Allah) not for personal benefit or revenge (Anees, 2006).

Avishai Margalit, an Israeli writer, has also commented that revenge through suicide bombing is an act that is celebrated by the community of the suicide bomber (2003). Frequently, such bombers are avenging a specific death of a friend or family member and will make it clear in their wills whom they are avenging. Margalit has illustrated one example in which the connection to revenge seemed clear: "Darin abu-Isa, a student of English literature who blew herself up in March 2002, lost her husband and her brother in the current Intifada; her family says that she did it to avenge their deaths." Margalit continues that revenge itself as a motivation, however, does not explain the attraction to suicide bombing, because there are other avenues. What is accomplished through this act has an additional value to the bomber: "that of making yourself the victim of your own act, and thereby putting your tormentors to moral shame."[8]

Merari (2005) has found from his study of friends and families of Palestinian suicide bombers between 1993 and 1998 that the personal history of these bombers (in regard to participating in demonstrations, stone throwing, distributing leaflets, etc.) "does not distinguish them from the average Palestinian youngster in the period under consideration" (p. 439). As Merari has noted, more than half of the thirty-four suicide warriors came from families who were politically active during the first Intifada. In most cases, a high level of militant feeling did precede a personal trauma that conceivably added to any preexisting wish for revenge. In addition, fifteen of the thirty-four suicide bombers had been beaten or injured by Israeli forces during demonstrations (Merari, 2005).

Khalid Sohail, a poet and psychotherapist, has suggested that the need for revenge evolves from a generalized anger toward "imperialistic and colonial countries" (Sohail, 2006). Other researchers (Fisk, 2001) have suggested that terrorists are motivated by revenge from suffering at enemy hands. However, Merari (2005) does not believe that the theory of revenge fits the terrorist attacks of September 11, 2001, even though it may still be true in regard to attacks in Lebanon, Israel and Turkey. We question Merari's conclusions in this case, however, based on the Marsella and Moghaddam (2005) studies. The latter quote bin Laden extensively, pointing to revenge as one of the causes of the 9/11 attacks. For example, "The people of Islam have suffered from aggravation, inequity, and injustice imposed upon them by Zionists, Crusaders alliance" (Marsella & Moghaddam, 2005, p. 22). Bin Laden also declared that the United States has occupied the holiest of places of Islam, the Arabian Peninsula. He believes that the United States has plundered Arabian riches, dictated to its rulers, humiliated its people, terrorized its neighbors, and turned the land into a spearhead through which to fight the neighboring Muslim people. In bin Laden's words, "What America tastes now is something insignificant compared to what we have tasted for scores of years" (Marsella & Moghaddam, 2005, p. 22).

Can the motivation of a suicide bomber be a defining factor in determining if this violent action is terrorism? Shergald (2007) has held that the Palestinian suicide bombers involved in the second Intifada had motivations that would not establish them as terrorists according to the 1999 U.N. Resolution definition that stated that terrorists were those who used their actions to promote terror. Further, he has differentiated their motivations from that of Al-Qaeda or the PLO before the Oslo Accords of 1993, whose motivations were connected to receiving political recognition. If their incentive was not primarily to cause terror or gain political status, what were their motivations? Doctor Abdel Aziz Rantisi, a Hamas suicide bomber coordinator and pediatrician who was subsequently killed by the Israelis, put forth that Palestinian suicide bombers of the second Intifada were motivated by "situational anger and the desire for vengeance and retaliation" (Wilson, 2005; Shergald, 2007). The desire for revenge often accompanies feelings of rage. Rantisi has stated that before the second Intifada, Hamas had trouble finding men for their missions, which was the reason why there were so few suicide bombings during the Oslo Accords, and no suicide bombings between 1998 and 2000.[9] Afterwards, when the peace process began to breakdown and Palestinians began dying, Hamas and other organizations experienced a sharp increase as more Palestinians wanted to participate. In the first year of the second Intifada more than fifty suicide bombers penetrated Israel (Wilson, 2005; Shergald, 2007), and many innocent Israeli citizens were killed.

Psychological literature has indicated that anger and rage can act as protective shields for the ego. In our opinion, it seems that revenge and anger also confer power to suicide warriors. By using their bodies for the ultimate sacrifice, they feel they can reverse the sense of national despair, hopelessness, and powerlessness.[10]

The Element of Psychic Trauma and Dissociation

If we could read the secret history of our enemies, we should find in each man's life sorrow and suffering enough to disarm all hostilities.
Henry Wadsworth Longfellow

Psychic trauma is an abrupt event and painful experience that the individual's ego cannot assimilate. Instead, the individual may repress and eliminate part of or the entire traumatic memory from consciousness. As a result of trauma, one also may experience "dissociation." The definition of dissociation according to the American Psychiatric Association is a "disruption in the usually integrated functions of consciousness, memory, identity, or perception of the environment" (American Psychiatric Association, 2000). In regard to trauma and dissociation in potential suicide bombers and political militants, Speckhard and Akhmedova (2005) have their own definitions. When one undergoes trauma—"personally witnessing death, torture, beating"—one can spontaneously enter a "trance state" whenever a reminder of the traumatic event appears. "This spontaneous defense of entering a trance state in response to posttraumatic recall is commonly referred to as dissociation" (p. 129). Speckhard and Akhmedova have reported that trauma has negative side effects and long-term psychiatric implications.

In addition, Volkan (2003) has explored various types of trauma. Of particular importance to understanding what may contribute to the creation of suicide bombers are "chosen traumas," which are "representations of massive traumatic events experienced by a group's ancestors" (cited in Hough, 2004, p. 825). These traumas can be triggered when a large group is under stress: "Feelings, perceptions, and thoughts about traumatic events experienced by ancestors become condensed into feelings, perceptions, and thoughts about the present . . . a 'time collapse' which may incite acts of terrorism" (p. 825). Both Israel and Palestine have citizens, although they may be in the minority, who are on a violent mission to "right the world." As Lifton has noted, these sentiments have been built on years of collective humiliation, rage, and displacement: "Jews in connection with the Holocaust [and thousands of years of dislocation], and Palestinians in connection with earlier European imperialism and with more recent losses of land and homes through wars with the Israelis" (2003, p. 18). These feelings of humiliation, while having historical roots, can trigger traumatic experiences in the present.

Speckhard and Akhemdova (2005) use the following example to illustrate the effects of trauma and how it can become a motivator for suicide bombing. Mustafa, a Palestinian boy in an Israeli jail, witnessed a cellmate being beaten to death and was pushed "beyond all sense of psychological normalcy" (p. 130). He has stated that he would be willing to become a suicide bomber against Israelis. In his own words, "Every moment when you pass the line of death, you are already dead" (p. 130). Another thwarted suicide bomber has described himself as "floating on air" while the bomb was strapped to him, illustrating that on such an occasions, dissociation from self can occur (p. 130). Zacharia Zubeidi, leader of the Al Aqsa Martyrs Brigade in Jenin, has found that the people he deploys as suicide bombers often have a "dissociate response." However, dissociation does not always lead to one-option thinking, suicide bombing only, for example. Zubeidi himself has experienced moments of dissociation, yet he feels that he can respond in various ways to these instances of stress; whereas, he sees that the bombers "have only one decision . . . the martyrs [are] . . . locked into an inflexible dissociate mode caused by traumatic stress" (pp. 130–131). Speckhard and Akhem-dova have illustrated that a "normal" person enters a state of dissociation only "when the threat becomes overwhelmingly horrific" (p. 131). However, the bombers that Zubeidi trains have been in modes of dissociation for long periods of time. They are unable, due to the severity of their pain, to find another answer.

Speckhard and Akhmedova (2005) also have interviewed Fatima, a woman living in Chechnya, who had experienced trauma and dissociation; her seventeen-year-old brother exploded on a Russian land mine. It is in reliving this traumatic event that thoughts of becoming a suicide bomber have entered her mind because of the hatred she has for the Russians. Speckhard and Akhemdova have illustrated that when one enters a dissociated state, the person has, in a sense, left herself; she does not feel anything, so fear and reason do not touch her. Fatima, for example, has described a situation in which she picked up a Russian soldier's gun and aimed it at him after she and others were ordered off their bus at a checkpoint: "They [the others on the bus] were very frightened, but I didn't feel anything. Now I understand that I could have been arrested or killed, but I don't know how I did it" (p. 131). She already had pent-up rage within her over the death of her brother. Then, after being asked to come off the bus at a checkpoint with guns pointed at her, as had happened so many times before, she entered into a trance of dissociation. By taking the gun, "She was re-enacting what had been done to her many times" (p. 132).

Simon (*CBS News*, 2003) has interviewed Doctor Merari, head of the Center for Political Violence at Tel Aviv University regarding the psychological state of a suicide bomber. Doctor Merari at that time stated, "The only abnormal thing about the suicide bomber is, at a certain point, a total absence of fear." There is no indication that these people are psychotic. As he has noted, "I doubt that this person under any circumstances would be fearless. On this mission, to which he was prepared for so long, like a coiled spring [he] just wants to be released." We wonder if it is possible that total lack of fear actually represents a state of dissociation and even self-hypnosis.

In some cases, suicide bombers reportedly may have been drugged so that they would commit these actions (Murphy, 2004). Russian reports have indicated that some of the Chechen women (suspected of being involved in suicide bombing missions) have appeared to be "dazed and unfocused" (Murphy, 2004). Although drug usage can result in symptoms such as confusion and dazed expressions, an alternative diagnosis could suggest that these conditions are those of a person in a state of dissociation.

From another perspective, Alan Krueger, a Princeton University economist, has suggested, "I think that in the West, we think very much in terms of materialistic terms. And we think . . . who could possibly want to give up their lives for a cause? It must be someone who has nothing to live for, whereas I don't think that's what's motivating the people who participate in terrorism" (National Public Radio, 2003). The biographies of 9/11 terrorists have indicated that they had "a lot" to live for, but still gave up their lives. According to Doctor Eyad Sarraj, people who turn to this type of action have experienced extreme trauma in their lives, like many Palestinian children, for example, who have watched helplessly as their fathers were humiliated and beaten up in front of them (NPR, 2003).[11]

From reviewing the lives of suicide bombers/warriors, it is clear that many of them have had a history of psychic trauma in addition to possibly experiencing physical assault. It is well documented in clinical literature that psychic trauma can be a cause of dissociation, where people can become dazed, fearless, high, or euphoric at the time of their mission. It is also clear that many of the people living in areas where there are significant suicide bombings have experienced multiple traumatic events. One may wonder if there is a certain breaking point for those who experience such significant traumas, with one group developing dissociation as a coping mechanism to ward off the pain, another group becoming suicide bombers, and a third possible group being a combination—suicide bombers with dissociation. One may wonder if the people who turn to suicide bombing feel that they do not have another outlet or a way out of this pain.

The Element of Religion

It is the martyrs who create faith rather than faith that creates martyrs.
Miguel de Unamuno

When I was crossing into Gaza, I was asked at the check post whether I was carrying any weapons. I replied: "Oh yes, my prayer books."
Mother Teresa of Calcutta

It is in dying that we are born to eternal life.
St. Francis of Assisi

We do not want churches because they will teach us to quarrel about God . . .
Chief Joseph (Nez Perce, Native American)

Religion for the suicide bomber can possibly resemble religion for some people when they fly in an airplane. If the engine fails and the aircraft descends, many begin to pray. People who are already religious may become even more so in these times, with this crisis increasing their commitment to their faith. Yet even those who are not religious may become religious, at least for those moments of danger and uncertainty. Religion in these times can provide hope and a comfort of a greater power taking control. As a chaplain once said in a field sermon at Bataan in World War II, "There are no atheists in foxholes." Expressed conversely by others, religions tend to disappear with man's good fortune. Clearly people become more religious during a crisis, as was documented after the tragedy of 9/11 when church attendance in the United States substantially increased.

Professor David Cantor, director of Liverpool University's Centre for Investigative Psychology, has determined that suicide bombing has been used as a weapon in many cultures and should not be exclusively identified with Islam, as is the popular view (*BBC News*, 2005).[12] Many Americans have wondered if the 9/11 attack was carried out by Islamic religious fundamentalists. However, such an act would be counter to the teachings of the *Koran*. As the text reveals, sacrifices should be for God rather than for personal vengeance: "And do not kill yourselves. Surely, God is most merciful to you. And whoever commits that through aggression and injustice. We shall cast him into the fire, and that is easy for God" (*Koran* cited by Anees, 2006, p. 277). It is well documented that suicide warriors who are Muslim do not consider their actions to be suicide (which is opposed by their religion). Instead, they believe it to be a self-sacrifice and a dedication of their body to the community and God (Anees, 2006). Muslims have not been the only people to confront the possible contradiction of their actions with their faith. Other religious texts also have clear statements regarding violence, yet violence still is committed by the people who claim these faiths. Kurlansky has pointed out that in Judaism "The sixth commandment is, 'You shall not kill.' It is one of the shortest commandments and offers no commentary, explanation, or variation. . . . It does not say . . . 'except in self-defense,' nor does it say 'except when absolutely necessary'" (2006, p. 13). Judaism, a religion believed to be more than 5700 years old, has layers of laws and rules regarding violence, and some of the texts themselves seem to be contradictory (Kurlansky, 2006). In order to cope with possible conflicts, rabbis focus on prioritizing certain writings or beliefs over others. It is interesting to note that ancient Jews, although they did engage in warfare, did not rejoice in their victories, as is done today in various modern cultures (Kurlansky, 2006).

Although various researchers have focused on religion, Roy (2004), has presented a potential counter point in his book, *Globalized Islam: The Search for a New Ummah*, in which he has mentioned that Al-Qaeda's violence against western countries is politically inspired, not religiously. He has added that after all, "Al-Qaeda did not target St. Peter's Basilica in Rome, but the World Trade Center and the Pentagon. It targeted modern imperialism, as the ultra-leftists [around the world] of the late 1960s and 1970s did with less success" (Roy, 2004, as cited in Mamdani, 2005).

In regard to the motives of the bin Laden organization, Hashmi (2003) has reported that "al Qaeda's goals appear to be far more mundane than religious, more political than theological" (p. 24). The guerrilla warfare tactics used by the perpetrators would not be expected from holy warriors on a jihad. Hashmi also has presented evidence from the *Koran* and Syrian scholar Wahba Zuhayli, who has put forth that Muslim teachings promote peace unless the enemy directly attacks you, that all individuals are innocent unless their actions are a direct threat to Muslims. Zuhayli also clearly disagreed with the tribal concept that all citizens of a country are responsible for the perceived wrongs of their government. Bin Laden, on the other hand, has supported this notion in restating that all Americans are targets and that there are no innocents in the name of retaliation (Hashmi, 2003, p. 27).

From another perspective, Sohail (2006) has suggested that for many suicide warriors, their ethnic, gender, or racial characteristics are less important than their religious identities. They feel that they are more a part of the "ummah" than they are a part of England or the United States. Because of this identification, they are more willing to forfeit their lives for a "jihad."[13]

Freud has acknowledged the power of religion and belief systems and has ex-plained that religious beliefs are "illusions, fulfillments of the oldest, strong-est, and most urgent wishes of mankind" (1927, 1961, p. 30). Meissner (1996) has explained that Freud's idea in regards to religion as illusion is considered part of "infantile dependence creating powerful gods to which man could turn to for support and reassurance in the face of the painful difficulties of life." These "painful difficulties" could be the issues of loss and ultimately death (Meissner, 1996, p. 241).

Although religion itself has possibly existed since the creation of humanistic cultures, the idea of a religion asserting control over politics and government is new to the post-Renaissance era, according to Atran (2003). The concept of a ruling ecclesiastical party has its clearest historical precedent in the Holy Inquisition. Present-day activists such as the Shia, Sunni, and Taliban are much closer in spirit to this concept than to religious fanaticism. Furthermore, Merari (2005) has suggested that religious fanaticism is neither necessary nor sufficient to explain suicide attacks; in fact, several nonreligious groups have used the tactic. History reveals that suicide attacks have been carried out by many groups, including leftist Marxists (e.g., the Kurdish PKK; and the Turkish People's Liberation Front). Also, Pape (2005a) has reported that the Tamil Tigers, a Hindu group whose ideology has Marxist and Leninist elements, accounted for 75 of the 186 suicide attacks between 1980 and 2001. Nationalism and separatism motivated these "tigers" rather than religious fanaticism (Merari, 2005). As Pape (2005b) has stated, "in speech after speech, by leader after leader, it is the real-world circumstances of foreign occupation that define how religious norms should be interpreted, not an individual's desire for personal salvation independent of this context" (Pape, 2005b, p. 189).

Israel and Palestine both share religious apocalyptic visions that have inspired terrorism in the Middle East. Lifton (2003) has maintained that for Palestine the Hamas group although operating under political motivations, has been influenced by an even greater force, that of a Holy War. Israel has also produced assassins whose actions directly reflect their religious affiliations and influences. Yigal Amir, a twenty-five-year-old Israeli college student, murdered Prime Minister Yitzhak Rabin on November 4, 1995 (Lifton, 2003). Although Amir has been considered in Israeli society to be a violent extremist living on the fringe of society, there were religious and political connections that linked him to mainstream society. For a year before the assassination, Orthodox rabbis had been discussing a principle in the *Torah* (considered obsolete by many) that suggested the removal of any person "interfering with messianic redemption," with specific implications to Yitzhak Rabin (Lifton, 2003, p. 99). Amir admitted to having connections to rabbis who encouraged him to commit this action. In addition, right-wing political groups were denouncing Rabin, and protestors claimed he was "murdering Zionism." Therefore, although Amir's actions may have seemed extremist, the politics that motivated him were shared by mainstream Israeli society (Lifton, 2003).

Holmes (2005) has noted that as an empirical matter apart from Islamic or other religious teachings, "life is brief, and therefore the human impulse toward self-preservation . . . in the end, proves futile" (pp. 144–145). It is this sentiment that Holmes has maintained is emphasized to suicide bomber recruits and is one of the recruiters' most effective tactics. Men who are already inclined to fight "for the cause" become willing to give up their life (which will end anyway) for such a glorified cause. It is also pointed out to potential suicide bombers that they could be easily killed from a random accident any day; therefore, why should they not take control of their lives so they can die meaningful deaths (Holmes, 2005), especially if their religion offers afterlife incentives? We feel the need to elaborate on Holmes' statement regarding self-preservation. Although it is true that humans are inclined to preserve themselves, it is necessary to understand how age and circumstance can affect this concept. Take, for example, the notion that young people in general often have a "belief" that they are immortal, in a figurative sense of the word. Young people may drive cars too fast or take risks that older adults would not because, as adults, they have come to see how real death can be. What has changed? For many people, the older one becomes, the more experiences one has with death, in other words, relatives or friends dying. On top of this age factor however, is a circumstantial one. A young American growing up in a "safe or war-free" community will have a completely different sense of death, immortality, fear, and reality than a Palestinian or Iraqi in occupied territory will have. The Palestinian and Iraqi may understand the reality of death because of all that they see around them, more so than a young American free from that direct trauma. Boys from these nations may in fact have a greater chance of dying sooner than an American and may be greatly aware of their circumstances. Therefore, it might take far less energy to convince a Palestinian or Iraqi that "life is brief" than it would for someone not in the same circumstance. The statement that "life is brief" is truly a relative one.

Clearly, religion does not always turn people toward revolution or war.[14] Speckhard and Akhemdova (2005) have provided a more personal example of how religion can also be the element that prevents someone from turning to violence. They interviewed a twenty-five-year-old Chechen woman who mentioned that since her brother was killed on a Russian land mine, she has considered becoming a suicide bomber. Yet her moral sense and faith hold her back. As she explained, "When I pray, I ask Allah to give me reason and patience not to do it" (Speckhard & Akhmedova, 2005). Thus, religion may have an impact on a person by reinforcing what is already there.

Religion, therefore, can be a tool that is used by some as a motivator for war and for others, peace.[15] Although there are those who, in their hearts, are committing these violent acts to honor their religious beliefs, there are those who may use religion to manipulate others. Religion cannot be the only factor in creating a suicide bomber. There have been suicide bombers who are religious, yet clearly, there are millions of religious people who are against suicide bombing; therefore, there must be other factors involved. In addition, there are suicide bombers who do not hold any religious beliefs. From our research, it is evident that what the people who have become suicide bombers have in common is that they are committing this act to right a perceived wrong.

The Element of Group Process, Support and Bonding

People who die are not buried in the fields; they are buried in the heart.
Ephrem Karangwa (mayor of Taba, Rowanda)

Merari (2005) has used the phenomenon of group commitment as an example of a social contract that is difficult to break. In doing so, he has referred to the martyrdom cells of the Palestinian Liberation and Tigers of Tamil Ealem (LTTE) warrior groups: the Black Tigers (males) and the Birds of Freedom (females). The cohesiveness of these Palestinian organizations seems comparable to that of the Japanese Kamikaze warriors of WWII. A review of these pilots' relationships with their families and the letters they wrote before their last missions reveals that although some of these soldiers looked forward to the suicide mission almost enthusiastically, others considered it a duty that they could not avoid (Inoguchi & Nakajima, 1958, p. 196).

In either case, such a commitment is binding and personal. "Personal commitment" from Merari's point of view constitutes a point of no return. In fact, once someone becomes a Palestinian suicide candidate, he is formally referred to as a "living martyr" while in the martyrdom cells. This title is often used in a videotape of farewell and also in letters the candidate writes to family and friends before the suicide mission begins (Merari, 2005). It is important to note that these warriors do not see themselves as committing suicide (which is against their religious tenets) but as rendering the sacrifice of sacred martyrdom (Sohail, 2006).

Merari (2005) also refers to the recruiting groups as "production lines for suicide." It has been suggested that the bonding that can occur within a group can have such a strong effect on its members that they can be driven to commit acts that they may not have considered before. Merari has examined the effects of group bonding in regard to the ten Irish activists in prison with Bobby Sands in 1981 who went on a food strike that eventually led to their deaths. These prisoners had demanded to be recognized as political prisoners rather than as common criminals, but their request was denied by the British government. Although it took the hunger strikers from fifty to seventy days to die, Merari thought that some force drove them to continue the strike until their eventual demise. In analyzing this phenomenon, he did not feel that all ten hunger strikers were suicidal before being jailed, nor did he feel it likely that all were religious fanatics. Rather, he concluded that the group pressure became stronger after the first hunger striker died, and from that point on the cohesiveness of the group could not be broken (Merari, 2005).

Americans use the expression "did not die in vain" to express a group's need to justify the deaths of their comrades by carrying on. This type of group commitment, Merari has said, is similar to the group pressure that led hundreds of thousands of soldiers to charge against enemy machine gun fire in WWI when it was almost certain that they would die (Merari, 2005).

We, along with other professionals (Volkan, 2004), maintain that it is helpful to explore the psychology of group versus individual dynamics. Clearly, political leaders have generally been more successful in convincing a group rather than individuals. It seems that within a group, individual opinions weaken, and instead the group judgment becomes the norm. One charismatic leader may be able to lead a group to death if he runs toward it; in such a case, others will follow without doubting the leader's judgment.

Forensic psychiatrist Marc Sageman (2004), who is also an ex-CIA officer, conducted a study following the 9/11 attacks. He found that most terrorist cells evolve from people who already have become disenfranchised from a country's policies yet develop a strong bond among themselves. In addition, Merari's research on Palestinian suicide missionaries found that organizations engage three main elements to prepare suicide bombers: group commitment, personal pledge, and indoctrination of nationalist themes (Merari, 2005). From our point of view, it seems that the most important element is timing. A person who would join these groups has already acquired the motivation and desire to be a "martyr." This process does not seem to differ greatly from what happens when someone joins a group such as the U. S. Marines Corps. Basic training includes indoctrination, a personal pledge, and group commitment. The motivations—heroism, patriotism, and sacrifice—are already there and may be intensified in the presence of a charismatic leader or mentor. So, is indoctrination only the final step? From our point of view, Merari (2005) and other writers have focused on this last factor and possibly have not given enough attention to the circumstances that can lead a person to want to be a "martyr" in the first place.

The Element of Poverty

Ten men in our country could buy the whole world and ten million can't buy enough to eat.

Will Rogers

Poverty is the parent of revolution and crime.

Aristotle

The presence of poverty as a motivational factor for suicide warriors/bombers is a controversial one. Several Western news media sources have reported that 9/11 terrorists were not "poor," so poverty was not their motivation. Yet these same reporters also suggested that the terrorists were jealous of our wealth and prosperity and wanted to destroy it.

On the other hand, Marsella and Moghaddam (2005) also cite an opinion popular among some western government officials, who claim that poverty does not cause terrorism. In pointing to the middle-class background of the 9/11 terrorists, however, these same officials failed to recognize that revolutions are often led by those who have the education to speak on behalf of the poor and the resources required for sustaining opposition. It is the injustice that these intellectuals and educated people recognize that encourages them to take action against powerful organizations. Formation of unions is such an example because the leaders come from positions of adequate status (Marsella & Moghaddam, 2005). Lenin, Marx, other socialist elites, and pro-poor activists of the past came from a higher, rather than a lower socioeconomic background. A similar situation is evident in the leadership of some U.S. political families, such as the Kennedys. They had an upper-class upbringing, and they sided with the laborers, the poor, the impoverished populations overall, whereas some of the procorporation and big business politicians came from lower-class backgrounds.

Psychiatric literature (Garbarino, 1998) has suggested that poverty causes "developmental trauma" because it negatively affects the educational, social, and physiological growth of the child. Such people, growing up without culturally and socially defined basic needs, assess their position in the social order as debased. As they view core issues of their family's poverty, such as reduced social status and inadequate income, they may experience feelings of low self-esteem and shame; social toxicity may result. Clearly, being poor means being different; it is not what one has but what one does not have that drives the psychology of poverty (Garbarino, 1998). We agree with Garbarino that it is not poverty itself that is detrimental. Rather, it is the injustice, shame, and humiliation resulting from indigence that sets up the conditions of violence and retaliation.[16]

Marsella and Moghaddam identify poverty as fertile ground for terrorist recruitment. Such privation, they assert, can breed hopelessness and helplessness, deprivation and shame, and prejudice and social injustice. In poverty, social cohesion breaks down; this disintegration frequently causes illness and social divergence, crime and loss, and revolution (Marsella & Moghaddam, 2005).

According to one source, in Morocco on April 14, 2007, two brothers blew themselves up, aimed at U.S. targets (*Aljazeera Net News*, 2007). These brothers had lived in the slums of Casablanca, where five suicide bombings had occurred in the same week. This area also was reported to be a "breeding ground" for fundamentalists (*Aljazeera*, 2007). The brothers had shared a single room with five other siblings and their mother. When looking for an explanation for this bombing, photojournalist Murad Borga, who knew the family, stated, "We went looking for the reasons behind what they did and found the details of their arrest, their poor treatment at the hands of the police and the suffering and poverty of living in such a place" (*Aljazeera*, 2007).

From reviewing the literature, one can see that although the issue of poverty may contribute to terrorism it is not apparently the primary motivating factor. Subsequently, the alleviation of poverty and creating equality among the citizens of the world, although an ideal method to decrease class struggle, may not decrease the proliferation of suicide bombers.[17]

The Element of Perceived Injustice, Humiliation, Shame and Despair

He who terrorizes is himself the more terrified.
Claudian

A Palestinian slogan or "death oath" states that shame is present "in every house." The following statement has been written on many walls in occupied Palestine:

> *I swear by the one who made fast your mountain*
> *and set your clouds in motion, O Palestine*
> *That I will erase shame*
> *in every house*
> *And from my blood and bones I will weave*
> *banners of victory for Islam.*

(Oliver & Steinberg, 2005, p. 61)

Psychiatric literature has indicated that shame is a very significant emotional factor in human aggression. In fact, Armstrong (2006) has explored the possibility that shame plays a significant role in motivating nations and governments to go to war. She has offered the example of the rise of Nazism in Germany. After WWI, the Treaty of Versailles triggered feelings of humiliation and despair in a generation of Germans. When Hitler opportunistically reminded the Germans of their defeat, pride of country became a potent rallying cry and possibly contributed to the creation of the next war (Armstrong, 2006).

In another case, Prusher (2005) has reported on the despair and hopelessness that has motivated Palestinian suicide bombers. Most Palestinians in the occupied territories, she has written, have had to cope with the death of a family member or friend. Feeling bitter about their world, "younger and younger Palestinians have turned to suicide bombing as the only way to express their despair" (Prusher, 2005). President Carter, in his recent book entitled *Palestine: Peace not Apartheid*, has reported that the condition of Palestinians in the occupied territories is more oppressive than what "blacks lived under in South Africa during apartheid" (Carter, 2006). Many Muslim youth are thinking that the only way to stop the imprisonment of their friends and families is by joining the "wave of retaliation" (Sohail, 2006). However, history has revealed that violence breeds more violence and may develop into a vicious cycle.

Adas (2004) also has focused on terrorist issues in citing an example of injustice in Palestine that possibly triggered further violence. As she has detailed, Baruch Goldstein, a Brooklyn-born Israeli settler, killed twenty-nine Palestinian worshipers in a Hebron mosque while dressed in his Israeli military uniform. He was eventually killed by a fire extinguisher wielded by the Palestinians. Goldstein's terror went unmarked: the Israeli government reacted by putting the Palestinians of Hebron, but not the Israeli settlers, "under total curfew" (Adas, 2004). After the forty-day mourning period, the first Palestinian suicide bomber detonated himself, possibly as a reaction to these situations.

Although she was widely criticized for condoning suicide bombings, Jenny Tonge, a member of the British Parliament, told a British TV reporter in 2004 that "I understand why people out there become suicide bombers– it is out of desperation . . . I might just think about it myself" (Aljazeera.net, 2004). She was echoing a previous statement by Cherie Blair, wife of the British Prime Minister at that time, who also acknowledged the desperation that Palestinians must feel in order to take the step of last resort–suicide (Aljazeera.net, 2004).[18]

Marsella (2003) has noted a related terrorist motivation, the collective memories of humiliation resulting from defeat. These memories become magnified in a culture that values and prizes the past. Marsella has voiced that these root causes have not been addressed by the U.N., the United States, Israel or the Arab nations. He further has contended that the memories of the oppression of the Palestinians in the West Bank and Gaza will be kept alive for generations in oral histories, myths, and legends and that one day those memories will become a source of new terrorist attacks (Marsella, 2003),[19] just as WWII possibly was a reaction of the Germans to their humiliation during their loss and defeat in WWI. History has illustrated that this type of scenario tends to produce deadly results.

Volkan also has explored the phenomenon of large group identity using images of Jack the Ripper and Slobodan Milosevic, president of the former country of Yugoslavia. Volkan has noted that since Jack the Ripper's horrific crimes were against individuals, his historical significance was limited and essentially forgotten. However, Milosevic's ethnic cleansing resulted in massive violence within Serbian society. Doctor Volkan further describes how President Milosevic had inflamed former grievances of the Serbs by parading the remains of their ancient leaders brutalized in the war with Kosovo 600 years earlier. The hatred that ensued inflamed the Serbs and precipitated their decimation of Bosnia. This example indicates that group members can pass on their hurts and humiliation to their children if those losses have not been psychologically resolved.[20]

Group loss and despair are notable in the territory of Gaza, which has 1.2 million occupants residing in only 360 square kilometers. It is one of the more densely populated places in the world, with most of its residents unable to move in and out of the territory (Hutcheon, 2004). Eyad Sarraj has noted that approximately 70 percent of the Gaza population is made up of refugees who were exiled from their homes since 1948, when Israel became a state. Many of these people feel a strong sense of injustice, which manifests itself in helplessness (Hutcheon, 2004).[21]

In conclusion it seems that the perceived injustice that results in humiliation, shame, and despair may be an important and prominent factor in creating suicide bombers. These are the internal feelings that can be the result of the external factor of occupation or invasion.[22]

The Element of Cultural Support

We do not support it when the Israeli kill our people, so we cannot support it when their innocent people are killed by us; we just cannot condone that kind of martyrdom.
Mother of deceased suicide bomber (Davis, 2005)

Suicide warriors can often have significant emotional and financial support. Several studies have determined the extent of this support. For example, after the failure of the Oslo Agreement of 1993, the amount of Palestinian support for suicide missions against Israel rose from 20 percent in May 1996 to 70 percent in May 2002 (Center for Palestine Research and Studies, 2000). Merari (2005) has explained that the increase in suicide attacks during the Second Intifada reflects the increasing number of Palestinian youths who consider such attacks as acts of ultimate patriotism and heroism for their community.

Sarraj has reported that children in his area have grown to idolize suicide bombers/warriors and others who have sacrificed their lives for the Palestinian cause. West Bank walls are covered with graffiti praising them; children role-play their actions and sing songs praising the "shahid." In fact, Sarraj has noted that 36 percent of twelve-year-old boys in Gaza believe the oxymoron that dying as a martyr is the best thing in life (Prusher, 2005). The Palestinian religious society also glorifies the martyr and may elevate him or her to the level of sainthood. Indeed, as Sarraj has noted, martyrdom is the ultimate redemption, the only model of glory powering the lives of Palestinians. This martyr's image compares harshly to the view these youths hold of their own fathers. Sarraj's studies have revealed that a number of Palestinian fathers appeared as "helpless, unable to protect their children in the face of the Israeli incursion" as they were beaten up by soldiers in front of their own families (Prusher, 2005, p. 21).

As a result of such enemy operations, 66 percent of 1179 West Bank and Gaza Palestinians in early 2002 increased their support for suicide bombers, according to one poll (Atran, 2003). By the end of 2002, 73 percent of Lebanese Muslims considered suicide bombers justified. Similarly, a U.N. report in December of 2002 credited large numbers of volunteers with revitalizing Al-Qaeda in forty countries. Al-Qaeda was supported by 95 percent of educated Saudis aged twenty-five to forty-one in October 2001. PEW Research Centers reported similarly that only 6 percent of Egyptians viewed America and its "war on terror" favorably. This emotional support overall translates into both supply and demand for martyrdom operations as well as financial benefit. For example, after a Jerusalem supermarket bombing by an eighteen-year-old Palestinian, a Saudi telethon raised more than $100 million for the Intifada (Atran, 2003).

According to a poll conducted among Palestinian adults in 2001 by Dr. Nabil Kukali and the Palestinian Center for Public Opinion, 76.1 percent supported suicide attack, whereas 12.5 percent opposed and 11.4 percent expressed no opinion (Shuman, 2001). Yet, Lifton (2003) has pointed out that there are sentiments of opposition to suicide bombings by Palestinians as well. The initial excitement of suicide bombings has dwindled and families find it hard to conceal their grief and bitterness. This practice has undergone criticism by Arab intellectuals and leaders because it is seen to kill innocent civilians and reflects a negative image of Arab culture and ethical standards. In addition, it has been thought that this practice may actually hinder the Palestinian cause because the suffering that is experienced by all Palestinians from the Israeli retaliation after each bombing (Lifton, 2003).

The Element of Remuneration

Some western news media possibly have exaggerated the element of financial or sexual rewards as a significant motivation for the suicide bomb-er or activist. Middle eastern news media in fact, have criticized Western media for assuming that these rewards are significant motivations for the suicide bomber and for ignoring or downplaying the importance of occupation or invasion and the consequent loss, rage, frustration, and humiliation that inhabitants experience daily. However, the news media in the Middle East may not be aware that the issues of "money and sex" are, in general, the focus of western news reports, regardless of the subject. Rather than being a blatant attempt to downplay other motivations, this focus has more to do with western culture's fixation on money and sex. It is for these reasons that many western news media have focused on a $25,000 reward offered to the family of a deceased suicide activist and the promise of the "virgin girls in heaven" for the Muslim activist. It is clear however, that by focusing on what may attract the most viewers, western media have compromised on the accuracy of their reporting. For example, in the case of the LTTE and the Kurdish militant suicide bombers there are no reported sexual awards. The emergence of a significant number of female suicide bombers, and secular and non-Muslim warriors refutes the western media's attempt to promote the importance of this "virgin girls" reward. In addition, Pape (2005b) has stated, "since 1998, Israel has systematically demolished the homes of suicide bombers' families" (p. 193). Although there may be claims that these families have received some cash compensation from groups such as Hamas, any amount would be incomparable to the greater amount lost through a demolished home. This information "sends a strong signal that the motive for the attack was indeed to promote the communal good. . . . Palestinian suicide bombers continue to reveal their identities although it is common knowledge that their families will suffer harsh consequences" (Pape, 2005b, p. 193). It is important to note that despite the suffering of families of suicide bombers and the subsequent demolition of their homes, the number of suicide bombers has not decreased.

CONCLUSION

The motivational factors for suicide bombing are varied and complex. Suicide warriors may have internal experiences such as trauma and humiliation that are triggered by what is occurring in their external environment. Although not everyone who is living in a country under occupation or invasion will choose to become a suicide bomber, this type of situation is a commonality among suicide bombers. When investigating this violent act, it is necessary to examine the two elements involved: killing one's self in addition to others, which distinguishes it from other types of violence that focuses only on killing others. To only acknowledge one of these elements would be to ignore the uniqueness of this complex act. Unfortunately, suicide bombing will continue as long as there are life situations in which people feel that this type of violence is the only way to change their world and to improve their nation or tribe's status quo.

NOTES

1. From Ihanus, J. (2005, Winter). Psychological aspects of terror and witnessing. *The Journal of Psychohistory, 32*(3), 268–277. Juhani Ihanus is a docent of the Department of Cultural Psychology (University of Helsinki) and of the Department of History of Science and Ideas (University of Oulu). He has published books on psychohistory, culture psychology, and the psychology of art and literature.
2. Ahmad Shah Massoud, considered to be a national hero by many Afghans, was possibly one of the greatest practitioners of guerilla warfare in the late twentieth century, according to Peter Bergen of *Time* magazine (2006). Described as being honest, charismatic, and humorous, Massoud's vision of Islam focused on a peaceful, tolerant coexistence with others. He was given the name "Lion of Panjshir" for his success in fighting back against the Soviets in Afghanistan. He was murdered several days before 9/11 by suicide bombers, possibly sent by bin Laden who wanted to get rid of his competitor. The suicide bombers detonated

a bomb hidden in their camera. For more information, *see* http://www.time.com/time/magazine/article/0,9171,1555018,00.html.

3. The quotes and conclusions from Eqbal Ahmad were taken from one of his last public talks in the United States entitled *Terrorism: Theirs and ours* in 1998. David Barsamian, the editor who put together a book that features this speech aired it nationally and internationally on his weekly *Alternative Radio Program*. Barsamian has commented that he replayed this near prophetic speech after 9/11, which resulted in listeners' calling in requesting copies. Almost all of them believed that the speech had just been given; in fact it was first aired three years before 9/11.

4. For more information regarding Palestine please see Chapter 12: "Palestine—A Nation Traumatized." For more concerning the Intifada, please see R. Baroud (2006). *The Second Palestinian Intifada: A chronicle of a people's struggle.* London: Pluto Press.

5. Doctor Eyad Sarraj is the founder and director of the Gaza Community Mental Health Program. The mission of this organization is to provide rehabilitation services for torture victims and those affected by the Intifada. Doctor Sarraj has also voiced his objection to the actions of the Palestinian Authority (PA) and its possible human rights violations. He is also a member of the International Rehabilitation Center for Torture Victims and the chairman of the Palestinian Independent Commission of Citizens Rights. This group has been critical of the Israeli occupation and its impact on Palestinians. Dcotor Sarraj has been arrested by the PA police and was tortured and threatened with death while in prison, as reported by *Aljazeera Net News*. (*See* http://english.aljazeera.net/NR/exeres/843D6B3C-65D2-428C-86B8-30A31478F405.htm)

6. Mahmud Darwish is a contemporary Palestinian poet whose words have gained him international recognition. His poetry has focused largely on his significant affection for his homeland. He has been arrested repeatedly for his political writings and activities. Darwish joined the Communist Party of Israel in the 1960s but is better known for his participation with the PLO. In 1988, his poem "Passers Between the Passing Words" was discussed in Israel's Parliament. He was accused of wanting the Jews to leave Israel, although he maintained that he meant they should leave the West Bank and Gaza. The poet wrote "So leave our land/Our shore, our sea/Our wheat, our salt, our wound." Interestingly in March of 2000, Israel's education minister suggested that some of Darwish's poems be included in Israel's school curriculum. Prime Minister Ehud Bark responded that "Israel is not ready." (*See* http://en.wikipedia.org/wiki/Mahmoud_Darwish)

7. The "Palestinian Dream" refers to the birth of a Palestinian nation after occupied lands have been returned. Their poets refer to Palestine as their "Mother Land." The PKK in Turkey and the LTTE of Sri Lanka are other examples of nationalist minorities who are fighting for the development of their own nation.

8. For further information please see Chapter 14 "Female Suicide Warriors/Bombers," which explains how female suicide bombers may induce an extra element of moral shame not only to Israelis (because Palestinian women and mothers are

choosing to die fighting them) but also to Palestinian men and "sleeping Arab Armies."

9. Begun in 1991 and ratified in 1993, the Oslo Accords were officially entitled the Declaration of Principles (DOP) or the Declaration of Principles on Self-Government Arrangements, according to *Wikipedia Encyclopedia.* After two years of negotiations, the final agreement between the PLO and Israel called for the withdrawal of Israeli forces from parts of the West Bank and Gaza Strip and created the PA for self-government within those areas. A time table of five years was set, during which a permanent agreement and the more complex issues of division of Jerusalem, refugees, and Israeli settlements were to be negotiated. It is these issues that created the breakdown in negotiations stimulating the return of violence.

10. There are various ways one may respond to being hurt or offended by another. One may be to inflict pain in a similar fashion (hand for hand, eye for eye) as a way of revenge. A second way can be to make one's offender feel guilty, so that he or she reflects on his or her actions. A third example is to respond in peace and actually make an offering to one's presumed offender. One example of the last type is that of a 12-year-old Palestinian boy who was shot by Israeli soldiers and died in November 2005 (*IslamOnline*, 2005). The Israeli army said that soldiers had mistaken the toy gun that the boy was brandishing for a real one and shot him. Only later did they discover that the weapon was plastic. Ismail, the grieving father, said, "The Israeli soldiers shot my son in the waist, he fell on the ground, when he tried to stand again, they shot him in the head." Ismail, nonetheless, decided to donate his slain son's heart, lung, kidneys, and liver to save Jewish lives (Wilson, 2005), "Israeli children are our children. . . . we are doing this because we believe in peace" (IslamOnline, 2005). "Despite the pain, (the family) made a very courageous decision, " the uncle of slain Ahmed Al-Khatib further told Israeli television as reported by Wilson (2005) in the Washington Post. " This is part of our culture," he continued. "As Muslims we can tell the world that we are not terrorists." Al-Khatib's father accused the Israel forces of perpetuating a war crime, appealing for the Israeli Knesset and "rights advocates" to unravel the truth in his son's murder case (IslamOnline, 2005).

11. According to Dr. Sarraj recent psychiatric studies have demonstrated that most of Gaza's population is traumatized by Israel's aggression. According to his group research, only 3 percent of the people of Gaza do not show symptoms of anxiety, depression, or PTSD. Children suffer from multiple layers of problems. He reported that these children feel vulnerable, and worst of all, they feel that their fathers are unable to protect them.

12. One of the first suicide bombers to attack Israeli forces in the Middle East was Loula Abboud, who defied all the stereotypes: she was secular, middle class, nineteen years old, from a Christian background. She blew herself up in front of a group of Israeli soldiers in Lebanon in 1985.

13. Despite some theories to the contrary, our observations reveal that religion in Middle Eastern countries contributes to revolution and war against the government (i.e., Iran, Egypt). Islamic clergymen may gain, or lose, religious followers

depending on their stance toward peace or violence. Immediately after the Islamic Revolution in Iran, it became evident that some revolutionary activists changed their affiliation from one Islamic organization to another in order to match their true feelings. For example, a revolutionary religious man told the news media that he was changing his imam (Islamic clergyman) and becoming a disciple of another clergyman because his previous imam was too forgiving. This religious activist had arrested the old regime's torturer and commander and brought them to his imam for severe punishment. Instead, the imam only asked them to apologize (*Tobeh*) and to denounce their support of the Shah, and then they would be forgiven. It was because of this imam's "pacifist" actions that the religious activist decided he would take his captives to a new imam who believed that they should be cut into pieces.

14. In addition, religious beliefs in India possibly are preventing the poor from revolting against the extremely wealthy because the "destiny" of the indigent, according to certain religious beliefs, is to remain poor and homeless. Some are born in the streets, grow up in the streets, marry, and die in the streets yet on the next street, there sits the lavish palace of a maharajah. The excessive difference in income and socioeconomic class would usually cause rebellion, revolution and class struggle, but because of religion, such conflicts do not arise in these sections of India.

15. In our opinion, Islam as a religion can be used as a vehicle to protest current political situations in a country. For example, during the last years of the Shah of Iran's monarchy, religious activists began protesting and eventually became a strong force in opposing the Shah's regime. They reminded their supporters of all the "anti-Islamic activities" the regime had conducted and further motivated them by declaring the responsibility of "each Muslim" to oppose the "infidel's government." Most interesting is that leftist female students at the University of Tehran started to wear traditional Islamic clothes to show solidarity with Muslims and to symbolize their opposition to the regime. Some of these girls were affiliated with the left wing or socialist organizations and had no beliefs in Islam or any other religion.

16. Looking at the Middle Eastern culture, there are an abundance of proverbs and sayings concerning poverty and wealth. Because there is wisdom in cultural proverbs, we refer to a few of them: An old Persian proverb states, "if injustice is equal for everyone, then it is justice." In other words, if everyone lives in poverty, then economic reasons for opposition and class struggle will not develop. Another proverb relates that the difference between a thief and a capitalist is that the thief will steal money from the rich, whereas the capitalist robs the poor. A philosopher once said that it does not matter how small or large a city is; eventually it will be divided into sections: the poor side and the rich side. It seems obvious that as the rich get richer, the poor get poorer because of the limitations of education, capital, and goods. As the saying goes, "rain falls on the poor and the rich in the same amounts, but the poor get wetter because the rich have acquired umbrellas."

17. Cooper has noted that the globalization of American cultural and economic

practices increase resentment to its policies. Rapid population growth combined with poor economic growth creates a disparity in many Arab and Muslim countries. Local economies cannot absorb unemployed college graduates, and the lower classes become militant against the United States. The States, they say, promote the rich and repressive government but do not relieve economic suffering of the "poor" people (from M. H. Cooper [2003]. Hating America: An overview. In M. E. Williams & S. Barbour [Eds.], *The terrorist attack on America* [pp. 57–59]. Farmington Hills, MI: Greenhaven Press).

18. Mouin Rabbani, Director of the Palestinian American Research Center in Ramallah, has also analyzed the motivations behind Palestinian suicide bombings. He has reported that the common thread uniting the bombers is the "bitter experience of what they see as Israeli state terror." Palestinian suicide bombers are neither products of a passive and unquestioning obedience to political authorities nor pressed into service against their will. Instead, Rabbani continues, when "confronted by a seemingly endless combination of deaths, destruction, restriction, harassment and humiliation, they conclude that ending life as a bomb–rather than having it ended by bullet–endows them, even if only in their final moments, with a semblance of purpose and control previously considered out of reach" (Rabbani as cited by Shuman, 2001).

19. Palestinian activists have claimed that Israel's policies and occupation of their land have caused much of the violence. Living under occupation may also create feelings of humiliation and shame. Palestinian activists have stated that even Israel's leaders have acknowledged the atrocity of the Palestinians' living situation.

20. Volkan has compared large group identity to the center pole of a large tent; its only purpose is to keep the tent from collapsing. When the large group (the pole) does fall, its occupants focus on fixing the tent, and individual identities recede (from S. Siassi & S. Akhtar [2006]. Identity, destiny and terrorism: The effect of social terror on identity formation. *International Journal of Psychoanalysis, 87,* 1709–1711). In addition, Volkan (Hough, 2004) has explained that an assault on the integrity of a large-group identity is a motivating factor for ethnic or religious terrorists. He has suggested that the focus of counterterrorism should be on group identity and not on individual psychology; repairing the integrity of the large-group identity may be beneficial for all (Hough, 2004).

21. Despite being repressed, dignity and honor remain important to Arabs living in Gaza. As Doctor Sarraj has stated, "You can be a beggar, you can be very poor, but you need to be treated with dignity." It is noteworthy that dignity for one's self and dignity for one's leader are both needed by the citizens of a nation. Yasser Arafat, for example, was basically imprisoned by Israelis who surrounded his offices and paralyzed his administration. Although Sarraj has admitted to publically criticizing Arafat in the past, he, along with many Palestinians, still felt humiliated because his leader (chief of tribe) had been imprisoned and isolated. Sarraj has also stated that one of the reasons Palestinian police were unable to maintain security in Gaza was because they felt demoralized by Arafat's imprisonment by the Israeli army (Hutcheon, 2004).

22. Palestinian psychiatrist Doctor Sarraj has stated in a Reuters syndicate news report that: religion, the humiliation of life, and their home occupation were the key motives for suicide bombers bent on starting a better life in paradise (Shuman, 2001). Doctor Sarraj has commented, "It is no wonder that some people are doing it. We should wonder why everyone is not doing it."

REFERENCES

BBC News (2005, November 18). Bombers not driven by religion [On-line]. Retrieved March 17, 2007. Available: http://newsvote.bbc.co.uk

Adas J. (2004, September 21). My life is a weapon: A modern history of suicide bombing. *The Christian Centur, 121*(19), pp. 44–45.

Ahmad, E. (2001). *Terrorism: Theirs & ours.* New York: Seven Stories Press.

Aljazeera.net (2004, January) British MP in suicide bomb row [On-line]. Retrieved August 28, 2006. Available: http://english.aljazeera.net/NR/exeres/878E7EF7-2AD6-437F-B3AF-274189598ADD.htm

Aljazeera Net News (April 15, 2007). Morocco slum "bred suicide bomber" [On-line]. Retrieved April 15, 2007. Available: http://english.aljazeera.net/News/aspx/print.htm

American Psychiatric Association (2000). *Diagnostic statistical manual of mental disorders-text revision,* [DSM-IV TR].Washington, D.C.: American Psychiatric Association.

Anees, M. A. (2006, Fall): Salvation and suicide: What does Islamic theology say? *Dialog: A Journal of Theology, 45,*(3), 275–279.

Armstrong, M. K. (2006, Summer). The connection between shame and war. *The Journal of Psychohistory, 34*(1), 35–42.

Atran, S. (2003). Genesis of suicide terrorism. *Science, 299,* 1534–1539.

Carter, J. (2006). *Palestine: Peace not apartheid.* New York: Simon & Schuster.

CBS News. (2003, May 25). Mind of the suicide bomber [On-line]. Retrieved February 10, 2007. Available: http://www.cbsnews.com/stories/2003/05/23/60minutes/printable555534.shtml

Center for Palestine Research and Studies. (2000). Public opinion polls 1-48 [On-line]. Retrieved March 15, 2007. Available: http://www.cprs-palestine.org

Cota-McKinley, A., Woody W. & Bell, P. (2001). Vengeance: Effects of gender, age and religious background. *Aggressive Behavior, 27,* 343–350.

Davis, J. M. (2005). Do they kill for their mothers? In Y. Danieli, D. Brom & J. Sills (Eds.), *The trauma of terrorism: Sharing knowledge and shared care, an international handbook* (pp. 79–82). New York: The Haworth Maltreatment and Trauma Press.

Fisk, R. (2001, August 11). What drives a bomber to kill the innocent child? *Independent (UK)* [On-line]. Retrieved March 17, 2007. Available: http://www.independent.co.uk/story=88134

Freud, S. (1961). The future of an illusion. In J. Strachey et al., (Ed. and Trans.) *The standard edition of the complete psychological works of Sigmund Freud, 21,* 1–56. London: Hogarth Press.

Garbarino, J. (1998). The stress of being a poor child in America. In B. Pfefferbaum (Ed.), *Child and Adolescent Psychiatric Clinics of North America: Vol. 7*(1), (pp. 105–119). Philadelphia: W. B. Saunders Co.

Hashmi, S. (2003). Political extremism led to the attack on America. In M. E. Williams & S. Barbour (Eds.), *The terrorist attack on America* (pp. 24–27). Farmington Hills, MI: Greenhaven Press.

Heskin, K. (1980). *Northern Ireland: A psychological analysis.* New York: Columbia University Press.

Holmes, S. (2005). Al-Qaeda, September 11, 2001. In D. Gambetta (Ed.), *Making sense of suicide missions* (pp. 132–172). New York: Oxford University Press.

Horney, K. (1948). The value of vindictiveness. *American Journal of Psychoanalysis, 8*, pp. 3–12. Quoted in D. Lotto (2006, Summer). The psychohistory of vengeance. *The Journal of Psychohistory, 34*(1), pp. 43–59.

Hough, G. (2004). Does Psychoanalysis have anything to offer an understanding of terrorism? *Journal of American Psychoanalysis Association, 52*(3) pp. 813–828.

Hutcheon, J. (2004, June 20). Correspondents report–Gaza and trauma. *ABC Online* [On-line]. Retrieved May 2, 2007. Available: http://www.abc.net.au/correspondents/content/2004/s1135718.htm

Inoguchi, R. & Nakajima, T. (1958). *The divine wind: Japan's kamikaze force in World War II.* Annapolis, MD: Naval Institute Press.

IslamOnline (2005, November 8). Palestinian donates slain kid parts for Israeli children [On-line]. Retrieved February 8, 2006. Available: http://www.IslamOnline.net

Jackson, R. (2005). Understanding suicide terrorism: Richard Jackson argues that terrorism cannot be attributed solely to religious extremism, hatred or mental illness. *New Zealand International Review* [On-line], *30*(5), 24+. Retrieved April 6, 2007. Available: http://www.questia.com/PM.qst?action=print&docId=5011210925.

Khouri, R. (2006). *Ehud Olmert's profound ethics and deep lies* [On-line]. Retrieved September 20, 2007. Available: www.ramikhouri.com

Kohn, H. (1944). *Idea of nationalism.* New York: Macmillan Publishers, p. 9. Quoted in V. Volkan (1997) *Blood lines: From ethnic pride to ethnic terrorism.* Boulder, CO: Westview Press, p. 150

Koran (4:29–30). Quoted in Anees, M. (2006, Fall) Salvation and suicide: What does Islamic theology say? *Dialog: A Journal of Theology, 45*(3), p. 277.

Kurlansky, M. (2006). *Nonviolence.* New York: The Random House Publishing Group.

Lifton, R. J. (2003). *Super power syndrome.* New York: Thunder's Mouth Press.

Lotto, D. (2006, Summer). The psychohistory of vengeance. *The Journal of Psychohistory, 34*(1), pp. 43–59.

Mamdani, M. (2005, January/February). Whither political Islam? *Foreign Affairs* [On-line]. Retrieved March 1, 2007. Available: http://www.foreignaffairs.org

Margalit, A. (2003, January). The suicide bombers. *The New York Review of Books* [On-line], *50*(1). Retrieved March 2, 2007. Available: http://www.nybooks.com/articles/15979

Marsella, A. J. (2003). Reflections on international terrorism: Issues, concepts, and directions. In F. M. Moghaddam & A. J. Marsella (Eds.), *Understanding terrorism* (pp. 11–47). Washington, D. C.: American Psychological Association.

Marsella, A. J. & Moghaddam, F. (2005). The origins and nature of terrorism: Foundations and issues. In Y. Danieli, D. Brom & J. Sills (Eds.), *The trauma of terrorism: Sharing knowledge and shared care, An international handbook* (pp. 19–31). New York: The Haworth Maltreatment and Trauma Press.

Marvasti, J. A. (1993). Please hurt me again: Posttraumatic play therapy with an abused child. In T. Kottman & C. Schaefer (Eds). *Play therapy in action: A casebook for practitioners* (pp. 485–525). Northvale, NJ: Jason Aronson.

Meissner, W. W. (1996). The pathology of beliefs and the beliefs of pathology. In E. P. Shafranske (Ed.), *Religion and the clinical practice of psychology* (pp. 241–267). Washington, D.C.: American Psychological Association.

Merari, A. (2005). Suicide terrorism. In R. I. Yufit, & D. Lester (Eds.), *Assessment, treatment, and prevention of suicidal behavior* (pp. 431–453). Hoboken, NJ: John Wiley & Sons, Inc.

Murphy, K. (2004). Chechen women are increasingly recruited to become suicide bombers. In L. S. Friedman (Ed.), *What motivates suicide bombers?* (pp. 77–83). New York: Greenhaven Press.

National Public Radio (NPR) (2003, March 7). Profile: Look at the mind of a suicide bomber. Retrieved May 2, 2007. Available: http://www.npr.org/progams/morning/transcripts/2003/mar/030307.joyce.html

Oliver, A. M. & Steinberg, P. (2005). *The road to martyrs' square: A journey into the world of the suicide bomber.* New York: Oxford University Press.

Pape, R. A. (2005a). Nationalism motivates suicide terrorists. In L. S. Freidman (Ed.), *What motivates suicide bombers* (pp. 44–49). New York: Thompson Gale.

Pape, R. A. (2005b). *Dying to win.* New York: Random House Trade Paperbacks.

Prusher, I. R. (2005). Despair and hopelessness motivate suicide bombers. In L. S. Freidman (Ed.), *What motivates suicide bombers* (pp. 19–23). New York: Thompson Gale.

Rai, M. (2006). *7/7 The London bombings, Islam & the Iraq war.* London: Pluto Press.

Reuter, C. (2002). *My life is a weapon: A modern history of suicide bombing.* Princeton, NJ: Princeton University Press.

Roy, A. (2003). Anger about the U.S. bombing of Afghanistan is justified. In M. E. Williams, & S. Barbour (Eds.), *The terrorist attack on America* (pp. 73–79). Farmington Hills, MI: Greenhaven Press.

Roy, O. (2004). *Globalized Islam: The search for a new Ummah.* New York: Columbia University Press. Quoted in M. Mamdani (2005, January/February). Whither Political Islam? *Foreign Affairs* [On-line]. Retrieved March 1, 2007. Available: www.foreignaffairs.org/20050101 fareviewessay84113a/mahmood-mamdani

Sageman, M. (2004). *Understanding terror networks.* Philadelphia: University of Pennsylvania Press.

Sarraj, E. (2006). *Understanding Palestinian terror* [On-line]. Retrieved August 27, 2007. Available: www.gcmhp.net/eyad/xyz.htm

Searles, H. F. (1956). The psychodynamics of vengefulness. *Psychiatry, 19,* pp. 31–39.

Shergald (2007, February 27). Mind of the palestinian suicide bomber. Retrieved April 20, 2007. Available: http://www.myleftwing.com/showDiary.do?diaryId=14547

Shuman, E. (2001, June). What makes suicide bombers tick? *Israelinsider* [On-line]. Retrieved February 10, 2007. Available: http://www.israelinsider.com/channels/security/articles/sec_0049.htm

Silke, A. (2003a). Becoming a terrorist. In A. Silke (Ed.) *Terrorists, victims and society* (pp. 29–54). London: John Wiley & Sons.

Silke, A. (2003b). The psychology of suicidal terrorism. In A. Silke (Ed.) *Terrorists, victims and society* (pp. 93–108) London: John Wiley & Sons.

Sohail, K. (2006, August). Psychology of suicide "bombers". Chowk [On-line]. Retrieved August 31, 2006. Available: http://www.chowk.com

Speckhard, A. & Akhmedova K. (2005, Fall). Talking to terrorists. *The Journal of Psychohistory, 33*(2), pp. 125–156.

Volkan, V. (1997). *Blood lines: From ethnic pride to ethnic terrorism.* Boulder, CO: Westview Press.

Volkan, V. (2003, June 22). Terrorism Panel discussion held at the Spring Meeting of the American Psychoanalytic Association, Boston, MA. Quoted in G. Hough (2004). Does psychoanalysis have anything to offer an understanding of terrorism? *Journal of American Psychoanalysis Association, 52*(3) pp. 813–828.

Volkan, V. (2004). *Blind trust: Large groups and their leaders in times of crisis and terror.* Charlottesville, VA: Pitchstone Publishing.

Wilson, S. (2005, November 12). *Life and hope flow from Palestinian boy's death* [On-line]. Retrieved September 30, 2007. Available: www.washingtonpost.com/wp-dyn/content/article/2005/11/11/AR2005111101624_p

Chapter 4

TRAUMA OF TERRORISM AND POLITICAL VIOLENCE ON CIVILIANS: DIAGNOSIS AND TREATMENT

Jamshid A. Marvasti and Valerie L. Dripchak

Kill one and frighten ten thousand.
Karl Seger

INTRODUCTION

There has been a shift in the battlefields of war from the military arena to civilian ground. These changes are due to the way conflicts are fought through suicide attacks and terrorism. The results include not only the physical harm but also the psychological and social impact that these actions have on the lives of people. Amsel and Marshall (2003) pointed out that the terrorist attacks are intentional psychological warfare that damages the well-being of a country. Moreover, because the suicide terrorist uses ordinary events to create symbols of fear, the impact is more greatly perceived.

Amsel and Marshall (2003) further discussed the "iconography of terrorism" to include the psychological advantages in the fearful messages that are sent with each suicide attack. These include the elements of surprise by targeting what seem very often to be random civilian groups. This element of surprise suggests that anyone may be at risk for attack. Lastly, media coverage is always available, so that maximum broadcasting of the event is achieved. This provides for the suicide warrior/bomber widespread publicity for a cause that would never have been achieved if not for this type of warfare.

Marvasti has suggested that the terrorism has less to do with the terror act and more to do with society's response to the act (Bates, 2003). It can be added that there have been many diverse psychological reactions to terrorism that may change over time. These responses influence and are influenced by the political climate.

This section will discuss some of the psychological responses within the broad population (including those at risk of trauma-related disorders), children, and the intergenerational transmission of trauma.

PSYCHOLOGICAL RESPONSES WITHIN THE BROAD POPULATION

Shortly after the terrorist attacks of September 11, 2001, many Americans reported symptoms of stress that included difficulties paying attention at work or at school, sleep disturbances, irritability, distress, hypersensitivity, and depressed feelings. Susceptibility to these symptoms was associated with being female, nonwhite, previous psychological illness, and proximity to the disaster sites. Most of these adults alleviated their distress by talking with others, attending religious services, and donating gifts to charities. Within weeks to months, most people's symptoms were abated and they recovered (Sadock & Sadock, 2003). Other people changed their behaviors as a way to try to manage their fears. Some people changed their travel plans or increased their cigarette smoking or alcohol consumption (Silver, Holman, McIntosh, Poulin, & Gil-Rivas, 2002).

Fraguas et al. (2006) found that victims who showed symptoms of PTSD following the March 11th attack in Madrid, Spain, and were treated at a hospital's emergency department had subjective psychological health involvement. They further discovered that PTSD symptoms were high and remained stable between one month and six months, whereas subjective evaluation of health improved significantly during this time. The correlation pointed out that the importance of PTSD symptoms and subjective health involvement are part of the psychological responses to trauma.

Verger et al. (2004) discussed the psychological impact of terrorism and the presence of PTSD in the victims of the 1995 to1996 bombings in France. They explained that a wave of bombings struck France during this period of time, killing 12 people and injuring more than 200. These authors conducted follow-up evaluations with the victims of terrorism in 1998 to determine the prevalence of PTSD and the factors associated with this response. Their research yielded a logistic regression analysis that indicated that the risk of PTSD was significantly higher among women, individuals between the ages of thirty-five and fifty-four, and people who endured severe injuries or cosmetic impairment or perceived a substantial threat during the attacks. These authors concluded that there was a high prevalence of PTSD approximately 2.6 years after the terrorist attacks. This indicated the need for improved health services to address not only the immediate but also the longer-term effects of terrorism.

Njenga, Nicholls, Nyamai, Kigamwa, & Davidson (2004) discussed the terrorist attacks that occurred in Nairobi, Kenya. They evaluated the psychological reactions of nonwestern individuals after the bombing of the U. S. Embassy in Nairobi. They discovered PTSD in 35 percent of their 2883 Kenyan subjects one to three months after the attack. Factors associated with PTSD included being female, being unmarried, having a lack of education, seeing the blast, being injured, not recovering from the injury, not confiding in a friend, and having bereavement and financial difficulties since the blast. These researchers concluded that the specific factors that are often cited in the literature to predict and identify short-term PTSD reactions to trauma were confirmed in this large, nonwestern study.

Although these studies showed important information, we know that there is no such thing as a universal response to terrorism. A number of people do not recover from their trauma, and their symptoms may develop into long-term psychiatric disorders that create some serious challenges to daily functioning. Research indicated that adults' pretraumatic risk factors are significant determinants for them to develop PTSD. According to the *New England Journal of Medicine*, it was found that an estimated 90,000 people had developed PTSD or clinical depression following the September 11 attacks. An additional 34,000 people met the criteria for both diagnoses. Individuals who lived close to the terrorist sites, individuals who suffered personal losses as a result of the attacks, or individuals who had experienced other stressful events during the preceding twelve months were most at risk for developing these disorders (Galea et al., 2002).

PSYCHOLOGICAL RESPONSES IN CHILDREN

According to the literature, children's reactions to trauma are similar to the responses shown by adults except that children are more susceptible to secondary exposure. This type of exposure is brought about through the influence of fearful responses by parents or other key people in the child's life and through the media. However, the most important considerations for children are the severity of the traumatic event and the child's developmental stage (Yehuda & Hyman, 2005).

Young children, in particular, have not yet developed adequate coping mechanisms to deal with a significant trauma. Their immature cognitive abilities influence their perceptions of what has occurred. Children, like adults, need to understand what has happened after a trauma. However, unlike adults, they are not able to use reason and problem-solving skills. Instead they resort to fantasy and magical thinking. Sometimes they may even believe that they are the cause for the event (Timberlake & Cutler, 2001). In our experience as clinicians who work with children who have been exposed to trauma, some mitigating factors for children include the amount of family support and the degree of consistency in the child's life before and after the trauma.

According to Marvasti and Dripchak (2004), other behavioral responses are developmentally classified and include the following. For young children (infancy-five years), children may become easily startled; irritable; and fearful of being left alone in a room, crying and clinging. As children grow older, they tend to be able to verbally identify their reactions. For children (six to eleven years), there may be present some generalized anxiety, school avoidance or an inability to focus in school, withdrawal from friends, aggressive acts, fears about personal harm or abandonment, and irritability. Older children (twelve years to adolescence) may experience confusion, anger, fears, school problems, and somatic complaints.

Children, like adults, may reexperience the traumatic event through nightmares, flashbacks, or intrusive thoughts. However, in children, these issues tend to be generalized to other fears. Moreover, children tend not to verbalize their fears about the trauma but will often act out their concerns in their play. The term traumatic play has been used to describe the repetitive actions that the child uses to reexperience the trauma or trauma-related themes. Some older children use a reenactment to fantasize actions of revenge that may lead to impulsive and often dangerous acts (Sadock & Sadock, 2003).

In spite of the risk factors that were identified previously, most children, as with most adults, tend to be resilient after trauma exposure. Only a minority will develop trauma-related disorders. In a study cited by Sadock and Sadock (2003), 8000 children whose ages ranged from ten to thirteen and lived in New York at the time of the terrorist attacks were interviewed. It was found that 11 percent had symptoms of PTSD nine months after the event, and an additional 15 percent had symptoms of agoraphobia.

Pfefferbaum and associates (2006) discussed the trauma, grief, and depression in Nairobi children after the 1998 bombing of the American Embassy in Nairobi. They wrote that this tragic event provided an unfortunate opportunity to examine the traumatic grief in children after the trauma of terrorism. Their report described the findings of 156 children–eight to fourteen months after the bombing–who knew someone who was killed in the incident. They found that the grief of these children was associated with bomb-related posttraumatic stress (e.g., bomb-related losses), as well as other negative life events. Their study supported the developing literature of traumatic grief and the need for studying this potentially unique aspect of trauma.

Miljevic-Ridjicki and Lugomer-Armano (1994) compared the reactions of preschool children from Zagreb with those of refugees from the war during 1992. They found that they could discuss the subject of war with children as young as three years old. They reported that war was constantly in the minds of the children, and the worst war-related experience for Zagreb children was the air raid alarms. However the displaced/refugee children felt worse during bombardments, destruction, and shooting. The researchers revealed that girls could admit their fear, but boys hoped to live up to the male stereotype and be brave without demonstrating any fear.

Punamaki (2002) has extensively researched the impact of military violence and war on children. She discovered that children show great differences in their ways of appraising threat or seeking help and expressing feelings and emotions in regard to exposure to traumatic events. She hypothesized that each developmental age provided children with special potential resources on one hand and also made them vulnerable on the other. There are indications that insecure-avoidant children are vulnerable because of their tendencies to ignore or deny dangers. In addition, they may distrust the help of others. Their coping mechanisms were distraction and withdrawal (Punamaki, 2002). Doctor Punamaki's research indicated that insecure-ambivalent children are at risk because they may exaggerate the danger and threat and overactivate their negative emotions. However, secure children generally and accurately perceived the traumatic event, trusted in their own resource and healing power, relied on others' resources and abilities to help, and generally demonstrated a balanced emotional, cognitive, and behavioral response to a traumatic event (Punamaki, 2002).[1]

CASE EXAMPLES OF 9/11 VICTIMS

The following cases (Dripchak & Marvasti, 2007) are examples of the responses to different levels of trauma that were and may be experienced by civilians after the September 11 attacks in New York City. In the first case, Rachel, was working as a manager for a company that occupied office space in the first World Trade Tower that was hit. She found herself running from the site in a state of fright, although her supervisor urged everyone to remain within the office area and not leave the building. Although Rachel received only minor abrasions from falling debris, she suffered more serious psychological reactions. Almost immediately, she began to have fears about dying and began to perseverate on the sights, sounds, and smells of that day. These intrusive thoughts began to interfere with her sleep, which increased her agitation and irritability. Rachel did not want to return to work after her company found temporary office space in another location, so her absenteeism began to create a problem. Approximately four months after the event, she sought mental health services. Rachel was showing symptoms of PTSD.

Rachel's case showed what can happen to an innocent civilian who was a direct victim of a terrorist attack, but there are other kinds of victims as well. For example, Richard was a young emergency medical technician living in New Jersey when the attacks were made on the Twin Towers (Dripchak & Marvasti, 2007). He volunteered right away to go to New York to help in the rescue and recovery efforts. By his own choice, Richard worked long hours for several days without much rest. When he did try to sleep, he began to have nightmares of burned and mangled bodies, which caused him to sleep even less and to do even more rescue work. By the end of two weeks, he began to exhibit increased agitation and to make some mistakes. He also avoided any contacts with his family and began to argue with his coworkers, which was not like Richard's usual disposition. When some of the other rescue workers wanted to talk about the horrors that they witnessed, Richard responded with detachment and refused to engage in the discussions. Richard eventually collapsed. When he was cleared medically, he was told to seek mental health services. He was diagnosed and treated for Acute Stress Disorder.

These cases demonstrate the wide-reaching psychological effects that terrorist attacks can have on civilians. Not only can harm be endured by a victim who is directly involved, but it also can be sustained by rescue workers, people who witnessed the event, family members of victims, and even by media exposure.

PSYCHIATRIC ASPECT OF POLITICAL VIOLENCE ON ISRAELI CIVILIANS

Within the traumatized nation of Israel,[2] children are the most vulnerable population and may also suffer the most because they are in the process of growing up and developing their personality. Traumatic experience and violence may be internalized during the tender years of childhood and become a permanent part of their personality. An illustration of this can be seen in a BBC news report, which told a story about two Israeli children, ten-year-old Sivan and her eight-year-old brother David (Lustig, 2003). It was reported that they were playing a game in which one person was the news reporter and the other the interviewee. Sivan opened with "Here is the news. We have just heard that there has been another suicide bombing in Jerusalem, and David has been killed." She then turned to her brother and asked, "David, what is it like to be dead?" In this report it was also noted that this Israeli family had a close family friend recently killed by a suicide bomber while he was in a Jerusalem café (Lustig, 2003).[3] This story has illustrated how the external experiences of children can become part of their internal world and reenacted in the games that they play.

In addition, in a recent survey of youth living in Jerusalem by the Israel Center of the Treatment of Psychotrauma, it was revealed that 50 percent of teenagers had been exposed to a militant attack (Winder, 2004). The survey concluded that although Israeli children are resilient, 5 percent had developed PTSD. These children lost their ability to play; were preoccupied with death; were depressed; and wandered around, unable to socialize and develop relationships. Doctor Roni Berger expressed concern for the future when she stated, "Children start to believe that violence is the only solution to conflict" (Winder, 2004).

It is not only the children in Israel who are suffering. Shalev Tuval, Trenkiel-Fishman, Hadar, and Eth (2006) have explored the continuous exposure to terror in two communities in Israel. Their research revealed that residents who were directly exposed reported more frequent exposure to terror and deeper destruction of daily living. However, the directly and indirectly exposed groups both reported comparable rates of PTSD and the same level of symptoms. The results showed that 26.95 percent of people who were directly exposed and 21.35 percent of people who were indirectly exposed met the *DSM* criteria for PTSD. One-third of those with PTSD symptoms reported significant distress and dysfunction. In the indirectly exposed group, exposure and disruption of daily living contributed to development of PTSD symptoms. These authors concluded that continuous terror created similar distress in both proximal and remote communities. However, they found that exposure to discrete events was not a necessary mediator of terror threat. A subgroup of those exposed developed serious symptoms; others were surprisingly resilient. They concluded that disruptions of the daily routine life were a major secondary stressor to many of these people.

Furthermore, Gidron, Kaplan, Velt, and Shalem (July, 2004) have described the prevalence and moderators of terror-related symptoms of PTSD in Israeli citizens. The goal of their research was to examine the prevalence, correlates, and moderators of PTSD-like symptoms following a terrorist attack in Israel. They collected a sample of 149 Israelis from five cities and evaluated them. They found that 15.4 percent of the people were directly exposed to a terrorist attack; 36.5 percent of them knew someone else who had been exposed to an attack. Clinically significant PTSD-like symptoms were reported by 10.1 percent of the sample. They evaluated the correlates of the PTSD-like symptoms and found these correlates were: (1) perceived control in men, (2) government control, and (3) education in women (all inversely correlated with PTSD symptoms) and the frequency with which women listened to the news (positively correlated with PTSD symptoms). They concluded that approximately 10 percent of Israelis in their sample had PTSD-like symptoms. Correlates between PTSD-like symptoms differed between men and women.

In an additional study, Shalev and Freedman (June, 2005) discussed PTSD following terrorist attacks in a perspective evaluation. Their research revealed that survivors of terrorist attacks have a higher incidence of PTSD than do motor vehicle accident survivors (37.8% versus 18.7%). They concluded that early symptoms are reliable risk indicators of PTSD across events and circumstances. Their research method was based on evaluating 39 survivors of terrorist attacks and 354 survivors of motor vehicle accidents. Subjects were evaluated upon admission to a general hospital emergency room, after one week, and again four months later.

In a longer-term study, Kaplan, Matar, Kamin, Sadan, and Cohen (2005, September) examined stress-related responses after three years' exposure of terror in Israel. They found that a deeply held belief system affecting "life views" may cause a significant resilience to developing stress-related disorders. Religion, combined with common ideological convictions and social cohesion, was associated with increased resilience as compared to secular metropolitan urban populations. This study collected research from the inhabitants of three different types of "population centers" in Israel and evaluated the stress-reported symptoms during 2003 to 2004. The "population centers" have been exposed to two distinct forms of violence: sporadic large-scale terrorist attacks in the metropolitan areas in the heart of Israel and daily "war zone" conditions in the settlements beyond the 1967 borders of Israel. The results revealed that the inhabitants of Gush Katif, in spite of their first-hand daily exposure to violent attacks, reported the fewest and least severe symptoms of stress-related complaints, the least sense of personal threat, and the highest level of functioning of all three samples. The most severely symptomatic and functionally compromised were the inhabitants of the Tel Aviv suburb, who were the least frequently and the least directly affected and exposed to violence. Because the Gush Katif population is exclusively religious, the data were reassessed according to religiousness. The religious inhabitants of Kiryat Arba had almost the same symptoms as the Gush Katif population had, whereas the secular inhabitants of Kiryat Arba reported fairing worse than either population in the Tel Aviv suburb (Kaplan et al., 2005). Doctor Roni Berger of the Israel Center for Victims of Terror and War has witnessed that having a strong national ideology has also helped Israeli settlers withstand greater levels of trauma and violence (Winder, 2004).[4]

INTERGENERATIONAL ISSUES RELATED TO PSYCHOLOGICAL RESPONSES

Pain that is not transformed is transferred.

Richard Rohr

There has been some controversy about the research related to the transmission of trauma across generations. Part of the controversy relates to a lack of consensus of what actually is transmitted from one generation to the next. Another part of the controversy is that much of the research is limited to anecdotal evidence and case studies. Some of the studies included the work of Solomon, Kotler, and Mikuliner (1988) who examined Israeli soldiers who developed PTSD during the Lebanese War. The research indicated that soldiers who were the second generation of Holocaust survivors had a more extended course of PTSD.

Subsequent research done by Yehuda, Schmeider, and Wainberg (1988) found that healthy descendants of Holocaust survivors were more likely to develop PTSD after traumatic events and report more symptoms. Some of these findings related to the conclusions that significant trauma may change the responsiveness of the hypothalamic-pituitary-adrenal axis before the onset of PTSD, setting up a possible genetic link and an increased vulnerability to additional trauma. There is a likelihood that if there is evidence to support transmission of traumatic responses across generations, then we may see these reactions in the future as we continue to study people around the world who are offspring of parents who experienced trauma.

Although more research needs to be done in this area, the concept of intergenerational transmission of trauma has warranted much attention in the clinical area. It is important to keep in mind that children may have parents with trauma-related disorders who are therefore less able to provide the supportive responses necessary to mitigate the impact of the new trauma on the child. From the forensic point of view, monetary compensation should be considered on the basis of the new findings that successive generations of traumatized parents and children may also develop symptoms and have a need for treatment. In the authors' opinion, this issue currently needs to be addressed for Holocaust survivors and new compensation should be considered for others affected as well.

TREATMENT PRINCIPLES OF TRAUMA VICTIMS

When working with individuals who have been exposed to trauma, it is important to recognize not only the symptoms of the presenting pathology but also the protective factors that may be available within the client's environment. In any treatment protocol, an assessment must be done as the first step in treatment. Moreover, intervention strategies are different for adults than they are for children. The following sections provide a summary of crisis intervention and treatment programs that are effective for children, adolescents, and adults. Each of these treatment programs offers positive outcomes in anecdotal and small-sample-size studies of participants. We advise the reader to consider cautiously each approach as an option for treatment and to find the "best fit" for the client.

Crisis Intervention Model

The effects of terrorism are not necessarily seen immediately following the events, and a crisis onset may occur any time within six to eight weeks of the traumatic event. According to Marino (1995), a crisis develops in three distinct stages: (1) a precipitating event occurs in which an individual's usual coping strategies are not effective; (2) the individual experiences increased stress and disorganization surrounding the event that escalates beyond the person's abilities to cope (3) a need is present to facilitate a process to bring about a resolution of the crisis.

Gilliland (1982) developed a six-step model that is widely used in the area of intervention work. The first three steps of crisis intervention involve active listening on the part of the crisis intervener. They include: (1) defining the problem, (2) ensuring safety, and (3) providing support.

The next three phases incorporate change strategies. They are: (4) examining alternatives in the areas of situational supports, coping mechanisms, and constructive thought processes, (5) creating with the client an action plan, and (6) obtaining a commitment from the client to engage in the plan. This short-term intervention process entails several meetings over a brief span of time. The goal of crisis intervention is to return the client to his premorbid level of functioning and to foster the development of additional coping skills.

Treatment for Adults and Adolescents: Cognitive Behavioral Therapies

When individuals present with symptoms of pathology that are evident for a longer period of time and are not subsiding, more intensive therapeutic interventions are required. The goals of therapy include the following:

1. Prevention of transference of victimization to the next generation (the most important therapeutic goal).

2. Provision of corrective emotional experiences that result in reshaping the survivors' "world view."
3. Disappearance of dissociative states and development of insight into the impact of the trauma.
4. Reworking of the trauma, resolution of the developmental issues, and establishing a sense of self.
5. Integration of the trauma into the consciousness.
6. Improvement in object relationships, boundaries, coping skills, and self image, thus empowering the victim/survivor.
7. The prevention of compulsion to repeat the trauma in real life and deidentifying the possible identification with the aggressor. (Marvasti, 1993)

Cognitive-behavioral therapy (CBT) is a treatment approach based on cognitive and learning theories. In the treatment of traumatized adolescents and adults, CBT is designed to reduce the negative emotional and behavioral responses that surround the trauma by correcting the "faulty beliefs" related to the abusive experiences. The CBT approach stresses the interrelatedness of thoughts, feelings and behaviors, and interventions in such a way that targeting one of these areas will also affect the other sectors (Marvasti & Dripchak, 2004).

Trauma-focused CBT was developed by Cohen, Mannarino, Berlinger, and Deblinger (2000) and is based on the principles of CBT. It comprises of four components: (1) exposure, (2) cognitive processing, (3) reframing, and (4) stress management.

This treatment approach is applicable to adolescents. There is also a parent component that parallels the interventions for teens (exposure, cognitive processing, and stress management).

Eye movement desensitization and reprocessing (EMDR) is an intervention developed by Francine Shapiro to treat PTSD. It is based on the concept of moving traumatic data from the right hemisphere of the brain to the left hemisphere, where the traumatic events may be analyzed and affective arousal may be modified. The use of EMDR techniques allows the client to "revisit" the traumatic memories (Amendolia, 1998).

EMDR treatment simultaneously focuses on three areas of the client in relationship to the trauma: (1) the client's memories of the trauma, (2) his or her negative views of self and the trauma, and (3) the related physical elements of the anxiety.

While this is occurring, the clinician asks the client to follow the clinician's moving finger, eliciting a series of rapid and repeated side-to-side eye movements. During the intervention, the client provides an evaluation of how anxious she or he is feeling, as well as how strong the thoughts are that relate to the traumatic memories. The clinician then utilizes cognitive restructuring techniques with the client to replace responses of fear, anxiety, and so on and to modulate the physiological arousal (Shapiro, 1995).

Dialectical behavioral therapy (DBT) is a form of CBT developed by Marsha Linehan. It was initially constructed as a comprehensive treatment program for chronically suicidal individuals who met the diagnostic criteria for borderline personality disorder (BPD) (Linehan, 1993). However, the many people with BPD have histories of trauma and also meet the criteria for PTSD (Wagner & Linehan, 2006).

DBT is based on a "biosocial theory" that views the core dysfunction as emotional dysregulation that develops out of the transactions between biological and environmental factors. The important biological factors produce an emotional vulnerability that is characterized by high sensitivity to stimuli; an intense response to stimuli and a slow return to emotional baseline after arousal have occurred (Linehan, 1993).

In Linehan's DBT model, she emphasized four components: skills training within a group process; concurrent individual psychotherapy; telephone consultations between the client and her therapist; and team consultation for therapists. The skills training incorporates the acquisition, strengthening, and generalizing of four areas of learning: core mindfulness skills; distress tolerance; interpersonal effectiveness; and emotional regulation skills (Linehan, 1993).

Within the DBT individual psychotherapy sessions, there are stages of treatment. Stage 1 focuses on severe behavioral dyscontrol along a hierarchy of needs: suicidal behaviors, therapy-interfering behaviors, and quality-of-life-interfering behaviors with the goal of achieving behavioral control. Stage 2 targets problems with emotional suffering, which may include PTSD-related symptoms, with the goal of increasing normative responses. Stage 3 incorporates the remaining problems in life with the goal of better management or resolution. Stage 4 targets the sense of incompleteness with the goal of increasing the capacity for freedom (Wagner & Linehan, 2006).

Treatment of Children: Play Therapy

When the child does not have enough resources or protective factors or they are insufficient to prevent more serious reactions from occurring, we use play therapy. Through the selection of materials and toys, children are able to express their thoughts, feelings, and concerns. Gil (1991) suggested that the aim of play therapy with children who have been traumatized is to have them overcome the negative impact of the trauma and to empower them. Play therapy also releases the psychic energy that was being used to suppress the trauma toward the child's own emotional growth. However, in the process of play therapy, there needs to be an emphasis on the therapy and not on the play. When children reenact a traumatic experience through play, they have the potential of changing the outcome of the experience and of arriving at a better resolution of the conflict (Dripchak & Marvasti, 2004). Although there are many different forms of play therapy, the authors have successfully used an integrative model of story telling with the principles of Milton Erickson in their work with traumatized children.

The utilization of tales and storytelling for the purposes of learning and healing is not a new phenomenon. In fact, one of the first examples of the healing effects of stories is the well-known book *1001 Nights*. Captive Scheherazade used these imaginative stories to heal a tyrannical ruler's thirst for blood. Although they were used to treat the ailing king, these tales may be considered "treatments" for the readers and listeners. As the lessons from these stories are absorbed and integrated into their consciousness, the readers and listeners may gain new attitudes about their circumstances (Peseschkian, 1986). Clinton (1986) attributed the success of Scheherazade's story to a "talking cure." He added that, unlike the Freudian school, the doctor does the talking, not the patient, and tells tales that address the patient's concerns. The first modem amateur psychotherapists were quite possibly barbers and bartenders, and their therapeutic tools, in addition to their listening skills, were anecdotes and life histories of other clients (Marvasti, 1997a, b).

The interspersed technique was originated by Milton Erickson in order to convey suggestions indirectly to his patients through the embedding of messages with different nonverbal aspects (O'Hanlon, 1987, p. 167). Interspersed suggestions are emphasized during the storytelling by way of shifting the tonal quality of therapist's voice to a softer or lower voice to the point that interspersed suggestions gain a "voice all their own" (Mills & Crowley, 1986, p. 140).

Many clinicians believe that since storytelling is free from confrontations and direct approaches to client symptoms, they may not evoke resistance. Instead, children integrate the components of stories and develop a new view of their conflicts. They may at an unconscious level use the skill and the solutions that the metaphor protagonists use in order to overcome their problems.

Children easily enter into the world of story through their imagery skills. These skills are the essential elements needed for change and healing. The metaphors of the story further activate the child's imagination and result in healing through strength, self-knowledge, and transformation (Mills & Crowley, 1986, p. 21). Stories enable change to occur so that the type of learning goes from abstract and theoretical concepts to vivid and imaginary modes of thought.

The therapist creates a story with a hero (protagonist) who owns the same conflicts, behavior, and ego weakness of the patient but who will master them by learning new skills and coping mechanisms. In this way, the end of the stories is always positive and successful. In other words, there is an emphasis on assets rather than losses, potential rather than weakness, hope rather than despair, solution rather than problem, and healing power rather than pathology. In using storytelling, the therapist's toy takes the child's toys into the dollhouse and develops a story. The therapist's toy gradually closes the other toy's eyes, relaxing them to the point that they appear to be in trancelike states. This may help the child to fall into a trance as well. The toy and stuffed animals are then left to relax and listen to the puppet's story about good days and happy endings. The puppet's story may contain metaphors and interspersed suggestions, emphasized in a slow, rhythmic voice, with vocal changes such as tone or volume shifts.

Several basic elements of storymaking, that are necessary in creating a metaphorical storyline include: (1) presenting a metaphorical conflict similar to that of the child conflict, (2) personifying unconscious processes via various characters such as heroes and villains, that represent the potentials and fears of the protagonist, (3) integrating parallel learning situations that result in the protagonist's victory and success, (4) presenting a metaphorical crisis that eventually becomes a turning point in the resolution of the conflict, (5) developing a new sense of identity for the protagonist since his victory, and (6) culminating this resolution into a celebration and a sense of new identity (Mills & Crowley, 1986, p. 138).

In closing the section on treatment, the authors need to again emphasize that not everyone who is exposed to a trauma is traumatized. Furthermore, it is important to point out that treatment programs need to match the client's needs versus the therapist's orientation towards a particular treatment approach. Last, the basic tenet in therapy is that individuals are always changing, and it is essential that the clinician value this fact.

CONCLUSION

As more and more civilians are becoming the intended victims of terrorist attacks, we must look to ways to treat not only their physical injuries but also their psychological wounds. This is no easy task and it will take time, energy, and money. Furthermore, the answers do not lie in a particular discipline of study but need to be the product of a society of people working together and caring about what happens to their people.

The obvious requirements include educational programs about the effects of terrorism-related trauma. People need to understand the potential of the psychological issues caused by terrorist attacks. We also must have professionals who are competently trained in trauma work who can provide crisis intervention strategies to attempt to prevent pathologies from occurring. However, in the case of the development of serious symptoms, there must be professionals who have skilled training.

There is a need for further research into areas of how terrorism affects the biological, psychological, social, and spiritual realms of the individual and the family. Perhaps, with more understanding of the various effects, there may be newer ways to bring about resolutions. Last, but so important, legislation is needed to allocate funding for these programs. Resources that are designated towards wellness versus destruction will reap benefits for this generation and for many generations to come.

NOTES

1. Doctor Raija-Leena Punamaki is a psychologist and native of Finland, an invited lecturer at universities in Belgium, Italy, Israel, and The Netherlands. For information about Doctor Punamaki's research on Palestinian civilians *see* R. J. Punamaki (2000) The conflict between horror and heroism: The suffering of Palestinian children. In J. Marvasti (Ed.), *Child suffering in the world.* Manchester, CT: Sexual Trauma Center Publication.
2. *The New York Times* has reported about the brutality done to Israelis. One example is of a sixteen-year-old Lebanese, who in 1979 infiltrated into Israel and attacked a family. He shot the father in the head in front of his four-year-old daughter and then crushed her skull with his rifle butt. The wife hid in a crawl space with her two-year-old daughter whom she tried to keep quiet and accidently smothered to death. This sixteen-year-old has been in an Israeli jail since 1979 (from The New York Times, 2006, p. A6).
3. Reporter Gregg Zoroya (2002) related the picture he saw of seven-year-old Palestinian twins giggling while playing a game where one was a martyred suicide bomber and the other a weeping mother. Zoroya reported that many of the children in the West Bank were negatively affected and had recurrent nightmares and insomnia. Many different PTSD symptoms and physical disorders developed, such as speech disorders, panic attacks, bedwetting, and skin rashes as reported by area physicians. Vacations were nonexistent. Curfews altered social development. The empty streets were filled only with Israeli military vehicles. School performance also was negatively affected. The children left for school wondering if they would return home. Their play focused on being fighters, soldiers, and martyrs. The children's lives were governed by their own fears (shaking and clinging to their parents) and by the fear they see constantly in their parents' faces (from G. Zoroya [2002, August 6]. Fear, rage fester inside for West Bank children: Curfew, occupation push generation toward radicalism. *USA Today*, p. A1). The previous example and the example mentioned within this section of the book demonstrate that children reveal what they are exposed to and

what is bothering them through their play. Although the children in these two news reports are from two different cultures, Israel and Palestine, the children's play is quite similar.

4. For more information about life situation of Israelis and Palestinian children *see* Laurel Holliday (1998). *Children of Israel, children of Palestine: Our own true stories.* (New York: Pocket Books). For information concerning the impact of violence on Palestinian children *see* Chapter 12: Palestine–A nation traumatized.

REFERENCES

Amendolia, R. (1998). A narrative constructionist perspective of treatment of posttraumatic stress disorders with Ericksonian hypnosis and eye movement desensitization and reprocessing. *The American Academy of Experts in Traumatic Stress, 23*, p. 1–5.

Amsel, L., & Marshall, R. D. (2003). Clinical management of subsyndromal psychological sequelae of the 9/11 terror attacks. In S.W. Coates, J. L. Rosenthal, and D. S. Schechter (Eds.), *September 11: Trauma and human bonds.* Hillsdale, NJ: The Analytic Press.

Bates, B. (2003). Knowledge dismal on terrorism. *Clinical Psychiatry News, June*, 28.

Clinton, J. (1986). Madness and cure in the *Thousand and one nights.* In R. Bottigheimer (Ed.), *Fairy tales and society: Illusion, allusion and paradigm*, (pp. 1–65). Philadelphia: University of Pennsylvania Press.

Cohen, J. A., Mannarino, A. P., Berlinger, L., & Deblinger, E. (2000). Trauma focused cognitive-behavioral therapy for children and adolescents. *Journal of Interpersonal Violence, 15*, 1202–1223.

Dripchak, V. L., & Marvasti, J. A. (2004). Treatment approaches for sexually abused children and adolescents: Play therapy and cognitive behavioral therapy. In J. A. Marvasti (Ed.), *Psychiatric treatment of victims and survivor of sexual trauma: A neuro-bio-psychological approach* (pp. 155–176). Springfield, IL: Charles C Thomas, Publisher.

Dripchak, V. L, & Marvasti, J. A. (2007). The multi-dimensional impact of terrorism on civilians: Treatment implications for nurses. *On the Edge, 13*, 3–9.

Fraguas, D., Teran, S., Conejo-Galindo, J., Medina, O., Sainz-Corton, E., Ferrando, L., Gabriel, R., & Arango, C. (2006). Posttraumatic stress disorder in victims of the March 11 attacks in Madrid admitted to a hospital emergency room: Six-month follow-up. *European Psychiatry, 21*, 143–151.

Galea, S., Ahern, J., Resnick, H., Kilpatric, D., Bucuvalas, M., Gold, J., Vlahor, D. (2002). Psychological sequelae of the September 11, 2001 terrorist attacks in New York City. *New England Journal of Medicine, 346*, 982–987.

Gidron, Y., Kaplan, Y., Velt, A., & Shalem, R. (2004, July). Prevalence and moderators of terror-related post-traumatic stress disorder symptoms in Israeli citizens. *Israel Medical Association Journal* [On-line]. Retrieved December 23, 2006. Available: http://www.ncbi.nih.gov

Gil, E. (1991). *The healing power of play.* New York: Guilford Press.

Gilliland, B. E. (1982). *Steps in crisis counseling.* Memphis, TN: Memphis State University.

Kaplan, Z., Matar, M. A., Kamin, R., Sadan, T., & Cohen, H. (2005, September). Stress-related responses after 3 years of exposure to terror in Israel: Are ideological-religious factors associated with resilience? *Clinical Psychiatry* [On-line]. Retrieved December 23, 2006. Available: http://www.ncbi.nlm.nih.gov

Linehan, M. M. (1993). *Cognitive-behavioral treatment of borderline personality disorder.* New York: Guilford Press.

Lustig, R., (October 24, 2003). Children of Oslo live in fear. *BBC News* [On-line]. Retrieved July 25, 2007. Available: http://news.bbc.co.uk/go/pr/fr/-/2/hi/middle_east/3210533.stm

Marino, T. W. (1995). Crisis counseling: Helping normal people cope with abnormal situations. *Counseling Today*, 38, 25, 40, 46 & 53.

Marvasti, J. A. (1993). Please hurt me again: Posttraumatic play therapy with an abused child. In T. Kottman, & C. Schaefer (Eds), *Play therapy in action: A casebook for practitioners.* (pp. 485–525). Northvale, NJ: Jason Aronson.

Marvasti, J. A. (1997a). Ericksonian play therapy. In L. D. Braverman, & K. O'Connor (Eds), *Play therapy theory and practice: A comparative casebook*, pp. 285–307. NY: John Wiley & Sons.

Marvasti, J. A. (1997b). Using metaphors, fairytales, and storytelling in psychotherapy with Children. In H. S. Kaduson & C. E. Schaefer (Eds), *101 favorite play therapy techniques* (pp. 35–39). Northvale, NJ: Jason Aronson Publishers.

Marvasti, J. A., & Dripchak, V. L. (2004). The impact of terrorism, terror and trauma on children: Implications for treatment. *Journal of Forensic Psychiatry, 25*, pp. 19–38.

Miljevic-Ridjicki, R., & Lugomer-Armano, G. (1994). Children's comprehension of war. *Child Abuse Review, 3*, pp. 134–144.

Mills, J. C., & Crowley R. (1986). *Therapeutic metaphors for children and the child within*, New York: Brunner/Mazel.

Njenga, F. G., Nicholls, P. J., Nyamai, C., Kigamwa, P., & Davidson, J. R. (2004). Post-traumatic stress after terrorist attack: Psychological reactions following the US Embassy bombing in Nairobi: Naturalistic study. *British Journal of Psychiatry, 185*, pp. 328–333.

O'Hanlon, W. H. (1987). *Taproots: Underlying principles of Milton Erickson's therapy and hypnosis.* New York: Norton.

Peseschkian, N. (1986). *Oriental stories as tools in psychotherapy*, Berlin: Springer-Verlag.

Pfefferbaum, B., North, C. S., Doughty, D. E., Pfefferbaum, R. L., Dumont, C. E., Pynoos, R. S., Gurwitch, R. H., & Ndetei, D. (2006). Trauma, grief and depression in Nairobi children after the 1998 bombing of the American Embassy. *Death Studies, 30*, pp. 561–577.

Punamaki, R. L. (2002). The uninvited guest of war enters childhood: Developmental and personality aspects of war and military violence. *Traumatology, 8*(3), pp. 45–63.

Sadock, B. J., & Sadock, V. A. (2003). *Synopsis of psychiatry*. Philadelphia: Lippincott Williams & Wilkins.

Shalev, A. Y., & Freedman, S. (2005, June). PTSD following terrorist attacks: A prospective evaluation. *American Journal of Psychiatry* [On-line]. Retrieved December 23, 2006. Available: http://www.ncbi.nlm.nih.gov

Shalev, A., Tuval, R., Frenkiel-Fishman, S., Hadar, H., & Eth, S. (2006, April). Psychological responses to continuous terror: A study of two communities in Israel. *American Journal Psychiatry* [On-line]. Retrieved December 23, 2006. Available: http://www.ncbi.nlm.nih.gov

Shapiro, F. (1995). *Eye movement desensitization and reprocessing: Basic principles, protocols and procedures*. New York: Guilford.

Silver R. C., Holman E. A., McIntosh D. N., Poulin M., & Gil-Rivas V. (2002, September 11). Nationwide longitudinal study of psychological responses to September 11. *JAMA; 288*: pp. 1235–1244.

Solomon Z., Kotler M., & Mikulincer M. (1988). Combat-related posttraumatic stress disorder among second-generation Holocaust survivors. Preliminary findings. *American Journal of Psychiatry 145*, pp. 865–868.

Timberlake, E. M., & Cutler, M. M. (2001). *Play therapy in clinical social work*. Bosston, MA: Allyn & Bacon.

Verger, P., Dab, W., Lamping. D. L., Loze, J., Deschaseaux-Voinet, C., Abenhaim, L., & Rouillon, F. (2004, August). The psychological impact of terrorism: An epidemiologic study of posttraumatic stress disorder and associated factors in victims of the 1995–1996 bombings in France. *American Journal of Psychiatry 161*, pp. 1384–1389.

Wagner, A. W., & Linehan, M. M. (2006). Applications of dialectical behavior therapy to post-traumatic stress disorder and related problems. In V. M. Follette & J. I. Ruzek (Eds.), *Cognitive-behavioral therapies for trauma* (pp. 117–145). New York: Guilford Press.

Winder, B. (2004, June 2). Young Israelis "traumatised" by conflict. *BBC News* [On-line]. Retrieved August 27, 2006. Available: http://newsvote.bbc.co.uk/mpapps/pagetools/print/news.bbc.co.uk/2/hi/middle_east/37663

Yehuda R., Schmeider J., & Wainberg, M. (1988): Vulnerability to posttraumatic stress disorder in adult offspring of Holocaust survivors. *American Journal of Psychiatry 155*, pp. 1163–1171.

Yehuda R., & Hyman S. E. (2005, July): The impact of terrorism on brain and behavior: What we know and what we need to know. *Neuropsychopharmacology, 30*, pp. 1773–780.

Chapter 5

HOMEGROWN "WORRIER" AND "WARRIOR": MUSLIMS IN EUROPE AND THE UNITED STATES

Jamshid A. Marvasti

In every country the dominant religion, when it does not persecute other religions, in the long-run engulfs them all.

Voltaire

INTRODUCTION AND DEFINITION

In this chapter, we have tried to classify European and American Muslims into two distinct groups, with a very small minority being the warriors or the suicide bombers, as opposed to the overwhelming majority of Muslims, who are highly concerned about the current situation and are classified as worriers. Our goal is to understand the differences between these two groups and the causation for the development and formation of warriors. This understanding may give us an insight into how worriers can use their efforts (in coordination with other concerned society members) to reduce and eliminate the risk of future warriors.

In light of the 9/11 disaster, which was followed by the train bombings in Spain, the July 7th attack in London (named 7/7), and other events, the Muslim population living in the United States and Europe has been scrutinized, and a deeper understanding of these populations is warranted.

Currently, the overwhelming majority of western Muslims, including people who were born in the West or have immigrated legally to western countries, would be classified as the Muslim homegrown worriers. They are concerned about a number of issues that have made them subject to discrimination, profiling, detention, human rights violations, and rejection in multiple ways within the community. The media and policymakers, including the leaders of the government, have perpetuated continuous and multiple attacks not only on the Islamic religion but also on respected figures of that religion. Moreover, these western Muslims are also concerned about the negative impact on their communities due to the potential of homegrown warriors. In addition, they face the challenge of helping westerners understand intrafaith and interfaith concepts as well as resolving cultural conflicts that may arise.

Homegrown warriors are defined as individuals born or raised in the West who have become disillusioned, for many reasons, and have started activities that harm the interests of western governments. These warriors work either individually or in an organized group.

In order to reduce the risk of creating warriors, one must understand their motives. It is critical to analyze this group in order to manage and ultimately avoid grave social consequences. We begin by examining the demographics of these two Muslim groups. From there, we explore how communities have been affected by terrorist attacks, what contributed to these effects; and what are some recommendations for the future.

DEMOGRAPHICS OF AMERICAN MUSLIMS

The American Muslim community includes about seven million people. This group is highly educated with 67 percent of American Muslims having a bachelor's degree or higher as compared to 44 percent of non-Muslim Americans. Of American Muslims, 33 percent hold an advanced degree (above a bachelors) in comparison to 8.6 percent of non-Muslim Americans. This group is also affluent, with an average income of $42,158 per year in the U.S. (Anwar, 2006). In addition, 66 percent of American Muslim households earn more than $50,000 a year, and 26 percent of American Muslim households earn more than $100,000 a year.

DEMOGRAPHICS OF EUROPEAN MUSLIMS

The 15 million Muslims in the European Union are almost twice the number of Muslims living in the United States. They have gradually become a powerful political, economic, and scientific force. They hail from different countries and have diverse religious tendencies.

The European Muslim population grew as an unintended consequence of policies undertaken about fifty years ago during the postwar labor shortage in the 1950s and 1960s. Europe was experiencing economic growth and immigration was encouraged. People from countries such as Algeria, Morocco, Tunisia, and Pakistan were essentially guest workers in the beginning and then became citizens of their adopted countries. Subsequently, new generations of Turks, Algerians, and Moroccans were born in Europe. Currently, it is believed that the Muslim growth rate in Europe is about three times higher than that of non-Muslims and may double itself by the year 2015.

In acknowledging that Muslims have become a very significant population within Europe, one must explore how Muslims have adapted to these new nations. Liat Radcliff Ross (2006) in the *Foreign Affairs* journal, has questioned Robert Leiken's claim that European Muslims are "distinct, cohesive, and bitter" and who could be supportive of terrorist activities (Leiken, 2005). Ross (2006) has pointed out that European Muslims who immigrated came from vastly different countries, such as Morocco, India, and Indonesia. In addition, a recent British census has illustrated that only 2.7 percent of Britain's total population are Muslim, and those Muslims are divided into at minimum five distinct communities. Within these communities, Ross has stated, there are various factors such as political ideologies and tribal affiliations that further divide European Muslims. Even in response to the Iraq invasion, as Ross has pointed out, certain Muslim organizations supported the war (such as the Iraqi Shia Al-Khoei Foundation), whereas others illustrated their opposition through meetings with Prime Minister Tony Blair, and still others protested in the streets. Therefore, as Ross has maintained, there is no cohesive community of European Muslims; rather, they are a diverse group that does not pose a coordinated threat to Europe or the United States (Ross, 2006).

Stephanie Giry, a reporter with *Foreign Affairs*, has similar sentiments to those of Ross. Giry has written that most of Muslims in Europe have nothing to do with the "radical Islam" but rather have been working to assimilate into their new nations while preserving their own faith and tradition. The overwhelming majority of these people have contributed to society's growth (Giry, 2006). However, several negative circumstances have led to socioeconomic consequences for Muslims. One such circumstance is the possible ghettoization and religious and racial discrimination of certain neighborhoods. Researchers disagree on whether this is a result of local, national, or international policies.

Rai (2006) has reported that in Britain the YouGov agency conducted several polls with British Muslims in regard to the 7/7 bombings. Although only 1 percent polled believed that western society should be brought down by any means necessary (including violence), "24 percent of British Muslims had some sympathy for the motives and feelings of the London bombers, and 26 percent . . . disagreed with the Prime Minister that the ideas behind the bombings were 'perverted' and 'poisonous'" (Rai, p. 80). Rai has therefore concluded that despite a low percentage of British Muslims who believe violent means should be used against the West there is a significant percentage that can relate to the frustrations of the bombers. It is therefore vital to explore the question, "How has this come about?" (Rai, p. 80).

PROFILE OF TERRORISTS IN THE 7/7 ATTACKS IN BRITAIN

It is known that many immigrant European Muslims felt that immigration was their only means to have certain freedoms. They also hoped that one day they could change the regime in their country of origin. These people are not thought to be interested in destabilizing the country that provided them refuge.

Furthermore, it is important to note that there is a distinct difference between the homegrown warriors or terrorists who were seen in Britain and the 9/11 terrorists. The terrorists responsible for the London bombing on July 7th were British citizens born there and apparently well-integrated. This profile is different from the perpetrators of the terrorist attack on September 11th. Most of 7/7 terrorists were of western background, having been born in Europe, and were British citizens. The London suicide bombers were not educated in madrasses (religious schools) and had not been raised in a traditionally Islamic culture. At least one of the London attackers was a convert to Islam. They were students of ordinary state schools and pursued a modern education. Although there has been some concern about 7/7 terrorists traveling to Muslim countries (including a short trip by one of the perpetrators to Pakistan), most experts state that they had already been radicalized prior to their travel.

To gain further clarity regarding the few British-born Muslim militants who chose to destabilize the British regime, it is important to look at the specific profiles of each of the people involved in 7/7 to understand who these people were, what their backgrounds were, and what the people who knew them, thought of them.

Mohammad Sidique Khan

Khan was a thirty-year-old, law-abiding citizen and teaching assistant who had a wonderful rapport with children (Herbert, 2006). He was also popular with the school administration who thought highly of his dedication to children and providing extracurricular activities. Earlier in his career, Khan had worked for the Department of Trade and Industry and studied business management at Leeds Metropolitan University. Even at this point, however, he worked on the side with community groups focused on youth. Khan became a liaison between the police and youth, defusing conflicts related to gangs and drug usage (Herbert, 2006). In 1999, Khan began to attend Mosque services consistently, and his transformation into radical Islam had started by 2002, which was one year after he joined the Hillside school. In the next few years, Khan's attendance became inconsistent and he would often take long leaves of absence without notification. It was during this time in 2004 that Khan travelled to Pakistan with fellow bomber Shehzad Tanweer and then resurfaced in Britain six months before the bombings took place (Herbert, 2006). Married with one child and another one on the way, Khan's actions took the people who knew him very much by surprise. Khurshid Drabu, who advised Khan's family as a member of the Muslim Council of Britain, has stated, "If Khan could be turned, it means anybody could be turned. That's what's terrifying" (Rai, 2006, p. 28). His family has expressed deep sympathies to everyone affected by this event. They too were in shock and believed that their son may have been brainwashed, as they have only known him to be a kind, loving person in their family (*BBC News*, 2005, July 17).

Shehzad Tanweer

Tanweer was twenty-two years old and another surprising suicide bomber (Raghavan, 2005). Tanweer played cricket, went to college, did not talk about politics, and seemed to have acclimated well to British life as part of a family that had emigrated from Pakistan. His uncle could not believe he was capable of this act. Just the day before 7/7, Tanweer had been in the park playing sports with his friends. He seemed to love living the British lifestyle and had the means and desires to enjoy western activities. His friends were a mix from various ethnic backgrounds, and they too claimed that Tanweer was not interested in politics or even Islam growing up. Yet, they did notice a change in him regarding his political and religious interests around age eighteen. His family has believed Tanweer must have been used by someone else to enact his or her own violent ideologies (Raghavan, 2005).

Abdullah Jamal

Jamal was nineteen years old, born in Jamaica, and was the least well-known of the group (Alvarez, 2005). He converted to Islam in 2001 when he was fifteen. He, like the previously mentioned bombers, enjoyed sports. Unlike the others, Jamal seemed to be enthusiastic about his religion. Some have said that Jamal did try to convert them to Islam and would reject certain western pleasures. Overall, his friends and family were shocked at the news of Jamal's involvement because he was seen as a nice guy who did not get into trouble (Alvarez, 2005). His wife, who was also the mother of his daughter, also had disbelief. She did acknowledge a change in him after he began attending a men's prayer group meeting in 2004. After this point, he would be gone for days and would be traveling to mosques around the country. She too believed his mind had been poisoned and because he was a sweet and innocent man, might have appeared to be a perfect target for this kind of mission (Rai, 2006).

Hasib Hussain

Hussain was only eighteen years old when he participated in the 7/7 bombings (Rai, 2006). Two years earlier Hussain had had a strong "conversion" experience that dramatically changed his life. At one point, Hussain had been westernized in terms of clothing, style, and participation in certain sports. He was also quiet. Some people noticed a distinct change as he moved towards fundamentalism, including a change in dress, minimal communication with non-Muslims, and involvement with a "gang," but all that could be observed of the group was that they wore white robes and prayed. Classmates' opinions seemed to vary; some viewed Hussain as a good person who kept to himself, whereas others viewed him as argumentative and an occasional bully. Interestingly, he has been remembered differently depending on the race of the speaker (Rai, 2006). His father was in disbelief as he has stated that Hussain was a perfect son who had plans for life, such as an upcoming arranged marriage and the start of university. His brother and his parents have been unable to understand how a soft-hearted, unassuming eighteen-year-old who was afraid of spiders and refused to kill flies or any insects could become a mass murderer (Armstrong, 2005).

Rai (2006) has questioned what could have happened to these four "nice men" to bring them to this type of end. Several of the suicide bombers' families have stated their sons must have been brainwashed in order to commit such an atrocity, so let us start the examination here. Brainwashing is defined as fundamentally changing a person's ideology through coercive means (Rai, 2006). Martyn Carruthers (n.d.) has also maintained that in cases of coercive persuasion, there are attempts to force people to alter their current beliefs through psychological pressure, threats, and intimidation. In cases of brainwashing, people are often kept in isolation to be controlled and undergo emotional manipulation from the uncertainty of their situation. The bombers of 7/7, however, do not fit this description; two of them were even living with their families up until the bombings. Rai has presented the idea that self-radicalization, not coercive brainwashing, can possibly offer some explanation to these men's actions. According to a friend of several of the bombers, they were seen to meet in a book store that sold underground videos that would show horrific crimes being committed against Muslims around the world. It is offered as a possibility that through meetings where these videos would be watched and discussed, these men began a path of political extremism. Jason Burke (2005), author of *Al-Qaeda*, has stated this of the 7/7 bombers, "Radical Islam provided them with an explanation of what was happening in the world and suggested actions that made sense to them" (cited in Rai, 2006, p. 56). Continuing this thought, Rai has suggested "The suffering of Muslims in Chechnya, Palestine, Iraq, Thailand, Kashmir, and so on is real. The question is what interpretation one puts on it. . . . The question is how a 'nice' person could conceivably come to choose such a path" (Rai, 2006, p. 56).

Mohammad Sidique Khan, the suicide bomber believed to have led the attack, had asserted that this violence will continue as long as there are violent and atrocious acts being committed against fellow Muslim brothers and sisters (Rai, 2006).

From the literature, it appears that there are some differences between the 7/7 suicide bombers' motivations and the motivations of others committing this type of act. For example, the 7/7 suicide bombers, like other British Muslims, were not living in an occupied territory. Although we cannot confirm whether there was one main reason or a buildup of several factors, at least several of these bombers were not living in poverty, nor did their actions seem to be motivated by dreams of "72 virgins in Heaven." Although they seemed to be well-integrated into British society, they could have experienced (directly or indirectly) discrimination because of their religious or ethnic background. These men were not seeing their neighbors and friends being blown to pieces on a daily basis such as people living in Iraq, Palestine, and Israel. Yet, they were aware of what was going on around the world; they were not ignorant to the "injustices" that were taking place in the world. They could feel what was occurring to the larger Muslim community to which they belonged and believed that Muslim sufferings were a result of western democratic governments and their policies (Rai, 2006). As Rai has suggested, the "potential suicide bomber . . . is someone who, despite despair, is unable to hand over to God their perceived responsibility for their brothers and sisters in their ummah [Islamic community]. The final element . . . is the very human desire to feel effective in the world" (Rai, 2006, p. 136).

In a similar line of thought, Jackson (2005) has stated that these young men from Yorkshire who became suicide bombers in London were deeply angered by frequent images of horrific violence against Muslims in the world (Palestine, Iraq, Afghanistan, Guantanamo Bay, Abu Gharaib, Fallujah, etc.). They may have been disappointed and in despair over the possibility of change in western government policies and attitudes towards the Middle East and Muslim countries. They were also exposed to extreme religious ideology and possibly felt that through suicide attacks a strong message would be sent to the leaders of the G8 (an international group of eight industrialized countries that represent 65% of the world economy) (Jackson, 2005).

These possible motivations are not the only ones presented by various media and governmental reports. One can see how varied the interpretations of these bombers' life circumstances and their motives can be, which can lead to distorted perceptions. For example, the *BBC News* reported in August 2006 that the four British bombers of 7/7 may have been motivated by self-destructive desires rather than religious or political motives. This report has suggested that the bombers were a small group of individuals who saw themselves as separate, weak, and having failed. They acted in a "heroic way," making a statement about what they were trying to achieve. Professor David Canter stated that "there are other ways of having influence than killing oneself. We can't blame religion for these individual's ways of seeing the world" (*BBC News*, 2005, November 18).

Other reports have indicated that the attacks on Spain and Britain were done to punish these governments for supporting the United States in the war in Iraq. However, an opposing view has stated that these young second-generation Muslims were from rundown suburban slums of Europe, motivated primarily by their own situation, moderately from international issues, but less so by the Iraq invasion. It is easy to see how varied perspectives on these suicide bombers from the media can lead to confusion regarding what really caused the European bombings (i.e., 7/7 bombing). Who is right? Is there really a "truth" out there?

Ordinary Muslims in the community undoubtedly consider Middle East conflicts, Western aggression, double standards in the international arena, the lack of a channel to voice their concerns, and the ghettoization in Europe as factors leading to anger and resentment. As various western governments move to the extreme political right, communication is stifled, increasing the likelihood that the new generation will seek other ways, some extreme, to communicate their anger.

Some U.S. governmental officials have had concerns about the next September 11-style attack coming from Muslims raised in European countries who are rebelling against their "second-class citizen" status and their alienation by a "colonial legacy," as suggested by U.S. Homeland Security chief, Michael Chertoff (Harnden, 2007). Chertoff has asserted that Muslims in the United States are better off than the general American population in terms of education and economic standards. As a nation full of immigrant populations, there is not a distinction between "us" and "them." However in Europe, Chertoff continues, "you had an influx of people that came in as a colonial legacy and may have always felt, to some extent, that they were viewed as second-class citizens, and they've tended to impact and be kind of clustered in some areas" (Harnden, 2007).

PROFILE OF THE 9/11 TERRORIST LEADER

A few minutes after the September 11 terrorist attack, the Federal Bureau of Investigation (FBI) opened one of largest investigations in its history. Within a matter of three days, the suspects were identified and their names and, in most cases, pictures, were available. They were identified as non-U.S. citizens coming from Saudi Arabia, United Arab Emirates, Lebanon and Egypt. According to the 9/11 Commission Report, twenty-six Al-Qaeda terrorist conspirators were thought to have entered the United States to carry out the suicide mission. The profiles of these terrorists varied greatly from the profiles of the terrorists in the European attacks. As the investigation of 9/11 continued, it became clearer that this was an external attack planned by individuals outside of the United States and approved by Osama bin Laden.

Because this group of individuals has been labeled as "religious fanatics" and "Muslim extremists," it was surprising to note that some western news media sources reported that these terrorists had gone out to bars, where they drank large amounts of alcohol (the night before 9/11) and while in Las Vegas had hired female escorts. Both of these actions are very much forbidden by Islam and are considered to be sins.

Mohamed Atta has been labeled by the FBI to be the main perpetrator in the 9/11 attacks and the pilot of the first plane to crash into the World Trade Center. Atta was born in Egypt and apparently well-educated, studying at a university in Egypt. Later he went to Germany to continue his architectural studies. German friends of his have stated that he held strong convictions about western policies concerning the Middle East. More specifically he appeared to be most concerned with Israeli politics and the support of Israel by the United States. Atta's father has vehemently rejected the media's portrayal of his son as the leading terrorist of 9/11. His father has maintained that his son, who was gentle and uninvolved in politics, was framed by others (*Wikipedia Encyclopedia*).

There are controversial ideas in the media regarding who actually led the 9/11 attacks. Did they know it would become a suicide mission, or were they under the assumption that this was only a hijacking?

THE IMPACT ON THE MUSLIM COMMUNITY IN THE WEST: WORRIERS

According to the Department of Justice's own Inspector General, there is no doubt that after September 11 the U.S. government systematically used its powers to detain hundreds of Muslims on minor immigration violations (Kuruvila, 2006). These actions had a direct impact on the American Muslim community. In 2001, about 1264 people were deported by U.S. authorities. This number increased in 2002 to about 2760; as many as 961 (more than 34 percent) were of Pakistani heritage, and all were essentially from Muslim countries. More than 600 immigration hearings were closed to the public because the government designated them as "special interest." The hearings regarding Muslim detainees raised various constitutional concerns. In addition, in many cases a parent or the wage earner in the family was deported, leaving the children behind alone without support or supervision (Kuruvila, 2006).

Jess Ghannam, a professor from the University of California in San Francisco, has identified various effects of this "psychological assault on one's identity" (Kuruvila, 2006). For example, the earnings of Arab men and families of Muslims in the United States have decreased by 10 percent in the past five years. In addition, an increasing number of Muslims are being treated for traumatic stress, depression and anxiety (Kuruvila, 2006). Becky Ham, a writer for Health Behavior News Service, has reviewed a study from the *Journal of Psychosomatic Medicine* that has recognized how immigrants' psychology can be affected once they have moved to the United States. This study illustrated that the more negative slurs and nicknames were applied to an immigration group, the more likely the members were to commit suicide. The suicide rates of these immigrants have been higher in the United States than were the rates of suicide within immigrants' own countries (Ham, 2004).

Brzezinski (2007) has stated that the entertainment industry has encouraged the negative sentiment towards Arabs and Muslims because of the presence of "war on terror" propaganda. He has reported how television series and movies create evil characters as having recognizable Arabic features, in addition to religious gestures that exploit public anxiety and paranoia and stimulate Islamophobia. From Brzezinski's point of view, Arab facial stereotypes, especially in news media cartoons, are reminiscent of Hitler's anti-Semitic campaign.

In earlier years, when the Soviet Union was a powerful enemy, many cartoon "bad guy" characters spoke with a Russian accent. After the Soviet Union became an ally, Arabic accents were substituted. Jack Shaheen has reported that in American television, "the Arab is depicted as pimp, cheat and backstabber . . . television helps to perpetuate the myth that there are no heroic Arabs, only heroic Exoduses" (Shaheen, 1978).

Brzezinski's (2007) has stated that the "war on terror" has encouraged legal and political harassment of Arab Americans, who are in general loyal Americans. Furthermore, Brzezinski has reported on cases of harassment toward the Council on American-Islamic Relations (CAIR) for its plan to imitate the Israeli-American campaign. "Some House Republican recently described CAIR members as 'terrorist apologists' who should not be allowed to use a Capitol meeting room for a panel discussion" (Brzezinski, 2007). It remains unclear as to what the guidelines are for holding meetings in the Capital, as is done by American Jewish organizations and other ethnic-based activists.

RACIAL DISCRIMINATION AND STEREOTYPING

We have interviewed a number of American Muslims (from different countries of origin) and discovered that among the American Muslims, Pakistani Americans reported the highest level of discrimination and government targeting, even more than those of Arab descent. Reports of discrimination in their schools, workplaces, and neighborhoods have increased substantially in the past few years.

Five years after 9/11, Kuruvila (2006) conducted several interviews in the San Francisco area in order to assess the continuing negative impact on American Muslims. Kuruvila has maintained that America's preoccupation with race has created a Muslim caricature. Actual nationality and faith are rejected as Americans' perceptions of bearded brown-skinned men and women with head scarves are all seen as Muslim. Paul Silverstein (an anthropology professor who studies the intersection of race, immigration and Islam) reported that Muslims are the "new Jews" in the United States (Kuruvila, 2006). Silverstein has seen a similarity in the stereotyping that has occurred; it is based on peoples' fears not reality. Unfortunately, people often may ignore their own individual experiences with certain groups of people (even when positive) and instead use stereotypical physical characteristics to judge others (Kuruvila, 2006). Our observations however, have indicated that unlike the Jews, who were a people discriminated against for many years, Muslims in the United States were not discriminated against before 9/11. The discrimination against them is a more recent phenomenon, directly traceable to the events of 9/11.[1]

As a result of some of the Muslim stereotyping in the United States, other light-skinned minorities, such as Hindus and Mexicans, have been affected. Slurs, suspicion, and violence toward people targeted as Muslims have increased as this country dances around the age-old racial identity question (Kuruvila, 2006). In one example of mistaken identity, a female Palestinian, who is a nonpracticing Muslim, reported that she has not been a victim of prejudice because people assume that she is "just" a Latina. Others have not been so "lucky." This negative caricature of Muslims has altered the life of a white, brown-haired, green-eyed, female Muslim from Modesto, California, who had previously converted to the religion of Islam. She has learned to remove her Hijab, (the traditional Muslim head scarf) for traveling and business, because people respond to her differently when she wears it. When she is wearing the Hijab, people assume she is Palestinian and have repeatedly told her to return to her own country. Ironically, this religious discrimination is occurring in a country whose values include "freedom of religion" (Kuruvila, 2006). In another example of racial discrimination following 9/11, Piven (2004, p. 187) has reported a case of a woman of Latin descent who had escaped from one of the New York World Trade Towers moments before the building collapsed. She developed PTSD and uncontrollable crying spells. The day after she escaped, a man unleashed his dog against her in revengeful action because she resembled a Middle Eastern person.

Kuruvila (2006) has stated that Muslims are wrongly typecast as a race. Muslims are a heterogeneous population as are Christians, Americans, and Arabs. Identifying faith as a race is based on lack of knowledge about Islam and the American Muslim community in general. One fourth of U.S. Muslims are African Americans, by far the largest group. A number of the Arabs in the United States, including Edward Said, Ralph Nader and many other prominent leaders, are not Muslims. Many of the prominent Palestinians in the United States, especially those who have been active politically, are Christian. Residents of the largest Muslim country in the world, Indonesia, are not all brown skinned and bearded Arabs. A California Muslim with Cham (East Asian) ethnicity has said that he has been misidentified as a devout Buddhist and therefore has not faced discrimination.

Even though only nineteen Muslims out of an estimated 1.3 billion Muslims in the world committed the atrocities of 9/11, all Muslims have been connected to the terrorists' violence by association. Radical racism produces harassment and even death to people of other faiths who fit the Muslim stereotype. On July 30, 2006, a Santa Clara (California) man stabbed a Sikh grandfather because, as the prosecutor said, the assailant wanted to seek revenge for September 11 and was trying to kill somebody who appeared to him to be a Taliban (Kuruvila, 2006). *The San Francisco Chronicle* has reported that many factors are responsible for religious generalizations such as considering all Muslims to be terrorists or violent. Some Evangelical Christians have labeled Islam as "evil" and have considered the war in Iraq as an opportunity to convert Iraqis to Christianity (Kuruvila, 2006).

Various news media sources also have reported that the terminology used by the government can affect the community. When President Bush says that Americans are at war with "Islamic fascism," he basically legitimizes the perspectives of the extremist. Categorizing people is a result of shallow thinking (Kuruvila, 2006). It has been suggested that Americans were persuaded, with help of the media, to support the ousting of Saddam Hussein as revenge for 9/11. The irony of the situation is that Saddam, although a dictator and a criminal by most perspectives, was not involved in the 9/11 terrorist attacks.

Interestingly enough, bin Laden (who was connected to 9/11) volunteered to fight Saddam in 1991, because he considered Saddam to be his enemy.

President G. W. Bush has purportedly banned racial profiling yet allows it to continue in U.S. immigration policies (Kuruvila, 2006). Winant, a professor from the University of Southern California has stated that a tendency toward international racial prejudice can easily turn a nation of immigrants that is diverse yet peaceful into one in which conflicts and quarreling become the norm. The barrages of violent images in the news can become internalized into an us versus them mentality that centers on the Muslim stereotype (Kuruvila, 2006).

Racial discrimination and harassment has also increased in Canada. According to Taneja (2006), minority groups such as African Canadians, in addition to Muslims, have felt that governmental antiterrorist acts passed after 9/11 have promoted racial profiling and have fueled racism. Various Arab and Muslims groups have felt that they have been "singled out and humiliated by their government," according to a survey conducted by the Canadian Department of Justice. Black and brown-skinned people have feared even wiring money home to their families in other countries. Sadly, immigrant communities are the most likely to receive the least amount of information regarding their rights (Taneja, 2006).

ELEMENTS OF RESENTMENT AND ALIENATION

Brzezinski (2007) has reported that the "war on terror" has gravely damaged the image of the United States in the world. A number of Muslims have developed a sense of hostility towards the United States, because they have seen similarities between the rough treatment of Iraqi civilians by the U.S. soldiers and that of the Palestinians by the Israeli army. As he has stated, "It is not the 'war on terror' that angers Muslims watching the news on the television, it is the victimization of Arab civilians." He has also referred to the resentment by non-Muslims populations. A recent BBC poll of 28,000 people in twenty-seven countries sought their assessment of which country had the most negative influence on the world. The results were Israel, Iran, and the United States (in that order). Brzezinski (2007) has stated that for some people, "that is the new axis of evil."

DISTORTION BY NEWS MEDIA

Certain Middle Eastern media have their own biases, distortions, and one-sided approaches to describe western government activities. For example, the Middle Eastern media have often written exclusively about the negative aspects of the western countries and has ignored the positive sides. It is important to note that except in Israel, there are very few real free media in the Middle East because they are controlled by the local government or special interest groups.

Along the same lines, many western Muslims have been angered by "one-sided" media reports in the United States and Europe.[2] It is not unusual to hear these Muslims express their frustration through claims that most of the U.S. news media organizations are controlled by "right-wing Zionists." Several Muslims have objected vocally to the labeling of Islam as a terrorist-producing and violent religion. We have reviewed two letters written to newspaper's editor; one was written by a Muslim and the other by a Christian minister.

Mudassir Siddiqui (personal communication, 2002) wrote a letter to the editor of *The New York Times* as a response to an editorial titled "Dancing with the Dictator." In his letter, Siddiqui objected to the common use of words such as "Islamic terrorism" or "Islamic terrorist," suggesting that by doing so, newspapers have already marked Islam and terrorism as synonymous. It was ironic, he stated, that the U.S. media did not consider Belgium's Leopold II's rule of the Congo between 1885 and 1908 as "Christian terrorism," even though it claimed between five and eight million victims under barbarian systems of forced labor and systematic terror. The killing and "ethnic cleansing" in Bosnia and Kosovo, which claimed 80,000 lives, also was not considered "Christian terrorism." Even though Hitler's regime killed millions of Jews, the media again did not refer to that as "Christian terrorism." Rather, the media declared Hitler to be a prejudiced man gone mad. Siddiqui has noted that Hitler's "madness" claimed a thousand times more lives than were lost on 9/11. This same rationale, however, has not been applied to "Islamic terrorists." Since these terrorists are not "mad" and prejudice does not drive them, by simply acting in the name of Islam, it has been concluded that they are "Islamic" terrorists.

Siddiqui has also blamed the United States for its blind unconditional support of the state of Israel. America has appeared to be two-faced because it bombed Iraq with one U.N. resolution against it, yet the United States did not respond to more than a dozen U.N. resolutions against Israel. In other situations, the U.S. government preaches democracy while tolerating the tyranny of its undemocratic allies. Siddiqui also has claimed that the news media and western governments closed their eyes when the Indian government allegedly massacred thousands of Muslims. The massacre was not condemned, he has asserted, and was not considered state terrorism because India is a natural ally to the west (Siddiqui, 2002).

In another letter to the editor in *The Day*, the Rev. Emmett Jarrett (2004,

September) has written that terror is an aspect of warfare: "When desperate people who have no recourse to conventional armies and weapons use suicide bombing, it is terrorism. To insist that 'terrorism' is intrinsically related to Islam is untrue. When a government bombs civilians of another nation to demoralize them (the British with Dresden, Germany and the U.S. with Hiroshima) it should be labeled as terrorism, no matter the source." Jarrett has noted the ease with which people have focused on good versus evil and us versus them, which has allowed them to avoid self-examination and has created a lack of multicultural understanding.

One may see evidence through the U.S. media's reporting of Islamic issues of possible misunderstandings and prejudiced sentiments about Islam. In January, 2007, a newly elected U.S. congressman used the *Koran*, instead of the *Bible*, to be sworn into Congress (in a private ceremony) (abcnews.go.com, 2007). Although *The Sacramento Bee* (2007, cited in *The Week*, 2007) editorialized that "the American Republic did not fall" as a result of this action, another publication printed that, "naturally, some conservatives went ballistic," citing various sources. In response to this event, one radio host, Dennis Prager (2007), stated that, "America is interested in only one book, the *Bible*," (cited in *The Week*, 2007) and warned America that the congressman's use of the *Koran* would "embolden Islamic extremists." A Republican representative from Virginia (Goode, 2007) requested tougher immigration restrictions, suggesting that otherwise "many more Muslims [could be] elected to office and demanding the use of the Koran" (as cited in *The Week*, 2007). *The Week* asked whether a congressman swearing on the *Koran* would be conflicted between his official duties and his allegiance to Islamic strictures that "sanction conquest of violence, oppression, and religious intolerance" (*The Week*, 2007).

Even President Bush has spoken of "Islamofascists" who seek to force people to convert to their faith. *The Week's* article then raised the question, "So what do we call those who want to keep Muslims out of public office and force nonbelievers to swear on the *Bible*? Judeo-Christo-fascists?" (*The Week*, 2007) In that same spirit, *The Miami Herald* has written about a streak of intolerance in the United States that "denies American values under the guise of defending them" (Pitts, 2007). *USA Today* has challenged the negative assumptions mentioned previously in its report that Congressman Keith Ellison, like most Muslims, is neither a terrorist nor a fanatic. He is a native-born American who converted to Islam in college (Turley, 2007).

A poll by the Pew Research Center of 1050 Muslims in the United States was released on May 22, 2007. Several media sources wrote articles summarizing the information gleaned from this survey. It is interesting to note, however, that even though each article was based on the same survey, each media source presented a slightly different slant on the information. Titles of these articles varied from "U.S. Muslims more assimilated than British," to "Poll finds some U.S. Muslim support for suicide attacks," to "What about the enemy within?"

JEWS AND MUSLIMS: EVIDENCE OF COLLABORATION

The news media have reported that Muslim extremists have named Israel's activity and the blind support given by the United States as the major causes of their anger and violent activities.

However, there has been evidence of collaboration between Jews and Muslims. Historically, there have been indications that Jewish and Muslim populations have gotten along with each other and, at times, even have protected each other. For example, during the Holocaust, the embassies of Iran in Europe independently asked the German authorities to not persecute any Iranian Jews. Their argument was that Iranian Jews (in Europe) were more Iranian than Jewish, meaning they had been Iranian "since the time of Cyrus the Great and therefore fell under protection of Iranian laws like any other Iranian." Their Iranian nationality was promoted as being more important than their religion. This request was granted. What is interesting is that many European Jews were issued Iranian passports by the Iranian embassy to make them "Iranian" so that they could escape persecution. Subsequently many European Jews were saved from the harsh Nazi measures (Hoveyda, 1997; *Iran Times*, 2007). It has been reported that this tactic was used by others, such as Egyptian embassies, to save European Jews.

In another historic example of Muslims creating a haven for Jews, Avnery (2006) an Israeli intellectual, has explained that the Jews that fled the flames of the Christian Inquisition in Spain were received with open arms by the Muslim Ottoman Empire. Their reception of Jews differs dramatically from the rejection of these people by many German Christians during WWII. Germany, one of the most cultured European nations, democratically elected Hitler who created the Holocaust. In addition, the Pope in the Vatican did not raise his voice in protest after the Holocaust atrocities began (Avnery, 2006).

Even in recent times there is evidence of positive relationships between Jews and Muslims. In the United States, Jewish groups exist who have shown sympathy to "Muslim worriers," because Jews themselves have experienced (and are still experiencing) similar negative propaganda, humiliation, and false accusations (a type of scapegoat phenomenon). These compassionate actions have been encouraged by their own faith, which has advised them to be compassionate to those in exile for they themselves were once exiled in ancient Egypt.

A number of Jewish organizations in the United States are in collaboration/alliance with Muslims to create foundations and peace groups that express sympathy toward Muslims (specifically Palestinian and Lebanese). "We Refuse to be Enemies" (www.we-refuse.org/index.html) is one such organization where Jews, Muslims, Christians, and others have come together to advocate for peace and friendship among these religions. In addition, in 2006 the International Jewish Solidarity Network created a "Petition for U.S. Jewish Solidarity with Muslim and Arab Peoples of the Middle East" (www.2.jewishsolidarity.info/en/petition). Through this petition, American Jews criticized the use of American armed forces in the Middle East to protect its oil supplies through the use of Israel without regard for the resulting innocent civilian deaths. "The everlasting violence ensures that there will never be safety for Jews throughout the world or in Israel, because the fear and hatred that has developed . . . perpetuates violence rather than tolerance and coexistence" (International Jewish Solidarity, 2006).

QUANTITATIVE DATA AND ANALYSIS OF RESEARCH ON THE AMERICAN MUSLIM COMMUNITY

Pew Research Center

A poll conducted by the Pew Research Center between January and April 2007 demonstrated that overall U.S. Muslims are well assimilated, moderate, and content (www.pewresearch.org, 2007). This nationwide survey of 1050 American Muslims illustrated that 80 percent felt that suicide bombing was a nonjustifiable act in defending Islam. Of young Muslim Americans (under 30 years), 15 percent felt that suicide bombing could be justified, as compared to only 6 percent of older American Muslims.

It is important to note that the question that was related to justification was focused on defending Islam from its enemies; there was not a specific focus or reference to the 9/11 attacks. As Farid Senzai from the Institute for Social Policy and Understanding has stated, "it's not something they see themselves engaging in. It's more of them seeing what's happening abroad and . . . feeling that in these situations, suicide bombings are justified for others" (Morgan, 2007). Other information gleaned from this survey illustrated that overall U.S. Muslims are more assimilated than are Muslims in certain European countries.

The Pakistani-American Public Affairs Committee Research

Members of the American Muslim community have been asked their opinions regarding the treatment of Muslims in America as well as their assessment of life quality for American Muslims (Anwar, 2006). The Pakistani-American Public Affairs Committee polled 2000 individuals by electronic means, ten percent of which responded. Below is a summary of the poll's findings, (the questions are listed in Appendix 1 of this chapter).

- 69 percent of respondents agreed that the American Muslims were more integrated than were the European Muslims, 21 percent were not sure, and 10 percent felt otherwise.
- 99.5 percent valued interacting with their fellow Americans. These numbers are much higher than those of their British counterparts.
- 84 percent wanted to maintain the identity and values of their religious and ethnic origin; 7 percent were not sure; and 9 percent said no. This suggests that American Muslims are more inclined toward integration than assimilation.
- 76 percent said American Muslims had not become more religious since 9/11; 19 percent said yes; and approximately 5 percent were not sure.
- 80 percent said they did not agree with American policies; 4 percent did; and 16 percent were not sure.
- 73 percent said Pakistani Americans and American Muslims have been perceived negatively in the United States, as opposed to 16 percent who felt otherwise; 11 percent were not sure.
- 88 percent said that their political and social interaction would improve the perception of American Muslims; 12 percent were not sure.
- 22 percent said they had a feeling of hopelessness; 58 percent did not feel hopeless, and 20 percent were not sure.
- 75 percent said they were comfortable talking to a law enforcement officer; 13 percent were uncomfortable; and 12 percent were not sure.

These data provide us with a glimpse into understanding Muslim sentiment in America. These findings have suggested that American Muslims overall feel somewhat integrated within American society, more so than their European counterparts. The percentage of American Muslims who felt marginalized was minimal at the time of the study.

It was also clear that most of the responders were in disagreement with the U.S. government policies. In addition, they have felt that the media's biased portrayal of Muslims has created a negative perception about them. More importantly, this sample felt that to overcome this negative perception, they would have to be more politically and socially active.

QUALITATIVE DATA OF RESEARCH

In the Pakistani-American Public Affairs Committee research (Anwar, 2006); qualitative insight was also sought from members of the Islamic community. Members of the community, not necessarily leaders, were polled in a second study. The questions can be seen in Appendix 2 in this chapter. Interestingly, many of the Muslim youth did not focus on their status as immigrant or American-born. In either circumstance, they just considered themselves as Americans. Overall, they did not experience profiling or prejudice among their peers.

Some expressed anger at information available through media sources, such as news about the war in Iraq, Abu Gharaib prison, the number of civilian deaths, the war in Lebanon, and the impact on individual lives. They felt that alternate media (even simple information through *BBC News*) were useful.

Many said that media and the policymakers should not attack religion as such. Some felt religion is the core of the people. Whenever any community is attacked, people seek refuge in religion. When religion is attacked, people tend to harbor anger. When religion is cited as the source of a problem, terrorists are given more legitimacy.

Most of the participants said that appropriate use of terminology, fair implementation of policies, and protection of rights would assist Muslim integration. They also recognized their own responsibility to educate westerners.

Most agreed that the negative portrayal of Islam and the Muslim population had to be stopped. They expressed an acute need to empower the moderate majority and legitimize the efforts of moderate Muslims. Muslims, rather than secular sources, they agreed, should be the ones to educate policymakers.

AMERICAN-PAKISTANIS SPEAK IN THEIR OWN WORDS

We have provided sections from three American Pakistani statements to further illustrate their own experiences (Anwar, 2006).

1. We should concentrate on the fact that we are Americans who also happen to be Muslims. . . . Most of our children are not radicalized due to the fact that they all belong to the privileged upper classes. The ones we have to worry about those that are members of relatively disadvantaged segments of society and cannot find acceptance as my son who went to Harvard and Yale does. . . . However we should learn not to oppose Israel as a knee-jerk reaction. My response to the question when Pakistan should recognize Israel is a simple one. Pakistan and all other Muslim countries should recognize Israel on the day a geographically viable

Palestine is admitted to the UN as full member and Israel votes for its membership. . . . We should start making alliances with other minorities both ethnic and religious. In the ultimate analysis it is the Jews that will be our best allies; we just have to figure out a way getting there. I can say without any sense of shame whatever that some of my best friends as well as supporters while in the U.S. were Jews. Most of them understand our problems better than any other minority and we should take advantage of their empathy and their understanding of our problems. After all during the height of McCarthy mania in the U.S., the anti-communist movement was just a thinly disguised expression of anti-Semitism.

2. In the U.S., American-Muslims generally feel they have the space to contribute to politics, professionally, and earn social mobility. All of this coincides with the fact that there is a sense that their children have access to good education. . . . This may not be true for Britain, France, Germany and Italy where many immigrant Muslims are locked into particular social groups. Access to education is possible but still professional fulfillment is not there, plus some feel that there is very little space for political participation. The process of assimilation is much racialized, and most European Muslim communities feel that there is pressure to compromise their culture to fit in.

3. England is very different from the United States of America or Canada. It is a small country. Immigrants who came to UK one or two generations earlier worked hard and made a success story. Times were good and there were ample opportunities for every one. With the passage of time, some of the areas have developed into isolated and insulated foci of different cultural entities. If one goes to Bradford, it looks more like Gawalmandi (old Lahore) than a part of Europe. Isolation from the main stream cultural tempo and lack of equal career opportunities in the thriving European economy has given them a sense of hopelessness. Strong religious commitment gives them hope and kind of satisfaction despite their material deprivations.

AMERICAN IRANIAN MUSLIMS IN THE UNITED STATES

Interviewing a number of Iranian Muslims who emigrated to the United States reveals several facts. The Iranians who were questioned have a high level of education, income, and social status; most have degrees in medicine, engineering, or accounting. Several respondents married American women with religions other than Islam and have family nearby. These Iranians are generally integrated with the American community but have not totally assimilated. Many said they love the American people and that their close friends are American, but they adamantly oppose the current foreign policy of the U.S. government. They differentiate between "the American people" and the foreign policy of the U.S. government, which they say has been discriminating and aggressive.

Several respondents stated that they have not faced discrimination as Iranians or Muslims. A few referred to problems about twenty years ago when American hostages were held in Iran. One person remembered the day when the U.S. government froze all Iranian assets in the United States. Some could not withdraw money from their own bank accounts until they had written a statement denying employment in the Iranian government.

One woman relayed an incident that she perceived as discriminating towards Muslims that she witnessed in an airport. An American airport worker pushed an elderly Iranian woman wearing traditional elderly clothing who was in line to pass through airport security. Her nephew, a young Iranian man, protested the behavior of that agent. When police arrived the nephew showed his identification; he was an American Marine on a two-week leave from Afghanistan.

A few respondents objected to the blind support of Israel by the United States,although many of them have Jewish friends. One of the Iranians felt that every minority group should have its own country, such as Jews and Armenians have; "unfortunately peoples such as the Kurds and the Gypsies do not."

Some Iranian Muslims said they have tried to educate other Iranians about America, especially when they go back to Iran to visit. They have stressed the difference between the American people and government policy, citing highly civilized, law-abiding, and church-oriented people in the United States who graciously accept immigrants. On the other hand, these Iranians also work to educate westerners and the news media to differentiate between Muslims and terrorism and to disconnect Islam and violence.[3]

AMERICAN IRANIAN MUSLIMS SPEAK IN THEIR OWN WORDS

In this section we have focused on the responses of a number of American-Iranian Muslims who relate their own experiences.

One Iranian stated that the coordination between the western governments and the news media (or control of the news media by the government) is to the point that one may joke that if there were a few Iranian or Syrians in New Orleans, they could be blamed for the Katrina disaster. This idea could be sold to the crowd, if one controls the media. In addition, he was disturbed by omissions in the U.S. news media that would reflect badly on the United States. For example, a few Iranian Government officials (diplomats) in Iraq were arrested in early 2007 by the U.S. army. The U.S. news media missed the statement from the President of Iraq (Talebani), who immediately announced these Iranian diplomats were invited by him to come to Iraq and were his "visitors" and should not be arrested by the U.S. Army. This Iranian also stated that if President Nixon had the news media that we have now, "no Watergate conspiracy would have been discovered!"

Another Iranian with a doctoral degree stated that he is puzzled when the west demonizes all Muslims and fears that if this viewpoint is not challenged then eventually all Muslims may be falsely connected to 9/11. In addition, this perspective ignores that the Iranian Islamic regime was the enemy of bin Laden and the Taliban regime. Years after the conquering of Afghanistan, the Taliban regime was defeated by NATO, and the United Nations thanked Iran for its assistance with the overthrowing of the Taliban and bin Laden's militants. Few Americans may know of this fact because it never appeared in the U.S. mainstream media.

A few Iranian Muslims were specifically critical of the Bush administration. One man stated that the words "crusaders" and "Islamist fascist" are used deliberately to irritate fundamentalist Muslims and militants, so they will do something "stupid," thus giving justification to this "war president" to extend the invasion to any Muslim country that is independent and not a puppet of the west.

Another Iranian stated he also was disappointed with the current U.S. government because it disproved a childhood ideal of America he had learned from watching western movies. In these movies, if a criminal was chased across the border into Mexico, he would laugh and make fun of the American Marshall chasing him because the criminal knew he would not cross the border into Mexico. The American Marshall would respect the border, knowing that once the criminal passed into Mexico, he was no longer in the U.S. jurisdiction. The border limited his authority. Yet the reality has been that the U.S. does not necessarily respect the boundaries of other countries. During the U.S. invasion of Iraq, the U.S. Army invaded Syria with no regard for its border. Several Syrian border guards were killed, and others were captured and arrested.

One Iranian was disturbed by the kidnapping of a clergyman from Italy in 2003 by twenty-six CIA agents who took him to Egypt, where he was tortured and interrogated. This responder also stated that the U.S. attacked Saddam Hussein because his government was torturing people, violating U.N. resolutions, using poison gas on his opponents, and arresting family members of a suspected criminal when the suspect himself could not be found. Yet the western news media has reported that the U.S. government and army did the same thing in Iraq. In Fallujah, the U.S. used poison gas but only admitted to this act months afterward. Pictures from Abu Gharaib clearly documented the United States torturing prisoners. In addition, a U.S. captain admitted to a newspaper that his platoon arrested the wife of a suspect they were looking for yet could not find. His wife was taken in the hopes that he would come to rescue her. Furthermore, the United States has violated the U.N. and Geneva Convention agreements during the invasion of Iraq.

The following statement came from a telecommunication professor in Iran (who has spent most of his adult life in the United States and Britain as a student or teacher). He stated that "even if we could understand the psychology of would-be terrorists, we may still not be able to control or prevent their proliferation, because we only are using military force and the terrorists are not afraid of dying. But what can reduce terrorism is to eliminate the objective reasons and motivations of terrorists. More specifically: to establish justice by giving the land of Palestinians back to them or at least part of it and to agree with the right of return of all Palestinians; to end occupation in Iraq and Afghanistan and not to threaten Iran; to close the Guantanamo prisons; and to support autonomy/ independence to minorities that are not willing to be part of another nation (such as the Kurds in Turkey and the Tamils in Sri Lanka.) Ultimately, this implies that the American political system has to change. It has to be based on justice and not be subservient to lobbies and special interest groups. Otherwise, I am afraid terrorism will stay with us for a long time to come" (Farokh Alim Marvasti, Personal Communication, 2007).

CONCLUSION

In this chapter we have identified two categories of western Muslims: home grown worriers and homegrown warriors. We have defined homegrown worriers as Muslims born or raised in western countries who are concerned about the many issues of discrimination, profiling, detention and the violations of their human rights. Muslim homegrown warriors are defined as individuals who are born or raised in the west who have become disillusioned, for many reasons, and have started activities that harm the interests of western governments. As we have illustrated, there are differences between the American and European Muslims. The American Muslims are much more integrated and assimilated into U.S. society than are their European counterparts. The European Muslims are more likely to be separated and marginalized than are American Muslims. We have referred to wrongful use of terminology by the news media in regard to Islam that has led to the alienation of Muslims. Wrongful use of terminology and implications that Islam is the cause of the violence help legitimize the activities of the terrorist and leads to the weakening of moderate voices among the Muslims. The policies that need to be undertaken should help prove and confirm that the current war and wars are not against any specific religion or group but are against terrorists.

One may consider the current situation in Iraq as a failed policy due to the lack of nonmilitary and diplomatic means. Policies can be developed to strengthen the moderates in every community and religious group. In addition, it is also known that policies of sanctions (which result in deaths of civilians) have failed in the past and should be avoided.

The results of research on American Pakistani and American Iranian Muslims have revealed interesting observations. They generally differentiate between American people and the foreign policy of the U.S. government. They also believe that the nineteen terrorists of 9/11 in no way represent the 1.3 billion Muslims in the world. Muslims in general are a heterogeneous population and there are various branches of Islam. Muslims therefore cannot be looked at as a one-dimensional entity.

NOTES

1. One may use the acronym of "JIM" which stand for Jews, Irish, and Muslim, all of whom experienced discrimination/prejudice in the United States from a historical point of view (the Jews were the first target, then the Irish immigrants, and now Muslims.

2. Western media, at times, has also chosen to focus on the negative and ignore the positive in regard to Muslim activity. In 2005 about 300 American Muslims got together in front of the Connecticut state capitol (in Hartford) to organize a rally focused on denouncing terrorism and extremism and the ideology of hate. When the media were contacted for covering the event, the response given by *The New York Times* representative was "this is not a newsworthy event." The organizers, who were Muslims, mentioned to *The New York Times* how ironic it was that if a Muslim individual (who does not represent the Muslim community) states something negative about the United States, it is covered in the front pages of the newspapers. Yet when a majority of Muslims stand up to denounce inaccurate words and misperceptions and publically show their support of the United States, they are told that this is not newsworthy.

3. In addition, American Muslims currently do have an important role in helping the U.S. government make more effective policies with Muslim majority countries; assisting in building bridges; and sharing the true American values with the rest of the world. U.S. domestic polices should help Muslims feel like partners who can take ownership of these responsibilities. Although some European Muslims are living in the so-called "ghetto" in poverty, this is not indicated in the United States. However, there are Muslim worriers in the United States who believe that if the present negative attitudes and humiliation toward Muslim communities continue, psychological ghettoization may develop in the United States.

APPENDIX 1

The Web-Based Questions

Q1: Do you think that the American Muslims are more assimilated and integrated than the European Muslims?

Q2: Do you enjoy and value interacting with other Americans?

Q3: Do you prefer to maintain the identity and values of your religious and ethnic origin?

Q4: Have you become more religious since 9/11 and the "War on Terror" has started?

Q5: Do you disagree with the U.S. foreign policies?

Q6: Do you think that the Pakistani Americans and American Muslims have a wrongful negative perception in the United States?

Q7: Do you think that if you are politically and socially active, you can help change improve the perception?

Q8: Do you have a feeling of hopelessness with the current situation?

Q9: Are you comfortable talking to a law enforcement officer?

APPENDIX 2

The Qualitative Questions

Q1: Do you think that the young Muslims in the developed world (Immigrant or indigenous) are slowly being radicalized?

Q2: If yes, why?

Q3: Is the situation different between England, Canada and United States?

Q4: If yes, why?

Q5: What can be done to protect this from happening?

Q6: What does the U.S. government need to do with respect to LOCAL policy regarding this?

Q7: If Q6: cannot be done, what is the best mechanism to protect people from the potential actions of the people who may choose to use violence to show their anger?

REFERENCES

Abcnews.go.com (2007, January 3). First Muslim in U.S. Congress to use historic Koran. *Reuters* [On-line]. Retrieved January 3, 2007. Available: http://www.abcnews.go.com/Politics/wireStory?id=2767827

Alvarez, L. (2005, July 19). New Muslim at 15, a bombing suspect at 19. *New York Times* [On-line]. Retrieved May 25, 2007. Available: http://tinyurl.com /cc8w3

Anwar, M. S. (2006). Immigrant American Muslims and European Muslims: Similarities and differences & homeland security implications [On-line]. Retrieved September 24, 2006.

Available: http://www.american-peace.org /Testimony.htm

Armstrong, J. (2005, August 2). My Hasib must have been brainwashed. *Daily Mirror* [On-line]. Retrieved May 25, 2007. Available: http://tinyurl .com/7s3o8

Avnery, U. (2006, August). America's rottweiler. *International Middle East Media Center* [On-line]. Retrieved February 10, 2007. Available: http://www.imemc.org/content/view/21141/1/

BBC News (2005, July 17). Statements from bombers' families [On-line]. Retrieved May 25, 2007. Available: http://newsvote.bbc.co.uk.mpapps/pagetools/print/news.bbc.co.uk/1/hi/uk/4690011.stm

BBC News (2005, November 18). Bombers "not driven by religion" [On-line]. Retrieved March 1, 2007. Available: http://news.bbc.co.uk.go/pr/fr//2/hi/uk_news/england/merseyside/4449686.stm

Brzezinski, Z. (2007, March 25). Terrorized by "War on Terror." *Manchester Journal Inquirer*. p. 23.

Burke, J. (2005, August 7). Seven ways to stop terror. *Observer* Quoted in M. Rai (2006). *7/7 The London bombings, Islam & the Iraq war*, London: Pluto Press.

Carruthers, M. (n.d.) Prevent coercive persuasion & mind control [On-line]. Retrieved June 8, 2007. Available: http://www.systemiccoaching.com/ coercion.htm

Egorova, Y. & Parfitt, T. (Eds.) (2003). *Jews, Muslims, and mass media: Mediating the "other,"* New York: Routledge Curzon Publishers.

Giry, S. (2006, October). France and its Muslims. *Foreign Affairs* [On-line]. Retrieved November 4, 2006. Available: http://www.foreignaffairs.org

Goode, V., Jr. (2007). Quoted in the *Koran*: Fit to swear on? *The Week* (2007, January 19) p. 16

Ham, B. (2004, August 12). Hate speech tied to immigrant suicide rates. *Health Behavior News Service* [On-line]. Retrieved November 6, 2006. Available: http://www.cfah.org/hbns/news/hate08-12-04.cfm

Harnden, T. (2007, May 4). Briton "could stage another September 11." Interview: America's new homeland security chief tells Toby Harnden of his fears of "clean skin" terrorists [On-line]. Retrieved April 6, 2007. Available: http://www.telegraph.co.uk/core/Content/displayPrintable.jhtml;jsessionid=KDOEYGSOSA

Herbert, I. (2006, March 11). Revealed: How suicide bomber used to work for the government. *The Independent* [On-line]. Retrieved May 21, 2007. Available: http://news.independent.cou.uk/uk/this_britain/article350613. ece

Hoveyda, F. (1997, December). My maternal uncle Abdol-Hossein Sardari Qajar and "Sardari's Schindler List [On-line]." Retrieved June 16, 1997. Available: http://users.sedona.net/sepa/sardarij.html

International Jewish Solidarity Network. (2006, August). Petition for U.S. Jewish solidarity with Muslim and Arab peoples of the Middle East [On-line]. Retrieved January 9, 2007. Available: http://www2.jewishsolidarity.info/en/petition

Iran Times (2007, September 14). State TV series shows Nazis murdering Jews. 37(26), p. 1, 3.

Jackson, R. (2005). Understanding suicide terrorism: Richard Jackson argues that terrorism cannot be attributed solely to religious extremism, hatred or mental illness. *New Zealand International Review* [On-line]. 30(5), 24+. Retrieved April 6, 2007. Available: http://www.questia.com/PM.qst?action=print&docId=5011210925

Jarrett, E. (2004, September). Letters to the editor: Terrorism and Islam not intrinsically linked [On-line]. The Day.com. Retrieved January 27, 2007. Available: http://www.the day.com

Kuruvila, M. C. (2006, September). 9/11: Five years later, typecasting Muslims as a race. SFGate.com [On-line]. Retrieved January 22, 2007. Available: http://sfgate.com/cgi-bin/article.cgi?file=/c/a/2006/09/03/MNG4FKUMR71.DTL

Leiken, R. S. (July/August 2005). Europe's angry Muslims. *Foreign Affairs* [On-line]. Retrieved November 4, 2006. Available: http://www.foreignaffairs.org/20050701faessay84409/

robert-s-leiken/europe-s-angry-

Morgan, D. (2007, May 22). Poll finds some U.S. Muslim support for suicide attacks [On-line]. Retrieved May 22, 2007. Available: http://www.reuters.com/article/topNews/idUSN2244 293620070522

PEW Research Study (2007, May). Muslim Americans: Middle class and mostly mainstream [On-line]. Retrieved August 30, 2007. Available: http://pewresearch.org/assets/pdf/muslim-americans.pdf

Pitts, L. (2007, January 11). Koran debate another reminder of intolerance [On-line]. Retrieved October 4, 2007. Available: http://www.ummah.com/forum/archive/index.php/t-109650.html

Piven, J. S. (2004, Fall). The psychosis (religion) of Islamic terrorists and the ecstasy of violence. *The Journal of Psychohistory, 32*(2), 151–201.

Prager, D. (2007). Quoted in the *Koran*: Fit to swear on? *The Week* (2007, January 19) p. 16.

Raghavan, S. (2005, July 29). Friends describe bomber's political, religious evolution. *Washington Post* [On-line], p. A16. Retrieved May 25, 2007. Available: http://tinyurl.com/7tc28

Rai, M.(2006). *7/7 The London bombings, Islam & the Iraq war.* London: Pluto Press.

Ross, L. R. (2006, January/February). Europe's divided Muslims. *Foreign Affairs* [On-line]. Retrieved November 4, 2006 . Available: http://www.foreignaffairs.org

Sacramento Bee (2007). Editorial. Quoted in the *Koran*: Fit to swear on? *The Week* (2007, January 19) p. 16.

Shaheen, J. (1978, May). The ugly Arabs: U.S. TV image. *The Middle East (London)* Quoted in Y. Egorova & T. Parfitt (Eds.) (2003). *Jews, Muslims, and mass media: Mediating the "other."* New York: Routledge Curzon Publishers

Taneja, P. (2006, October). Global war on minorities [On-line]. TomPaine.common sense. Retrieved November 4, 2006. Available: http://www.tompaine.com/articles/2006/10/02/global_war_on_minorities.php

The Week (2007, January 19). Talking points: The Koran; Fit to swear on? p. 16.

Turley, J. (2007, January 04). The truth about oaths. *USA Today* [On-line) Retrieved October 4, 2007. Available: http://www.usatoday.com/printedition/news/20070104/opquranbible.art.htm

Wikipedia Encyclopedia: Mohamed Atta [On-line]. Retrieved May 25, 2007. Available: http://en.wikipedia.org/wiki/Mohamed_Atta

Chapter 6

PSYCHOLOGICAL AUTOPSY OF THE SUICIDE BOMBER

Jamshid A. Marvasti and Valerie L. Dripchak

And Samson said, 'Let me die with the Philistines!' And he bowed himself with all his might; and the house fell upon the lords, and upon all the people that were therein. So the dead which he slew at his death were more than they which he slew in his life.

Judges 16:30

Suicide bombing is the crack cocaine of warfare. It doesn't just inflict death and terror on its victims; it intoxicates the people who sponsor it. It unleashes the deepest and most addictive human passions—the thirst for vengeance.

David Brooks

INTRODUCTION

When Don Stewart-Whyte was arrested outside of London on August 8, 2006, along with twenty-three other suspects in an alleged plot to blow up ten airplanes inflight, people who knew him reported their "shock." He was described as a good-looking, carefree and sociable twenty-one-year old who worked as a bartender. He was born in England and raised in a prominent family—his father was a politician and his mother is a gym teacher (Tresniowski & Hammel, 2006). How can seemingly ordinary people become suicide terrorists?

This case is not unique. The purpose of this chapter is to explore the psychiatric and demographic data of suicide warriors/bombers. Neutrality is the main goal of this writing. We will present several different perspectives, rather than just the western news reports or commentaries. Suicide warriors/bombers and activists, in this chapter, are not limited to the Israeli-Palestinian conflict (the one that has had the most disinformation and subjectivity). We reviewed information on Japanese pilots (kamikazes); Kurdish fighters; Sri-Lanka's Tamil Tigers; Iranian "suicide battalions" in the Iran-Iraq War; the Chechen suicide fighters against Russia; and the Afghan, Iraq, Palestinian, and Lebanese suicide attackers.

PROFILE OF THE SUICIDE TERRORIST/ACTIVIST

A common response to suicide bombers is to assume that they are from a lower socioeconomic class, poorly educated, outcast from mainstream society, and motivated by despair. President George W. Bush and Senator John Warner, as well as other U.S. government officials, have described suicide terrorists as "irrational cowards and extremists" (Von Drehle, 2002). However, this description is not a true picture of the complex phenomenon. We need to make a closer examination of the myths and facts about this group of individuals by first looking at the demographic data.

Age and Gender

In 2001, Yediot Aharonot presented demographics of Palestinian suicide bombers/warriors: 47 percent have an academic education; 29 percent have at least finished high school; 83 percent are single; 64 percent are between the ages of eighteen and twenty-three; most are under age thirty; and 68 percent are from the Gaza Strip (Shuman, 2001).

Most individuals who are attracted to suicide warrior groups are young, between their late teens and early twenties. Silke (2003a) suggested that this range also correlates with the fact that most violent crimes throughout the world are committed by individuals who fall within this age group. Further research (Junger-Tas, 1994) in this area indicated that when delinquency rates are compared across cultures, at least two-thirds, and possibly as high as 90 percent, of young men admitted to committing at least one criminal offense. These astounding figures make it appear that a high risk for criminal activities exists for this age group that is almost considered "normative." However, it also should be noted that these rates decreased significantly as individuals got into their late twenties and early thirties.

Although violent crimes tend to be committed by young adults, we want to point out that this is the same age group used to volunteer or draft people into the military. The best soldiers or warriors, including war heroes, are also in this same age category. One need only look at the average age (which was also in the late teens and early twenties) of the Israeli pilots during the "Six-Day War" to realize the fighting prowess of this age group.

In general, the reported mean age of Palestinian suicide warriors/bombers is twenty-two, with a range of seventeen to thirty-eight years; Lebanese suicide attackers were between sixteen and twenty-eight years old, with a mean age of twenty-one. Palestinian female suicide warriors/bombers have an age range of seventeen to twenty-seven (Merari, 2005). Although most suicide bombers have been men, women also have carried out an increasing number of attacks since 1985. In fact, this may be a growing trend, because women tend to draw less suspicion than men do and go through less-rigorous security checks (*Wikipedia Encyclopedia*). The LTTE has special women's fighter units who are assigned to suicide missions and are called the "Birds of Freedom."[1]

Education

To understand the level of education of suicide attackers, let us look at the historical evidence. Atran (2003b) found in his research that the kamikazes (which in the Japanese language means "divine wind") were educated pilots, who were well read in western philosophy and literature. Moreover, the research conducted by Krueger and Maleckova (2003) suggested that a lack of education may not be correlated with supporting suicide terrorism.

In a poll taken in December 2001, 1357 West Bank and Gaza Palestinian adults who had at least twelve years of education supported suicide attacks by 68 percent, those who were considered to have little or no education supported the attacks by only 46 percent. Merari (2005) reported that Palestinian suicide bombers had education levels higher than the community norm; 26 percent had at least a partial college education compared with 11 percent within the general population. Scott Atran is an anthropologist who worked at the University of Michigan and the National Center for Scientific Research in France collecting surveys of failed suicide bombers and their families. It was found that suicide bombers did not fit the fanatic stereotype. As Atran has stated, "These people are fairly well educated, most from a middle class and not acting at all in despair" (*National Public Radio* [NPR], 2003).

As Ken Heskin has illustrated, terrorist leaders, in general, have been more educated than the larger population is. Specific terrorists groups of the past such as the German Baader Meinhof gang, the American Weatherman, and the Japanese Red Army were composed mostly of intellectuals. However, there are the exceptions. "The Provisional IRA is exceptional in being almost entirely devoid of intellectual elements and contemptuous of what little intellectual support they have had. The same is true, as far as one can see, of Protestant paramilitary organizations in Northern Ireland" (Heskin, 1980, p. 77). In addition, when Post (2003 cited in Hough, 2004, p. 819) interviewed the captured Palestinians suicide bombers, he found that these seventeen to twenty-two-year-olds were "uneducated, unemployed, unmarried–

they were uninformed youth." These examples illustrate that suicide bombers are indeed a heterogeneous population.

Family Structure and Socioeconomic Status

Another idea presented in the media is that suicide bombers come from "broken homes" or dysfunctional families. However, this conclusion is also questionable. In fact, there have been arguments made that suicide bombers/warriors come from cohesive and stable families (Silke, 2003b). The more prominent factor regarding their families is that one or more of their kinship has been harassed, injured, or in some way persecuted by their enemy. This in turn has motivated the would-be suicide attacker to consider giving up his or her own life as a form of revenge. The family is usually not in a position to either encourage or discourage this terrorist action because of the secrecy surrounding a suicide bombing event. Family members tend not to know what their relative is planning until after the attack is over. Possibly, this is the main reason that many human rights activist groups such as the Israeli Committee Against House Demolition (ICAHD) and the Jewish Rabbis for Human Rights (RHR), continue to protest the demolition of the homes of the suicide bomber's family.[2]

From a socioeconomic point of view, Palestinian suicide attackers represent the entire society of the occupied territories as Merari (2005) reported in his research. Twelve percent of the suicide attackers were very poor, 21 percent were poor, 26 percent were from the lower middle class, 32 percent were from the middle class, and 9 percent were from the upper class.

Religion and Political Ideology

Men never do evil so completely and cheerfully as when they do it from religious conviction.

Blaise Pascal

There has been much speculation that suicide terrorists are strongly influenced by religion, particularly Islam. However, both past and recent histories have illustrated that suicide attackers are extremists from many of the major religions, Marxism, or Communism. As Silke (2003b) pointed out, Hindu terrorists have carried out more suicide attacks during the past twenty years than extremists from all other religions combined. He further stated that although it is true that some Islamic warriors believe that a person who dies in carrying out a suicide attack becomes a martyr (a shahid), the attack has to be carried out primarily for the honor of Allah. In other words, to commit such an act for personal or family rewards or for political retaliation serves to undermine the value of the sacrifice. Moreover, Merari (2005), who actually interviewed some surviving suicide bombers, concluded that religion had little importance for this group.[3]

Hecht (2003) explained that violence is neither integral to religion nor an organic part of religion. He wrote that "bad" people use religion to accomplish evil. Hecht further suggested that the medicalization or pathologization of the suicide bomber changes the responsibility from the offender to the environment, which breeds the symptoms. He identified such an environment as the Israeli occupation of the West Bank and Gaza. Hecht referred to Mansdorf, who quoted a Palestinian psychiatrist stating that, from the medical point of view, "suicide bombing and all these forms of violence are only the symptoms, the reaction to this chronic and systematic process of humiliating people in an effort to destroy their hope and dignity" (Hecht, 2003). In other words, this is the illness, and unless it is treated and resolved, there will be more and more symptoms of pathology. In contrast to these findings, the Singapore Parliament study (White Paper-The Jemaah Islamiyah Arrests, 2003), although supporting the "normality" of captured suicide attackers, also reported that their one consistent characteristic was the importance of religion as their main personal value.

Merari (2005) explained that suicide attacks in Lebanon were initially conducted by the radical Shia group, which later formed the Hezbollah party. From this basis, public and professional perceptions of suicide attackers in the Middle East have assumed that religious fanaticism was the main personality element. However, by 1986, it became evident that almost two thirds of the attacks in Lebanon were performed by secular groups. Suicide attacks in other areas have been carried out by individuals with Marxist ideology and by many nonreligious organizations.

PSYCHOPATHOLOGY AND PERSONALITY FACTORS

Oh madmen of Gaza-A thousand welcomes to madmen if they liberate us. Truly the age of political reason slipped away long ago, so then teach us madness . . .

Nizar Qabbani[4]

Research on Captured Suicide Bombers

Most of the research on suicide warriors/bombers has been retroactive. This means that our knowledge has been obtained by a psychological "autopsy" of a successful activist (one who has died). We believe that the psychological research on captured or future suicide bombers is not entirely valid in regard to the presence of any specific psychopathology, including mood disorders. There are multiple reasons that we would like to explain further. First, many of these captured individuals are systematically tortured in detention and mistreated or abused. This is a psychological trauma that can cause psychiatric, biochemical, and anatomical changes in the brain. Second, captured suicide bombers may have an unconscious (or conscious) wish to survive and therefore unconsciously (or consciously) may arrange to get caught or for their explosive device to fail. These individuals are, therefore, not representative of suicide bombers who complete their mission. Third, captivity and isolation create a paranoid tendency in some individuals, plus the failure of a mission, may contribute to a sense of failure, self-blame and depression. Even if a mood disorder or anxiety is present, it is difficult to determine whether it was present before captivity. Last, there is the possibility that captured prisoners may not give the right answer to their enemy or anyone (including a clinician) who is connected with their enemy. The element of manipulation or even a "hostage syndrome" may be present during and after interrogation (Marvasti, 2007; MacNeil, 2007).

Review of Literature on Psychopathology and Personality Factors

Normal people, given the right circumstances or right set of friends, can become suicide bombers.
                    Marc Sageman (ex-CIA officer, forensic psychiatrist)

Although the public view would be that terrorists must be insane, most of the academic writing reveals that suicide attackers are not suffering from any notable mental illnesses and do not qualify to have any *DSM-IV* diagnostic categories. Experts continue to state that suicide bombers/activists are not necessarily irrational and many different societies honor those who choose to kill themselves in order to kill enemies; for example, the Japanese kamikaze pilots and Samson, in *The Bible*, who pulled down a temple to kill his enemies despite killing himself (*ABC NEWS*, 2005).

Are suicide bombers driven by "a cocktail of religious fanaticism and outright insanity?" Many experts say that anyone, under the right circumstances, could become a suicide bomber. Clark McCauley, Bryn Mawr College professor, affirmed that this "is normal psychology, normal group dynamics." He further stated that suicide bombers see themselves as sacrificing their lives for a greater good. Merari, stated that "none of the suicide bombers would be put in a mental asylum on the order of a district psychiatrist"(*ABC NEWS*, 2005).

Since 9/11 the American public has wondered how anyone in his right mind could consciously go after the innocent civilians in the Twin Towers. What would possess someone to not care about human life to such a great degree that he or she is willing to destroy the innocent in search of political revenge? Why do terrorists see violence as their only option for change? Do Americans themselves not undergo a psychological change when exposed to trauma, which leads to reactions that could be labeled irrational, extreme or insane? As Peter Fonagy has pointed out, Americans who would normally be considered "sophisticated" or rational, after 9/11 appeared to "lose their minds" and spoke in terms of rage and revenge (Fonagy, 2003, cited in Hough, 2004, p. 817). Piven (2004, pp. 188–189) has given us a few examples of immediate reactions to 9/11 by well-known Americans:

1. There is only one way to begin to deal with people like this, and that is you have to kill some of them even if they are not immediately directly involved in this thing (Former Secretary of State Lawrence Eagleburger, CNN, 9/11/01).

2. America roused to a righteous anger has always been a force for good. States that have been supporting if not Osama bin Laden, people like him, need to feel pain. If we flatten part of Damascus or Tehran or whatever it takes, that is part of the solution (Rich Lowry, *National Review* editor, to Howard Kurtz, *Washington Post,* 9/13/01).

3. This is no time to be precious about locating the exact individuals directly involved in this particular terrorist attack. . . . We should invade their countries, kill their leaders and convert them to Christianity (syndicated columnist Ann Coulter, *New York Daily News,* 9/12/01).

4. An interview between Bill O'Reilly and Sam Husseni (Institute for Public Accuracy):
   Bill O'Reilly: If the Taliban government of Afghanistan does not cooperate, then we will damage that government with air power, probably. All right? We will blast them, because . . .
   Sam Husseini: Who will you kill in the process?
   O'Reilly: Doesn't make any difference (The O'Reilly Factor, Fox News Channel, 9/13/01).

The previous examples demonstrate how someone's psychology can change under fear of terrorism or vengeful anger. As reported in psychoanalytical literature, "By viewing terrorism as an effort to deprive its victim of the capacity to mentalize, we can see that terrorists often deprive us of our capacity to perceive them as thinking and feeling human beings" (Hough , 2004, p. 817).

Reviewing the literature in regard to suicide bombers or terrorists' psychopathology has revealed that most writers see these people as "not sick." For example, Atran (2003b) has reported that in comparison with violent racist individuals, suicide attackers demonstrate no socially dysfunctional attributes such as being fatherless, friendless, and jobless or having any suicidal symptoms. Hassan (2001) also studied Palestinian suicide bombers/warriors and found that they appeared to have normal mental health before recruitment to their terrorist organization. Oliver and Steinberg (2005), who lived with a Palestinian refugee family in the Gaza Strip for six months, arrived at the same conclusions. They interviewed a number of leaders and followers, including a Hamas suicide bomber whose bomb failed to detonate on an Israeli bus in Jerusalem. These writers discovered that Hamas would only take "normal" people as potential suicide attackers. In other words, a potential suicide bomber could not be depressed or suicidal or exhibit any other pathology.

Pies (2001) has speculated on the general ego defense mechanism of terrorists (not specific to suicide attackers). He felt that they exhibited two main mechanisms: (1) paradoxical narcissism and (2) projective identification. In paradoxical narcissism, the individual appoints himself or herself as judge, jury, and executioner of his or her cause. The terrorist feels the world must conform to his or her needs, and if it does not, someone must pay the price to make it fit. From our point of view, this narcissism would not explain how the same persons will then "sacrifice" their "self" and their life for the "welfare" of others, as many suicide activists perceive that they do. The other criticism of Pies' theory is that these qualities are not exclusively seen in terrorists. One may speculate that some western governments have used this same ego mechanism in regard to the invasion and control of other countries (e.g., France with Algeria; Belgium with the Congo; and the United States with Granada, Panama, and Iraq) and dictating to other nations what kind of governmental system they should have.

Splitting off the "bad part" and projecting it onto others may be another psychodynamic explanation. John Sanford indicated that all of us may have "inner feelings" that we do not discuss with anyone. However, most of us are able to detect a way to compromise and live in peace with this "inner adversary." The terrorists disown their inner adversarial parts and split and project them outward onto others (e.g., "Evil Empire"). Terrorists simply cannot accept these adversarial inner feelings and the co-occurring anxiety without decompensating. The split and projection of this bad part promotes an "intact" sense of self (Sanford, as cited in Herzog, 2002).

Heskin mentioned that it is difficult to typify Provisional IRA members into a certain category, although one common trait noted was a pervasive authoritarianism. In addition, depression and guilt were common. The accused racketeering was not, however, "Indeed, dedication and material sacrifice appeared to attend Provisional [Sect of the IRA] involvement normally" (Heskin, 1980, p. 83).

There are terrorists, however, whose behavior has indicated paranoia and delusional thinking. For example, Timothy McVeigh was definitely suffering from a severe mind disturbance and could have been labeled mentally ill. He thought that the Army had implanted a computer chip in his buttocks (Persaud, 2004). It is surprising that he was executed even with this history of mental illness and paranoid delusions. He is an exception to the rule that large-scale attacks are planned by groups. Most mentally ill individuals become isolated (and not a good team player) because others cannot understand their abnormal beliefs system.

Silke (1998) and Atran (2003a, b) argued against the premise that all suicide attackers have some type of psychopathology or psychological problems. The researchers in this area agree with the position that suicide bombers are basically "normal" individuals. Indeed, those individuals who have mental illness would not be good candidates to carry out the attacks. Moreover, prior to their selection, the suicide bombers exhibited no suicidal symptoms, nor did they express hopelessness or a sense of "nothing to lose." In addition, they exhibit no socially dysfunctional traits (e.g., having no friends or being unemployed).

Fink (2003) agreed that the "fanatics" that become terrorists are not crazy but that they have a completely different value system from the norm. His belief is that religious extremism is the suicide bombers' primary motivation.

Doctor Eyad Sarraj, was interviewed by correspondent Bob Simon about suicide bombers (Simon, 2003). Families come to see Doctor Sarraj for assistance after their son or daughter completes a suicide mission. Doctor Sarraj has commented that suicide bombers are not especially violent. Instead, he has found them to be timid, and introverted with weak communication skills and an inability to express their feelings (Simon, 2003).

Doctor Sarraj revealed that recruiters of suicide bombers make themselves known at local mosques for anyone who is interested in joining. "Whoever joins a holy war is considered a martyr and is worthy of entering Paradise" (Simon, 2003). As Atran has pointed out, it is also necessary to study psychological conditions that entice thousands of ordinary people into the "martyr-making web" (Atran, 2003a, p. 1538). As Simon has reported, it is not only a vision of paradise that draws in young men, because many of them were not religious before deciding to become suicide bombers. Instead, a cult has formed in Gaza around suicide bombing. It is idolized and the pictures of martyrs are placed on walls and worshipped (Simon, 2003). Doctor Sarraj has mentioned, "It is something to aspire to be, a martyr." He recounted his own teenage years when rock stars were the idolized symbols: "then it changed . . . the guerilla, the fighter, then it was the stone thrower, and today it is the martyr" (Simon, 2003). Similarly, Jerrold Post (2003) has found that in asking young people why they joined resistance movements, their general reply was, "everyone was joining–it was the popular thing to do." (cited in Hough, 2004, p. 819). These responses, as Post has noted, indicate that terrorism is a "deeply rooted social phenomenon, not an instance of individual psychology" (Hough, 2004, p. 819). Simon also interviewed Doctor Merari, who stated "the only abnormal thing about the suicide bomber is, at a certain point, a total absence of fear." There is no indication that these people are psychotic, although he doubts that lacking fear is a common personality trait. "I doubt that this person under any circumstances would be fearless. On this mission, to which he was prepared for so long, like a coiled spring just wants to be released" (Simon, 2003). In the chapter entitled,

"What Motivates the Suicide Bomber" (Chapter 3), we explained that this lack of fear may be an episode of a dissociation state in some individuals.[5]

One may wonder, from a psychoanalytical point of view, whether suicide may be a kind of "hate turned inward." The person develops anger or resentment towards the self to the point that he or she wishes "to kill" and destroy the self. In the case of suicide bombers, we have speculated that a certain amount of hate or resentment towards self may develop, because of the lack of any power in the self to change the perceived injustice and oppression.

JUSTIFICATION AND RATIONALIZATION

98% of the adults in this country are decent, hard-working, honest Americans. It is the other lousy 2% that get all the publicity. But then, we elected them.

Lily Tomlin

Can the intentional killing of innocent civilians ever be justified? Is it only done by the insane or antisocial? History reveals that under certain circumstances mentally stable people (e.g. those who made the decision to bomb Hiroshima) have felt justified in deliberately killing nonmilitary citizens (Marvasti, 2007). Bandura (2003) stated that bin Laden claimed his attack was only a defense and "this is defensive Jihad." Bandura compared bin Laden to both Jewish and Christian assassins. The Prime Minister of Israel, Yitzhak Rabin, was killed by a Jewish terrorist trying to prevent the transfer of occupied land back to Palestinian control. The assassin claimed that he was following the "rabbinical pursuer's decree" as moral justification. "Maybe physically I acted alone, but what pulled the trigger was not only my finger, but the finger of this whole nation, which, for 2000 years, yearned for this land and dreamed of it" (p. 125). As he stated in his trial, "Everything I had done, I have done for Israel, for the Torah of Israel, for the people of Israel, and for the land of Israel—it is a knot that will never be untied" (Volkan, 2006, p. 118). It seems that this decree is the rationalization for the death of "traitors" who reject their people and surrender their land to the enemy.

Paul Hill, a Presbyterian minister, also justified his killing of a doctor and his elderly assistant outside an abortion clinic as carrying out God's will: "God's law positively requires us to defend helpless people. God has used people who were willing to die for their cause to save human life. I am willing to do that" (Bandura, 2003, p. 126). Therefore, he felt that the killing of two people was worth rescuing many unborn fetuses.

The assassin of Mahatma Gandhi used similar justification. His brother pointed out that he (Gandhi) had insulted the Hindu nation, "We wanted to show Indians that there were Indians who would not suffer humiliation that there were still men left among the Hindus."[6]

Post and Sprinzak (2002) published an article that contained an interview with Hassan Salameh, a captured Arab fighter. During the interview, Salameh explained that he did not consider himself a murderer even if civilians are killed. His reasoning included a firm statement that he is not "blood-thirsty," but that killing and death become "facts of life" when people struggle against a foreign occupier. He added, "A suicide bombing is the highest level of jihad and highlights our faith. Bombers are holy fighters" (Hecht, 2003, p. 36).

One needs to look to the cultural aspects of the Middle East to further analyze this issue through two kinds of justification. The first is the concept of the tribal tradition of "an eye for an eye" justice. This is an important factor that needs to be considered in regard to how the suicide bomber justifies killing innocent people. The same situation can be seen in the Arab and Israeli conflict. When a child is killed (even if it is collateral damage), the family or the victim tribe may claim a kind of permission or entitlement to kill a child of their enemy which justifies perpetuating the conflict.

Hashmi (2003, p. 27) provided a further example in this quote from bin Laden, "We do not differentiate between those dressed in military uniforms and civilians. Because U.S. aggression is affecting Muslim civilians, not just the military." This indicated that all Americans are targets.

The second rationalization occurs when the suicide bomber justifies killing civilians because they may be future combatants. These civilians are perceived to be the past, present, or future enemy soldiers, prison guards, or torturers, so killing them is a defensible policy. Sohail (2006) also wrote that the western democratic process allows the suicide warrior a rationale for killing civilians, because the inhabitant populace is responsible for electing leaders who are implementing the policies that the suicide activists oppose. For example, Khan's (a London suicide bomber) videotape of his last message revealed that the invasion of Iraq by the British Government was the motivation for him to kill an innocent British civilian (Rai, 2006).

However, from a psychological point of view, there are indications that one may first develop desires to kill (murderous wishes) and then look for justification or rationalization. In these cases, feelings come first and then one looks for plausible causes, motivation, or justification, because human beings have difficulty in accepting their actions without having the "right reasons."

DOCTOR MILGRAM'S STUDY ON UNITED STATES STUDENTS

The main questions that were presented in this study included the following: How can an individual who is not suffering from any mental illness resorts to killing himself or herself plus many other civilians? Is a normal person capable of doing torture and atrocities on innocent civilians? During the Korean Conflict in the 1950s, a number of American soldiers did not actually fire their guns at the Koreans. During the military training for the Vietnam conflict, draftees were conditioned by repeatedly shooting at enemy facsimiles in order to bypass their natural inhibitions against killing. However, many normal, nonviolent people can be influenced into violence under the right circumstances (Persaud, 2004). Milgram's research from Yale University has been helpful in understanding how this phenomenon develops. In a closely observed research experiment, Milgram (1974) recruited college-educated adults to help other people learn better. When the learners failed to memorize the words fast enough, the instructors were ordered to administer what they were told was an electric shock to the student. The voltage was increased with each erroneous response. Most instructors complied with the instructions to give potentially lethal shock despite the learners' (who were really actors) screams and pleas. This experiment was replicated by Kilham and Mann (1974) with similar results. In addition, they found participants were more willing to give an order to another person to administer the shock versus administering the shock themselves. Zimbardo Haney, Banks, and Jaffe (1973) did research focusing on another aspect of behavior. They set up an experiment involving college students, half of whom were to be "prison guards" and the other half, were the "prisoners." As the experiment unfolded, the guards became authoritative and penalizing. The prisoners withdrew and experienced emotional distress.

These experiments show that ordinary citizens of the United States can obey potentially harmful orders under the right circumstances. In addition, these studies may help to explain the atrocities that "educated and civilized" German officers inflicted on the innocent Jewish population during WWII. However, Heskin has suggested that one should not judge the character of people simply on the basis of their overt behavior (1980, p. 89).

CASE HISTORY OF A SUICIDE BOMBER

Bob Simon (2003) reported about a nineteen-year-old Palestinian refugee with the name of Murad. He tried a suicide action but he failed and was arrested. He stated that his older brother recruited him: "He wants me to become a martyr. Because martyrdom is the most exalted saying in our religion. Not just anyone gets a chance to become a martyr." Murad explained how happy he was when he was accepted to become a suicide bomber. "I was very happy and couldn't wait for the time to come. I was counting the seconds before I went down. I felt very calm, as if nothing were happening. When I put on the belt of explosives, it felt like it was nothing at all. My brother put it on me and I was watching him, looking for tears in his eyes, but there weren't any. He was smiling and encouraged me more." When Murad went for his mission, it took thirty minutes to drive to the border. He explained that during thirty minutes, "I was just thinking about saving the Palestinian people. That's all . . . I never felt so calm in my life. It was the will of God." Murad also mentioned, "when my mother hears on television that I've become a martyr, she will burst with joy and make cries of joy" (Simon, 2003).[7]

CONCLUSION

Our conclusions indicate that the suicide warrior/bomber is not detectable by race, religion, pathology, education, socioeconomic status, or gender and actually is in a heterogeneous grouping. This variety of elements in the population should prevent us from any profiling or "indexing" to determine possible offenders. Perhaps the idea that many individuals, and not just a particular group, may be a risk for committing acts of political violence is too frightening for us to contemplate. The effect of long-term violence in a population concerns everyone–Christian, Moslem, Jew, and secular. On all sides, people are affected by the uncertainty of ongoing violence. The issue that remains is what attracts an individual such as Don Stewart-Whyte, an English-born citizen, to kill others by killing oneself? Is anyone capable of such actions given a certain set of circumstances?

It seems that suicide terrorism is both an individual and a group set of interacting dynamics that incorporate many complex issues. There is much evidence to support the notion that the suicide warrior/bomber is acting in a rational manner given his or her set of circumstances and beliefs. For the individual, there is a deep feeling of oppression and a need for revenge, particularly if ongoing violence and deprivation have become a way of life and conventional tactics do not work. When the individual meets the militant group that promises an elevation in status and achievement for a cause that is greater than one's life, the combination may become a suicide bomber.

NOTES

1. Please see Chapter 14, "Female Suicide Warriors/Bombers" for more information about this group.
2. For more about the Israeli Committee Against House Demolition, please go to www.ICAHD.org. For the Israeli organization of Rabbis for Human Rights, please go to http://www.rhr.israel.net and for the North American site, please go to http://www.rhr-na.org.

3. It is conceivable that extreme religious values have been used to support and maintain and reward the suicide bomber rather than to be the main motivation factor.   It seems that the most important elements in creating a suicide bomber are still political and ideological factors. We do not see any suicide bombers from Kuwait, an Islamic country. However, if the Iraqi occupation of Kuwait in the 1990s had lasted for years and its citizens had been interred in refugee camps, it may have been a different story. For more information please refer to the "Element of Religion" section in Chapter 3.

4. Nizar Qabbani was a Syrian diplomat and poet. His poetry explored themes of love, feminism, religion, and Arab nationalism. One of his most famous poems, "The Face of Qana," was written in the wake of the 1996 Qana invasion by Israel. By reading only a section of this long poem, one may gain a   perception of the " other side" and their opinions:

> *The face of Qana*
> *Pale, like that of Jesus*
> *and the sea breeze of April . . .*
> *Rains of blood . . . and tears . . .*
> *They entered Qana*
> *Like hungry wolves*
> *Putting to fire the house of the Messiah*
> *Stepping on the dress of Hussain/ and the dear land of the South . . .*
> *Blasted Wheat, Olive-trees and Tobacco*
> *and the melodies of the nightingale . . .*
> *Who ever will write about the history of Qana*
> *Will inscribe in his parchments*
> *This was the second Karbala . . . .*

(http://bloggingbeirut.com/archives/586-Nizar-Qabbani-The-Face-of-Qana.html)

5. The experience of "lacking" fear and dissociation can be seen in events that would usually cause anxiety. In Iran some murderers have been hanged in public. These individuals had committed multiple murders and armed robberies for many years before they were arrested and sentenced to death. The news media that covered this event reported that these people did not seem frightened or depressed. On the contrary, some of them were singing songs on the way to their death and even as they stood under their own hanging rope. A possible psychological explanation could be that these people who had been involved in armed robbery and murder for years, had also visualized for years their future arrest and hanging. Therefore, when this did become their reality, they may have already been desensitized to it. The other possibility is that they were in a state of dissociation. Dissociation in psychiatry is the separating out of thoughts, feelings, and fantasies from the individual's conscious awareness. In desensitization, the person gradually lessens the emotional responses to a situation or object through repeated exposure paired with some form of relaxation or imagery.

6. This quote has been obtained from Doctor Ansar Haroun. Psychiatric Evaluation of Suspected Terrorist (PEST). Unpublished article.

7. Murad's statement in regard to his brother is interesting. He mentioned that when his brother put the explosive belt on him, Murad looked for his brother's tears but did not see any. On the contrary, he saw that his brother was smiling. As to what could be in the mind of his brother at that moment, we can never know. Yet, one may wonder if his brother was in a dissociated state, which is common among traumatized individuals.

REFERENCES

ABC News (2005, August 6). Experts: Suicide Bombers Not Crazy [On-line]. Retrieved August 26, 2006. Available: http://abcnews.go.com/Nightline/print?id=1004809

Atran, S. (2003a). Genesis of suicide terrorism. *Social Science, 299*, 1534–1539.

Atran, S. (2003b). Genesis and future of suicide terrorism. *Interdisciplines* [On-line]. Retrieved on December 12, 2006, Available: http://www.interdisciplines.org/terrorism/papers/1

Bandura, A. (2003). The role of selective moral disengagement in terrorism and counterterrorism. In F. M. Moghaddam & A. J. Marsella (Eds.), *Understanding terrorism* (pp. 121–150). Washington, D.C.: American Psychological Association.

Fink, P. J. (May, 2003). The anxiety of terrorism. *Clinical Psychiatry News, 31*(5), p. 18.

Fonagy, P. (2003, June 22). Terrorism Panel discussion held at the Spring Meeting of the American Psychoanalytic Association, Boston, MA. Quoted in G. Hough (2004). Does Psychoanalysis have anything to offer an understanding of terrorism? *Journal of American Psychoanalysis Association, 52*(3) pp. 813–828.

Hashmi, S. (2003). Political extremism led to the attack on America. In M. E. Williams & S. Barbour (Eds.), *The terrorist attack on America* (pp. 24–27). Farmington Hills, MI: Greenhaven Press.

Hassan, N. (2001, November). An arsenal of believers: Talking to the "human bombs." *The New Yorker Fact* [On-line]. Retrieved March 2, 2007. Available: http://www.newyorker.com/fact/content/?011119fa_FACT1

Hecht, R. (2003). Deadly history and deadly actions and deadly bodies: A response to Ivan Strenski's sacrifice, gift and the social logic of Moslem human bombers. *Terrorism and Political Violence Journal, 15*, pp. 35–47.

Herzog, A. (2002) Essay: The mind of a terrorist. *Connecticut Medicine, 66*(4), pp. 237–239.

Heskin, K. (1980). Northern Ireland: A psychological analysis. New York: Columbia University Press.

Hough, G. (2004). Does psychoanalysis have anything to offer an understanding of terrorism? *Journal of American Psychoanalysis Association, 52*(3), pp. 813–828.

Junger-Tas, J. (1994). Delinquent behavior among young people in the Western World. Amsterdam: Kugler.

Kilham, W., and Mann, L. (1974). Level of destructive obedience as a function of the transmitter and executants roles in the Milgram obedience paradigm. *Journal of Personality and Social Psychology, 29*, pp. 696–702.

Krueger, A., & Maleckova, J. (May 29, 2003). Poverty doesn't create terrorists. *New York Times*. Business Section, p. 1

MacNeil, J. S. (2007, July). Suicide bombers don't fit psychological profile. *Clinical Psychiatry News, 7*, 35, p. 35

Marvasti, J. A. (2007, April 26) *Psychological autopsy of a suicide bomber*. Paper presented at the 25th annual symposium in forensic psychiatry of the American College of Forensic Psychiatry, Santa Fe, NM.

Merari, A. (2005). Suicide terrorism. In R. I. Yufit & D. Lester (Eds.), *Assessment, treatment, and prevention of suicidal behavior* (pp. 431–453). Hoboken, NJ: John Wiley & Sons, Inc.

Milgram, S. (1974). *Obedience to authority.* New York: Harper & Row.

National Public Radio (NPR) (2003, March 7). Profile: Look at the mind of a suicide bomber [On-line]. Retrieved May 2, 2007. Available: http://www.npr.org/progams/morning/transcripts/2003/mar/030307.joyce.html

Oliver, A. M., & Steinberg, P. (2005). *The road to Martyrs' Square: A journey into the world of the suicide bomber.* New York: Oxford University Press.

Persaud, R. (2004, September). Inside the mind of a terrorist. *BBC News* [On-line]. Retrieved February10,2007. Available: http://news.bbc.co.uk/go/pr/fr/-/2/hi/uk_news/magazine/3699826.stm

Pies, R. (2001). Special forum: 9/11 and everyday life–A simple way to end terrorism. *Journal of Mundane Behavior, 2,* 3, Oct. Retrieved July 20, 2006. Available: http://mundanebehavior.org/issues/v2n3/9-11/pies.htm

Piven, J. S. (2004, Fall). The psychosis (religion) of Islamic terrorists and the ecstasy of violence. *The Journal of Psychohistory, 32*(2), pp. 151–201.

Post, J. (2003, June 22). Terrorism Panel discussion held at the Spring Meeting of the American Psychoanalytic Association, Boston, MA. Quoted in G. Hough (2004). Does psychoanalysis have anything to offer an understanding of terrorism? *Journal of American Psychoanalysis Association, 52*(3) pp. 813–828.

Post, J. & Sprinzak, E. (2002, July 7) Terror's aftermath. *Los Angeles Times,* p. M1.

Rai, M. (2006). *7/7 The London bombings, Islam & the Iraq war.* London: Pluto Press.

Sanford, J.A. (1982). *Evil: The shadow side of reality,* New York: Crossroad Classic

Shuman, E. (2001, June). What makes suicide bombers tick? *Israelinside* [On-line]. Retrieved February 10, 2007. Available: http://www.israelinsider.com/_channels/security/articles/sec_0049.htm

Silke, A. P. (1998). Cheshire-cat logic: The recurring theme of terrorist abnormality in   psychological research. *Psychology, Crime and Law, 4,* pp. 51–69.

Silke, A. (2003a). Becoming a terrorist. In A. Silke (Ed.), *Terrorists, victims and society* (pp. 29–54). London: John Wiley & Sons.

Silke, A., (2003b). The psychology of suicidal terrorism. In A. Silke (Ed.), *Terrorists, victims and society* (pp. 93–108). London: John Wiley & Sons.

Simon, R. (2003, May 25). Mind of the Suicide Bomber. *CBS News* [On-line]. Retrieved February 10, 2007. Available: http://www.cbsnews.com/stories/2003/05/23/60minutes/printable555344.shtml

Sohail, K. (2006, August). Psychology of suicide "bombers." *Chowk* [On-line]. Retrieved August 31, 2006. Available: http://www.chowk.com

Tresniowski, A., & Hammel, S. (2006). The bomber next door. *People, 66,* pp. 81–82.

Volkan, V. (2006). *Killing in the name of identity: A study of bloody conflicts.* Charlottesville, VA: Pitchstone Publishing.

Von Drehle, D. (2002, October 7). Debate over Iraq focuses on outcome. *Washington Post.* p. A4.

White Paper–The Jemaah Islamiyah arrests (2003, January 9). *Singapore ministry of home affairs, Singapore.* Retrieved August 25, 2007. Available: http://www2.mha.gov.sg

Wikipedia Encyclopedia: Female suicide bomber. Retrieved on December 5, 2005. Available: http://en.wkipedia.org/_wiki/Female_suicide_bomber

Zimbardo, P. G., Haney, C., Banks, W. C. & Jaffe, D. (1973). *The psychology of imprisonment: Privation, power and pathology.* Unpublished manuscript, Stanford University.

Chapter 7

SUICIDE AND SELF-DESTRUCTIVE BEHAVIORS: LEARNING FROM CLINICAL POPULATIONS

Valerie L. Dripchak

I think of suicide as neither arbitrary nor meaningless. I think of it as a way out. . . .

statement made by a clinical patient

INTRODUCTION

Suicide and self-destructive behaviors are difficult topics to discuss. These issues bring up uneasy feelings in all of us because there seems to be a natural inclination to value human life. This subject matter is made even more problematic by the complexities of terrorism and war with suicide bombers literally at our doorsteps.

Although suicide bombers are usually studied by the forensic sciences, it is also important to examine this topic from a clinical view in order to better understand the "enemy." There are many areas, that surround this complicated action of self-destruction, and that cross into different spheres of life. Some of them include legal, philosophical, religious, environmental, and demographic factors, to name a few. This chapter will explore the different facets of suicide and self-destructive behaviors that are demonstrated in the clinical populations and attempt to discover what we can learn from the clinical groups in relation to the suicide bombers.

DEFINITIONS

The word suicide incorporates different components. Generally, suicide is considered to be an act that ends one's own life. It is derived from the Latin term *sui caedere*, which means to kill oneself (Dickinson & Leming, 2007). However, this term includes not only the act of harm but also the idea of harm. A suicidal thought or ideation is used when an individual is thinking about ending his or her life. A suicide threat is when a person verbalizes that she or he wants to kill herself or himself but has yet to act on it. The threat may include a plan to do it, but no act has taken place. Roberts (1991) referred to this phase as "potentially dangerous," and this is the phase that is encountered by many clinicians. It is a time when one-to-one mental health intervention is necessary.

The actual nature of a completed suicide is when the individual concludes the act and dies. Completed suicides often depend on the lethality of the method used and the chance of rescue. Jobes and Berman (1996) explained that high-lethality methods tend to have a low degree of reversibility and include, for example, using a gun or hanging. The lower-lethality methods have a higher degree of reversibility and include overdosing or cutting. In suicidal behavior, when an act or plan has already been carried out but death has not occurred, it is considered imminently dangerous, and the patient must be initially evaluated for medical care before considering mental health treatment. The latter act, if it does not conclude in death, may be termed a suicide attempt.

Further distinctions may be made between suicide and parasuicidal acts, in which the latter also are referred to as suicidal gestures. Kreitman (1977) introduced the term parasuicide to describe the nonfatal but intentional self-injurious behaviors that may result in physical damage, illness, or risk of death. It is distinguished from suicide because there is no intention to cause death. Linehan (1993) suggested that the term parasuicide is preferred over suicide gestures or manipulative suicide attempts because the former term does not communicate the patient's motivation and is a less-pejorative descriptor.

Another type of suicide that does not fit into the terms mentioned earlier is assisted suicide. Assisted suicide is the completion of suicide by a terminally ill or suffering individual with the aid of another person (*Suicide & Grief Glossary*, 2006). A closely related term is euthanasia, which is the act of ending the life of a person or animal who has been suffering from either a terminal illness or a chronically painful condition. Euthanasia may occur with or without the full consent of the patient (Dickinson & Leming, 2007).

There is another element of suicide known as cluster suicide. It is defined as the occurrence of a number of completed suicides within a given geographical area that is greater than what would be expected on the basis of statistical prediction. These deaths tend to be sensationalized, which may promote further suicidal behaviors (*Suicide & Grief Glossary*, 2006).

According to acceptable definitions of suicide, one's death is the central issue not the intention of the act. Therefore, the literature (*Wikipedia Encyclopedia*: Suicide) makes a distinction between suicide and the suicide bomber. In suicide bombing, terrorism and the death of others are the intentions of the bombing. The death of the suicide bomber is a certain outcome of the act, although not its primary focus.

Before the clinical suicide group is compared with suicide bombers further, a closer examination of some of the background aspects is necessary in order to gain a full appreciation of the complexities of the factors that are involved in suicide. Let us begin by reviewing the historical and legal issues related to this topic.

HISTORICAL AND LEGAL ASPECTS OF SUICIDE

The act of suicide has been around since ancient times. In early Egypt, suicide was considered an acceptable way to escape unbearable conditions. However, the early Roman government was ruled by emperors who were considered to have both secular and religious powers. Roman law made suicide illegal and promised "eternal torture" to those individuals who took their own lives (*Suicide & Suicidal People*, 2005). As European societies developed through the centuries and many heads of states were separated from religious rule, laws were passed making attempted suicide illegal. In some jurisdictions, it was punishable by imprisonment and, ironically, even death. If a person was successful in completing suicide, legal consequences might still remain. For example, until 1961, the United Kingdom forfeited the estates of people who died by suicidal acts (Dickinson & Leming, 2007).

The Suicide Act of 1961 decriminalized the act under English law, so that those individuals, who attempted suicide and failed would no longer face criminal sanctions (*Wikipedia Encyclopedia*: Suicide Act of 1961). In the United States, every state decriminalized attempted suicide and suicide by the 1990s, although some states continue to view it as a "de facto common law crime." As an unwritten common law crime, suicide may prevent financial damages from being awarded to the family of a suicidal person (e.g., malpractice law suits), unless the suicidal individual is proven insane (*Wikipedia Encyclopedia*: Legal Views of Suicide).

The Suicide Act of 1961 also created a new criminal offense to assist someone, either directly or indirectly, in taking his or her life (Humphrey, 2005). In England and Wales, there is a possibility of up to fourteen years of imprisonment for anyone who assists in a suicide. Assisted suicide, or the "right to die," is a hotly debated issue throughout the world. The controversial issue is sometimes met with no affirmative legislation or with another part of the criminal code that is extended to fit the act that has been brought to the attention of the authorities.

According to Humphrey (2005), there are only four places that have legalized active assistance of suicide to dying patients: Switzerland passed a law in 1941, allowing physician and nonphysician-assisted suicide; Belgium passed a law in 2002 permitting euthanasia but does not define any method; the Netherlands passed a law in 2002 legalizing voluntary euthanasia and physician-assisted suicide, but the courts had permitted such acts since 1984; and Oregon passed its Death with Dignity Act in 1997, allowing physician-assisted suicide, but it has been met with federal criticism and attempts to overturn the legislation. In the United States, the right to die groups in Washington, Michigan, California, Maine, Hawaii, and Vermont have attempted to pass laws allowing assisted suicide for dying patients. However, to date, these states have not passed the legislation.

DEMOGRAPHIC CHARACTERISTICS IN THE CLINICAL POPULATION

According to Stone (1999), approximately 2000 people kill themselves each day throughout the world. The U. S. Department of Health and Human Services (2003) reported that about 30,000 individuals kill themselves each year in the United States. Yet, the U.S. rates rank in the mid range as compared with other industrialized countries throughout the world. In addition, between 300,000 and 600,000 Americans "survive" a suicide attempt each year. Some of these survivors subsequently go on to complete the act. Most data emphasize that suicides are underreported.

With these startling figures, it is important to view suicide along a continuum. One might say that the suicide ideas of yesterday may become the suicidal attempts of today and the completed suicides of tomorrow. Although not every individual who attempts suicide will end up dying, more research is needed to focus on the distinguishing intervening variables that would give rise to the differences between life and death. Some of the data that are already known are discussed below.

GENDER DIFFERENCES

There are decided differences between men and women regarding self-destructive behaviors and suicide. According to the American Foundation for Suicide Prevention (2004), the rates for men who commit suicide were higher for every year of the past century. In fact, according to this source, men were three to five times more likely to commit suicide, although women reported making more attempts. Another factor that was noted in this report was that men have a greater variance from one year to another, whereas the rates for women remained relatively flat. Theses rates correlated to an increase in economic problems in 1908 and in 1930 and dropped during the two world wars.

During the first half of the twentieth century, wartime was considered to be a time when suicide rates dropped, because WWI and WWII seemed to unite people around a common cause. However, in recent U. S. military conflicts, there has been an increase in suicides among people serving in the armed forces. The figures indicated that the number of military who took their lives in 2005 rose over the previous year and was the highest since 1999 (Waters, 2005).

The rate of completion of suicide was related to the methods used. Men tended to use a higher lethality method (e.g., firearms, hanging or jumping from high places). Women, on the other hand, tended to overdose on substances or poisons (Sadock & Sadock, 2003).

LIFESPAN ISSUES

The National Institute of Mental Health (2004) reported that although suicide rates for young people tripled over the last thirty years, people who were sixty-five years and older had the highest suicide rates. Although older individuals attempted suicide less often than younger people did, they were more likely to complete the act.

As stated previously, the suicide rate is rapidly rising for young people. In fact, suicide was found to be the third leading cause of death in the fifteen- to twenty-four-year-old age group, following accidents and homicides. Attempted suicides, in this same age group, ranged between one million to two million annually (Sadock & Sadock, 2003).

SITUATIONAL FACTORS

Rich, Warstadt, Nemiroff, Fowler, and Young. (1991) found that the most powerful situational factors for suicide are significant losses or traumatic events. Losses were related to the death of a loved one, a divorce, or the loss of personal property. Traumatic situations included an arrest, a scandal, or a failure. However, the actual precipitating events varied across the lifespan. For young people, the situation that usually preceded a suicide was most apt to be an interpersonal conflict or rejection. In the midlife range, situational factors that were associated with suicide were financial stressors, such as the loss of a job. For older adults, the predominant factor seemed to be related to chronic or terminal medical illnesses.

It is important to keep in mind that suicide is not necessarily the result of a single event but may be due to the lack of actual or perceived coping resources to deal with the situation. Moreover, patients often report that there was a series of situations that placed them in a position of hopelessness, and suicide was viewed as the only way out.

MENTAL HEALTH ISSUES

According to Sadock and Sadock (2003), approximately 95 percent of all individuals who either completed or attempted suicide had a diagnosed mental disorder. Some of their findings indicated the following links to psychiatric problems within this grouping: 80 percent of the individuals had mood disorders, 10 percent were found to have a diagnosis of schizophrenia, and 5 percent had either dementia or delirium. In addition, among this population, 25 percent were considered to have a dual diagnosis that included a mental disorder and alcohol dependence (p. 915).

Although this list demonstrates important data, it is by no means inclusive of all the mental health issues that a suicidal patient might endure. Suicide may be linked to other diagnostic areas such as anxieties, personality disorders, and phobias. In addition, many of our patients had more than one psychiatric condition. At the same time, this information cannot lead us to conclude that every one who presents with mental illness will commit suicide.

Demographic factors are important to examine because taken together they provide some important information about at-risk groups. This information may allow clinicians to intervene at primary and other early levels of prevention work. At the same time, one must acknowledge that there are multiple factors to consider. In other words, each clinical suicide is idiosyncratic, and there are no universal truisms in this work. Furthermore, the fact that an individual is not currently in one of the high-risk groups does not mean that the individual may not commit suicide. This issue is the same for the suicide bomber. Although certain variables—age, gender, family, and so on—are discussed in Chapters 3 and 6, we must conclude that like clinical suicide, suicide terrorism may be carried out by anyone. This is the issue that causes concern. If these demographics serve to provide information regarding the profiles of individuals who committed suicide, what are some of the other characteristics that point to the beliefs of individuals and society about suicide? Let us turn now to some of the philosophical and religious views related to suicide.

PHILOSOPHICAL AND RELIGIOUS VIEWS OF SUICIDE

In order to understand an individual's actions in attempting or completing suicide, it is necessary to discuss the different philosophical and religious views of suicide. The idea that all suicide is irrational is not accepted by many people. Emile Durkheim published his well-known book *Suicide* in 1897. In his works, Durkheim studied the suicide rates of different groups of individuals and discussed different types of suicide: egoistic, altruistic, anomic, and fatalistic.

In egoistic suicide, individuals depend more on themselves and do not recognize any rules of conduct beyond their own interests. Durkheim noted that egoistic suicide often occurred in societies that were weak or under unstable conditions in which the religious, domestic, and political groups did not integrate the individual into society. In other words, excessive individuation can lead to suicide. In contrast, altruistic suicide involves insufficient individuation. Examples of altruistic suicide existed in cultures in which the person killed himself or herself because of duty. This duty was imposed by society for social purposes. There is a similar point of view with cluster suicides that encourages people to imitate another's actions. Anomic suicide is similar to egoistic suicide in that it is the result of insufficient integration into society. However, in addition to integrating its members, societies must regulate and control its members' beliefs and behaviors. During times when there was a disturbance in the financial or social areas of equilibrium, people resorted to suicide. For example, it could be during significant financial changes that occur in economic decline or in economic prosperity. In fatalistic suicide, there is no hope for change and there is no relief from the oppression that the individual experiences (Jones, 1986).

Pretti (2006) has suggested that (in addition to Durkheim's work) there is literary evidence to support the idea that suicide also may be an act of revenge. Throughout literary history, there have been stories that involved the suicide of an individual who wanted to take vengeance on those held responsible for some suffering and for whom there was no other recourse. Along with the suicide, there would be some evidence of a "curse" denouncing the oppression that may be seen more in suicide bombers than in the clinical population.

RELIGIOUS ASPECTS

The major religions of the world have integrated one or more of these philosophical views of suicide as they formulated their policies. In Judaism, there is a great emphasis on the sanctity of life. Suicide is forbidden by Jewish law in all circumstances. Consequently, assisting in suicide and requesting assistance are also prohibited. Even in Conservative Judaism, the value of life is affirmed. Their Committee on Jewish Law and Standards published a *teshuva* on suicide and assisted suicide in the summer of 1998 that stated that although people become ill with pain, most individuals do not resort to suicide. The Conservative paper advocated better ways to control pain without committing suicide. It also stated that rather than assisting the patient in dying, the proper response is to provide the patient with people who will reaffirm the patient's living (Bernstein, 2000).

In Roman Catholicism, suicide is considered a mortal sin. By the sixth century, people who committed suicide were denied a Christian burial, which was a requirement in order for the soul to go to heaven. In the following century, even an attempted suicide became an ecclesiastical crime that could be punished by excommunication. The argument is that an individual is the property of God and to take one's life is an act against God. However, the Catholic Church also teaches that there is no moral obligation for a person to select extraordinary means of saving one's life. In 1997, The Catechism of the Catholic Church stated that suicide might be the result of a person who has serious psychological disturbances and therefore cannot be viewed as entirely morally culpable. The Church also had lifted its ban on prohibiting Christian burials (U. S. Conference of Catholics, 1997).

In the Protestant sects of Christianity, some conservatives argue that suicide is considered "self-murder." Anyone who commits murder of any type perpetrates a grievous act and will go to hell after death. However, more liberal Protestant sects hold that God forgives all sins without the need to ask forgiveness. Consequently, people who do complete suicide can go to heaven (Anglican Church in America, 1996).

In the Hindu religion, suicide is considered equally as sinful as murdering another human being. In fact, according to Hindu beliefs, to die by any type of violent act, which includes suicide, results in becoming a ghost and never being at peace. However, Hinduism does permit *Sallekhana*, which is the practice of ending one's life by fasting. This practice requires time and willpower and requires the individual to settle worldly affairs and to draw closer to God (Jayaram, 2006).

The Islamic religion views suicide as sinful and detrimental to one's spiritual journey on earth. In the *Koran*, the Islamic holy book, Allah is said to be "most merciful" and forgiving of all sins. However, any person who contemplates suicide and shows no regret for this wrongdoing before she or he completes the suicide will spend eternity in hell reenacting the behavior that took her or his life. A small minority of Muslim scholars, however, consider that this conduct, when taken in the course of jihad (in which death is inevitable such as in suicide bombing), is not an act of suicide. These deaths are viewed as a form of martyrdom, even though there is evidence in the Koran to the contrary. Certain scholars have asserted that these acts are seen as the only alternative action against "unjust oppressors," rather than an act focused on killing oneself (*Comparative Index to Islam*, 2006).

In the doctrine of karma, Buddhists believe that a person's past actions influence what is experienced in the present and the present behaviors influence future experiences. Therefore, all people experience suffering that originates from their past bad deeds. For Buddhists, one must realize the true nature by Enlightenment and refrain from any destruction of life. Despite this religious precept, there is an old ideology that oppressed Buddhists may select suicide as an "honorable act" (Keown, 1996). An example of a resurgence of this ideology occurred during the Vietnam conflict. There were Buddhist monks who committed acts of suicide by setting themselves on fire as political protests of American soldiers in their country.

With some noted exceptions, one may conclude that the major religions of the modern world condemn the act of suicide. However, identification with religion or religious beliefs is often brought up in the news media when discussing acts of terrorism such as suicide bombings. Perhaps we need to examine not the religious affiliation of the suicidal individual but the degree of integration that religious values have on the individual. We may then conclude that religious values actually may be a protective construct for not resorting to suicide, rather than a risk factor. Let's examine other misconceptions that surround suicide.

MISCONCEPTIONS REGARDING SUICIDE

Although suicide is common throughout the world, it is also surrounded by a number of misconceptions. One misconception is that an individual who attempts suicide and fails to complete the act is not serious about ending life. Approximately 40 percent of all completed suicides have had previous attempts or threats (Maris, 1992). Furthermore, the research (Goldstein et al., 1991) shows that the more prior attempts there have been, the greater the likelihood of a completed suicide.

Another myth about suicide is that people who threaten suicide never actually kill themselves. We know that many individuals who have completed suicide tend to communicate their intentions within three months before the fatal act (Isometsa et al., 1994). When people threaten suicide, they need to be taken seriously.

The last two misconceptions about suicide are associated with people's emotional responses to it as an "incomprehensible act." There is a misconception that suggests that if we talk about suicide, individuals, who did not consider this alternative before will turn to suicide as an option now. We know, however, that this is not true. If we do question clients about suicide in a nonjudgmental way, it allows them to begin to talk about the issues that are affecting them. However, this "restricted" topic often reflects the general public's discomfort to discuss these issues. When this happens, consideration is not given to those people who are contemplating suicide. We need to understand the importance of providing clients with the opportunities to talk about their hopelessness and so on.

Another example of this taboo is seen in many adults who think that children who are the survivors of a caregiver's or a relative's suicide do not grieve. Perhaps, it is too overwhelming for adults to consider that children's feelings go as deeply as their own. We know, however, that children experience the same range of emotions as adults do about suicidal deaths. However, given their developmental ages, children may be less likely to put their feelings into words. Secrecy about suicide, in the hopes of protecting children, may lead to further complications. It is important to offer age-appropriate explanations to children, but adults may first have to reach their own "comfort" level in this process (*Survivors of Suicide Fact Sheet*, 2005).

COMPARING SUICIDE NOTES BETWEEN CLINICAL POPULATIONS AND SUICIDE BOMBERS

In the examination of the information gathered from the clinical populations about suicide, we may draw some interesting comparisons with the suicide terrorist. Overall, there are more differences than there are similarities. We also must acknowledge that both groups contain heterogeneous aspects. Despite the variations, the analysis did reveal some interesting similarities and differences.

Sneidman (1985) provided six aspects of clinical patients who commit suicide that may be considered in understanding suicide bombers. These include situational characteristics, motivational traits, affective responses, cognitive characteristics, relational factors, and serial characteristics.

The most common predisposing situational characteristic in suicide is an "unendurable psychological pain." As described earlier, most clinical patients who commit suicide have serious psychiatric disorders. Although it was noted that suicide terrorists do not tend to have mental disorders, their psychological pain may emanate from what they perceive to be a more powerful oppressor. Over time, this feeling of oppression may create its own "unbearable psychological pain."

Within this schema, there is the motivational trait of "attempting to seek a solution." The solution for the clinical population may be to use suicide as a means to stop consciousness. The solution for the suicide bomber is to overcome powerlessness with his only weapon—himself. The suicide bomber causes the death of others by dying himself.

The affective responses noted in the clinical population seem to be a sense of "hopeless and helplessness" within the context that they have "nothing to lose." These traits also may be applied to the suicide bomber but in a different context. With their impending deaths, the suicide bombers may experience feelings of hopelessness, but at the same time they may be hopeful that there might be much to gain over the political oppression that they or their tribe may be experiencing.

The cognitive characteristics of suicide individuals include a kind of "tunnel vision" in which no other alternative ideas can emerge. This tunnel vision may also be the view of the circumstances of the lives of the suicidal bombers. Suicide provides not only a way out of the oppression for the potential suicide bomber but also a way into an act of glory. The individuals within both groupings who turn to suicide view their worlds in conflicted and narrowed states and are not able to see other options.

The relational factors of suicide focus on the interpersonal behavior of the act. In other words, suicide is a form of communication to those who are living. In our clinical work, the act of suicide often signified the pain and lack of options that the patient was experiencing. It also communicated anger or revenge towards someone—a final message that can have no response from the living. Perhaps this same sentiment is being expressed by the suicide bomber. It is the communication of pain, a lack of options and revenge. However, instead of intending the message for someone who is known, the target is someone known as the "enemy" and the message is one of terror.

In serial characteristics, a person shows specific lifelong coping patterns when the individual is upset, distressed, threatened, and enduring some psychological pain. As issues increase and are perceived to be unsolvable, they may be combined with how oriented the person is toward dying and lethality increases. This seems to be another common factor with the suicide bomber, who also experiences these serial characteristics. However, their view of death often is linked toward a political end, which serves to provide more impetus to the act.

Similarities

Overall, both the clinical population and the suicide bombers perceive themselves to be victims of discrimination who suffer unfair treatment in their lives. These issues produce deep wounds and possible feelings of hopelessness, frustration, anger, and helplessness, as well as other kinds of emotional pain.

Another similarity between the two groups is the effect that their deaths have on their loved ones who are alive. To "plan" a death by suicide brings out a variety of emotions such as sadness, anger, emptiness, and so on towards family members or close friends. These concerns were illustrated in the written notes that some individuals, who resorted to suicide, left behind. The following note was written by "Paul" to his wife prior to his act of clinical suicide:

> My Darling,
> Please don't blame yourself for my death. It was my only solution. I tried just about everything else, but it doesn't get better. I am trapped in the memories that we had and know that they can never be again. Things are really getting worse. I know that you will find a way to move on. That is your nature, but it isn't mine. (Reprinted with permission by the surviving spouse who sought psychotherapy to overcome her grief after her husband's death.)

The sentiments expressed by Paul are not very different from the last letters of two suicide warriors, who showed the same sense of grief toward their remaining family members, and what impact their deaths may have on those whom they love. BBC correspondent, David Powers (2001), provided the following portion of a letter written by a twenty-three-year-old kamikaze to his mother just prior to his suicide attack:

> I am pleased to have the honor of having been chosen as a member of a Special Attack Force that is on its way into battle, but I cannot help crying when I think of you, Mum. When I reflect on the hopes you had for my future . . . I feel so sad that I am going to die without doing anything to bring you joy.

A more Modern-day suicide bomber wrote the following before his death (Ganor, 2001).

> Dear family and friends! I write this will with tears in my eyes and sadness in my heart. I want to tell you that I am leaving and ask you for your forgiveness because I decided to see Allah today and this meeting is by all means more important than staying alive on this earth.

Differences

Although some of their internal responses may be similar, there are still marked differences between a person who resorts to suicide and a suicide bomber. As stated earlier in this article, the focus of suicide in the clinical population is death, whereas the focus of the suicide bomber is the death of other people and to terrorize countless numbers of others. Death for the suicide bomber is a "by-product" of the act.

Another key distinction between these two groups is that in the clinical populations, there are serious mental health issues, whereas the suicide bombers have political motives for their actions. Moreover, it is important to note that even society reacts differently toward both groups. In the clinical population, suicide is often covered up or not discussed. However, the suicide bombers actually rely on the publicity that their actions will have throughout the world.

Although internal feelings of hopelessness, revenge, and so on may be similar in both groups, their targets are different. For example, when persons with pathology resort to suicide as a form of revenge, they are usually targeting one or a small number of individuals whom they know well. In suicide bombing, the target is the "enemy" who is not known as an individual to the bomber but represents a larger military force.

CONCLUSION

Suicide is a complex problem for clinicians in the mental health field. This chapter examined many aspects of suicide that included demographics, history, law, philosophy, and religion. These areas help us to understand that there are strong universal systems that make suicide the alternative action for someone who is in deep emotional pain or social isolation, or both. In spite of the very strong arguments against suicide, suicide and suicide terrorism have become an ever-growing problem throughout the world. Although some of the internal emotions may be similar to those of the clinical populations, the suicide terrorist is, indeed, different. The fact that the suicide terrorists, who arguably have no reported pathologies, need to take revenge on their enemies is a very powerful motivation and a threat to innocent people. In conclusion, it is important to research further the issues that lead to the preventable deaths in both the clinical suicide and the suicidal bomber groups. We need to have a better understanding of people who look to self-destruction as a remedy for their conflicts. It is also imperative that we continue to seek answers that help to preserve life and not destroy potential, to seek solutions and not destruction.

REFERENCES

American Foundation for Suicide Prevention. (2004). *U.S. Suicide Rates: 1900–1999* [On-line] Retrieved on November 6, 2006. Available: http://www.afsp. org/statistics/USA.htm

Anglican Church in America. (1996). Statement on the moral implications of suicide [On-line]. Retrieved on November 6, 2006. Available: http://www.acahome.org/suicide.htm

Bernstein, S. (2000). Stopping a suicide: Jewish perspective [On-line]. Retrieved November 6, 2006. Available: http://www.aish.com/societywork/sciencenature/Stopping_a_Suicide.asp

Comparative Index to Islam (2006). Suicide [On-line]. Retrieved on November 6, 2006. Available: http://www.answering-Islam.org/Index/S/suicide.html

Dickinson, G. E., & Leming, M. R. (2007). *Death, dying and bereavement.* (Contemporary Learning Series). Dubuque, IA: McGraw-Hill.

Ganor, B. (2001). Suicide attacks in Israel. In The International Policy Institute for Counter-Terrorism (Ed.), *Countering suicide terrorism* (p. 138). Herzlia, Israel: The International Policy Institute for Counter-Terrorism.

Goldstein, R. B., Black, D. W., Nasrallah, A., & Winokur, G. (1991). The prediction of suicide. *Archives of General Psychiatry, 48*, pp. 418–422.

Humphry, D. (2005). Tread carefully when you help to die: Assisted suicide laws around the world [On-line]. Retrieved May 12, 2006. Available: http://www.assistedsuicide.org/suicide_laws.html

Isometsa, E. T., Henriksson, M. E., Aro, H. M., Heikkinen, M. E., Kuoppasalmi, K. I., & Lonnqvist, J. K. (1994). Suicide in major depression. *American Journal of Psychiatry 151*, pp. 530–536.

Jayaram V. (2006). Hinduism and suicide [On-line]. Retrieved November 21, 2006. Available: http://www.hinduwebsite.com

Jobes, D. A., & Berman, A. L. (1996). Crisis assessment and time-limited intervention with high risk suicidal youth. In A. R. Roberts (Ed.), *Crisis management & brief treatment* (pp. 60–82). Chicago, IL: Nelson-Hall Publishers.

Jones, R. A. (1986). *Emile Durkheim: An introduction to four major works.* Thousand Oaks, CA: Sage Publications.

Keown, D. (1996). Buddhism and suicide. *Journal of Buddhist Ethics, 3*, pp. 1–23.

Kreitman, N. (1977). *Parasuicide.* Chichester, UK: Wiley.

Linehan, M. M. (1993). *Cognitive-behavioral treatment of borderline personality disorder.* New York: Guilford Press.

Maris, R.W. (1992). The relation of nonfatal suicide attempts to completed suicides. In R. W. Maris, A. L. Berman, J. T. Maltsberger, & R. I. Yufit (Eds.), *Assessment and prediction of suicide.* New York: Guilford Press.

National Institute of Mental Health (2004). U.S. *Suicide rates by age, gender and racial group.* Bethesda, MD: National Institutes of Health, U.S. Department of Health and Human Services.

Powers, D. (2001). Japan: No surrender in World War Two [On-line]. Retrieved March 13, 2006. Available: http://www.bbc.co.uk/history/war/wwtwo/_japan_no_surrender_05.shtml

Pretti, A. (2006). Suicide to harass others: Clues from mythology to understanding suicide bombing attacks. Crisis: *The Journal of Crisis Intervention and Suicide Prevention, 27*, pp. 22–30.

Rich, C. L., Warstadt, G. M., Nemiroff, R. A., Fowler, R. C., & Young, D. (1991). Suicide, stressors and the life cycle. *American Journal of Psychiatry, 148*, pp. 524–527.

Roberts, A. R. (1991). *Contemporary perspectives on crisis intervention and prevention.* Englewood

Cliffs, NJ: Prentice-Hall.

Sadock, B. J., & Sadock, V. A. (2003). *Synopsis of psychiatry.* Philadelphia, PA: Lippincott Williams & Wilkins.

Sneidman, E. S. (1985). *Definition of suicide.* New York: Wiley.

Stone, G. (1999). *Suicide and attempted suicide: Methods and consequences.* New York: Carroll & Graf.

Suicide & grief glossary [On-line]. Retrieved July 4, 2006. Available: http://members.tripod.com/~LifeGard/index-2.html

Suicide & Suicidal People [On-line]. Retrieved December 5, 2005. Available: http://www.soul work.net/sw_articles_eng/suicide.htm

Survivors of Suicide Fact Sheet (2005). Washington, D.C.: American Association of Suicidality.

United States Conferences of Catholics (1997). *Catechism of the Church.* Washington, D.C.: United States Catholic Colleges Public Services.

United States Department of Health and Human Services (2003). *Suicide in the United States.* Atlanta, GA: Centers for Disease Control.

Waters, R. (2005). The psychic costs of war. *Psychotherapy Networker, 29*, pp. 13–14.

Wikipedia Encyclopedia. Legal views of suicide [On-line]. Retrieved July 5, 2006. Available: http://en.wikipedia.org/wikiLegal_views_of_suicide

Wikipedia Encyclopedia. Suicide [On-line]. Retrieved December 5, 2005. Available: http://en.wikipedia.org/wiki/Suicide

Wikipedia Encyclopedia. Suicide Act 1961 [On-line]. Retrieved May 12, 2006. Available: http://en.wikipedia.org/wiki/Suicide_Act_1961

Chapter 8

COUNTERTERRORISM: VIOLENCE BREEDS VIOLENCE AND INCREASES TERRORISM AND DISCONTENT

Jamshid A. Marvasti

Any government reduced to meeting its enemies only on the battlefield would soon be destroyed.

Alexis de Tocqueville

An eye for an eye only makes the world blind.
Mahatma Gandhi

INTRODUCTION

An old Chinese proverb teaches us, "When seeking revenge, dig two graves." A serious mistake is to ignore the cause of terrorism and hostility and attend only to the effect. As Marsella (2003) has mentioned, terrorism may be caused by past or present anger, religion, economics, politics, culture, racism, poverty, inequality. As an analogy, a somatic pain (e.g. headache) needs to be alleviated by a painkilling drug but simultaneously, a skilled physician will look for the cause and etiology of the pain.

Western governments should know that fighting the cause of terrorism is beneficial, but fighting only "terrorists" is treating the effect in order to destroy the cause. Martin Luther King, Jr. has stated, "Violence may murder the murderer, but it doesn't murder the murder. Violence may murder the liar, but it doesn't murder lies; it doesn't establish the truth. . . . Violence may go to the point of murdering the hater, but it doesn't murder hate. . . . It may increase the hate. This is the ultimate weakness of violence: It multiplies evil and violence in the universe. It doesn't solve problems" (Wheels of Justice, n.d.).

WHAT DOES NOT WORK: KILLING LEADS TO MORE KILLING

When valor preys on reason, it eats the sword it fights with.
Shakespeare

By militarizing the problem of terrorism, our leaders have dangerously obfuscated its political, social, and historical dimension.
Robert Lifton

If your people are involved in brutality on the outside, the cruelty and hatred is certain to reverberate on the inside of your community as well.
Rabbi Michael Lerner

The security and safety of a nation require more than military strength. After five years of war in Iraq, the new commander of U.S. troops has warned, "military force alone will not be enough to quell the country's violent insurgency" (*CNN News*, 2007). Violence breeds violence, and killings lead to revenge, retaliation, and eventually more killings. Conflicts continue when countries act as if peace can only be accomplished through war and military domination.

Marsella (2003, p. 13) in particular has identified vigilance, counterterrorism, and elimination of resources as the tactics that the governments of the United States, Great Britain, and Israel believe will defeat terrorism. Yet terrorism probably arises from human discontent, resentment of inequalities, and a belief that violence is justified. Logically, then, Marsella and several others have concluded that any military action must be combined with economic, cultural, and diplomatic activities focused on establishing opportunities and providing social justice (Marsella, 2003). He has suggested that this analysis is not meant to justify international terrorism but "rather to call attention to how individual and group terrorists might justify their own actions" (p. 35). Marsella has advocated the need to study not only terrorism, but the need to study peace: "History still remains the best predictor of future action. Why did we not respond to the warning signs before 9/11, and what are we doing now to promote peace?" (Marsella, p. 46).

REVIEWING THE LITERATURE

The first line of defense against terrorism is to prevent people from becoming terrorists. To begin with, Atran has presented several possibilities of what may not help to accomplish this goal (2003, p. 1538). Although usually thought of as only beneficial, increasing literacy rates may actually work in favor of recruiting organizations because there will be greater exposure to terrorist propaganda. In addition, Atran has explained that lessening poverty may have no effect or could even result in a redistribution of wealth that leaves those who were better off with less than they had before. Alan Krueger, an economist with Princeton University, has also studied bombers and the views of Palestinians on terror attacks against Israelis and does not see a connection between terrorism and poverty or literacy (*National Public Radio* [NPR], 2003). In fact Krueger has stated, "I think there's very little connection between economic circumstances and support for terrorism or maybe even an opposite relationship, from what most people suspect" (*NPR*, 2003).

Furthermore, as Atran has maintained, ethnic profiling and preemptive attacks are unlikely to ameliorate the problem, especially in regard to a long-term solution, and may prove to be quite costly (Atran, 2003). Although reducing the number of military occupation troops can help, it does not guarantee success. Atran has stated that "ending occupation or reducing perceived humiliation may help, but not if the population believes this to be a victory inspired by terror (e.g., Israel's apparently forced withdrawal from Lebanon" (Atran, 2003, p. 1538).

George Soros (2006), an American multibillionaire, has written that the failure of Israel to subdue Hezbollah in the 2006 invasion of Lebanon demonstrates the many weaknesses of the war on terror concept. One weakness of the war on terror concept, Soros has explained, is that it relies on military action and ignores the need for political intervention and negotiation. Hezbollah and Hamas were strengthened as a direct consequence of that approach.[1] The approach also separates "us" from "them" and denies that our actions help shape their behavior (Soros, 2006). The second weakness of the war on terror is the target. Even if the target is terrorists, the victims are often innocent civilians, and their suffering reinforces the terrorist cause. Civilian casualties and property damage inflamed world opinion against Israel and converted Hezbollah from the aggressor to the hero of resistance (Soros, 2006a). The situation in Afghanistan provides a further example to illustrate this weak spot in the war-on-terror approach. As the governor of Baluchistan province has explained, "The foreign presence in Afghanistan was initially popular. But due to indiscriminate bombings and other mistakes, you've lost the high ground and turned the public against you. The current policy will continue to radicalize society and increase violence" (Siddiqui, 2007).

The late activist Eqbal Ahmad has illustrated how problematic this second weakness can be, because often the person who is sought after is not the one killed; instead innocent people are. "They [the U.S.] tried to kill Saddam Hussein. Instead they killed Laila bin Attar, a prominent artist, an innocent woman. They tried to kill bin Laden and his men. Twenty-five other people died" (Ahmad, 2001, p. 25). Missiles intended for one country, fall into another. The point is that military attacks are completely fallible, not full proof. Even if the capture or defeat of one person would change everything, how many innocent people are killed in the attempt (Ahmad, 2001)? It has been reported that during the second Intifada (Palestinian uprising), "more than 4,000 Palestinians [were] killed in five years, 80 percent were classified as innocent civilians. . . . In the same period roughly 1000 Israelis were killed, with the same proportion, 80 percent being innocent adults and children" (Shergald, 2007).

Carroll (2006) has clearly stated that "both Israel and the United States have been at the mercy of the same illusion, that the hammer of military force is the tool to use against every threat." During the 2006 failure of Israel's attack on the Hezbollah of Lebanon, it became apparent that Israel has not learned from recent American misadventures in Iraq. In fact, Israel's decision to wage war against Lebanon has only shown the increasing political vulnerability of a nation that relies exclusively on military force. "Since WWII, wars have been waged for no significant purpose or gain. In fact, enemies have been empowered, not defeated" (Carroll, 2006).

The literature (Marsella, 2003; Atran, 2003; Chomsky & Achcar, 2007) also has documented how the pressure of globalization creates serious societal threats that Western countries have ignored in favor of temporary fiscal gain. Even if Al-Qaeda fighters and bin Laden are captured and defeated, the conditions that developed and encouraged terrorism remain, so other terror-based groups will continue to evolve. A military reaction will always come too late. Instead, there must be a plan to prevent the emergence of terrorism (Marsella, 2003). Also problematic are government policies concerning counterterrorism that can promote discontent and opposition. As Soros once mentioned, the United States' war against terror is misnamed, as it causes terrorism on its own (Soros, 2006b).

Looking at the Middle East conflicts may lead us to a similar conclusion: that a military-based solution focused on the capture of certain individuals may not bring peace. During the Israeli-Lebanon-Palestine war of 2006, an Israeli newspaper, *Haaretz* (2006), printed its opinion that bombing, airport seizure, destruction of the power station, and arrests of elected Palestinian officials would not help to release the one soldier kidnapped by Palestinians.

The editorial stated that the Israeli government has deported many Hamas activists but that they have returned to leadership in their organization. The editorial sought to remind the Israeli government that arresting leaders only strengthens them and their supporters. The editorial concluded that arresting people for use as bargaining chips is the act of a gang, not of a state.[2]

Reuter (2002) has concluded that a massive military response only enhances the appeal of Al-Qaeda, and any such attacks are used to justify and encourage more suicide bombing. Reuter has suggested that the war on terror is therefore not the solution. His sentiments are echoed by Stephane Dion, a political leader in Canada, who has stated "the Taliban will not be defeated solely through the barrel of a gun" (Siddiqui, 2007). Reuter has quoted an Arab poet, Adonis, who stated, "Our wars should only be against oppression, injustice, poverty, ignorance, and violators of human rights" (Reuter, 2002). When western governments themselves violate human rights (e.g., kidnapping, torture), the cultural difference between terrorists and the counterterrorism of the West fades.

Gershman (2006) has presented several factors to explain the failure of the George W. Bush administration:

- Overemphasis on military responses: only a third of the defense budget is spent on homeland security, to protect America from terrorism; two thirds, twice that, is assigned for overt military action;
- Failure in intelligence communication: lack of coordination between departments;
- Diminishing values of democracy and civil liberties: the 2001 Patriot Act is now considered un-American;
- Weakening international institutions: The prime example is the lack of U.S. support for the current Geneva Convention edicts;
- Failure to attack root causes: Military focus has evaded the issues of repressive regimes; the U.S. role in those regimes; and the conditions that facilitate terrorism such as poverty, inequality, and economic issues.[3]

Arundhati Roy has criticized the western governments' counterterrorism approach as counterproductive and potentially akin to terrorism. She has stated that President Bush has said that "we're a peaceful nation." Prime Minister Blair has echoed him, saying, "we're a peaceful people." Roy (2003) has written that these "peaceful people" have decreed that "War is Peace," as evidenced by the invasion of Middle East countries. These leaders have justified the invasion by "evidence that they shared with friendly coalition/invasion members," yet this "evidence" would not have been viable in the International Court of Law. As Madeline Albright (previous U.S. Secretary of State) once stated, "The U.S. acts multilaterally when it can, and unilaterally when it must" (Roy, 2003, p. 73).

In conclusion, unilateral military invasion, bombing, kidnapping, destroying the infrastructure of a nation, and forcing a type of puppet government on a nation are not productive steps. On the contrary, they are probably the very activities that terrorists anticipate and desire.

WHAT MAY INCREASE TERRORISM AND DISCONTENTMENT?

The fox condemns the trap, not himself.
Blake

Although it has been suggested that religious and cultural differences are the major causes of conflict or discontentment among people of the world, we would like to challenge this concept of much evidence proving the contrary. Avnery (2006) a former member of the Israeli Knesset (Parliament), has referred to Samuel Huntington's concept, the "Clash of Civilizations" (Huntington, 1996). In this book, Huntington has presented a theory that the major sources of conflict in the post-Cold War world are peoples' cultural and religious identities. However, this idea has been criticized for not acknowledging the role of occupation, invasion, and exploitation.[4] In addition, there is a lack of evidence to suggest that people's differences of culture and religion will result in conflict.[5] In a series of British Broadcasting Corporation polls (*BBC World Service Poll*, 2007) taken from people around the world, 52 percent of 28,000 people surveyed held that political interests were the largest factors contributing to the tension between Muslims and westerners, compared with only 29 percent who believed religion and culture were to blame. 56 percent of these people, felt that Muslims and westerners could find areas of agreement to build better relations, whereas only 28 percent felt that conflict was inevitable (*BBC World Service Poll*, 2007). Avnery has asserted that there is no "clash of civilization" between, for example, the Muslims of Indonesia and Christians in Chile. Huntington admitted that "the West won the war not by the superiority of its idea or values or religion, but rather by its superiority in applying organized violence. Westerners often forget this fact; non-Westerners never do" (Avnery, 2006).[6]

"He who controls the oil controls the world," Avnery has said, adding that the U.S. government would viciously attack Iran even if Iran were peopled with pigmies devoted to the religion of the Dalai Lama.

Occupation and Invasion Increases Terrorism

Terrorism is the war of the poor and war is the terrorism of the rich.

Peter Ustinov

Egyptian President Mubarak advised the United States not to invade Iraq because that action would create hundreds of "bin Ladens." After five years, his advice and prediction appear to be accurate. Zinn (2003, p. 130) has explained that the "old way of thinking," meaning the usage of military intervention, never worked. For instance, President Reagan bombed Libya, President George H. Bush made war on Iraq, and President Clinton bombed Afghanistan and Sudan to "send a message" to terrorists. "Then comes this horror in New York and Washington. Isn't it clear by now that sending a message to terrorists through violence doesn't work, that it only leads to more terrorism?" Zinn has also referred to the Middle East problem, asking, "haven't we learned anything from the Israeli-Palestinian conflict" (Zinn, 2003, p. 130).

Chomsky (2001, 2002, p. 17), in response to 9/11, has remarked that European leaders (NATO members) recognized that a massive assault on the Muslim population would be "the answer to the prayer of bin Laden and associates" and may lead the United States and its allies into a "diabolical trap" as the foreign minister of France has stated.

Mueller (2005, 2006) has referred to the Israeli occupation of southern Lebanon as another example. After a series of attacks by Palestinian forces based in bordering Lebanon, the Israelis moved in with a massive force in 1982 and occupied southern Lebanon. Many Arabs, according to Mueller, resented the Palestinian presence in the Middle East as much as the Israelis, and in some way they welcomed the Israelis with flowers and smiles. However, as Mueller has explained, indiscriminate Israeli brutality and arrogance quickly reversed the welcoming tone. Numerous Arab villages were overrun, and some 1900 civilians were killed in the war. The invasion of southern Lebanon forced most Palestinian fighters to flee the country, but within a year more than 5000 had returned. In 2000, Israeli forces withdrew because of the number of Israeli soldiers killed. By the time Israeli soldiers withdrew, many more of their occupying forces had been killed than terrorists had killed before 1982 (Mueller, 2005, 2006).

In another case, the Indian government massively overreacted to Sikh terrorism in 1984 by invading the Sikh's holiest place, called the Golden Temple, and used excessive military force. As a result, Sikh rage increased. Eventually, two Sikh bodyguards assassinated the Indian prime minister, and an Air India plane exploded from a bomb planted by Sikhs that caused the deaths of 329 passengers.

Double Standard

We feel that there are two standards of morality being applied . . . one for America and the West and the other for the rest.

N. Al-Musawi (Hezbollah activist)[7]

Where is the justice of political power if it executes the murderer and jails the plunderer, and then itself marches upon neighboring lands, killing thousands and pillaging the very hills?

Khalil Gibran

Eqbal Ahmad suggested that the United States avoid the practice of double standards, as the United States will receive them in return. "A superpower cannot promote terror in one place and reasonably expect to discourage terrorism in another place" (Ahmad, 2001, p. 24).[8]

Professionals and governments may illustrate an inconsistency that many find hard to trust. They occasionally discourage violence if a certain group uses it as a tactic but then make no mention of it when utilized by their own governments or allies. Post (2003) attended a workshop with Palestinian children and spoke with group facilitators on what promoted and encouraged violence (cited in Hough, 2004). He asked what are we teaching Palestinian children if we encourage or reward them for throwing stones against the Israeli enemy. Does that encourage peace or more violence? Post has commented that this type of behavior, reacting to violence with violence, results in a "training to hate and to attribute problems to the other" (Hough, 2004, p. 827). What then is to be thought of the way that Americans were encouraged to respond to 9/11 events by their own government? Did the U.S news media not proudly report the capturing or killing of potential "terrorists?" Did the U.S not then reelect a president who would fight the enemy to the bitter end, hunt them out, and capture them "dead or alive?" In the early history of the United States, American colonists defended "their" land against the British, and did more than just throw stones. It is necessary to look at this double standard. Violence is deemed to create more violence by certain groups, yet it is promoted as a profitable strategy when used to win against one's enemies.[9]

Critics suggest that the U.S. government exhibits a double standard overseas. The United States claims that the goal of invading Iraq was to bring democracy to the country, yet, conversely, the United States has supported some of the most dictatorial regimes in the Middle East (e.g. Saudi Arabia, Egypt). Apparently democracy is good for Iraq but not so good for Saudi Arabia, Egypt, or Jordan, countries with prowestern dictatorship regimes. Actually, democracy versus dictatorship is not the issue; rather, it is a question of a country's independence from the West.[10]

As many authors have documented, people in countries that have a pro-West dictatorship "hate the West," and people who are under an oppressive regime that is hostile to the United States or the United Kingdom are pro-West. It is not surprising that if western governments help an unpopular dictator, they will be hated by the oppressed people of these countries. Western governments have declared their support for democratic elections in the Middle East, yet their actions suggest this support is conditional. If these democratically elected leaders are not pro-West, then an economic boycott and covert military actions are the frequent procedures used to topple them. In 2005, President G. W. Bush was internationally criticized when he declared that President Arafat should be removed from power. Critics stated that Arafat was the democratically elected leader of Palestine and that only Palestinians had a legitimate right to remove him. The Algerian government elections serve as another example. Western countries supported a "democratic election" in Algeria, and the religious fundamentalist party of Algeria won over the military regime. The military regime did not relinquish power to the elected party, however, and western governments supported the military regime's decision to hold fast, thereby negating the "democratic election." A similar situation occurred in Palestine. Western governments did not accept the legally elected democratic government of Palestine (Hamas), and military skirmishes between Israel and Palestine increased. In this sense, the meanings of democracy and democratically elected governments are blurred. Some western governments only accept and support elected officials if the native people elect the choice of the western governments.[11, 12]

Chomsky (2001, 2002) has mentioned that in the 1980s "radical Islamic extremists," who are often called, "fundamentalists," were one of the United States favorites, "because they were the best killers who could be found." Chomsky has added that in those years, the prime enemy of the United States was the Roman Catholic Church, "which had sinned grievously in Latin America by adopting, 'the preferential option for the poor' and suffered bitterly for the crime." He has declared that "the West is quite ecumenical in its choice of enemies. The criteria are subordination and service to power, not religion" (Chomsky, 2001, 2002).

Double standards have also been evident in regard to international policies and resolutions. For example, Marsella (2003) has stated that double standards were also at work when Israel rejected the U.N. Security Council's resolution of September 23, 2002. This resolution requested a withdrawal of Israel's troops from the vicinity of President Yasser Arafat's compound and a halt to bombing. Israel dismissed the resolution. Although the United States argued that Iraq's failure to comply with U.N. resolutions justified an invasion, Israel's failure to comply had no consequence (Marsella, 2003).

For another case of conflicting policy, one can look to Iran and the United

States when the Shah of Iran fled his country and the Islamic revolution began, the Iranian government requested the Shah's return so that he could be put on trial for the alleged murder and torture of political prisoners. However, the United States politely informed the Iranian government that international law was the standard for extradition from the United States, and the government needed legal documents to prove the Shah's guilt. When the United States made a similar request of the Taliban of Afghanistan to arrest and extradite bin Laden for the 9/11 attacks, the Taliban government requested comparable documents to prove that bin Laden was responsible for 9/11 before they would comply. The United States government then initiated military strikes on Afghanistan and the Taliban government before negotiations could begin.[13]

Modern governments that practice double standards may only be repeating history. In 1917 radical journalist John Reed related how the United States was quick to point out the atrocities of the Germans, such as exploding ships of innocent people. In addition, the invasion of Belgium was seen as an offensive wrongdoing. How could the Allies explain their own similar actions, such as invading neutral Greece and Iran, the Russian atrocities that rivaled the Germans, or England's setup of exploding mines that killed ships full of innocent people (Zinn & Arnove, 2004, p. 290). Reed also asked, "Why was it a violation of international law for the Germans to establish a 'war-zone' around the British Isles, and perfectly legal for England to close the North Sea?" (Zinn & Arnove, 2004, p. 290). The propaganda created by a country at war presents its actions in the best light possible, which includes shining a disgraceful light at the actions of the opposition.

Language Distortion Concealing Double Standards

A half truth is a whole damned lie.
                                        Middle East Proverb

Political speech and writing are largely the defense of the indefensible . . . Defenseless villages are bombarded from the air, the inhabitants driven out into the countryside . . . the huts set on fire with incendiary bullets: this is called pacification.

                                        George Orwell

The use of language distortion as a strategy to advance one's own goals has historical roots. As noted by Native American Black Hawk in his dealings with early American settlers, "How smooth must be the language of the whites, when they can make right look like wrong, and wrong like right" (Nerburn & Mengelkoch, 1991, p. 12). As Heskin (1980) has explained, the difference between force (legitimate) and violence (illegitimate) makes only a little sense from a psychological point of view. We know that legitimacy is in the eyes of the beholder; therefore, "violence is what you use on me; force what I use on you" (Heskin, 1980, p. 90).

Language carries emotional weight. To understand the literature and reports on suicide bombers one must understand the denotative language used as well as the connotative message. Bandura (2003) has written that a person's thoughts, positive or negative, are based largely on the language used to describe a situation. Action or opinion, then, is affected by those thoughts. He referred to Lutz's comment in 1987 that "euphemistic language is used widely to make harmful conduct respectable and to reduce personal responsibility for it" (Lutz, 1987). Professor Ralph Slovenko (2005) noted that euphemisms that mislead or deceive are known as doublespeak (or words of mass deception). Slovenko has aptly stated that "Euphemisms provide clean words which are used to cover atrocious deeds" (p. 547); for example, removing responsibility from the attacking nation is called a "preemptive strike." "Euphemism" derives from the Greek words "eu," meaning good, and "pheme," meaning saying or speech; therefore meaning to speak with good words. A dysphemism is defined as an expression that is offensive (Slovenko, 2005).[14]

Several authors, such as Slovenko (2005), Gambino (1973), Bandura (2003) and others have identified several varieties of euphemistic language. When language is "sanitized," the word killed is changed to wasted, bomb is changed to vertical anti-personal device, civilian deaths become collateral damage, and soldiers mistakenly killed by their own troops become victims of friendly fire (Gambino, 1973). A governmental cover up of illegal operations or questionable conduct is called damage control or containment. President George H. Bush committed to "no new taxes" ("read my lips") in his campaign speeches yet acknowledged that he would "seek new revenues" (Slovenko, 2005). Some of the news media reported that President Nixon's assistants relayed that Nixon never gave the order to kill Castro or other Cuban Leaders; instead he used the words "get rid of them."

During Reagan's presidency, the U.S. government policy of support for South Africa was termed constructive engagement even though South Africa was the leading terrorist state in the 1980s. This government terrorized its black population and was funding terrorist organizations in other African states such as RENAMO in Mozambique (Herman, 2002). As Herman has pointed out, the United States actively supported UNITA in Angola (close allies to the apartheid government of South Africa) while condemning the PLO for its terrorist actions. The U.S. news media, however, never described the Reagan War as a "war of terrorism," even though the United States supported the Cuban terrorist network, the Contras in Nicaragua, Savimibi in Angola, and other terrorist activities (Herman, 2002). "The operative rule for the press . . . terrorism is what the U.S. government says is terrorism, however bad the fit to any definition you might name . . . the media and experts were serving as an arm of government policy" (Herman, 2002).[15]

Bandura (2003, p. 125) has reported that bin Laden also uses this technique by referring to terrorist acts as the "winds of faith." The Israeli invasion of Lebanon in the summer of 2006 was coded euphemistically as "Summer Rain." The code name for the Nazi extermination of Jews was called "Operation Harvest Festival." Harre (2003) has mentioned that the words we choose can entrap our beliefs. Syntax and semantics clearly influence our thoughts, especially when we speak of terrorism (Harre, 2003).

It is significant to note, then, the extent of distortion embedded in military-style language. For example, the invasion of Iraq was called a war. Even the bombing of Serbia was labeled a humanitarian intervention, according to Chomsky (2001, 2002, p. 14). Government lies have been termed disinformation or misspeak, while the torture of detainees is called tough interrogation. Military activities strikingly similar to terrorism are called low intensity warfare in official military manuals.

War propaganda is the label for lies and deception that governments use to deceive the enemy but not the government's own people (unless they are also considered an enemy or if the government wants to hide the true nature of its activities).[16] Political scientist Michael Stohl has noted that "coercive diplomacy" is used to describe a great power threatening to use force, as opposed to a form of terrorism (Chomsky, 2001, 2002, p. 16). During the first Gulf War, the government spoke of smart bombs that were programmed to strike only the intended target–regardless of the presence of civilians. If civilians got in the way, the result was labeled collateral damage, not "the deaths of innocent people." Similarly, Gambino (1973) has pointed out how the military spoke positively of surgical strikes, meaning that a target was as finely distinguished as a critical cut made by a surgeon.[17] The intended effect was to connect a life-saving medical procedure to government-sanctioned killing. The use of the passive voice also influences the way a listener perceives a thought, while absolving the speaker from blame. "Mistakes were made," for instance, does not identify the person responsible for the mistake. "I made a mistake" is much more difficult to say.

In implicating the terminology of the American news media in covering the Arab-Israeli conflict, Fisk (2005) commented that "occupied territories" changed to "disputed territories," Jewish illegal settlements transformed to Jewish "neighborhoods," Palestinian militants became "terrorists," and Israeli militants were just "extremists" or "fanatics." Civilian casualties caused by Israeli armies are described as "caught in the crossfire" (Cohn, 2002). In the same manner, Donald Rumsfeld, former U.S. Secretary of Defense, used the words "so-called occupied territories," which many challenged, including former President Jimmy Carter, who wrote a letter protesting the use of "so-called."

Shergald (2007) has pointed out that the United States is the only country in the West to categorize Hamas and Hezbollah as "terrorists," seemingly forgetting that these groups were created to fight military occupation by Israel. European countries on the other hand, refer to these groups as militants, resisters, or even freedom fighters. Because of this difference, CNN broadcasters have used different terms to describe these groups' activities depending on if they are reporting to the United States or Europe (Shergald, 2007).[18]

Further, in 2006 when Lebanese or Palestinians captured one or two Israeli soldiers, the western news media labeled it kidnapping. Television reporters sympathetically interviewed the parents of these captured soldiers; but critics claim that the same news media ignored the Israeli capture of as many as 10,000 Palestinians (300 of them children) and 1000 Lebanese (being held without trial). Israel even captured a Palestinian-elected official, but the word kidnapping was only applied to the Arab group action. In a similar pattern, critics claim when Israeli civilians are killed, the act is called terrorism, but when the Israeli army kills Palestinian civilians, it is labeled as self-defense. The western news media has been accused by critics as being reluctant to mention words such as *settlers in occupied territories, violation of U.N. resolutions*, and *Geneva Convention* when referring to the Israeli government.

Doctor Toine van Teeffele (2003) has reported that in western news media, Palestinian victims are less prominently reported than are Israeli victims. For example, when the news media reports that there is a period of calm, it means that there are no Israeli victims; at the same time there may be numerous Palestinian victims. The Palestinian violence is dramatized. However, the illegitimacy of the Israeli occupation and the structural violence inherent in it are deemphasized. The occupied territories in Palestine are labeled as disputed. Doctor van Teeffele has mentioned that such linguistic representation of the Middle East clash steers the readers' understanding of the cause and effect relationship and their interpretations of the conflict (van Teeffele, 2003).

The previous examples illustrate that the target is what actually determines the label, regardless of the atrocities or violence. Therefore the issue seems to be who you kill, not how you kill or why you kill.[19]

THE ISSUE OF ISRAEL AND PALESTINE

Jews did not climb out of the gas chambers to be oppressors of another people. The deepest values of our people have been shaped by the history of our own oppression; yet in the past weeks we've become brutalizers without constraints .

Rabbi Michael Lerner[20]

Looking at the broader aspect of the Middle East conflict, we see that numerous experts have expressed the need for the Israel-Palestine conflict to be resolved before any lasting peace is found. It is believed that this resolution will untie the knot of terrorism. In addition, politicians such as Tony Blair, Britain's previous Prime Minister, have confirmed that "brokering an Israeli-Palestinian peace deal would help diminish the anger fueling Islamic militants in places outside the Middle East. . . . This global extremism is an ideology that exploits grievances" (Stringer, 2006). Blair's comments were echoed by Pakistan President Musharraf, who mentioned that these issues of terrorism took a generation to grow and may possibly take a generation to be defeated (Stringer, 2006).

The paradoxical nature of the news media and official government policies is a troubling phenomenon in the West and the East. Middle East news media rarely criticize Arab extremist violence toward Israel. Furthermore, at times they can totally ignore the positive aspect of U.S. policies, such as when the United States helped Bosnian Muslims through their attack on the former Yugoslavia. Alternately, rarely is there criticism of the Israeli regime by U.S. officials or the western mainstream media. In fact, there is more criticism of Israel's government policies by Israeli congressmen than by any member of the U.S. Congress.

Marsella (2003) has suggested that although disproportionate Western support toward Israel may bring Israel closer to the West, it serves to inflame Arab hatred and widens its separation from the West. For example, one of the U.S. presidents attended several memorials for Israeli children who were killed in the conflict by Palestinians. Yet he never attended memorials or acknowledged any of the Palestinian children who were killed. Some Middle East analysts have called this behavior racism, although we believe it more resembles a double standard. Marsella thus concludes, "It is only a matter of time before terrorists decide to move beyond Israel to attack Jews and Israel's supporters throughout the globe" (Marsella, 2003, p. 13). This notion is similar to one held by the International Jewish Solidarity Network (2006), which has stated, "Israel's tactics of fueling hatred and inciting fear, not least where tolerance and coexistence were once longstanding rules, cannot ensure Jewish safety but will endanger the lives of Israeli citizens and residents and of Jews around the globe."

John Gershman, co-director of Foreign Policy in Focus for the Interhemispheric Resource Center, has affirmed that present U.S. policies make Americans more vulnerable rather than more secure. "There is a distinction between Israel's right to exist and support for the occupation in the West Bank and Gaza." Washington's continued approval of the occupation, however, adds fuel to anti-American sentiments, which terrorists use to their advantage. To improve the situation, Gershman has described specific initiatives that include ending U.S. financial and military assistance for the occupation, promoting Palestinian self-determination, setting a timetable for U.S. troop withdrawal, and channeling reconstruction and development efforts through the United Nations (Gershman, 2006).

The president of Syria, Bashar Al Assad, has stated recently, "Every new Arab generation hates Israel more than the previous one" (Avnery, 2006). Although Avnery, an Israeli intellectual, has said that Al Assad may not be one of the world's greatest thinkers, the thirty-three days of the Israeli war in Lebanon in 2006 should give pause for thought. He has cited mangled bodies of babies, woman weeping over the ruins of their homes, Israeli children writing "greetings" on the shells about to be fired at villages, and Israeli leaders talking about "the most moral army in the world" while television showed a heap of bodies (Avnery, 2006).[21]

Avnery (2006), a former member of the Israeli Knesset (Parliament), has reported that feelings of pity and empathy for non-Jews in Middle East have been blunted in the United States for a long time. He compared the whole Zionist enterprise to an organ transplant. A person's natural immunity system normally fights the "foreign" tissue, so doctors use powerful medications to overcome the rejection of the newly implanted organ. One wonders if Avnery might illustrate this analogy with the Middle East as the patient and Israel as the foreign tissue. The United States is the doctor attempting to stabilize this union with support and arms. Avnery stated this battle may continue indefinitely, sometimes until the eventual death of the body, as well as the transplant organ (Avnery, 2006).

Avishai Margalit, an Israeli writer, has pointed out that suicide bombing has indeed hurt Israel severely, not only in human lives, but with the result that "Israel may now be the most hated country in the world." Moreover, "throughout the world . . . the suicide bombings have often been taken more as a sign of desperation of the Palestinians than as acts of terror" (Margalit, 2003).

Rabbi Michael Lerner wrote more on this subject in the *Los Angeles Times* in 2001. Every human being is created in the image of God, Lerner has written, and the brutality toward the Palestinian people is as much a tragedy as the brutality carried out by Palestinian terrorists on Israelis (Lerner, 2001). He has admitted that some Jews insist that "no suffering is like our suffering" and their past suffering warrants present insensitivity to the Palestinian people. Many of these Jews are unwilling to acknowledge that Israel is the only party in this struggle with an army. Moreover, Palestinians have had ten times as many deaths as Israelis, and Palestinian people are enclosed in small areas as Jews once were, denied food, education, and medical care. Lerner has stated that it seems so much easier to blame the victims and become angry at the messengers who are raising serious moral objection to Israel's behavior (Lerner, 2001).

Many concerned Muslims and Jews have jointly expressed their feelings that unconditional (and blind) support for all Israeli government activities is detrimental to Jews, Israel, and the West. Through the use of its veto power in any U.N. resolution or discussion that may point to a wrongdoing by Israel, the United States is engaging in a double standard while undermining the United Nations.

If Palestinians used the techniques of Nelson Mandela, Gandhi or Martin L. King Jr., would it be possible for them to "disarm" the rightwing Israeli militants? Reacting with violence has shown to only increase violence. Some years ago there were indications that some Israeli citizens explored the history of the establishment of Israel and discovered that some Palestinian villagers were victimized and coerced by Israel into leaving their land (rather than by legitimate means). This discovery could have eventually encouraged sympathy toward Palestinians as victims. When the Intifada (Palestinian uprising) started, however, the violence changed many people's mindset, negating the view of Palestinians as civilian victims.

In conclusion, peace in the Middle East cannot be accomplished without a fair and legitimate solution for the Arab-Israeli conflict. To resolve this conflict, supporters of both sides may need to look more objectively at this situation. In doing so, each side may be able to acknowledge its own mistakes and work to right its own wrongs; as opposed to simply blaming the other side, which accomplishes very little.

STATE-SPONSORED TERRORISM AND STATE-CAUSED TERRORISM

I love America more than any other Country in this world, and exactly for this reason, I insist on the right to criticize her perpetually.
James Baldwin (Notes of a Native Son)

Perhaps the so-called dark ages will be thought of as including our own.
Lichtenberg

State-sponsored terrorism is a widely accepted term to define the government's involvement in terrorism. We would like to suggest a second category, state-caused terrorism, to further identify government involvement.

State-Sponsored Terrorism

State-sponsored terrorism has been documented in Third World countries. In El Salvador, in November of 1989, six priests and two of their colleagues were assassinated on the campus of the University of Central America (UCA). The assassination was reportedly organized and conducted by the Atlacatl Battalion, an elite army unit that was established, equipped and trained by the U.S. government (Emam, 2006). In another example of state-sponsored terrorism, the U.S., Pakistani, and Saudi Arabian governments supported bin Laden and Taliban militants while fighting a pro-Soviet Union government in Afghanistan. Many civilians, intellectuals and nationalists were massacred.

Government policies can have as great an impact as military support does in contributing to terrorism. Montiel and Anuar (2002) have asserted that U.S. policies have promoted global poverty, which has cultivated resentment that lead to terrorism. They have charged that these policies have perpetuated U.S. dominance and exploitation of developing countries. Further they have suggested that the United States has grown to be a leader in state-sponsored terrorism because of its support for rightist groups who have destabilized legitimate governments in South and Central America and the Middle East. Several other writers, including Noam Chomsky, have echoed that idea (Chomsky & Achcar, 2007).

Montiel and Anuar (2002) have further pointed out that Israel is also a government that has practiced state-sponsored terrorism. At one time the Israeli government supported the activist Palestinian group Hamas, to counterbalance the perceived secular success of the PLO. This attempt to support an Islamic religious group ultimately wounded Israel. Hamas subsequently established social services that supported Arab communities. Israel's attempt to then label Hamas as a terrorist group due to its aggression against Israelis is similar to the switch the U.S. government made in regard to bin Laden and Al-Qaeda (Montiel & Anuar, 2002, p. 203). The United States originally supported bin Laden and the Taliban regime against the Russian Army in Afghanistan.

State-Caused Terrorism

The phenomenon of state-caused terrorism, occurs when a government, with the intention of fighting terrorism, actually causes more terrorism, or their actions further entice terrorists and thereby diminish that government's own image in the world. An example of state-caused terrorism is depicted humorously in a caricature in *The Hartford Courant* (Oliphant, 2006): bin Laden and his assistant are resting in a cave and talking to each other. The assistant says to bin Laden, "Isn't it wonderful . . . the more Bush talks, the less we have to do."

Although President Bush's statement in defense of his policy declared that "you do not create terrorism by fighting terrorism," available evidence seems to suggest otherwise (Raum, 2006). For example, a *National Intelligence Estimate* document produced in April 2006 gave the testimony and findings of sixteen government agencies with their consensus of the effect of the U. S. government's war on terror in the Arab world. Parts of the document were leaked to the public in the fall of 2006. This report stated that the war on terror in Iraq has made America less safe and has increased the number of terrorists.

Furthermore, according to a *Providence Journal* editorial from October 1, 2006 (Projo.com), the war in Iraq has actually multiplied the number of "Islamist terrorists" and freelancers recruited into violent organizations. The use of unlimited detentions at Guantánamo Bay, along with the U. S. government's rejection of the ban on torture from the Geneva Convention, and Abu Gharaib prison images of tortured Iraqis have deterred potential U. S. allies. The United States' actions have actually helped develop new terrorist organizations inspired by the work of bin Laden. As General Colin Powell has noted, by disregarding the Geneva Convention, the U. S. administration could make others "doubt the moral basis of our fight against terrorism" (Projo.com, 2006).

ARE WE LEARNING FROM HISTORY OR JUST LEARNING TO REPEAT IT?

> *Vietnam [war] was hopeless enough but to repeat the same arrogant folly 30 years later in Iraq is unforgivable. The Swedish statesman, Axel Oxenstierna, famously said, "Behold, my son, with how little wisdom the world is governed."*
>
> Arthur M. Schlesinger (2007)

In a satirical broadcast in November 2006, U.S. radio host Jerry Klein suggested that all Muslims be identified with a distinctive crescent sign. He was amazed at the vehemence and vituperative comments from many listeners who not only supported the idea but also suggested that Muslims be incarcerated in camps and be forced to live in exile. He then revealed that his initial statement was made to completely mock this idea. Through this experience, Klein has stated he could see the similarity between how Muslims are being viewed in recent times and the sentiments many Germans had about Jews in WWII (Debusmann, 2006). It is sad and incredible to see how the technique that the Nazis used to "brand" Jews could be seen, by some, as an appropriate action against Muslims today. It is clear that despite the horror of the Holocaust, many people have missed a vital lesson from that period. We maintain that western governments could learn much from history's lessons, specifically from the experience of Iran at the time of the Shah's regime. Citizens during this time were requesting freedom of speech and freedom of the press. In response to their appeals, the Shah and his regime closed down the news media and journals that printed mild criticism and oppositional ideas. Then the Shah banned the competitive political party, and he changed the parliamentary structure to a one-party system. It was reported that he felt that no one should criticize his regime so there was no need for two parties. When all the nonviolent means of protest and resistance had failed, small groups of dissidents took up arms and started a guerrilla movement in the "Siahgal" jungle against the regime. The Iranian government, rather than considering this development as a wake-up call and exploring the causes of the uprising, became more oppressive. The Security Service (SAVAK) arrested and jailed some of the opponents who criticized the government.[22] Eventually, several of these militants were killed by SAVAK during the crackdown or were executed after trials on charges of armed resistance. A few of these militants at their trial bravely defended their uprising and issued the now famous statement: "From every drop of our blood, a militant will be created." History has revealed that their prediction was right. As the Iranian regime continued to execute them, their numbers increased. The regime blamed "outsiders" who gave the militants training or arms, but it never explored the rationale of people sacrificing their lives or the source of their message, pain, or grievance.

LIMITING CIVIL LIBERTIES, A SIDE EFFECT OF COUNTERTERRORISM

Those who give up essential liberties for temporary safety deserve neither liberty nor safety.

Benjamin Franklin

Terrorist attacks may have several political ramifications. During such a crisis some citizens inevitably will protest that government responses infringe upon human rights and limit civil liberties. Our observations have indicated that terrorized populations gradually tolerate that sacrifice, especially if they believe it will make them safer. Atran (2003) has quoted Carmichael (1982), who stated that "democratic societies face the monumental moral dilemma of how to justify countermeasures that are taken to stop terrorist atrocities without violating the values of the society, in defense of those values."

The United States currently faces such a dilemma: the Patriot Act (Public Law 107-56) is considered by many human rights activists as abusive and un-American, giving the executive branch too much power over people. Although the intent of this law was to protect the United States, the actual provisions of the act expanded the authority of law enforcement in many areas in order to increase security. The law has not been without its critics, especially in the areas of the "sneak and peek" searches and claims of infringement upon freedom of speech, freedom of the press, human rights, and the right to privacy (*Wikipedia Encyclopedia*: USA Patriot Act). Olivier (2007) has maintained that in theory this act was meant to be preventative. The government would monitor Americans phone calls and e-mails to sabotage any possible planning of future attacks against the United States. Yet a truly preventive act, she has stated, would start by inquiring why there are people from other countries, or even within the U.S., who would want to attack America in the first place (Olivier, 2007).

Some U.S. citizens are already asking whether the government's measures against terrorism are too extreme. What is the balance between fighting terrorism and protecting civil liberties? Some Americans have expressed fears that their government is being too intrusive in their lives and some measures threaten individual freedoms. A Gallup Poll in 2005 (Saad, 2005) revealed that most of Americans disapprove of government access to massive databases that contain records of billions of telephone calls made by ordinary citizens. Approximately two-thirds of those who were interviewed are worried that the program may be an indication of another not-yet-disclosed method of obtaining personal information. Even political candidates are concerned that incumbent government officials may obtain e-mail messages and communication information on their opponents' private and professional lives, thereby exposing challengers' election strategies. Human rights activists have also avowed that governments allowed a victory for the terrorists by limiting civil liberties. The enemy was able to successfully change our society from a free and liberal state to a police state in which law enforcement officials have unlimited authority over its citizens. Opposition to this change may be one of the main reasons that the "torture proposal" was rejected in the U.S. Congress despite personal campaigns from the White House for its approval (Zinn & Arnove, 2004). Citizens in other countries have also protested their nation's inhumane policies. There are, for example, Israeli citizens who were disturbed that their own government violated human rights and spoke out against these violations (see the websites for Rabbis against torture [www.rabbisagainsttorture.com] and Rabbis for Human Rights [www.rhr.israel.net]). Such opposition supports the adage "in the time of war, the worst mistake is silence."

Other political ramifications of an act like the Patriot Act include an increase in racist sentiments against people of Middle East origins. Olivier (2007) has commented that there are certain Americans who believe that a slight decrease in their civil liberties is a small price to pay for being kept "safe." In response, she has asked if Americans are actually safer from this act and, more specifically, which Americans are safer. It is likely, she has commented, that the people who are willing to "give up" certain freedoms for safety are citizens who do not need to fear that their specific rights will be compromised by the Patriot Act. As Olivier has noted, "a brown skinned, U.S. citizen, attending Mosque, wearing a turban, named Hussein, has a much greater chance of being arrested, then a white male named Johnson, who goes to church" (Olivier, 2007).

Minority communities of many diverse religions and ethnicities have also suffered from the war on terror in the United States. It has allowed more subtle and indirect expression of racism and discrimination. The declaration of this war gave government officials complete freedom to disregard the individual rights of its citizens (Taneja, 2006). This increased discrimination was exactly what Congresswoman Barbara Lee was afraid would happen (Lee, 2007). Three days after September 11, 2001, Lee gave a speech to Congress expressing her opposition to the United States's "Use of Force Act," which was basically a go ahead to President Bush to wage war. She was the only member of Congress to vote against this act (Lee, 2007). Lee cautioned the United States in stating that Americans cannot let their justified anger, "inflame prejudice against all Arab Americans, Muslim, Southeast Asian, and any other people because of their race, religion, or ethnicity" (Lee, 2001). In her near-prophetic words she stated, "I am convinced that military action will not prevent further acts of international terrorism against the United States" (Lee, 2001).

Other countries besides the United States have participated in this type of violation of citizen's rights with similar consequences. The Australian Security Intelligence Organization, for example, has demonstrated its disregard for private citizens' rights. In 2002, after the Bali bombings, forty Muslims were incarcerated without due process. In 2003, the Australian Human Rights Commission reported more than 1400 incidences of racism, abuse, and violent behavior against Muslims since 9/11 (Taneja, 2006).

The limiting of civil liberties is not a new method used by governments. Zinn and Arnove (2004) have noted that in WWI, governments passed legislation that placed antiwar protesters in prison. Using the Espionage Act of 1917 and the Sedition Act of 1918, the government sent close to 1000 people to prison for expressing their opinions against the war; many of them were labor activists and radicals. This prison list included socialist Helen Keller. Although the Espionage Act was passed by the U.S. Congress to prevent spying, it was used to silence American critics of the war (Davis, 2003, p. 314). In 1918 the socialist leader and presidential candidate, Eugene Debs, was arrested and sentenced to ten years in jail for making a speech that "obstructed recruiting." He received support from many notable Americans, especially Helen Keller, who wrote, "I want you to know that I should be proud if the Supreme Court convicted me of abhorring war, and doing all in my power to oppose it" (Davis, 2003, p. 318). Debs ran for President again in 1920 from prison. After thirty-two months in jail he was pardoned by President Harding (Davis, 2003).

In April of 1917, John Reed wrote an article entitled "Whose War?" in which he spoke out against WWI. He stated, "War means an ugly mob-madness, crucifying the truth-tellers, choking the artists, side tracking reforms" (Zinn & Arnove, 2004, p. 289). In addition, he pointed out that citizens who opposed entering the war were called "traitors." Those who protested curtailing of free speech were labeled as "dangerous lunatics." He complained about censorship in the news media and mentioned "The press is howling for war. The church is howling for war. Lawyers, politicians, stockbrokers, social leaders are all howling for war" (Zinn & Arnove, 2004, p. 289). John Reed added that poor men were sent to jail for long terms without trial and even without any charge. Peaceful strikers and their families were shot to death. These people did not want the war. He asked the question, "Whose War is this? Not mine."

CONCLUSION

Only the dead have seen the end of war.
Plato

Of one Essence is the human race,
Thusly has Creation put the Base;
One Limb impacted is sufficient,
For all Others to feel the Mace.
Saadi Shirazi (13th century CE Persian poet)[23]

War of any kind reawakens our animalistic and "primary process" thoughts. Even though our civilized minds know that war instigates more conflicts and "killing brings more killing." Researchers have worried that it will only be after another nuclear bomb has been dropped in a battlefield that people will get the message and wonder if a world without war must be made a possibility. As Albert Einstein stated, "I know not with what weapons World War III will be fought, but World War IV will be fought with sticks and stones, indicating the end of civilization" (Angier, 2003). War historians have stated that there was only a brief 100-year period of world peace, from A.D. 100 to 200, which was due to "the Roman Empire's having everyone, fleetingly, in a thrall" (Angier, 2003).

Governments continue to use military-focused counterterrorism as a quick fix for stopping terrorist attacks. Yet Olivier (2007) has concluded that the United States's reaction to 9/11 has created "enemies abroad, and discontented people within our borders." The U.S. government had two buildings destroyed and, in response, ended up destroying two countries. Olivier has stated that Americans, like any other nation's citizens, want their government to protect them from harm. Yet "how" America becomes a safer country for all of its citizens is a controversial topic. Any true solution may depend more on the U.S. government's international policies, than on its national ones (Olivier, 2007). Negotiation, compromise, and recognition of the perceived injustices of the combatants could be the beginning of the peace process as documented by many professionals in the field. It has been suggested that governments expand their objectives and prioritize the resolution of the political, social, and economic discord of our contemporary world, which would be the ultimate long-term solution to terrorism, so that we can avoid "digging two graves."

NOTES

1. As Soros has mentioned, it is easy to see where Israeli policy went wrong: None of the points of peace were implemented, contributing to Hamas' victory. The U.S. administration at that time, having pushed Israel to allow the Palestinians to hold elections, then backed Israel's refusal to deal with Hamas government. The effect was to impose further hardship on the Palestinians (Soros, 2006a).
2. As Soros has mentioned, the time has come to realize that current policies are counterproductive. Israelis must realize that a military strategy is not sufficient. The Palestinian people yearn for peace and relief from suffering (2006a).
3. John Gershman (2006) has presented recommendations to change current U.S. policy. Gershman suggests a "new framework," a coordinated strategy to counterterrorism (p. 239): Strengthen international and national legal systems to hold terrorists accountable by expanding international cooperation; adopt prosecution principles for crimes against humanity; strengthen international law tribunals; provide global technical assistance to prevent financial support; defend and promote democracy at home and abroad by reevaluating the Patriot Act of 2001; proactively limit international human rights violations through established courts; attack root causes by addressing the socioeconomic, political issues from which terrorism emerges; clarify differences between Al-Qaeda and other terrorist causes; change the "war on Islam" to a "war on terrorism," not a war on religion; end support for repressive regimes; deal with failed military operations by appropriate withdrawals; enhance the U.N. role for peacekeeping; reorient the U.S. policy in the Middle East and Central Asia (Gershman, 2006).

4. Doctor Hamid Dabashi, a Columbia University professor discussed both Samuel Huntington's concept and also that presented by Francis Fukuyama (once employed with the U. S. Department of State). He criticized Huntington's assertion that there should still be one more victory over Islam as well as Fukuyama's phrasing that "the West had won and the Rest had lost" (p. 212). Dabashi characterized Huntington's concept as one of "fabricated civilizational categories" (p. 4) and Fukuyama's idea that history has ended because "Western liberal democracy" (p. 3) had triumphed over its political alternatives as a short-sighted analysis of world events (from H. Dabashi [2007]. *Iran: A People Interrupted*, New York: The New Press).

5. If we followed Huntington's cultural line of thinking then one could conclude that Israel and Palestine would have always been doomed to military conflict. It has been suggested that despite military occupation, however, violent retaliation was not the only method considered by Palestinians. Polls taken by Palestinians illustrated that they had been very open to focusing on a peace process with Israel as opposed to becoming suicide bombers for years after the 1993 Oslo peace accord. This accord "brought limited self-rule to the Palestinians and the prospect of an independent state." It was when the peace process appeared to be breaking down in 2000 and the second Intifada began, that would be suicide bombers began to proliferate (Rees & Jala, 2002; Shergald, 2007).

6. In addition, as Herman has pointed out, President Bush has increased military production, pursing a National Missile Defense program that promotes the use of nuclear weapons in warfare. "Terrorism includes not just killing but instilling fear and these plans . . . project U.S. power by producing fear of noncompliance with U.S. demands. . . . [These types of projects will encourage] even more violence and terrorism because they will divert resources from human needs at home and abroad" (Herman, 2002).

7. Nawaf al-Musawi, a Hezbollah representative, said in an interview, "We condemn the killing of civilians, all civilians–Americans and Muslims alike–why were all those voices of humanity and morale silent when Israel bombed and massacred Lebanese and Palestinian civilians? Where was the American public opinion and conscience?" (from F. A. Gerges [2006]. Inside Muslim Militancy. *Journey of the Jihadist* (pp. 186-187). New York: Harcourt, Inc.)

8. In the Iraq war, western news media and the American government objected to Arab television broadcasting pictures of dead U.S. soldiers. They stated that this was against the Geneva Convention. Yet within hours of the deaths of Saddam's sons, the U.S. government released horrific images of the two dead brothers for the entire world to view. As Tim Predmore has mentioned, this is a "do as we say, and not as we do" scenario (Zinn & Arnove, 2004, p. 615).

9. Double standards are not limited to government officials and the news media. Special interest groups and citizen activists also exhibit this two-sidedness. For example, antigun control movements in the United States have supported the deregulation of weapons as exemplified in the slogan "guns don't kill people, people kill people." Conversely progun lobbyists have agreed that the number

of terrorists could be diminished by controlling their guns, ammunition, and money. Such lobbyists have suggested finding out who gives the terrorists the guns, rather than who causes their anger, rage, and revenge. It would be more appropriate if attention were focused on determining the source of hatred, humiliation, victimization, and need for revenge–the very roots of terrorism.

10. In 1999, a military coup by General Musharraf ended democracy in Pakistan. The major U.S. news media reported that Musharraf was a pro-west general and again revealed their double standards by supporting (legitimizing) this coup rather than denouncing it. In the fall of 2007 civilians demonstrated against the dictatorship governments in both Myanmar and Pakistan. The main U.S. news media exaggerated the demonstrations in Myanmar which resulted in a request by western governments to the United Nations to investigate the issues. The U.N. then sent a delegation to Myanmar. However, the brutal suppression of civilians (most of them educated professionals) in Pakistan was ignored.

11. This situation developed in reverse in Nicaragua during the 1980s. The Socialist Party, which the U.S. government resented, released government control to the elected opposing party, but after twenty years, Socialist party was reelected to take leadership.

12. As historians such as Doctor Fakhreddin Azimi have documented, the goal of the 1953 CIA coup in Iran (which resulted in the overthrow of the Iranian national hero, Doctor Mosaddeq) was not only to settle the issue of the western wish for oil, but "also to subvert the very desires and struggles of the Iranians to achieve national sovereignty and move in a democratic direction." From the coup organizers (CIA and domestic supporters) Iran was "saved" as part of the "free world," but as Doctor Azimi (2004, p. 101) explained "it began to deny its citizens basic political freedoms" and established a brutal pro-west dictatorship. Unseating Mosaddeq: The Configuration and Role of Domestic Forces in M. J. Gasiorowski & M. Byrne (Eds.), *Mohammad Mosaddeq and the 1953 Coup in Iran*, [pp. 27–101]. Syracuse, NY: Syracuse University Press).

13. In another case, former Haitian dictator Emmanuel Constant was tried and convicted by the present Haitian government in the deaths of more than 4000 innocent people. Because Constant currently resides in the United States, Haitians have asked for his extradition. Chomsky has stated, that despite documentation, the United States will not allow extradition because Constant has been supported by both the Bush and the Clinton administrations (Chomsky, 2001).

14. Our words and thoughts can have even farther reaching effects, as suggested by these poetical verses:

> *Watch your thoughts, they become words.*
> *Watch your words, they become actions.*
> *Watch your actions, they become habits.*
> *Watch your habits, they become character.*
> *Watch your character, for it becomes your Destiny*
> (author unknown)

15. In another example, when bin Laden and Taliban fighters jointly fought the pro-Soviet puppet government in Afghanistan to gain back their land, they initiated suicide missions, atrocities, and human rights' violations while killing civilians (e.g., the bombing of the technical college of Kabul) and eventually forced the Soviet Union to leave their country. The West supported their actions because they too were against the Soviet Union. Yet after conquering Afghanistan, the Taliban, who were labeled "freedom fighters" by the Western media, established the fanatical religious government that continued similar atrocities. Interestingly, the reverse labeling occurred in the Middle East when Israel occupied southern Lebanon in the early 1980s. The partisan resistance movement (Hezbollah) that developed to regain its own land and independence was labeled by the western media as "terrorism" and not "freedom fighting." Although both organizations (Taliban and Hezbollah) have used the same means for fighting and had similar goals, the West has labeled the two differently.

    It is important to note that in the first few days of Taliban victory, Taliban members killed ten Iranian diplomats. Western media did not refer to this violence as "terrorism" (at the time, the Taliban had enormous financial and military backing from the United States and other prowestern regimes).

16. In March of 2007, the Pentagon announced its "misstep" regarding the distortion in reporting the death of Army Ranger Pat Tillman. For the first eleven days after his death, his family and the nation were told persistently that Tillman was killed in a conventional ambush, even though several soldiers knew at the time of his death that this was not the case. The use of the word "misstep" softens the more blunt, yet accurate words, "cover up." (From L. C. Baldor [2007, March 24–25]. Pentagon finds missteps after Tillman's death. *Manchester Journal Inquirer*.)

17. In the winter of 2007, fifteen British marines and sailors were arrested by the Iranian government while their military boat was in Iranian waters (as the Iranian government claimed). Western news media reported this event as the "Illegal arrest of 15 British sailors." Attention was not given to whose "law" was being violated. If it was international law, then the presence of British sailors in that area was by itself illegal, because the United Nations never endorsed the invasion of Iraq. The western news media also ignored a statement from the Iraqi general, who stated that British sailors were in Iranian territory. In addition, several mainstream U.S. news media did not report on what was uncovered during the British media's interviews with the sailors. During these interviews, the sailors stated that their mission was to spy on Iranian activities.

18. *The Washington Times* reported that a Syrian singer and his band were detained by the FBI terrorism task force during a recent flight to Los Angeles (from A. Hudson [2004, July 29]. Syrian music star sings praise of suicide bombers. *The Washington Times* [On-line].Retrieved January 7, 2007. Available: www.washingtontimes.com). The singer had written a song about the "glorification" of suicide bombers liberating Palestine, ending with chants of "Allah Akbar" which means "God is great," a common Muslim expression. However, Hudson

also reported that "those were the last words shouted by September 11 hijackers before the plane crashed into the Pennsylvania field and have been the last words of many suicide bombers in Israel." One may assume that the reporter was connecting this common Muslim expression of praise of God to hijacking and terrorism, especially since the article did not mention that the expression had been used by Afghan freedom fighters that attacked the Soviet Union Red Army. They gave their lives to eradicate possible Communism from Afghanistan with the help of the U.S. government. When the Afghanis said, "God is Great" while attacking the Red Army, they were considered "Muslim freedom fighters" by the western news media.

19. Jerrold Post (2003, as cited in Hough, 2004) has spoken of the resistance by the Algerians of a French takeover. Although Post has acknowledged that this was an anticolonial struggle, he labeled the Algerians, who were fighting for their homeland, a "small group of terrorists" (p. 821). When counter actions were taken by the French, more individuals joined "the terrorist network," as Post has described it (Hough, 2004, p. 821). Yet it is clear Algerians were fighting against the colonization by the French; they were second-class citizens in their own land. Eventually, the French left Algeria when it was clear they could not win (Hough, 2004). When Algeria became independent, many of the people Post had referred to as "terrorists" became the leaders of Algeria and were respected by the United Nations and the global community. How similar is this situation to a young America fighting off the British? Americans were fighting for their freedom; would George Washington also be considered a terrorist?

20. For more information on Rabbi Michael Lerner's writing, please see www.tikkon.org. This quotation refers to the invasion of Lebanon by the Israeli army.

21. As Baroud has pointed out, for those who receive only half of the news coming from the Middle East, Israeli "checkpoints" may sound like a logical idea (from R. Baroud [2006] T*he Second Palestinian Intifada: A Chronicle of a People's Struggle* London: Pluto Press). How else can Israel contain the crimes committed by Palestinians and potentially slow the rate of bombers into Israel's vulnerable state? U. N. Envoy Terje Roed-Larsen on a visit to the Middle East showed a sharp contrast in recommendations given to Palestine and Israel. Palestinians were urged to stop terrorism and reform their political governance, while Israel was encouraged to "ease travel restrictions" (p. 68). Larsen did however acknowledge that"Israeli roadblocks and checkpoints were 'the single largest impediment to the Palestinian economy'" (pp. 68–69). Yet Baroud has questioned if this whole Middle East conflict is thus believed to be about removing a few checkpoints. In his own words, "Checkpoints are indeed provocative and frustrating, but Mahmoud Annani didn't choose to blow himself up near an Israeli military base in Gaza because he couldn't stand the long wait in a taxi near an Israeli army checkpoint" (p. 70). Baroud has illustrated another example of blatant favoritism. Douglas Feith, U.S. Undersecretary of Defense for Policy, has commented that "Israel will always maintain a level of

'moral superiority' over the Arabs" (p. 88).

22. SAVAK, the secret service of the Shah regime in Iran, was founded in 1957 and disbanded after the Islamic Revolution in 1979. Its mission was to place opponents of the regime under surveillance, many of whom were arrested, tortured, or killed. SAVAK had virtually unlimited power and control over civilians in Iran. It operated its own prison centers and routinely subjected its detainees to torture as reported by many prisoners and their families.

23. Saadi Shirazi was an Iranian poet and a philosopher of the 1300s. He is well-known for his poetry, which used humor, cynicism, and wisdom (*see* www.iran chamber.com/literature/saadi/saadi.php).

REFERENCES

Ahmad, E. (2001). *Terrorism: Theirs & ours.* New York: Seven Stories Press.

Angier, N. (2003, November 11). Is war our biological destiny? *New York Times,* p. D-1.

Atran, S. (2003). Genesis of suicide terrorism. *Social Science, 299,* pp. 1534–1539.

Avnery, U. (2006, August). America's Rottweiler. *International Middle East Media Center* [On-line]. Retrieved February 10, 2007. Available: http://www.imemc.org/content/view/21141/1/

Bandura, A. (2003).The role of selective moral disengagement in terrorism and counterterrorism. In F. M. Moghaddam & A. J. Marsella (Eds.) *Understanding Terrorism,* (pp. 121–150). Washington, D.C.: American Psychological Association.

BBC World Service Poll (2007, February 19). Global poll finds that religion and culture are not to blame for tensions between Islam and the West [On-line]. Retrieved May 23, 2007. Available: www.globescan.com/news_archives/bbciswest/

Carmichael, D. J. C. (1982). Of beasts, gods, and civilized men: The justification of terrorism and of counterterrorist measures. *Terrorism, 6,* 1–26. Cited by Atran (2003), Genesis of suicide terrorism. *Social Science, 299,* pp. 1534–1539.

Carroll, J. (2006, September 6). War's reckoning. *Manchester Journal Inquirer,* p. 19.

Chomsky, N. (2001, October). The new war against terror. *Chomsky.Info* [On-line]. Retrieved February 12, 2007. Available: www.chomsky.info/talks/20011018.htm

Chomsky, N. (2002). *911.* New York: Seven Stories Press.

Chomsky, N. & Achcar, G. (2007). *Perilous power: The middle East and U.S. foreign policy.* Boulder, CO: Paradigm Publishers.

CNN News. (2007, March). No military solution to Iraq–U.S. chief [On-line]. Retrieved March 8, 2007. Available: http://www.cnn.com/2007/WORLD/meast/03/08/iraq.petraeus/index.html? eref=ss_topstories

Cohn, M. (2002). Understanding, responding to and preventing terrorism. *Arab Studies Quarterly* [On-line]. pp. 25+. Retrieved October 24, 2006. Available: http://www.questia.com

Davis, K. C. (2003). *Don't know much about history.* New York: HarperCollins Publishers Inc.

Debusmann, B. (2006, December). Radio hoax exposes anti-Muslim sentiment. *U.S. Reuters News* [On-line]. Retrieved December 6, 2006. Available: http://articles.news.aol.com/news/-a/radio-hoax-exposes-anti-muslim-sentiment/20061202

Emam, A. (2006, October). On the assassination of the Jesuits of El Salvador. *GhasedakOnline* [On-line]. Retrieved October 9, 2006. Available: http://ghasedakonline.com

Fisk, R. (2005). *The great war for civilization: The conquest of the middle east.* New York, NY: Random House, Inc.

Gambino, R. (1973, November-December). Watergate lingo: A language of non-responsibility. *Freedom at Issue, 22,* 7–9, 15–17.

Gershman, J. (2006) A secure America in a secure world. In J. T. Rourke (Ed.), *Taking Sides: Clashing Views on Controversial Issues in World Politics* (12th ed.) Guilford, CT: McGraw Hill/Dushkin.

Haaretz (2006, June). The government is losing its reason. *Le Monde Diplomatique* [On-line]. Retrieved March 14, 2007. Available: http://mondediplo.com/2006/06/19palestine?var_recherche=palestinian%20children

Harre, R. (2003). The Social Construction of Terrorism. In F. M Moghaddam & A. J. Marsella (Eds.), *Understanding terrorism: Psychosocial roots, consequences, and interventions* (pp. 91–102). Washington, D.C.: American Psychological Association.

Herman, E. S. (2002, July/August). The world confronts U.S. wars of terrorism. *Z Magazine* [On-line] 15(7). Retrieved March 14, 2007. Available: http://www.zmag.org/ZMag/articles/julaug02herman.html

Heskin, K. (1980). *Northern Ireland: A psychological analysis.* New York: Columbia University Press.

Hough, G. (2004). Does psychoanalysis have anything to offer an understanding of terrorism? *Journal of American Psychoanalysis Association, 52*(3), pp. 813–828.

Huntington, S. (1996). *The clash of civilizations and the remaking of the world order.* New York: Simon & Schuster.

International Jewish Solidarity Network. (2006, August). Petition for U.S. Jewish solidarity with Muslim and Arab peoples of the Middle East [On-line]. Retrieved January 9, 2007. Available: http://www2.jewishsolidarity.info/en/petition

Lee, B. (2001, September 14) Rep. Barbara Lee's Speech opposing the post 9-11 use of force act [On-line]. Retrieved June 12, 2007. Available: www.wagingpeace.org/articles/2001/09/14_leespeech.htm

Lee, B. (2007) Congresswoman Barbara Lee [On-line]. Retrieved June 12, 2007. Available: http://lee.house.gov/index.cfm?SectionID=6&SectionTypeID=2&

Lerner, M. (2001, May 18). Threats dehumanize Jews who question Israel. *CommonDreams.org Newscenter* [On-line]. Retrieved December 30, 2006. Available: www.commondreams.org views01/0518-02.htm

Lutz, W. D. (1987). Language, appearance, and reality: Doublespeak in 1984. In P. Boardman (Ed.) (1987) *The legacy of language–A tribute to Charlton Laird,* Reno, NV: University of Nevada Press, pp. 103–119.

Margalit, A. (2003, January). The suicide bombers. *The New York Review of Books* [On-line]. *50*(1). Retrieved March 2, 2007. Available: http://www.nybooks.com/articles/15979

Marsella, A. J. (2003). Reflections on international terrorism: Issues, concepts, and directions. In F. M. Moghaddam & A. J. Marsella (Eds.), *Understanding Terrorism* (pp. 11–47). Washington, D.C.: American Psychological Association.

Montiel, C. J. & Anuar, M. K. (2002). Other terrorisms, psychology, and media. *Journal of Peace Psychology, 8*(3), pp. 201–206.

Mueller, J. (2005). *Reactions and overreactions to terrorism* [On-line]. Retrieved February 10, 2007. Available: http://psweb.sbs.ohio-state.edu/faculty/jmueller

Mueller, J. (2006). *Overblown: How politicians and the terrorism industry inflate national security threats, and why we believe them.* New York: Free Press.

National Public Radio (NPR)(2003, March 7). Profile: Look at the mind of a suicide bomber [On-line]. Retrieved May 2, 2007. Available: http://www.npr.org/progams/morning/transcripts/2003/mar/030307.joyce.html

Nerburn, K. & Mengelkoch, L. (1991). *Native American wisdom*. Novato, CA: The Classic Wisdom Collection.

Oliphant, P. (2006, September 18). Oliphant's view. *The Hartford Courant*, p. A10.

Olivier, C. C. (2007, June 22). Are Americans really safer? *Manchester Journal Inquirer, Reader's Forum*, p. 18.

Post, J. (2003, June 22). Terrorism Panel discussion held at the Spring Meeting of the American Psychoanalytic Association, Boston, MA. Quoted in G. Hough (2004). Does psychoanalysis have anything to offer an understanding of terrorism? *Journal of American Psychoanalysis Association, 52*(3), pp. 813–828.

Projo.com (2006, October 1). Intelligence test [On-line]. Retrieved September 30, 2006. Available: http://www.projo.com/cgi-bin/bi/gold_print.cgi

Raum, T. (2006, September). The plain dealer: Bush denies Iraq war inspires terror, calls claim "the enemy's propaganda." *Cleveland.com* [On-line]. Retrieved February 10, 2007. Available: http://www.cleveland.com/printer/printer.ssf?/base/news/115961736590170.xml&coll=2

Rees, M. & Jala, B. (2002, August 19) Where to now? [On-line]. Retrieved September 22, 2007. Available: www.time.com/time/printout/0,8816,1003045,00.html

Reuter, C. (2002). *My life is a weapon: A modern history of suicide bombing*. Princeton, NJ: Princeton University Press.

Roy, A. (2003). Anger about the U.S. bombing of Afghanistan is justified. In M. E. Williams & S. Barbour (Eds.), *The terrorist attack on America* (pp. 73–79). Farmington Hills, MI: Greenhaven Press.

Saad, L. (2005, August 08). Americans reject extreme anti-privacy security measures [On-line]. Retrieved October 3, 2007. Available: www.galluppoll.com/content/?ci=17686&pg=1

Shergald (2007, February 27). Mind of the Palestinian suicide bomber [On-line]. Retrieved April 20, 2007. Available: http://www.myleftwing.com/showDiary.do?diaryId=14547

Siddiqui, H. (2007, March 4). Memo to Canada: Might won't win in Afghanistan [On-line]. Retrieved March 5, 2007. Available: http://www.thestar.com/printArticle/187723

Slovenko, R. (2005). Euphemisms. *The Journal of Psychiatry & Law, 33*, pp. 533–548.

Soros, G. (2006a, August). Blinded by a concept. *GeorgeSoros.com* [On-line]. Retrieved February 10, 2007. Available: http://www.georgesoros.com

Soros, G. (2006b). *The age of fallibility: Consequences of the war on terror*. New York: Public Affairs.

Stringer, D. (2006, November 19). Blair: Moderate policies defeat terror. *The Associated Press* [On-line]. Retrieved March 27, 2007. Available: http://abcnews.go.com/International/print?id=2665549

Taneja, P. (2006, October). Global war on minorities. *TomPaine.common sense* [On-line]. Retrieved November 4, 2006. Available: http://www.tompaine.com/articles/2006/10/02/global_war_on_minorities.php

van Teeffele, T. (2003, October). Israelis better at manipulating media. Aljazeera.net [On-line]. Retrieved March 20, 2007. Available: http://english.aljazeera.net/NR/exeres/0944B35C-4811-4F44-88EF-F96684DF85F7.htm

Wheels of Justice. Nonviolence [On-line]. Retrieved November 9, 2006. Available: http://wheelsofjusticetour.org/nonviolence

Wikipedia Encyclopedia: USA Patriot Act [On-line]. Retrieved February 13, 2006. Available: http://wikipedia.org/wiki/USA_PATRIOT_Act

Zinn, H. (2003). Reject violence and war as a means of resolving conflict. In M.E. Williams, & S. Barbour (Eds.), *The terrorist attack on America* (pp. 129–131). Farmington Hills, MI: Greenhaven Press.

Zinn, H., & Arnove, A. (2004). *Voices of people's history of the United States.* New York: Seven
    Stories Press.

Chapter 9

THE FAILURE OF COUNTERTERRORISM: THE NEED FOR A PSYCHOSOCIAL AND NONMILITARY SOLUTION

Jamshid A. Marvasti

An activist used the analogy of a bird to describe the present direction the U.S. government is taking: "It's not about the right or left wing because a bird needs both wings to fly. The problem is that we've had a one-wing bird—a right wing rather than a balanced bird."

The Hartford Courant (2006, August 3)

All the cities of the earth should rise up against the man who ruins one.

Landor

We are investigating the outcome, not the cause of a war.

Seneca

To kill one man is to be guilty of a capital crime . . . to kill ten men is to increase the guilt ten-fold. . . . This the rulers of the earth all recognize and yet when it comes to the greatest crime—waging war or another state—they praise it!

Mozi

INTRODUCTION

In 1986, threats such as President Gadhafi's statement that Libyans will attack "American citizens in their own streets" created the initial war on terrorism (Szumski, 1986, p. 20). Twenty years later, the U.S. government is still struggling to determine the techniques and policies that will make this "war" successful, the amount of sacrificed civil liberties U.S. citizens should accept, and the number of policies they should overlook. Roy (2003) has addressed a human rights issue that can be overlooked or justified in the name of fighting terrorism. In referencing the thousands of Afghani civilian deaths since 9/11, Roy has stated, "Nothing can excuse or justify an act of terrorism, whether it is committed by religious fundamentalists, private militia, people's resistance movements–or whether it's dressed up as a war of retribution by a recognized government." Each person killed in these attacks becomes an additional casualty of 9/11, not the result of a revenge killing (Roy, 2003, pp. 73–74). Roy's comments seem to echo the warnings given by Congresswoman Barbara Lee, the only member of the U.S. Congress to vote against going to war in September 2001. As Lee stated in her speech to Congress on September 14, 2001, "If we rush to launch into a counter-attack, we run too great a risk that women, children, and other noncombatants will be caught in the crossfire" (Lee, 2001).

In the previous chapter we explored what has not worked in the battle against terrorism, methods that may have produced more harm than good. In this chapter we seek to further decipher the issue of counterterrorism by analyzing what may work in alleviating terrorism. To do so we look to the "other side," to the voices of people who may not have had a space to express their opinions. In addition, we discuss the variety of methods that may decrease terrorism and alleviate future sufferings, which lead to terrorism. The necessity to resolve the psychic trauma of future terrorists is one aspect that requires psychological and sociological attention. Moreover, we focus on supporting "moderates" and implementing economical and political reform into our counterterrorism policies. We acknowledge that the concept of nonviolence is considered a viable yet underused method for change. Furthermore, we maintain that, by and large, it is crucial to listen to those who could be future terrorists, in order to understand their perceived injustice and grievances in order to discover how to deter terrorist proliferation.

We begin our exploration with an attempt to understand the view from the other side, the relevance of which has been succinctly described by a Native American (in a conversation with the early American settlers): "You who are so wise must know that different nations have different conceptions of things" (Nerburn & Mengelkoch, 1991, p. 13). Hearing this other side may shed some light on new perspectives, understandings, and alternative responses to terrorism.

VIEW FROM THE OTHER SIDE

Every man sees through his own glasses.
Korean proverb
Only judge when you have heard all.
Greek proverb

The United States has been viewed in a negative light by various countries and news media due to its foreign policies and military actions. Yet it is important to make a distinction between the sentiments of the U.S. government and its citizens. Furthermore, it is necessary to make a second distinction between U.S. citizens who support the actions of their government and those who believe that U.S. policies are problematic. This latter group may be viewed as the other side. The other side comprises Americans and Westerners who believe that certain U.S. policies may be the cause of hostility against the U.S. In addition, the other side includes non westerners who also disagree with certain U.S. policies and actions. It is helpful to read the sentiments of a former lieutenant colonel in the U.S. Air Force, Robert Bowman, who flew many bombing missions in Vietnam before he became a Catholic priest (Zinn, 2003). He was quoted in an article in the *National Catholic Reporter* three years before September, 11, 2001:

> . . . *We are not hated because we practice democracy, value freedom, or uphold human rights. We are hated because our government denies these things to people in Third World countries whose resources are coveted by our multinational corporations. That hatred we have sown has come back to haunt us in the form of terrorism.* . . . *Instead of sending our sons and daughters around the world to kill Arabs so we can have the oil under their sand, we should send them to rebuild their infrastructure, supply clean water, and feed starving children.* . . . *Who would hate us? Who would want to bomb us?*. . . *(Bowman, 1998)*

It is this other side that would disagree with certain sentiments held by the U.S. administration and its president. For example, President G. W. Bush in his "call to war" after 9/11 presented a simple explanation that our enemies hate us because they dislike our freedoms: religion, speech, voting, assemblage, and the ability to disagree with each other (Everest, 2003). However, Everest, an American author, has maintained that his experiences reporting in the Middle East for more than twenty years dispute this claim. In addition, as Cohn (2002) has noted, the attackers of 9/11 did not attack the Statue of Liberty, a symbol of freedom and democracy for the United States. Instead, they destroyed the World Trade Center and the Pentagon, two places which symbolized "the U.S. led global economic system . . . and the heart of the United States military."

Moghaddam and Marsella (2003) have written that much to the consternation of the American people, the international media have often suggested that the United States government activities at times become similar to terrorism in the "eyes of some nations and peoples."

It is well- known that many people worldwide differentiate between "the American people" and the U.S. foreign policy.[1,2] In addition, critics have identified several incidents in which U.S. government officials allegedly have deceived their own citizenry in order to perform activities that most American people would never approve of (torture of prisoners, support of brutal foreign regimes, kidnapping, and other such practices).[3] Khaled El-Masri, a German citizen of Lebanese descent, is one man who has experienced the warmth of the American people in contrast to the cold treatment by the U.S. government. El-Masri was abducted while on vacation, taken to a secret prison in Afghanistan and tortured. There he was held without counsel for five months, until he was released after being found innocent of having terrorist ties. El-Masri has since traveled to the United States and Germany to participate in court cases that investigate probable CIA involvement in his abduction. In visiting the United States El-Masri stated, "I'll never forget an elderly couple in Richmond, Virginia, who came to support my case against the government, holding signs that read 'Stop the Torture Flights.' That's the real face of the United States. The people who kidnapped me represent the hidden and false face of America" (Abadi, 2007).

In another example, the CIA's coup d'état in Iran was considered a "successful" operation by the U.S. government, but it removed the democratic government of Dr. Mosaddeq, and brought back the Shah's dictatorship.[4] Many U.S. citizens would have disapproved of this act, had they known. It was fifty years later when President Clinton's Secretary of State apologized to the Iranian people for overthrowing their democratic government.[5] However, this coup d'état is still considered a sore wound for many Iranian nationalists, and possibly a simple apology was not enough for the healing of old injuries. In the book, *All the Shah's Men*, Stephen Kinzer (2003) has connected this United States-induced coup in Iran to the 9/11 terrorist attacks. He has explained that intellectuals and nationalists in the Middle East lost their trust in the U.S. government's claim that although it is prodemocratic, the United States would not attempt to dictate a government style for other nations.[6]

Numerous Americans may have a hard time understanding why they were attacked on 9/11 unless the act is attributable to something as straightforward as religious differences. With so many possible motivations contributing to the 9/11 terrorist attacks, why did so many Americans assume it was solely connected to religious fanaticism? As Holmes has pointed out, "some Americans . . . think more easily in Biblical terms than in secular terms. They certainly know much more about 'the end of days' than about political intrigue in Saudi Arabia" (2005, p. 133).[7]

WHAT MAY WORK

There is nothing wrong with America that cannot be cured with what is right in America.

William J. Clinton

Make peace with your enemies, not your friends.

Yitzhak Rabin

The best way to fight hate is to put out more love into the world. Even the haters are people who are severely wounded, and those wounds can best be dealt with by compassion rather than by hating back.

Rabbi Michael Lerner[8]

Alleviation of Trauma

What then could work to decrease terrorism? From the psychiatric point of view, it is clear that traumatic experiences have been a motivational factor in turning people towards terrorism.

Many suicide bombers have had a personal history of severe and multiple emotional traumas besides possible physical assault and injuries. Therefore, addressing this issue of trauma could potentially help to alleviate the suffering that may lead to terrorism. Salman Akhtar (2003, as cited in Hough, 2004), a psychoanalyst, has suggested that interventions into a traumatized community should be focused on:

- decreasing the level of hatred
- encouraging the capacity to reflect and empathize
- increasing listening to "oppressed" group
- decreasing humiliating factors to "oppressed" group and encouraging actions to restore pride and sense of capability
- integrating empathetic mindset into educational materials along with a more balanced view of the "other"
- acknowledging stereotyping and prejudicial thinking/writing
- invite artists and filmmakers to create material that depicts times when the two opposed groups lived in peace

Support Moderate Activists and Policies

What the British government means by the term "moderate Muslim," on the other hand, is a Muslim who rejects the use of violence for political purpos-

> *es–unless that purpose accords within the wishes of the United States and Britain.*
>
> Milan Rai (2006, p. 135)

Atran (2003) has stated that empowering moderates from within a culture may permanently reduce terrorist groups. Numerous analysts and professionals have indicated that support of moderate activists around the world may substantially decrease the danger of extremists and their proliferation. As the governor of the Baluchistan province (in Pakistan) has suggested, "Initiate backdoor political and diplomatic moves with the resistance groups who are not hard-core Taliban. Develop a level of accommodation" (Siddiqui, 2007). In addition, former British Prime Minister Tony Blair has maintained that the United Kingdom supports moderate policies because they are seen as an effective strategy against terrorism (Stringer, 2006). "More aid, moderate Islamic role models, and a lasting resolution of the Israeli-Palestinian conflict," Blair has asserted, "were key to defeating Islamic extremism" (Stringer, 2006). One must consider, however, that the word moderate is a controversial term and that possibly its definition is in the eyes of the beholder. For example, Kessler (2007) has reported that many of the countries that President George W. Bush has considered to be moderate, such as Egypt and Saudi Arabia, "are autocratic dictatorships rated among the worst of the 'not free' nations by the nonpartisan Freedom House." Yet, supporting the moderates can also be used as a way for western governments to "do something" without really doing anything. Rai (2006) has pointed out that Britain's creation of "Operation Contest" was aimed at managing Muslim discontent with minimal political cost. This government plan supported moderate Muslim student and youth organizations, in addition to encouraging public Muslim representation. Yet Rai has contended that "the purpose is manipulative: to give the appearance of influence" (p. 134). There is no plan to have a dialogue with Muslims about the wars in Iraq and Afghanistan or to discuss other key issues of Muslim concern such as the "global war on terror" (p. 134).

A number of observers have accused some Western government officials of deliberately opposing moderates in order to create extremism in antiwestern regimes. If a moderate government is not supported it may be overthrown and replaced by a more extreme militant one. This is actually advantageous to prowar officials because it is easier to persuade their nation to wage war against extreme militants than it is against moderates. Through war, a government can pursue its own agenda. Critics of this type of practice have cited the example of Iran's President Khatami. Khatami was a moderate and peace-oriented leader while in power (from 1997 to 2005) yet western governments did not approve of him. On the contrary, Iran was labeled an "axis of evil" by the U.S. government during Khatami's presidency, and U.S. policies undermined his peaceful and nonmilitary style. Perhaps in part as a result, an extremist was elected to succeed him. A similar situation occurred in Palestine, when Hamas was elected and the moderate Palestinian fraction lost the election.

Somewhat paradoxically, the United States, has supported moderates at other times. Up until 1937 the U.S. State Department had labeled Hitler as a moderate who needed the support of the United States as he stood in-between the extremists on the left and the right and created balance, preventing the masses from taking over (Rai, 2006). Rai has suggested that it is necessary to, "distinguish between political 'moderation' in the propaganda sense, which means 'obedience to U.S. and British power,' and in a more neutral sense of being in the mainstream of global opinion or aligned with liberal, humanistic values" (Rai, 2006, p. 135).

THE CONCEPT OF NONVIOLENCE

Nonviolence, exactly like violence, is a means of persuasion, a technique for political activism, a recipe for prevailing.

Mark Kurlansky

Nonviolent protest has been effective for minority groups for decades, if not centuries. The success of Mahatma Gandhi in changing British policies through peaceful activities indicates the value of this method for change. So why has nonviolence stayed a "minority group practice?" (Kurlansky, 2006). Why, as Kurlansky has questioned, is there not even a word for nonviolence, other than to say it is "not" something else?

The only possible explanation for the absence of a proactive word to express nonviolence is that not only the political establishments but also the cultural and intellectual establishments of all societies have viewed nonviolence as a marginal point of view, a fanciful rejection of one of society's key components, a repudiation of something important but not a serious force in itself. It has been marginalized because it is one of the rare truly revolutionary ideas, an idea that seeks to completely change the nature of society, a threat to the established order (Kurlansky, 2006, p. 5).

Yet even if nonviolence has been deemed a weak force by some, there are organizations and individuals that are committed to this method for change. Wheels of Justice, a peaceful, moderate Palestinian-American organization, has defined nonviolence as "the willingness to confront a wrongdoing without submitting or imposing our will on the wrongdoer; to confront an injustice and a wrongdoer to reach a win-win situation rather than a win-lose situation." By avoiding the degradation and annihilation of the enemy, nonviolent actions effect social and political change. Opinions and belief systems determine how government actions are perceived. When nonviolence is chosen, marginalized and oppressed people are assisted. To enact nonviolent strategies it is necessary to: (1) recognize an injustice; (2) refuse to cooperate with that injustice; (3) listen willingly to the wrongdoer and the wronged; and (4) state the confrontation in an open, direct, and compassionate manner (*see* www.wheelsofjustice.org).

   Nonviolence can take the form of standing between tanks and civilians; staging an authorized government protest; refusing to accept one group as "good" and the other as "bad." and refusing to allow taxes and monies to support war, terror, and occupation of others' lands (*see* www.wheelsofjustice.org). As Atran (2003) has maintained, it is essential to engage the communities involved in war. He has made it clear that local communities must withdraw their support for suicide attackers. In addition, Pape (2005) has asserted that recruitment by terrorist organizations can be impeded by concessions to national grievances held by terrorists' communities. However, Pape has warned that partial concessions or concessions that stretch out over too long a time may backfire and fail. This is not unlike the Oslo Peace Accords[9] between Israel and Palestine in which delays and lack of actual peace progress resulted in the second Intifada. Even true concessions may not result in an immediate end of terrorism, because terrorist leaders may believe this "victory" is due to their violent tactics (Pape, 2005).

   In a speech given long before 9/11, Eqbal Ahmad stated "Do not condone the terror of your allies. Condemn them. . . . Avoid covert operations and low-intensity warfare. These are breeding grounds for terrorism and drugs. Try to look at causes and solve problems. Avoid military solutions. Terrorism is a political problem." (Ahmad, 2001, pp. 24–25). Ahmad's words resonate in those of Congresswoman Barbara Lee, who advocated against a military attack. As she has stated in a speech given after the 9/11 attacks, "This crisis involves issues of national security, foreign policy, public safety, intelligence gathering, economics, and murder. Our response must be equally multifaceted" (Lee, 2001).

   Certain Israeli soldiers have seemed to take the nonviolence concept to heart. These soldiers used another form of nonviolence to assert their disapproval of the domination of Palestinian people. It began as a letter published in the Israeli daily newspaper *Haaretz* by fifty-two Israeli soldiers and officers on January 25, 2002. The purpose of this letter was twofold: to announce that they would no longer serve in the Palestinian-occupied territories of the West Bank and the Gaza Strip and to invite their fellow comrades to join them in refusing to contribute to the unjust domination over another people (Chacham, 2003).[10]

Reactions by Israel society have ranged from approval to rejection, and more soldiers, called "refuseniks," have joined this movement labeled, "Courage to Refuse." They assert that the Palestinian problem is a reality, not to be wished away, but also not to be dealt with through starving, demolishing, humiliating, and killing the Palestinian people (Chacham, 2003).

Atran (2003) also has continued to question the effectiveness of revenge or military retaliation, especially if those seeking retribution desire allies. The Allied Coalition must address the community's feelings of grief and humiliation, especially in Palestine, where daily violence has made it the focus of Muslim attention globally (Atran, 2003). On the same subject, Hecht (2003) has written that the cycle of violence can only be retarded or suppressed by extraordinary ritual confessions, such as those from the South African Truth and Reconciliation Commission. This extraordinary procedure in South Africa prevented a bloodbath.[11]

Marjorie Cohn, a law professor and member of the Executive Committee of the National Lawyers Guild, has suggested several important steps the United States can take to stop the violence in the Middle East and prevent terrorism. She recommends preventing terrorism with alternatives to military force: (1) immediately stop bombings in Iraq and Afghanistan; remove ground forces there and avoid invading other countries; (2) contribute people and money to the U.N. peacekeeping forces; (3) refuse to trample on the Bill of Rights and U.S. citizens in the name of national security; (4) refuse to allow racial profiling and intimidation of Middle Eastern émigrés (Cohn, 2002).

There have been various suggestions, as just illustrated, as to what will work to stop terrorism. Certain tactics, however, have been viewed as more controversial than others. Jerrold Post (2003 has presented a four-point strategy to counterterrorism: "inhibit potential terrorists from joining groups . . . produce dissension within terrorist groups . . . facilitate exit from the group through amnesty arrangements . . . and reduce support for the group and its leader" (as cited in Hough, 2004, p. 820). On the surface these may appear to be rational and potentially helpful strategies, but we would like to challenge Post by suggesting that he has ignored the main causes of terrorism in his counterterrorism strategy. Major motivating factors are perceived injustice, occupation, and the invasion of one's homeland. The methods that Post has suggested are the same techniques being used by western governments. For example, certain governments have focused on how these groups are supplied with money and weapons and have enacted a wide spread freeze on the money of organizations some of which are charities that they "assume" are financing these groups. Why not focus instead on what enrages them to use these weapons? It seems to be suggested by Post that the issue of "invasion" is a given fact, and there would be no point in discussing "not invading" as an option. In a sense, stating that the western government and its allies are going to invade regardless, so let's look at what other ways terrorism can be dealt with.

Michael Scheuer (2005), who headed the CIA's bin Laden unit from 1996 to 1999, has a different approach than Post has; one that reflects an examination of the root causes of terrorism (Rai, 2006). Scheuer has concluded that it is necessary to look at U.S. foreign policies, because it is these policies that are motivating the people who are fighting the United States. These policies must be revisited: "in an open and democratic way [to decide if they still serve the interests of the U.S.] we need a shot of democracy inside the United States. . . . The American people, I think, deserve to at least have a voice in policies that have basically been on autopilot for twenty-five years, whether toward Israel, energy policy, support for the Saudis and the Egyptians–all of that–I think deserves a debate. . . . I think it would make a difference if there was some kind of change in our policy towards Israel" (cited by Rai, 2006, p. 163).

When asked, what if these policies were reviewed by the citizens of the United States and then were voted to remain the same, Scheuer responded, "I think that might be a mistake, . . . if that's what the country would want, then at least the country would be going into war against Islamic militancy with its eyes open, knowing that those policies, more than anything else, motivate our enemy" (Scheuer, cited by Rai, 2006, p. 164). The notion of informing the American public so that they could be more involved is one that was also promoted by U.S. Congressman Wayne Morse, who opposed the Vietnam War. In 1968, Morse appeared on a *CBS* program, on which he argued that foreign policy belongs to the American people, not the president: "I have complete faith in the ability of the American people to follow the facts if you'll give them. And my charge against my government is, we're not giving the American people facts" (Solomon, 2002).

Doctor de Waal (a primatologist and professor of psychology) and others have put forth another avenue leading to nonviolence. Encouraging interdependency among nations promotes peace because each country involved does not want its economy to plummet: "Imagine if France were to invade Germany now, that would upset every aspect of their economic world. It's not as if Europeans all love each other, but you're not promoting love, you're promoting economic calculations" (Angier, 2003).

We may need to look no further than to our friends in the animal kingdom to see nonviolence being enacted with success. Possibly some of the war-oriented leaders need to learn from animals such as the bonobo chimpanzee. As a primatologist reported in *The New York Times*, bonobos "choose love over war, using a tantric array of sexual acts to resolve any social problems that arise" (Angier, 2003). Similarly, the hamadryas baboons are peace-loving animals. Although a peanut thrown to one male will be eaten happily, when thrown in front of two males it will be ignored to avoid even the chance of a fight.

Critics of nonviolence may claim that this method cannot truly be effective because it would take too long to implement in nations who have used war for centuries. However, it is actually quite possible that a country can change its national temperament, regarding war, quite rapidly. Take the example of the Vikings who "slaughtered and plundered; their descendents in Sweden haven't fought a war in nearly 200 years, while the Danes reserve their fighting spirit for negotiating better vacation packages" (Angier, 2003). As Peter Fonagy, a psychoanalyst, has noted, in the Middle Ages, Sweden often attacked Russia, with disappointing results. Eventually it became clear that this was not an advantageous policy. The Swedish feudal lords then removed their king and created a more peaceful relationship with Russia (Hough, 2004).

THE PSYCHOLOGY OF SOFT POWER

Joseph Nye (1990) has explained the use of "soft power" as a tool and a possible alternative to military intervention. Soft power utilizes nonmilitary strategies to shape international relations and behavior. Lennon (2003) has edited a book entitled *The Battle for Hearts and Minds: Using Soft Power to Undermine Terrorist Networks*. In this book, four authors from around the world have explained the limitation of "hard power" (military force) to combat terrorism. Although they do not argue that military actions are always useless, they have suggested that military operations are not panaceas. In their book an Australian writer (Dibb, 2003) has questioned how long an international coalition (of several western countries) against terrorism would last when only the United States (out of these member countries) has suffered severe attacks (9/11). Since the British government has become the victim of terrorism, however, this issue may be extended to how long other European countries would maintain military in Afghanistan and Iraq when they have not been targets. This book has suggested that political, economical, and ideological measures are a necessity to successfully fight terrorism. Soft power tools such as postconflict reconstruction, public diplomacy, and foreign assistance are elements that possibly need to be implemented in the war against terrorism rather than relying solely on military strength (Lennon, 2003).

CONCLUSION

Words fly faster than Arrows.
Middle Eastern proverb

There never was a good war, or bad peace.
Benjamin Franklin to John Quincy Adams

If the distant peoples do not submit, then build up culture and character and so win them, and when they have been won give them security.
Confucius

What would happen if people in the United States tried to consider Osama bin Laden as human and forgive him? During a panel discussion of psychoanalysts, this topic was broached (Hough, 2004). Salman Akhtar (2003), a psychoanalyst, has suggested that before we could try to forgive bin Laden, we would need to fully listen to his side of the story; one may wonder if that has been done to any extent. Furthermore, the next question is can anything be accomplished by listening to the "other" side? As Peter Fonagy (2003), a psychoanalyst, has noted, "in the United Kingdom, when officials finally sat down and talked with terrorists in Northern Ireland, the terrorists activities began to subside" (as cited in Hough, 2004). Many hostile conflicts may be resolved if "West meets East" and the two faithfully "talk," so negotiation replaces violence. As the Middle East proverb says, "Words go faster than arrows."

Because of all the negative propaganda regarding Islam that has surfaced since 9/11, it is surprising that an Islamic poet (and a qualified clergyman) may be the person people turn to for hope and peace-inspiring words. The popularity of Mevlana Jalaluddin Rumi, a Persian poet and Islamic authority from the thirteenth century, has increased dramatically in America in the six years since 9/11 (Curiel, 2007). Despite the fact that terrorism and genocide are what surrounded Rumi in his own time, his poetic words and stories did not turn to revenge or retribution. Instead, he chose to focus on love, commonality of humanity, and the opportunity that existed through war–to love one's enemy and heal one's self from hatred. Rumi has shown a side of Islam to which people unaffiliated with this religion might never be exposed: the stories, spiritual dancing, music, and fellowship among people. It can give one hope to see people around the world embracing this nonviolent, love-centered poet (Curiel, 2007).

Every facet of hostility and every injustice against human beings have provided the plausible motivations for terrorism. Reacting to violence with violence has been shown to be a fallible technique. Negotiation, compromising, support of moderates, and recognition of the perceived injustices of any and all citizens can be the beginning of the peace process. Certain peace-focused organizations would suggest that responding to one's perceived enemies with love versus hatred may change enemies into friends. In addition, as Rumi has suggested in his Persian poetry, " From love, thorns become flowers. "

NOTES

1. Some news media are using and distorting the term "anti-American" and claiming that whoever criticizes U.S. foreign policy must also be against everything "American." For example, when there were demonstrations against the United States in South Africa, an American reporter criticized these demonstrators for smoking Marlboro cigarettes, as if anyone who criticized U.S. foreign policy should not have any interest in any U.S. products.
2. Shirley Telhami, an American Middle East expert, has clarified that there is "pervasive anger at the United States, but not pervasive hatred. The majority of Middle Eastern people like America, want American products and want to be liked by America." They differentiate between the American people and the foreign policy of the U.S. government (from M. H. Cooper (2003). Hating America: An overview. In M. E. Williams, & S. Barbour (Eds.), *The terrorist attack on America* [pp. 57–59]. Farmington Hills, MI: Greenhaven Press).
3. Doctor Hamid Dabashi, an Iranian scholar and professor at Columbia University reported that there was an attempt to justify the human rights violations due to the demands of counterterrorism policies. Yet "the eventual revelations about the United States torture chambers in Bagram Air Base in Afghanistan, in Abu Ghraib in Iraq, in Guantanamo Bay in Cuba and throughout an entire network of interrogation dungeons in Europe" plus discoveries of sporadic war crime incidents (rape, murder and massacre of civilians in Fallujah, Haditha and Mahmoudiya in Iraq) have entirely "discredited the United States as an arbitrator of human rights abuses." Doctor Dabashi also referred to western writers and politicians who "theorized the legal and moral necessity of torturing people" to support these policies (from H. Dabash, p. 239. [2007]. *Iran: A People Interrupted*, New York: The New Press).
4. From the aftermath of WWI through WWII, the French and British governed the oil fields of the Middle East in separate "spheres of influence" or colonies. Everest (2003) has stated that the United States became "imperialists" as the spoils of war were divided. The global conflicts of the 1950s and 1960s between the Soviet Union and the United States emerged to protect those spoils while dealing with the proliferation of new independent countries (former colonies) around the world. Everest (p. 61) has maintained that the United States dealt with these challenges "mercilessly." He identifies the overthrow of Doctor Mosaddeq's government in Iran in 1953 by the CIA as an example of the covert policies. The United States installed Shah Mohammed Reza Pahlavi in Iran and thereby increased their military, economic, and political control of the region. A similar instance with the CIA occurred in 1949 in Syria and in

1963 in Iraq.

5. Fakhreddin Azimi is a historian who has researched the era of Doctor Mosaddeq and the CIA coup d'etat extensively. As he has stated, "The coup is widely seen as a rupture, a watershed, a turning point when imperialist domination, overcoming a defiant challenge, reestablished itself, not only by restoring an enfeebled monarch but also by ensuring that the monarchy would assume an authoritarian and antidemocratic posture" (from F. Azimi, 2004). Unseating Mosaddeq: The Configuration and Role of Domestic Forces. In M. J. Gasiorowski & M. Byrne (Eds.), *Mohammad Mosaddeq and the 1953 Coup in Iran*, [pp. 27–101]. Syracuse, NY: Syracuse University Press). Mosaddeq was prime minister of Iran from 1951 to 1953. He was passionately opposed to intervention by foreign countries. He nationalized the Iranian oil industry and is considered a hero and model for nationalists in the Middle East and North Africa.

6. Native Americans were also aware of what the U.S. government was trying to promote to them. "Much has been said of the want of what you term 'civilization' among the Indians. Many proposals have been made to us to adopt your laws, your religion, your manners, and your customs. We do not see the propriety of such a reformation. We should be better pleased if we could actually see the good effects of these doctrines in your own practices rather than hearing you talk about them, or reading your newspapers on such subjects" (Old Tassel, a Cherokee, as cited by Nerburn & Mengelkoch, 1991, p. 77).

7. Doris Haddock has reported what a friend of hers did to help American students understand the sentiment against the United States. This West Virginian teacher used an analogy: A Mideast country poises itself against West Virginia, which is rich in natural resources. This distant country buys almost all of West Virginia's resources inexpensively. Because this Mideast country saves money on energy costs, it can use its leftover wealth to buy off and manipulate West Virginia's government and its officials and help imprison any citizens who oppose the process. Meanwhile, the citizens of that distant country get richer and richer and ignore the effect on West Virginia citizens. This analogy has stimulated poignant thought about the United States and its global role (from D. Haddock [2003]. Anger about American dominance is justified. In M. E. Williams, & S. Barbour (Eds.), *The terrorist attack on America* [pp. 67–72]. Farmington Hills, MI: Greenhaven Press).

8. Michael Lerner is a political activist and also the editor of *Tikkun*, which is a progressive Jewish and interfaith magazine based in California. The intention of the magazine is to challenge the Jewish conservative population and encourage understanding of the spiritual and religious concerns of ordinary Americans. Lerner has described some of his own views as "very controversial," specifically his thoughts on building peace in Israel and Palestine. (*See* http://en.wikipedia.org/wiki/Rabbi_Michael_Lerner. For more information about the writings of Rabbi Michael Lerner, go to www.tikkon.org; *see also* Cohn [2002].)

9. Begun in 1991 and ratified in 1993, the Oslo Accords were officially entitled the Declaration of Principles (DOP) (or the Declaration of Principles on Self-

Government Arrangements according to *Wikipedia Encyclopedia*). After two years of negotiations, the final agreement between the PLO and Israel called for the withdrawal of Israeli forces from parts of the West Bank and Gaza Strip and created a Palestinian Authority for self-government within those areas. A timetable of five years was set during which a permanent agreement and the more complex issues of division of Jerusalem, refuges, and Israeli settlements would be negotiated. However, after the signing of the Accords, Israeli settlement expansion accelerated and terrorist events in Israel escalated, creating more mistrust between the two governments. It is these issues that created the breakdown in negotiations stimulating the return of violence and the second Intifada (from *Wikipedia Encyclopedia* [On-line], Retrieved January 27, 2007. Available: http://en.wikipedia.org/wiki/Oslo_Accords).

10. Israel possibly has been the only democratically elected government in the Middle East. It is surrounded by kings and dictatorships although Iran and Turkey have attempted to include a type of democracy in their governing systems. Some observers have reported that Israeli democratic guidelines surpass the United States in the freedoms they allow. Israel's news media and its parliament (The Knesset) routinely criticize the Israeli government and its strategies, although criticism of the Israeli government is rarely heard in the United States main news media or by members of Congress.

11. The Truth and Reconciliation Commission (TRC) was a court-like body assembled in South Africa after the end of apartheid. The TRC was set up by the 1995 Promotion of National Unity and Reconciliation Act, No. 34, and was seen by many as a crucial component of the transition to full and free democracy in South Africa. The mandate of the commission was to bear witness to, record, and in some cases grant amnesty to the perpetrators of crimes relating to human rights violations, reparation, and rehabilitation. Although there was some opposition from antiapartheid activists who feared that the government would not be held accountable for its atrocities, it is generally considered successful. In 1998, the final Commission report condemned both sides for committing violence and murder (from *Wikipedia Encyclopedia* [On-line]. Retrieved March 27, 2007. Available: http://en.wikipedia.org/wiki/Truth_and_Reconciliation_Commission)

REFERENCES

Abadi, C. (2007, Spring). Disappeared but not silenced. *Amnesty International*, pp. 12–15.

Ahmad, E. (2001). *Terrorism: Theirs & ours.* New York: Seven Stories Press.

Akhtar, S. (2003, June 22). Terrorism Panel discussion held at the Spring Meeting of the American Psychoanalytic Association, Boston, MA. Quoted in G. Hough (2004). Does Psychoanalysis have anything to offer an understanding of terrorism? *Journal of American Psychoanalysis Association, 52*(3) pp. 813–828.

Angier, N. (2003, November). Is war our biological destiny?" *New York Times*, p. D-1.

Atran, S. (2003). Genesis of suicide terrorism. *Social Science, 299*, pp. 1534–1539.

Bowman, R. (1998, October 2). Truth is we're terrorized because we're hated. *National Catholic*

Reporter [On-line]. Retrieved September 22, 2007. Available: www.natcath.com/NCR_Online/archives/100298/1002981.htm

Chacham, R. (2003). *Breaking ranks: Refusing to serve in the West Bank and Gaza Strip.* New York: Other Press.

Cohn, M. (2002). Understanding, responding to and preventing terrorism. *Arab Studies Quarterly* [On-line] p. 25+. Retrieved October 24, 2006. Available: http://www.questia.com

Curiel, J. (2007, April 1). Can Rumi save us now? Life and words of the popular 13th-century Persian poet have special meaning for a 21st-century world torn by war, genocide and hatred. *San Francisco Chronicle,* p. E-3.

Dibb, P. (2003). The future of international coalition: Useful? How manageable? In T. J. Lennon (Ed.) *The battle for hearts and minds.* Cambridge, MA: MIT Press. pp. 29–44.

Everest, L. (2003). Anger toward America is justified. In M. E. Williams & S. Barbour (Eds.), *The terrorist attack on America* (pp. 60–66). Farmington Hills, MI: Greenhaven Press.

Fonagy, P. (2003, June 22). Terrorism Panel discussion held at the Spring Meeting of the American Psychoanalytic Association, Boston, MA. Quoted in G. Hough (2004). Does psychoanalysis have anything to offer an understanding of terrorism? *Journal of American Psychoanalysis Association, 52*(3) pp. 813–828.

Hecht, R. D. (2003). Deadly history, deadly actions, and deadly bodies: A response to Ivan Strenski's 'sacrifice, gift and the social logic of Muslim "human bombers."' *Terrorism and Political Violence, 15*(3), pp. 35–47.

Holmes, S. (2005). Al-Qaeda, September 11, 2001. In D. Gambetta (Ed.), *Making sense of suicide missions* (pp. 132–172). New York: Oxford University Press.

Hough, G. (2004). Does psychoanalysis have anything to offer an understanding of terrorism? *Journal of American Psychoanalysis Association, 52*(3), pp. 813–828.

Kessler, G. (2007, January 24). President's portrayal of "the enemy" often flawed [On-line]. Retrieved January 27, 2007. Available: http://www.washingtonpost.com/wp-dyn/conent/article/2007/01/24/AR2007012400006

Kinzer, S. (2003). *All the Shah's men: An American coup and the roots of Middle East terror.* Hoboken, New Jersey: John Wiley & Sons, Inc.

Kurlansky, M. (2006). *Nonviolence.* New York: The Random House Publishing Group.

Lee, B. (2001, September 14) Rep. Barbara Lee's Speech opposing the post 9-11 use of force act [On-line]. Retrieved June 12, 2007. Available: www.wagingpeace.org/articles/2001/09/14_leespeech.htm

Lennon, A. T. J. (2003). *The battle for hearts and minds: Using soft power to undermine terrorist networks.* Cambridge, MA: The MIT Press.

Marsella, A. J. & Moghaddam, F. (2005). The origins and nature of terrorism : Foundations and issues. In Y. Danieli, D. Brom & J. Sills (Eds.), *The trauma of terrorism: Sharing knowledge and shared care, an international handbook* (pp. 19–31). New York: The Haworth Maltreatment and Trauma Press.

Moghaddam, F. M., & Marsella A. J. (2003). Introduction. In F. M. Moghaddam & A. J. Marsella (Eds.), *Understanding terrorism* (p. 3). Washington, D.C.: American Psychological Association.

Nerburn, K. & Mengelkoch, L. (1991). *Native American wisdom.* Novato, CA: The Classic Wisdom Collection.

Nye, J. S. (1990, Fall). Soft power. *Foreign Policy, 80,* pp. 153–171.

Pape, R. A. (2005). *Dying to win.* New York, NY: Random House Trade Paperbacks.

Rai, M. (2006). *7/7 The London bombings, Islam & the Iraq war.* London: Pluto Press.

Roy, A. (2001, September 29).The algebra of infinite justice. *Manchester Guardian,* p. 1.

Roy, A. (2003). Anger about the U.S. bombing of Afghanistan is justified. In M. E. Williams

& S. Barbour (Eds.), *The terrorist attack on America* (pp. 73–79). Farmington Hills, MI: Greenhaven Press.

Scheuer, M. (2005, January 5). Michael Scheuer, ex-CIA bin Laden Unit Chief, Explains why insurgents are willing to die fighting us . . . maybe it's not our freedom they hate. . . Buzz Flash [On-line] Retrieved October 4, 2007. Available: http://www.buzzflash.com/interviews/05/01/int05001.html

Siddiqui, H. (2007, March 4). Memo to Canada: Might won't win in Afghanistan [On-line]. Retrieved March 5, 2007. Available: http://www.thestar.com/printArticle/187723

Solomon, N. (2002, August 2). Where is the voice of dissent? As we weigh an attack on Iraq, we need someone like the Vietnam era's Wayne Morse. *Los Angeles Times* [On-line]. Retrieved June 12, 2007. Available: http://www.purewatergazette.net/waynemorse2.htm

Stringer, D. (2006, November 19). Blair: Moderate policies defeat terror. *The Associated Press* [On-line]. Retrieved March 27, 2007. Available: http://abcnews.go.com/International/print?id=2665549

Szumski, B. (1986) *Opposing view points: Terrorism* (pp. 16–21). St. Paul, MN, Greenhaven Press.

Zinn, H. (2003). *A people's history of the United States.* New York: Harper Perennial Modern Classics.

Chapter 10

WESTERN LEADERS AND TERRORISM: PSYCHO-POLITICAL IMPACT AND INTERACTIONS

Jamshid A. Marvasti

When we read the speeches of Osama bin Laden and George W. Bush, we are struck with a number of similarities. Each believes he is fighting for justice and peace. Each believes the other is a terrorist. . . . Both have declared a Holy War, and are willing to kill. . . . One calls it a crusade, and the other a jihad. Both believe God is on their side.

Khalid Sohail[1]

INTRODUCTION

A nation and its leader can be traumatized by war, terrorism, or political violence occuring in their country. Ample research and assessments exist in regard to the effects of trauma on individuals. Studies on a traumatized group, nation, or its political leaders are limited, however. Leaders are first and foremost human beings, and therefore, just like ordinary citizens, they are subject to acute stress disorder, PTSD, excessive anger, narcissistic revenge, and impulsive retaliation after experiencing trauma. They may suffer from blows to their ego and its protective shield, as well as from threats to their integrity. Leaders may employ ego defense mechanisms to ward off the pain of perceived trauma and loss. They are also subject to the universal reaction to trauma: fight, flight, or freeze. One must continue to ask such questions as: Do leaders demonstrate "identification with the aggressor" or a "compulsion to repeat" the trauma?[2,3] How does a nation and its leader collectively react to trauma and victimization? How long does the impact last?

One wonders what the impact of psychic trauma is on the capacity to adapt, compromise, and place oneself in another's shoes. Do past or present traumas contribute to brutality and hatred? Could the reason for the inflexibility of Israel and Palestine's leaders be the collective trauma both have experienced? Israel is one example of a traumatized nation. Palestine is another. In order to fully understand the effects of trauma on these nations and their leaders, it might be beneficial for future research to be aimed at investigating the impact of old, new and collective traumas in regard to decision-making and judgment.

In this chapter we explore the public and personal reactions of leaders to the trauma of terrorism and war. Leaders who may be traumatized by terrorism may be retraumatized if their strategies to defeat terrorism fail and become a subject of criticism by their nation.[4]

PUBLIC REACTIONS OF LEADERS

In crises, leaders employ strategies to reverse the feelings of powerlessness and helplessness in people. Although a nation may feel helpless and powerless, it does not become "parentless," because its citizens look to their leader as a parental figure.[5] A leader may mobilize the nation's anger and desire for revenge by promising retaliation and punishment for the offenders. Anger is in the service of ego for restoration, so that revenge may glue the shattered and fragile pieces of the ego together. As Lifton has pointed out, war can become an antidote: "War then becomes heroic, even mythic, a task that must be carried out for the defense of one's own nation, to realize its special destiny and the immortality of its people" (Lifton, 2003, p. 111). "War-fever," Lifton has maintained, can be connected to disillusionment. What is behind or beneath it is anxiety and fears of new terrorist attacks (2003).

The leader needs to be immediately "visible" to the nation and display an image that is decisive, active, and in control, although inside, this head of state may be as shaky as the other citizens.[6] Further, the leader's response may turn into a mission to hunt down perpetrators while simultaneously transforming the nation's culture and economic environment from one of despair to hope. In so doing, the ruler can therefore reverse the collective feelings of helplessness and powerlessness in the nation. Leaders may focus on decreasing the country's pain by transforming the image of "passive victim" into that of "active avenger," mobilizing the nation's anger and need for revenge into promises of punishment.[7] In this situation, people may blindly believe everything that their leaders tell them, and their capacity to doubt, criticize, or challenge government officials decreases. Such avengers need to "degrade" and "dehumanize" the enemy offenders, so that no ambivalent feelings exist about destroying them.

SUPPOSITIONS ABOUT LEADERS' INTERNAL STRUGGLES

The trauma of terrorism may change the mood, behavior and world view of a nation and possibly its leaders. After the trauma of aggression, people enter the first response stage and may behave in an insecure, frightened, and distrustful manner. The affective components of depression, and anxiety and panic states may also emerge after this first response stage. Members of the victimized or traumatized groups also show regressive behaviors with feelings of hopelessness, helplessness, and powerlessness. Some people may resort to religion because church attendance can be soothing (as a coping mechanism). Political leaders may respond to trauma with the same emotions and ego defense mechanisms as those of the country's citizens. Grinfeld (2001) in *Psychiatric Times* has written that the reactions of leaders are further complicated by their need to decide the nation's response to the violence or aggression. The nation may then move to the next response stage—anger, rage, and retaliation—especially if encouraged by leaders, because people at this stage tend to lean on their political and religious leaders for support and direction. A worst-case scenario occurs if such leaders are killed, injured, or unable to perform the role of a strong, protective, punitive parent, because a nation looks for guidance from its leaders in times of crises.

As human beings, leaders are not exempt from being traumatized by terrorism. They too may develop anxiety, nightmares or flashbacks, depression, guilt feelings, and self-blame, especially if they feel that they are partially responsible for the event or failed to prevent it. It is evident that political leaders rarely discuss their personal reactions with the media. For example, we do not know Churchill's reaction to the London bombings of WWII, nor are we aware of the personal response of the Prime Minister of England, Tony Blair, to the London subway bombs by English citizens.[8]

The rare example we have is that of former mayor of New York, Rudy Giuliani (2002) as he described his experiences on September 11, 2001: "There was no time to spend actually experiencing an emotion. There were moments of anger, fear and sorrow, but with so much to do it was impossible to dwell on those feelings" (p. 23). Later in his account of that day, after he was forced to evacuate both his family's residence and City Hall (both considered possible targets), Giuliani wrote about his reactions while at Ground Zero: "Several times, I closed my eyes and expected to open them and see the twin towers still standing. This is not real. This is not real. This is not real. Then I'd shake myself. Damn right it's real, and I had better figure out what I'm going to do about it" (p. 25).

EMOTIONAL AND POLITICAL RESPONSE OF LEADERS

Under the trauma of terror, leaders may become rigid and develop the psychological condition of "splitting." Splitting is a phenomenon in which the leader divides everything into "good or bad," "friend or enemy," "all or nothing." This attitude also exists in children and in regressed adults under the threat or trauma of violence. Regardless of their age or rank, however, individuals in this condition ignore the gray areas and abandon "relativity." It becomes difficult for such people to process the fact that there are different degrees of friendship and animosity.[9]

Grinfeld (2001) has presented several theoretical opinions by psychiatrists regarding what happens to leaders in response to terrorist attacks. Arthur Rousseau has spoken about the emotional volatility of world leaders. He related seeing President George W. Bush tear up about the 9/11 attacks. Rousseau also mentioned even long time allies can snipe at each other. Israeli Prime Minister Ariel Sharon lashed out when comparing the United States' attempt to build alliances with the Arab nations to the European attempts to appease Hitler preceding his assaults. Spencer Eth's discussion about leaders' coping techniques has suggested that "hopefully" we elect leaders who are more mature, controlled and less emotionally reactive than the rest of the nation.

In regard to stress and leadership, Peter Coleman has stated that high stress tolerance is part of the training and conditioning of our leaders (Grinfeld, 2001). Therefore, world leaders' ability to manage stress would ideally allow them to be less likely to react in emotional ways. However, exposure to trauma may impair the ability to make rational decisions. In addition, David Singer has reflected on the limited psychological reaction of these leaders: "They're not attractive human beings. They tend to be cool cats and they like to see and present themselves that way. Their intense self-control has allowed them to develop an affect-less demeanor" (Grinfeld, 2001).

Paul Wallace has identified two types of political reactions by government leaders to terrorism attacks (Grinfeld, 2001). A total reliance on force or "shooting from the hip" is one methodology. The other tactic is analysis, understanding of the problem, and arrival at a solution without a military response. Wallace has suggested that the choices made by our leaders reflect both their own personalities and their psychological responses to a crisis (Grinfeld, 2001). A leader's personality traits, beyond just the nation's interests, may dictate how danger is portrayed and to what degree people should be anxious (Volkan, 2004).

One may wonder if it is the personality of a leader that determines a peaceful or warlike reaction, or if it is outside circumstances, or a combination of both? Several presidents have had the opportunity to be "war presidents," yet have chosen to be "peace presidents." For example, President Carter did not bomb Iran during the hostage situation. President Reagan also did not storm into Iran with military, although there are speculations and allegations that the Iraqi invasion of Iran and their Eight-Year War was spurred on by the United States as retaliation for U.S. hostages taken by Iran. If ideology is a reflection of personality, one speculates what difference there might have been if President Carter had been in charge of the White House during the 9/11 tragedy instead of President Bush. There are differences in the personalities of these two presidents. Would President Carter have used phrases such as "Bring'em on," "dead or alive," or "Axis of Evil" to describe countries with whom the United States has differences (Iran, Iraq, and North Korea)? Would he have initiated a "War on Terror" (with code name of "shock and awe") or would he have thought of war in itself as a terror? Would he have refused to meet the mother of one of the fallen heroes who wanted to question the President about why her son was killed in Iraq? Would he have refused to admit in public that he had made any mistakes? Would he have supported the "rough interrogation" of detainees? Would he have allowed his vice president to imply that "water torture" (dunking someone under water until they are almost to the point of suffocation) was "all right"?

The power of a leader's personality to dictate the role and actions of a nation are made evident through examining Winston Churchill's leadership decisions. Eth has used Winston Churchill as an example of a leader who suffered from depression and possibly alcoholism throughout his career, conditions that Churchill named his "Black Dog." Eth also has speculated about "Churchill's motivation to fight on with 'blood, toil, sweat and tears.' Was it because he was depressed and drinking too much? Was it despite being depressed and drinking? Who knows?" Although these questions remain unanswered, it is possible that politicians tend to be just as traumatized by war and terrorist events as the rest of us (Grinfeld, 2001). Ko and Kim (2007) have referred to three war-oriented historic events over which Churchill had significant, if not total, control: the Dardanelles campaign, the approval of the Dresden Carpet bombing, and the first decision to drop the atomic bomb. These authors have suggested, "Churchill had a tendency not only to enjoy war but also to minimize the value of human lives." It may very well be the case, as psychohistorian Lloyd deMause has indicated, "Wars are clinical emotional disorders" (Ko & Kim, 2007). In addition, a leader's own physical and mental disorder can dramatically influence the fate of a nation as pointed out by Vivian Green, Oxford professor. "Winston Churchill's childhood of neglect stimulated his will to succeed and drive to remain in charge, until he finally had to step down after three strokes" (Garces, 1996).

As Green has mentioned, the events from a leader's childhood may be looked to as the explanation for current actions. Take for example the response of Hillary Clinton in reference to her husband's affair, "There was a terrible conflict between his mother and grandmother. . . . The incident loomed in his unconscious" (Kaminer, 1999). Ex-President Nixon is another example of a leader whose strong childhood experiences of loss and adversity may have affected his adult behavior.[10] Volkan (2004, p. 316) has suggested that these nonideal childhood experiences, and the personality that was formed from them, were echoed in his behavior as a president where shame and humiliation were unbearable.[11]

Repeating a Past Trauma and Transforming the Defeat into Victory

A dejected Vietnam veteran goes into a bar and gets into a fist fight. He may or may not realize that he is repeating the trauma of the war. What he does know is that this time he wants to stand up for himself and ensure that he will be a winner. So, he chooses an enemy he thinks he can overcome. Even if he starts to lose the fight, he knows that the police will come to break it up before he is seriously hurt or killed. This is different from how he might have felt in Vietnam, when he did not feel like he had support if he was losing a battle.

A similar reaction to defeat that may be seen on the national level has been labeled in the United States as the "Vietnam Syndrome." Vietnam Syndrome is considered to be a pattern which can develop after one's defeat, such as the United States defeat in the Vietnam War. Defeat may become a traumatic quality, and yet the impact of a trauma can be diminished by repeating the trauma and trying to change its outcome from defeat to victory. As Lotto has explained, the myth that underlies this syndrome is that after the United States defeat in Vietnam there was a sense of loss and low self-esteem experienced by U. S. leaders and civilians, resulting in a "kind of collective depression" (Lotto, 2006, p. 291).

We have noted that after the Vietnam conflict ended, the U.S. government's leaders "repeated" the war in Grenada and Panama, which resulted in favorable outcomes but only partially compensated for the failure in Vietnam, because of the insignificant size of these countries. The most significant "repeat," however, was created in the first Gulf war. In this conflict, many Vietnam War situations were re-arranged in a favorable way, for example,[12]

1. The United States had support of the United Nations and many world governments including neighboring Arab regimes.
2. The United States had a coalition of several other armies (including Egypt), so the isolation and international criticism of the Vietnam War was reversed.

3. The time of attack was decided by the United States.
4. Enemy soldiers were identifiable.
5. The war front was delineated (versus Vietnam, which was called a front-less war, as enemies were "all over," including inside the South Vietnamese army).
6. The war was considered a "just war" and not an "imperialistic war." Soldiers returned as saviors of Kuwaiti civilians rather than as "baby killers," as in the Vietnam War.

This "defeat syndrome" may also be evident in Hitler's motivation to create WWII as a response to losing in WWI; Hitler blamed the Jews and Communists for this loss. As explained by Lotto (2006) in both cases the bad feelings from being traumatized resulted in an aggressive use of military power to recover from and remedy this sense of weakness.[13]

Leaders' Communication With God: A Possible Genuine Feeling That is Misunderstood

Recently, it has become the fashion for leaders to "talk to God" or to declare that God directed their actions. We speculate that leaders become more religious when they are facing national crises. For example, Richard Nixon, in the crisis of Watergate, knelt down on the floor in the White House with Henry Kissinger and they both prayed. The White House is traditionally about discussing politics, not showing religious expressions. At that time, however, Nixon was losing his dignity (besides all that he had worked for in office), and religion was one of the few things that could give him comfort. In another example of how religion can be soothing and rehabilitating to the shattered ego of a leader, the Shah of Iran reportedly became "more religious" during the last episode of his monarchy as he was being overthrown by his own people.

Similarly, both President George W. Bush and British Prime Minister Tony Blair hinted that "God" told them to attack Iraq. Several critics from opposing parties immediately criticized President Bush because they felt he was violating the separation of church and state by making this statement. Various people felt that they could not criticize his policies if they were indeed inspired by God. Yet other critics suspected that he was exploiting people's belief in God and religion and was trying to justify his actions after he was accused of lying about WMD. Still there were those who, although they possibly could accept the President's explanation of God's command, asked why the United States was losing the war if God was on America's side and how God could approve the deaths of thousands of innocent civilians.

Resorting to faith, with the justification that "I did it for God" or "God told me to do it" may be a genuine feeling that leaders develop to balance a shaky "self-concept" equilibrium. President G. W. Bush and Prime Minister Tony Blair, for example, may have been exposed to multiple instances of "psychic pain" that damaged their concept of self. Instances of such pain could include guilt over the deaths of thousands, recognition of the pain of fallen soldiers' families, realization that there were no WMD in Iraq, the failure to create a pro-western government in Iraq, the creation of thousands of "bin Ladens" because of the invasion of Iraq; the possibility of being labeled "worst President" (*Washington Post*, 2007), and loss of the Parliamentary election to the opposition party. When circumstances become critical, and one is losing the battle, the concept of leaning on and communicating with God may restore and soothe a damaged ego. U.S. leaders are not the only ones to have received criticism for their actions in Iraq. Lynda Gilby in covering Prime Minister Blair's farewell, has commented that he barely showed any remorse at having "dragged us into an illegal war [in Iraq], making war criminals out of every last one of us" (Gilby, 2007).[14]

Do Leaders Believe Terrorists Are Cowards?

President Bush was criticized for identifying the 9/11 terrorists as "cowards." In our opinion, however, he has a point, according to the historical documentation and definition of the word coward. The word coward comes from the French *cuard* which literally means, "someone who runs with his tail between his legs." Goldberg (2001) presented a short history of coward, using the crossbow as an example. In 1097, Pope Urban II banned the use of the crossbow. Forty years later Pope Innocent II outlawed all archery techniques in war, citing their use as cowardly. This ban came in response to complaints by the aristocratic knights of the era. Arrows (shot by peasants) reduced the performance of the armored knight in battles. The use of a crossbow and arrow defied the code of chivalry, which stated that one had to face the enemy and make one's combative intentions clear. In a similar way, modern terrorists also defy the chivalric code with the secrecy and disguise of their attacks. *The Weekly Standard* in 1996 reported that the tendency of leaders to denounce terrorists as "cowardly" began in 1969 when Pope Paul VI condemned the Maoist bombings in Rome and Milan as "cowardly and wicked" (Goldberg, 2001).

Despite the classic definition and examples of cowardice, Goldberg (2001) contradicted President Bush's statement and concluded that terrorists are often considered daring because they sacrifice their own lives for their cause. *The Weekly Standard* also deduced that there was something "weird" about calling terrorists "cowardly," referring to the beheading of the four convicted terrorists in Saudi Arabia at that time. The *Standard's* view was that an activist would not participate in an event that could cause his beheading unless he was courageous, not cowardly (Goldberg, 2001).[15]

Do Opportunistic Leaders Exploit Terrorism?

In times of crisis and terror, leaders can heal or poison their followers.
Vamik Volkan (2004, p. 13)

It is part of the general pattern of misguided policy that our country is now geared to an arms economy which was bred in an artificially induced psychosis of war hysteria and nurtured upon an incessant propaganda of fear.
General Douglas MacArthur (in a speech on May 15, 1951)

Volkan (2004, p. 11) has explored how a society (large group) can regress when put under the pressure of terror and how a society's leader may take advantage of this regression. "Patriotic" actions such as displaying a flag or rallying around one leader provide ways for large groups to purify themselves and dissociate from the enemy. Regression in and of itself is not necessarily negative. However, it is during regression that groups may become more susceptible to their leader's manipulation (Volkan, 2004, p. 13). Volkan has skillfully explained that between a leader and her or his society there is usually an exchange of information, a flow that travels in both directions because both the leader and the public inform and influence each other. During times of crisis, however, the information tends to travel in one direction, from the leader to the public. This trend, with time, can create dependency on the leader, who is looked on as a savior for all the answers, unconscious to the fact that before this crisis both the public and the leaders created the nation's solutions. Therefore, it is during a crisis that a leader may have the most power over her or his nation (Volkan, 2004).

In any government there are officials who believe that terrorism can and should be eradicated by military force alone. Some Middle East intellectuals refer to this attitude as the "cowboy" style similar to what they have seen in western movies. These films show no episodes of negotiation, understanding, or communication between cowboys and Indians. The cowboy relies on his gun and horse and never shows any empathy or sympathy for the suffering of the Indian tribe's people. Similarly, some leaders may consciously or unconsciously exploit terrorist violence and become violent themselves, as if there were no coping strategy other than military retaliation. Some critics further speculate that in any war, regardless of victory or defeat, certain groups will reap benefits and profit. Therefore war, in that regard, is not necessarily considered a tragedy but an opportunity for certain corporations, industries, or individuals. To facilitate the United States involvement in WWI, *The Wall Street Journal* printed a statement from a member of the New York Stock

Exchange, who attempted to create the impression that war was a beneficial move for the country. This statement put forth that in entering the war, the stock market would have great benefits and obviously the economy as well (Davis, 2003). In this sense, any terrorist activity (even if not welcomed) could still be exploited to create war and aggression.

Mueller (2005, 2006) has considered many governments' reactions to terrorism as overreactions. Military attacks do not prevent or destroy terrorism but may actually increase it. Furthermore, Mueller has maintained that often a government's overreaction is a merely a political ploy. Terrorism can be used as an excuse to push forth policies desired for other reasons. He has postulated that terrorist acts do not "trigger" or "cause" these ventures, but actually facilitate them (Mueller, 2005, 2006).

Critics have suggested that the U.S. government used the 9/11 attacks to further its own agenda. Bob Woodward has reported that long before 9/11 many people in President Bush's administration had been planning to depose Saddam Hussein in Iraq (Woodward, 2006). September 11 gave them the opportunity they had been waiting for. Lifton (2003) has pointed out that after 9/11 the United States rejected the offered responses by the United Nations, which incidentally were methods of force, short of war. Did the United States reject these offers because it actually wanted to promote its own agenda besides "preventing" more terrorism? Although President G. W. Bush has declared this to be a "preemptive" war, Lifton has suggested that the invasion of Iraq was not a preemptive but a "preventive" war, in the sense that the Iraqi government was "preventing" U.S. domination in the Middle East (versus any actual physical danger to America) (Lifton, 2003).

Lifton (2003) also has raised questions regarding the quality of western leaders. Did they have their citizens' best interests in mind when, in the earliest stages of the war, they took pride in the fact that only a couple hundred American and British soldiers died compared to the thousands of Iraqis? Lifton has also criticized the U.S. leaders when "we wallow in triumphalism-as though this had been a true contest between military equals and a glorious victory, rather than a slaughter as the world's most powerful military machine simply overwhelmed a relatively small and weak nation" (p. xi). Furthermore, those who questioned this war were judged by political leaders to be "unpatriotic" and "ungrateful" to the western soldiers who were fighting. Is wanting peace or a nonmilitary solution consequently considered to be anti-American?

In Israel, a number of military personnel dared to challenge their country's leader, possibly because they felt that leaders, like anyone else, may be wrong at times. These conscientious Israeli soldiers, who disobeyed their leaders and refused to fight in the occupied territories of the West Bank and Gaza, experienced a lack of support from mainstream society (Chacham,

2003). To these soldiers, however, it was clear that there was a limit to what they were willing to do in the name of their country. These "refuseniks" signed a petition, refusing to serve in the occupied territory of the West Bank and Gaza because they felt it served no purpose beyond humiliating and dominating the Palestinian people.[16] They maintained that "there is a limit to obeying orders when the lawful borders of their country were not being threatened" and challenged their leaders strategies (Chacham, 2003, p. 3).

Mueller (2005, 2006) has also examined cases in which terrorism (aggression) is used as an excuse to further a leader's own agenda. He has compared the U.S. government's actions in the Middle East after 9/11 to Vladimir Putin's actions in Russia in 2004. At that time Vladimir Putin seized the political opportunity afforded by some Chechen terrorist acts to abruptly enhance his control over the Russian political system. Mueller has maintained that this act probably had nothing to do with the behavior of the Chechen terrorists; rather than cause Putin's response, the terrorists' actions simply facilitated it. Mueller has also referred to earlier historical examples of violent attacks as justification to react aggressively. The reaction of Austria and Germany in 1914 to the assassination in Sarajevo is one case study that has been viewed by historians at large as an excuse for initiating WWI. This assassination also gave some Austrian leaders an excuse to impose the Serbian punishing policies that they were seeking to carry out anyway (Mueller, 2005, 2006).

As was made clear after the 9/11 attacks, fear is a common tactic that could be used by leaders in order to rally a nation or community around certain causes or actions. Heskin (1980, p. 100) has referred to the "politics of paranoia" in regard to the conflict between Great Britain and Ireland. He has explained that politicians constantly endeavor to explode public fears and misapprehension in regard to certain aspects of the community. For example the British Conservative Party exploited public fears in regard to the strength of the trade unions, whereas the Labor Party exploited public fears concerning the greed and authority of big corporations. Examples of using fear also have been seen in the United States, when U.S. Senator McCarthy successfully exploited popular fears and misconceptions about communism to his political advantage (Heskin, 1980). By creating a paranoid culture, McCarthy successfully divided the population into those who supported communism and those who did not and sided one against the other. By doing so, he could leverage the support of anticommunists to manipulate communist supporters and promote his political agenda.

Brzezinski (2007), who was the national security advisor to President Carter, has stated that the war on terror has created its own culture of fear in America. Constant reference to the war on terror accomplished a negative element: it stimulated the creation of a culture of fear. Unfortunately, "fear obscures reason, intensifies emotions, and makes it easier for demagogic politicians to mobilize the public on behalf of the policies they want to pursue" (Brzezinski, 2007). Brzezinski has referred to the Iraq war as the "war of choice" and reported that it could never have gained Congressional support without the psychological linkage between the shock of 9/11 and the postulated existence of Iraqi WMD. He has explained that these three words–war on terror–have created a classic self-inflicted wound to America, that is greater than any wild dream that 9/11 terrorists had fantasized. Brzezinski has reported that the U.S. government has stimulated the paranoia at every level. He has referred to the electronic billboards over highways urging motorists to "report suspicious activity" and questions if this is referring to drivers in turbans (Brzezinski, 2007).

THE FEAR OF DEATH MAY INCREASE SUPPORT FOR AGGRESSIVE LEADERS

The war on terror has created fear among Americans. It is possible that this fear is specifically a fear of death, and has been amplified by opportunistic leaders. It also has been suggested that this type of fear can bring people to support extreme actions that they otherwise would reject. Three experimental social psychologists, Sheldon Solomon, Thomas Pyszczynski, and Jeffrey Greenberg, conducted a study of the biological and cultural perspectives of human aggression. They investigated cultural anthropologist Ernest Becker's theory that human awareness and denial of death guides human behavior. Numerous studies, including ones in Iran and Israel, have supported the theory that the fear of death is behind human aggression (Stone, 2006). Terror Management Theory states that existential terror derives from human awareness of the inevitability and finality of death. These findings have been applied to political surveys after exposure to "death images" (mortality salience). In each case, stimulating respondents' fear of death increased their choice for a more militant political leader. Additional knowledge came from this same study conducted by Abdollahi (a professor at Zarand Islamic Azad University in Iran) involving forty Iranian students. This study examined how answering questions about one's own death (versus another unfavorable topic) could have an impact on one's feelings of support for martyrdom. Conclusions revealed that students who had been reminded of death were more likely to support actions of martyrdom attacks (suicide bombers). A similar study in New Jersey produced the same results. Reminders of one's own death increased politically conservative American students' support for extreme military interventions that could kill thousands of civilians. Interestingly, mortality salience did not increase politically liberal students' support for extreme military interventions (Pyszczynski, Ab-dollahi, Solomon et al., 2006). From this study it is clear that "despite their differences, Americans and Iranians have something in common–thoughts of death increase the willingness of people from both nations to inflict harm on citizens of the other nation" (Stone, 2006).

EXAMPLES OF APPROPRIATE AND PEACEFUL REACTIONS OF LEADERS

> *We must face the fact that the United States is neither omnipotent or omni-scient–that we are only 6 percent of the world's population; that we cannot impose our will upon the other 94 percent of mankind; that we cannot right every wrong or reverse each adversity; and therefore there cannot be an American solution to every world problem.*
>
> John F. Kennedy

Not all political leaders have overreacted aggressively after terrorist incidents. For example, President Reagan showed restraint after the bombing of U.S. Marines in Lebanon; President Clinton withdrew U.S. troops from Somalia without acts of aggression after the loss of American lives there in 1993. One wonders whether President Clinton decided not to bomb Somalia because he possibly felt: (1) it would be the wrong decision to involve the United States in a war between two long-standing rivals; (2) that the United States was not the world's "gendarme;"(3) that Somalians themselves should decide their leadership; (4) that economic sanctions could have the same or a better effect than a military invasion of the country; or (5) that the lives of U.S. soldiers were more valuable than placement of a pro-West government in Somalia.[17]

Looking at the Nicaraguan government's reaction to the U.S. government, which was supporting the Contras (a terrorist group), gives us another example of nonviolent response. The impact of the Contras' terrorist activities on Nicaragua was much more severe than the tragedies of 9/11. Yet, as Chomsky (2001, 2002) has explained, Nicaragua did not respond by bombing Washington; instead, they approached the World Court, which ruled in their favor by ordering the United States to desist and pay them substantial reparations. The U.S. government rejected the court's judgment with contempt, and the Contras escalated their attacks. Nicaragua then approached Security Council of the United Nations. This agency presented a resolution requesting the United States respect international law. The U.S. government vetoed this resolution as well. Then Nicaragua went to the General Assembly and received a similar resolution that passed with the United States and Israel opposed. Chomsky has stated that if Nicaragua had been powerful enough it could have set up another criminal court. He has suggested that those are the measures that the United States could have pursued as a reaction to 9/11 (Chomsky, 2001, 2002).[18]

Looking at the Iranian conflict with the Afghanistan government provides another illustration of the success of nonviolent means to respond to aggression. In 1998, ten Iranian diplomats were massacred by the Taliban regime. At that time, Iran and Afghanistan were on the edge of war, but the Iranian president was able to use diplomacy, negotiation, communication, and requests for apology by the Afghanistan government. Through the use of these nonviolent methods, these countries were able to resolve this conflict and avoid war (salam Iran, 1998).

Davis (2003) has related the history of the U.S. entrance into WWI as an example of how President Wilson first attempted to avoid the war. As Davis has detailed, the British ship *Lusitania* was torpedoed by a German boat off the coast of Ireland and 128 Americans died. President Wilson resisted the indignant clamor for mounting a war against Germany following this sinking. Instead, he attempted to deal with the Germans through a series of diplomatic notes demanding reparations and German abstention from attacking passenger ships and boats. Secretary of State William Bryan thought that even these notes were too severe a response, and he protested and resigned. Nevertheless, the German government agreed to make reparations (Davis, 2003). However, they also claimed that the *Lusitania* had been carrying armaments and therefore was a war vessel. Although the British government, which owned the ship, denied this, it later became clear that the *Lusitania* had indeed carried 4200 cases of ammunition and 1250 shrapnel, which exploded when the German torpedoes hit (Davis, 2003).

When President Wilson was running for reelection, his campaign carried the slogan "He kept us out of war" (Davis, 2003). In February of 1917, however, the Germans began war against all merchants' shipping, including American ships, and so Wilson broke off all diplomatic relations. In March of 1917 the German navy sank five more American ships without warning. The critical change in Wilson's mind came with the revelation of a telegram that apparently showed that the German government was plotting to instigate a war between Mexico and the United States. Although the British had discovered the telegram earlier, they had waited for a more opportune time to give it to the Wilson government. Many historians assume that this telegram pushed Wilson past his wavering neutrality and into war. Almost two years after the *Lusitania's* sinking, in April 1917, America entered WWI, although it was already in its closing stages (Davis, 2003).

Although President Wilson responded to the pressure finally and entered the war, he tried admirably to restrain both sides and mediate a peace. Yet

Davis (2003) has reported that this eventual engagement in war was no surprise, "as in almost every other war America has fought, powerful forces in industry, banking, and commerce cynically thought that war was healthy. And if the world was going to be divided up after the fighting was over, America might as well get its fair share of this spoils" (p. 307). Furthermore, when President Wilson presented the war authorization in Congress, his speech was met with wild applause, and the U.S. Congress overwhelmingly approved war a few days later. It is reported that Wilson after delivering his speech in Congress and hearing the applause told an aide, "My message today was a message of death for our young men. How strange it seems to applaud that " (Davis, 2003, p. 313).

Although Congress overwhelmingly approved entering WWI, Senator Norris from Nebraska spoke against the declaration of war and mentioned that this fight was for profit rather than for principles.[19] He quoted from a letter written by a member of the New York Stock Exchange in the *Wall Street Journal* that favored the war for the bull market it would produce: "Here we have the man representing the class of people who will be made prosperous should we become entangled in the present war, who have already made millions of dollars, and who will make hundreds of millions more if we go to war. . . . Their object in having war and in preparing for war is to make money. Human suffering and sacrifice of human life are necessary, but Wall Street considers only the dollars and the cents. . . . The stock brokers would not, of course, go to war. . . . They will be concealed in their palatial offices on Wall Street, sitting behind mahogany desks. (Davis, 2003, p. 313; Norris, n.d.).

WWI was called the war to end all wars, but it did not prevent future wars.[20] In fact, the divisions of the "spoils of war" among the Allied Powers set the stage for almost a century of conflicts over the deadly divisions in the Middle East, Africa, Eastern Europe and Indochina (Davis, 2003).

CONCLUSION

Nations place their military and political decisions in the hands of their leaders. We "trust" them to act without self-interest but in the interest of the people they lead. We also expect the leaders in democracies to act in ways that reflect their countries' will, not their own. We expect such leaders to react without human frailty and with power and intelligence not available to all of us. Are we really asking too much from our leaders? Perhaps. A leader is a human being with human frailties common to all of us and should not be idolized as far superior to average citizens. They are experiencing the same amount of trauma in response to terrorism as the people of their nation (if not more so because of their role). Peaceful leaders may have had a different type of childhood, than did those leaders who tend to focus on war as a constant solution (cowboy style). Leaders, like ordinary citizens, are working to resolve their childhood issues and possible traumas. Their actions in response to terrorism may reflect how successful they have been in this endeavor. For leaders, childhood events, personality, and ideology may be more significant factors in anticipating how they will respond to terrorism than the actual terrorist events that have taken place will be. Opportunistic leaders may exploit terrorism and force their own agenda as explained in detail by Mueller (2005, 2006).

NOTES

1. Khalid Sohail is a poet and psychotherapist. We have included a portion of one of his poems (from K. Sohail [2006, August]. Psychology of Suicide "Bombers." *Chowk* [On-line]. Retrieved on August 31, 2006. Available: http://www.chowk .com).

"We Are All Children of Mother Earth"
When would we realize?
We are all children of Adam and Eve
Our enemies are our distant cousins
Alienated by ethnic and religious walls
Separated by linguistic and national borders
Divided by the history of Holy Wars.
When would we become aware?
We all belong to the same race
The same tribe
The same family
The Human family . . .

2. There are indications that a victim may identify with his aggressor and become an aggressor himself. Two rabbis from Rabbis for Human Rights, Rabbi Ascherman (founder) and Rabbi Walt, spoke in West Hartford, CT. It was during their lecture that one of the rabbis mentioned, "Now we are the victim and also the offender." Identification with the aggressor may occur at the individual level but may also occur at the group or national level. Algeria, for example, fought against the French for a number of years and lost several hundred thousand people while attempting to gain its independence. After the war, the next generation (those who were children during the war) began to dress in clothing reminiscent of French soldiers. One may speculate that this behavior demonstrated how people can identify with their aggressor.

   Do leaders also identify with the aggressor and imitate previously criticized behavior? Some of the United States' current leaders were also involved in politics or in the military during the Communist era, when the United States was preoccupied with the Soviet Union and its "evil" empire (who defeated the United States in the Vietnam War). Is it possible that some of the current western leaders have "picked up" the Soviet Union's unacceptable behavior and policies from the Communist era? Is it conceivable that western democratic leaders have identified with the aggressor and have repeated some of the offenders actions (e.g., practicing torture, kidnapping, establishing secret prisons, spying illegally on their citizens, violating international laws)?

3. Some Palestinians have accused Israeli leaders of identification with their former aggressor (Hitler and his generals). Although there may be validity in this theory, one must also consider the aggressive and hostile surroundings of Israel. Israel originally was established as a symbol of human rights, democracy, and fairness. At first Israel was excessively sensitive to discrimination, abuse, and human rights violations. However, over time it has changed to resemble a few hostile surrounding regimes (identification with the aggressor?). For example, in many areas of the Middle East, assassinations and coup d'etats are the way to change the governments if one disagrees with their policies. As we have seen in Israel, however, Prime Minister Rabin was also assassinated by a Jewish terrorist because of policy disagreements. So at least in this case, the bullet has become the method for change instead of the ballot for modern day Israel.

4. It is necessary to clarify two key terms: (1) Psycho-political Impact: A change in the political view or action which results from the impact of trauma on the personalities of leaders. (2) Trauma: (A) Trauma can be traced to the Greek word for wound. (B) Freud described trauma as a state of psychic helplessness caused when the traumatic experience is powerful enough to break through the ego's protective shield (from S. Freud [1920]. Beyond the Pleasure Principle. In *The Standard Edition of the Complete Works of Sigmund Freud* [*18*, pp. 26–33]. London: The Hogarth Press, 1955). (C) Kris proposed the concept of "strain trauma" for the dramatic impact caused by the long-term accumulation of frustrating tensions. He differentiated strain trauma from "shock trauma," which is due to a single painful experience. Strain trauma is similar to "cumulative trauma," which is described in psychoanalytic literature (from E. Kris [1956]. The recovery of childhood memories in psychoanalysis. *Psychoanalytic Study of Child, 11*, pp. 54–88). (D) "Psychic trauma" is the result of an abrupt and painful experience that the individual's ego cannot assimilate. Instead, the individual may repress and eliminate part of or the entire traumatic memory from consciousness. (E) War, terrorism and political violence, for example, are known to create terror and are considered psychic trauma.

5. After traumatic national events, leaders may project themselves as strong father figures in public. In addition they may gain citizens' support by promoting an image of their nation as an innocent victim that deserves to take revenge. How a political candidate presents himself or herself in public can strongly influence voters' opinions of the candidates, especially in times of crisis. For example, two candidates in the 2004 U.S. presidential elections presented opposing images. One, the incumbent, posed as an authoritarian, puni-

tive, powerful father figure who saw himself as infallible. Conversely, his counterpart, a senator, presented himself as a compassionate, benevolent father figure. One may wonder if the former candidate won because the United States was in a time of crisis and fear. In such times, people have a tendency to favor an authoritarian, punitive father figure rather than an affectionate and compassionate paternal one. They look for a firm and rigid attitude rather than a thoughtful and flexible approach. Even if a rigid decision proves to be wrong, the leader's decisiveness helps alleviate the suffering of a traumatized and victimized nation. In such a situation, people who are religious may also tend to lean toward a leader who plays the role of a godlike, "powerful, omnipotent" figure.

6. When President Ronald Reagan was shot in 1981, his secretary of state, General Alexander Haig, appeared on several TV channels. He was nervous and exhibited rapid breathing as he declared, "as of now I am in control here in the White House" (from P. A. Rinfret [2006]. People I Have Known: General Alexander Haig. Much less than life [On-line]. Retrieved March 1, 2007. Available: http:www.rinfret.com/ah.html). He was wrong in that regard, however, because from a constitutional point of view, he could not be next in charge. That role would go to the vice president, not secretary of state. One may wonder, however, what was in the mind of this obviously shocked general? Was he worried that the assassination attempt was part of an attack on the United States by the Soviet Union? Did he wonder who was in control of "the black box," which could order missiles with atomic bombs to fly toward the enemy? Did he want to show to a "perceived enemy" that a general was in the White House and in charge and that there was no disruption in the leadership of the U. S. government? Or was he so anxious that he simply forgot the chain of command issued in the Constitution of the United States?

7. After a national trauma, leaders generally attempt to crystallize the anger of their nation and direct it toward the enemy for revenge. We know that a victim's anger is in the service of the victim's ego and that anger can be used constructively. To survive torture, for example, political prisoners are often instructed to get in touch with their hate and anger for the torturer. The sufferers can then use their anger to give them the strength and power to hold their broken selves together and to tolerate rather than submit to the torture (from J. A. Marvasti [1993]. Please hurt me again: Posttraumatic play therapy with an abused child. In T. Kottman & C. Schaefer (Eds.) *Play therapy in action: A casebook for practitioners* (pp. 485–525). Northvale, NJ: Jason Aronson).

8. We cannot know how political leaders react personally to terrorist events in their countries (such as 7/7 in England). Yet an analogy that comes to mind is the probable reaction of a physician whose patient has committed suicide. We know that the physician frequently will develop guilt, self-blame, and fear of possible retaliation (such as malpractice charges). The physician also may wonder if the patient's family has developed negative feelings about his competence. The issue of "damage control" also may be indicated because the doctor will review the medical record to look for anything that would make him

or her appear neglectful or responsible for the suicide. It is possible that polit-ical leaders have similar reactions. Responding to guilt, a leader may ask, could I have prevented it? To self-blame, did I alienate my own citizens by attacking or occupying another country? To fear of retaliation, I may not be reelected. Leaders even might review their past and present documents and attempt to change their history by rewriting them. They would not want their popularity to decrease, nor would they want their counterparts to assign blame to them.

9. President Bush's statement that "if you are not with us you are against us" reminds us of John Foster Dallas who, in the 1950s, felt that countries were either "with us or were communist." He ignored neutral regimes that appreci-ated some of the United States' democratic qualities and also certain aspects of communism.

10. The final remarks given by President Nixon at the White House after he resigned may be the only speech that his speechwriter did not write. In this speech, he spoke about his mother who took care of his brother who had tuber-culosis. She was also taking care of several other children who were sick. From a psychological point of view, one wonders if the rejection by his nation re-minded him of rejection from his mother, who may have been overwhelmed taking care of so many children. Was his possible abandonment by his over-worked mother perceived by Nixon as a rejection and an emotionally trau-matic experience? Was he repeating this trauma unconsciously by setting up a situation in which he would be exposed and therefore rejected by the nation?

11. The issue of childhood personality has been captured in caricatures of various leaders, such as President G. W. Bush (from D. Granlund [2007, February 23]. George W. Bush at age 5. *Manchester Journal Inquirer*, p. 19). In February of 2007, President G. W. Bush rejected the U. S. Congress' war recommendations and disputed their challenge that Congress would decide if the war in the Middle East would be limited or not. President G.W. Bush declared that in regard to war or peace, "I am the Decider!" That same week a caricature was printed that illustrated George W. Bush as a 5-year-old in his pajamas screaming at his father, "I'm the decider! I'm not going to bed!!" while his father, President George Bush, is desperately thinking, "Hope he grows outta this!"

In regard to individual personalities, one may be strongly influenced by one's family upbringing and childhood experiences. For example, a leader who criticizes another regime for violation of human rights principles (e.g., tor-ture or kidnapping) and then himself tries to justify and legalize it in his own country may have grown up in a family with characteristics of the "it is differ-ent for me" mentality. For instance, when a father teaches his child not to pick up food with his fingers but later on does so himself, the child may challenge him. The father's response tends to be "it is different for me." When a mother punishes her child for lying but then lies herself (e.g., someone calls on the tele-phone, and she tells her child to tell him she's not home), she claims "mine is different" if the child challenges her.

12. Hamid Dabashi addressed the issue of the Vietnam syndrome and the events that took place after the United States "finally emerged from its Vietnam syn-

drome and began flexing its military muscles around the globe" in his recent book, *Iran: A People Interrupted*. Doctor Dabashi referred to "the two monsters that President Reagan created, Saddam Hussein and Osama bin Laden, soon came back to haunt" subsequent Presidencies (p. 211) (from H. Dabashi [2007]. *Iran: A People Interrupted*, New York: The New Press).

13. Some analysts have speculated that the Israeli attacks on Palestinians represent a similar attempt to erase previous victimization by Hitler's army and to become a superior military force.

14. It is interesting to point out that almost all U.S. Presidents in some way maintain (or at least pretend) that for them war is the last resort. However, President George W. Bush, who has been presented as more religious that his last several predecessors, considered war as the first choice by using the phrase preemptive strike as is claimed by his opponents. It is surprising that one who states that he follows the Christian dogma (and is in spiritual connection with God) is not turning his other cheek, but instead slaps the enemy's cheeks. Again one wonders if personality is more influential in determining leadership quality than are religious orientation and faith. Leaders also are less likely to credit God's help when they are winners of a war (because they want full credit for the victory).

15. Labeling terrorists cowards is a type of name calling. Name calling is not unusual for politicians. Yet Bill Richardson, presidential candidate for 2008, criticized President Bush's for calling North Korean leader Kim Jong-II, who has a short stature, names. He made the suggestion to the president, "Don't call Kim Jong-II a dwarf. He doesn't like it. And when he doesn't like something, he shoots missiles off" (from *The Citizen of Laconia* [2007, April 6] Richardson would approve medical marijuana [On-line]. Retrieved April 11, 2007. Available: http://www.citizen.com/apps/pbcs.d11/article?Date=20070406& Category=CITIZEN_01&A).

16. Although these Israeli soldiers were not leaving the military completely, they were acknowledging that the occupation of Palestine was not creating peace or a solution to this conflict. In their own words,

> "We . . . who have been on reserve duty throughout the occupied territories and were issued commands and directives that had nothing to do with the security of our country, and that had the sole purpose of perpetuating control over the Palestinian people. We, whose eyes have seen the bloody toll this exacts from both sides. . . . We who believed that the commands issued to us in the territories destroy all the values we had absorbed while growing up in this country. . . . We who understand now that the price of occupation is the loss of the IDF's human character and the corruption of the entire Israeli society, We shall not continue to fight beyond the 1967 borders in order to dominate, expel, starve, and humiliate an entire people. . . . We hereby declare that we shall continue serving in the Israeli Defense Forces in any mission that serves Israel's defense. The missions of occupation and oppression do not serve this purpose, and we shall take no part in them" (Chacham, 2003, p. 2).

17. Governments and their leaders could learn much from certain animal's peaceful behavior. As primatologists have pointed out, hamadryas baboons, while

happy to eat a peanut if thrown in front of one male, will ignore the peanut if thrown in front of two males to avoid the chance of a fight (from N. Angier, [2003, November 11]. Is War Our Biological Destiny?" *The New York Times*, p. D-1).

18. Mueller (2005) has explained that even in extreme cases such as Pearl Harbor or the 9/11 tragedy, the leaders could have pursued more patient and gradual policies. Looking back in history, one can see a multitude of instances in which extreme violence was not the only option. Mueller has referred to the British and Argentinean war over the Falkland Islands (with a population of less than 2000). Mueller has suggested, that during this conflict, the British could have chosen compromise rather than war because what they were fighting over was insignificant to both countries. Mueller has quoted Argentinean writers who have said the war was "like two bald men fighting over a comb." Although fewer than a thousand people died in the ten-week war, the cost was disproportionate to the value and made that war quite possibly the most brutal in history.

    Italy has seen the benefit of choosing peace. The Falkland war decision in the 1980s was exactly the opposite of Italy's response toward Libya's increasing antagonism. Instead of mounting a military campaign, Italy initiated an economic one. The country increased its trade with Libya to show that it was advantageous to maintain friendly relations and to retain preferred nation status.

19. There are also more current examples of leaders in Congress who spoke openly against the war. Congresswoman Barbara Lee from California, was the only member who three days after September 11, 2001, rejected giving the President authority to go to war (for her full speech *see* www.wagingpeace.org/articles/2001/09/14_lee-speech.htm). Congressman John Larson from Connecticut, was also one of several members who voted against the war in Iraq. He maintained his opposition to the war and felt that "what we need is a surge of diplomacy in the region" and not a surge of more troops (for more information *see* www.ctnewsjunkie.com/iraq_at_home/frustration_and_optimism_expre.php).

    Senator Christopher Dodd, although he originally voted for the Iraq war, later became concerned that the actions that the administration was taking were making America more vulnerable, not less. He has stated that "America doesn't start wars–we end them. . . . And we don't continue torture–we condemn it." He believes this was true until the current administration. He has become a candidate for the 2008 presidency and his slogan is "Restore the Constitution, Restore American's Moral Authority" (for more information *see* http://dodd.senate.gov/).

20. After the war ended in 1918, President Wilson delivered a speech that is now well-known as the "Fourteen Points for Peace" speech (Davis, 2003). In it, he suggested creating a kind of peace association of the nations. These points become a basis for the League of Nations. Yet, allied governments' reactions were tepid at first. For example, French Prime Minister said that the fourteen points "bore him" and referred to the Ten Commandments when he men-

tioned "even Almighty God has only 10" (Davis, 2003, p. 314). However, in October of 1918, Germany began peace overtures based on Wilson's Fourteen Points project.

REFERENCES

Brzezinski, Z. (2007, March 25). Terrorized by "War on Terror." *Manchester Journal Inquirer*, p. 23.

Chacham, R. (2003). *Breaking ranks: Refusing to serve in the West Bank and Gaza Strip*. New York: Other Press.

Chomsky, N. (2001, October). The new war against terror. *Chomsky.Info* [On-line]. Retrieved February 12, 2007. Available: www.chomsky.info/talks/20011018.htm

Davis, K. C. (2003). *Don't know much about history*. New York: Harper Collins Publishers Inc.

Garces, L. (1996, Winter). Book reviews. *The Journal of Psychohistory, 23*(3), pp. 338–342.

Gilby, L. (2007, May 25). United Kingdom: Why no one is weeping for Tony Blair. *The Week* p. 17.

Giuliani, R. W. (2002). *Leadership*. New York, Miramax Books.

Goldberg, J. (2001, August). Crossbows & suicide bombers: Stem-cell-free zone. *National Review Online* [On-line], Retrieved May 6, 2007. Available: http://www.nationalreview.com

Grinfeld, M. J. (2001). World leaders not immune to trauma. *Psychiatric Times, 18*(12). pp. 1–6

Heskin, K. (1980). *Northern Ireland: A psychological analysis*. New York: Columbia University Press.

Kaminer, W. (1999, December 15). The 12-step campaign, *Wall Street Journal*, p. 22.

Ko, Young-Gun & Kim, Jin-Young (2007, Spring). Churchill's childhood and his political legacies. *The Journal of Psychohistory, 34*(4), pp. 314–324.

Lifton, R. J. (2003). *Super power syndrome*. New York: Thunder's Mouth Press.

Lotto, D. (2006, Winter). Book reviews. *The Journal of Psychohistory, 33*(3), pp. 290–299.

Mueller, J. (2005). Reactions and overreactions to terrorism [On-line]. Retrieved February 10, 2007. Available: http://psweb.sbs.ohio-state.edu/faculty/jmueller

Mueller, J. (2006). *Overblown: How politicians and the terrorism industry inflate national security threats, and why we believe them*. New York: Free Press.

Norris, G. W. (n.d.). Opposition to Wilson's war message. Retrieved April 6, 2007. Available: http://teachingamericanhistory.org/library/index.asp?documentprint=649

Pyszczynski, T., Abdollahi, A., Solomon, S., Greenberg, J., Cohen, F. & Weise, D. (2006). Mortality salience, martyrdom, and military might: The great Satan versus the Axis of Evil. *Personality and Social Psychology Bulletin, 32*(4), pp. 525–537.

Salam Iran (1998, September 11). Iran mourns the diplomats murdered by the Taliban [On-line]. Retrieved on March 21, 2007. Available: www.salamiran.org/events/Afghan_crisis

Stone, K. (2006, November). Anatomy of human destructiveness. *NeuroPsychiatry Reviews, 7*(11). pp. 8–9.

Volkan, V. (2004). *Blind trust: Large groups and their leaders in times of crisis and terror*. Charlottesville, VA: Pitchstone Publishing.

Washington Post (2007, May 20). Bush Is 'the worst in history' in foreign relations, Carter says. Retrieved June 1, 2007. Available: http://www.washingtonpost.com/wp-dyn/content/article/2007/05/19/AR2007051900212_pf.html

Woodward, B. (2006). *State of denial: Bush at war, part III*. New York: Simon & Schuster.

Chapter 11

SOWING THE SEEDS OF WAR: ISRAELI AND PALESTINIAN CHILD DEATHS IN THE CONTEXT OF SEPTEMBER 11

Justine McCabe

There are many ways to consider the consequences of war and protracted ethnic violence. One is to attend to the children raised under such circumstances. Indeed, civilians—especially women and children—far outnumber armed combatants as victims in these conflicts today.[1] Consequently, there has been a growing interest among social scientists in the individual and societal effects of political violence on children maturing under such conditions. In sum, intuition that war is not good for children continues to be empirically demonstrated (Alkhatib, Regan, & Barrett, 2007; Dyregrov, Gjestad, & Raundalen, 2002; Garbarino, Kostelny, & Dubrow, 1991; Goldson, 1993; Leavitt & Fox, 1993; Masalha, 1993).

In addition to looking at the impact of violence on children's health and development, it is important to consider what violence towards children means, and what it arouses and symbolizes for both those living in and outside the conflict, as well as for the prospects for peace.

Today, violent ethnic conflict occurs mostly in the developing world. By contrast, residents of western industrialized nations can choose, mainly through news media, to relate to these hostilities safely from a distance, or not at all. Still, it is their governments that significantly influence the outcome of such conflicts, particularly wealthy European nations and the world's only superpower, the United States. Thus, a question arises: What effect does the killing of children in these conflicts have on members of societies who are at once safely removed from their violence, yet are citizens of those nations that have a significant impact on their resolution? That is, how do we translate the gravity of the loss of these children at a distance in terms that can be meaningful to citizens of such politically influential societies as the United States?

Perhaps no modern conflict has been more intractable than that between the Israelis and Palestinians. As the second Palestinian uprising, the *Al-Aqsa Intifada*, continues in opposition to Israeli military occupation, its violence echoes that of the first (1987–1993). This chapter takes a comparative look at the violence to Palestinian and Israeli children during the first and present uprisings and *translates these losses into terms meaningful to Americans–the September 11, 2001, attacks.* What are the consequences for peace and reconciliation between warring parties when their children are killed? Furthermore, what is the effect on peacemaking when the proportion of civilian casualties–specifically child deaths–is highly imbalanced between the parties?

In considering these questions, I seek to highlight the intense feelings inevitably aroused between Israelis and Palestinians by the mutual killing of their children are highlighted in a way that may bring the gravity of this conflict home to Americans.

THE FIRST INTIFADA

Between 1987 and 1993, the first mass civil uprising by Palestinians in the Occupied Palestinian Territories, (OPT) (West Bank, including East Jerusalem, and Gaza), occurred in response to twenty years of Israeli military occupation (Farsoun & Landis, 1990; Graff, 1997). In 1990, *Radda Barnen* (Swedish Save the Children) published an exhaustive report (Nixon, 1990) of that uprising's impact on Palestinian children in its initial two years.[2] This study established that children–then defined as those *under 16*–accounted for 21 percent of all Palestinian deaths and 38 percent of all casualties (death and injuries combined).

The report also found that 159 Palestinian children died from gunshot, beating, or tear gas, with most killed by gunshot: 67 percent over the two years and 78 percent in the last 18 months of that period. The average age of all those killed was ten, 12.5 for those shot (Nixon, 1990, pp. 225–226). According to this report, Israeli "military personnel were responsible for 94 percent of the children's deaths" (Nixon, 1990, p. 226). In Israeli population terms, those Palestinian child deaths were the equivalent of 251 Israeli child deaths and 70,000 to 99,000 Israeli child injuries over that two-year period. More dramatic still, in U.S. population terms, those 1987 to 1989 Palestinian child deaths and injuries represented an equivalent of 9680 American children (i.e., under 16 years) killed and 3 to 3.8 million American children injured over a two-year period (Nixon, 1990, pp. 292–293).

Radda Barnen did not collect data on Israeli child deaths for the study period. However, the Israeli human rights group, *B'Tselem* reports that during those two years, there were four Israeli child deaths: three within the OPT and one within the Israeli "Green Line."[3] Despite the fact that the *B'Tselem* aggregated data extends the *Radda Barnen* cohort to those Israeli minors *under seventeen*, there were nearly forty times more Palestinian than Israeli children killed during the same period (*B'Tselem*).

During the 1990s, the number of children killed declined. However, the asymmetry in fatalities continued between the formal end of that first uprising–the signing of the Oslo Peace Accords on September 13, 1993–and the outbreak of the second (*Al-Aqsa Intifada*) on September 29, 2000. According to *B'Tselem* figures, 3.7 times more Palestinians than Israelis under age seventeen were killed (44 to 12). How have Israeli and Palestinian children fared in the renewed uprising *Al-Aqsa Intifada*?[4]

PALESTINIAN AND ISRAELI CHILD DEATHS: THE FIRST TWO YEARS OF AL-AQSA INTIFADA

The first Intifada was characterized largely by nonviolent resistance by Palestinian civilians–adults and children–to the Israeli soldiers in their midst. As a result of the Oslo Peace Accords, by mid-2000 Israeli forces (IDF) had redeployed to the periphery of the main Palestinian population centers ("Area A"), whose local security was left to the Palestinian Authority (PA), although the IDF continued to be present and control most of the OPT (Areas B, and C), most prominently at places such as checkpoints and Jewish-only settlements.

Palestinian psychologists Ahmed Baker and Hana Kanan (2003) note that when the second, *Al-Aqsa Intifada* broke out, "a tactical shift" occurred on both sides: "Although it began in a similar manner (widespread demonstrations by civilian, including children) as its predecessor, it soon escalated to the use of firearms and weapons, reaching new magnitudes of destruction in March 2002, when Israeli forces began to make repeated and systematic 'incursions' into Palestinian cities and towns. The Israelis resorted to the use of Apache helicopters, F-16 fighter jets, and tanks and armoured personnel carriers to target buildings, installations, individuals and vehicles. The Palestinians, on the other hand, countered by employing light weapons (mainly AK-47 rifles) and suicide bombings" (Baker & Kanan, 2003, p. 14).

To study the deaths of Israeli and Palestinian children of the *Al-Aqsa Intifada*, I used data from Remember These Children, a consortium of Israeli, Palestinian, and American peace groups devoted to ending the killing of children in the Israeli-Palestinian conflict.[5] Since September 29, 2000, they have maintained a detailed list of each Israeli and Palestinian child under age eighteen[6] killed in the conflict, as well as the child's age, place of residence, date and circumstance of death.[7]

Their figures reveal that in the first two years of the present uprising (September 29, 2000 to September 29, 2002), 344 Palestinian and 70 Israeli children under age eighteen were killed, maintaining the asymmetry of loss between the two societies from the first uprising, even in the midst of unequivocal tragedy for each: Palestinian child deaths were five times as many as Israeli deaths.

Of note–and in contradiction to professed Israeli security fears justifying deadly force in response to the uprising–93 Palestinian children were killed before the first Israeli child was killed on January 17, 2001 (by Palestinian gunfire in the OPT). Of those 93, most (83 or 89%) were killed by IDF gunfire, mainly to the head and chest. Only 6 children (6.5%) were engaged in stone throwing at checkpoints (N = 4) or other direct, although unarmed, confrontations with Israeli soldiers (N = 2).

In comparison with the *Radda Barnen* study, my analysis of the Remember These Children data indicates that on average Israeli and Palestinian youth killed in these first two years were about the same age: 12.4 and 12.8 years, respectively. Although similar to the average age of Palestinians shot dead in the first Intifada (12.5), these average ages are higher than those of Palestinian children killed overall (10) between 1987 and 1989.

With regard to cause of death, of the 70 Israeli children killed in those first two years, the majority (66%) were victims of Palestinian suicide bombings, virtually all within the Green Line. Another 29 percent were killed by Palestinian gunfire, all within the OPT, of which 75 percent occurred at military-guarded Jewish settlements.[8]

Describing the psychological effect of suicide bombings on Israelis, Israeli professor of philosophy, Avishai Margalit (2003) writes, "In the minds of Israelis, suicide bombing colors everything else. . . . The suicide bombers make most Israelis feel not just ordinary fear but an intense mixture of horror and revulsion as well."

In some Palestinian suicide attacks, Israeli families have lost many of their members; for example the five surviving children of the Schijveschuurder family whose parents and three siblings (age two, four, and fourteen) were killed on August 9, 2001, in a pizzeria in Jerusalem (Pickett, 2001). The terror that Israeli families feel while going about ordinary activities (riding on a bus or eating in a restaurant) should not be underestimated. It stands in sharp contrast to the otherwise safe and very orderly functioning of their society.

With regard to Palestinians, the 344 child deaths that occurred during those first two years reveal patterns noted in the first uprising. Significantly, like the *Radda Barnen* study, the present data do not support allegations (made in 1990 as well as now) that the high Palestinian child death toll results from the deliberate use of children by Palestinians in confrontations with the IDF or that the children were armed.

For example, in the first uprising, 52 percent of Palestinian children were not in or near a protest activity when killed. Another 28 percent of the children killed were engaging in nonviolent activities such as observing or passing a demonstration, hanging a flag, dismantling a barricade, participating in a silent march, dispersing from a demonstration, fleeing from soldiers, marching in a funeral (Nixon, 1990, p. 226). Thus, 80 percent of the children killed were not engaged even in throwing stones when killed.

Similarly, of the 344 Palestinian children killed during the first two years of the Al-Aqsa uprising, 63 percent were not engaged in confrontations with the IDF or any protest activities when killed, most by IDF gunfire to head or chest.[9] Another 28 percent were demonstrating nonviolently when killed, again most shot in the chest or head by the IDF. In fact, of the 344 Palestinian children killed, only 7.3 percent were in direct confrontation with members of the IDF via actions such as throwing stones at checkpoints.[10] In sum, for Palestinians, the second uprising repeats the pattern of the first: Israeli military-soldiers on the ground, in helicopters, and shelling from above-were responsible for virtually all the deaths of mostly unarmed Palestinians under age eighteen. For Israelis, the origins of the Israeli-Palestinian conflict in 1948 created and sustained a bellicose atmosphere for their society in relation to their Arab neighbors.[11] Still, Israeli children were virtually untouched directly (killed or wounded) by Palestinians during the first uprising. By contrast, the second Intifada saw a dramatic increase in the killing of Israeli children, most of them by Palestinian suicide bombings within the Green Line and to a lesser extent by gunshot mainly in or near Jewish settlements in the OPT.

TOTAL PALESTINIAN AND ISRAELI CHILD DEATHS TO DATE

In the years following September 29, 2002, peace continues to elude Palestinians and Israelis, and their children have been dying in greater numbers. According to Remember These Children, between September 29, 2000 and April 5, 2007, 118 Israelis under the age of eighteen were killed, the last in March 2006. During the same period, 930 Palestinians under eighteen were killed, the last (at this writing) on April 5, 2007, nearly eight times the number of Israeli child deaths.[12]

Because Israel and Palestine represent such relatively small populations and territory, it is sometimes difficult to appreciate the gravity these losses represent in their societies as a whole, especially in the eyes of Americans, whose population and territory are vast.

To put these child fatalities in high relief, as in the *Radda Barnen* study, child death rates for: (1) the first two years of the Al-Aqsa Intifada; and (2) Israeli and Palestinian children killed from September 29, 200 to April 2007 were calculated as proportions of Israeli, Palestinian, and U.S. populations under eighteen.[13]

Child Death Rates for September 29, 2000 to September 29, 2002

From the Israeli population perspective: 70 Israeli child deaths over two years are the equivalent of 64 Palestinian child deaths (there were 344). Seventy Israeli child deaths are the equivalent of 2650 American child deaths. At the Israeli child death rate, the equivalent 2650 Americans would be killed at the rate of 110 American children per month for twenty-four months.

From the Palestinian perspective: 344 Palestinian child deaths over two years are the equivalent of 376 Israeli child deaths over two years (there were 70). Over two years, 344 Palestinian child deaths are the equivalent of 14,231 American child deaths. At this Palestinian death rate, the equivalent 14,231 Americans would be killed at the rate of 593 American children per month for twenty-four months.

Child Death Rates for September 29, 2000 to April 5, 2007

From the Israeli population perspective: 118 Israeli child deaths over 6.5 years are the equivalent of 129 Palestinian child deaths. (There were 930.) The 118 Israeli child deaths are the equivalent of 4355 American child deaths. At this Israeli child death rate, 54 American children would be killed each month for seventy-eight months.

From the Palestinian population perspective: 930 Palestinian child deaths are the equivalent of 856 Israeli child deaths (there were 118). The 930 Palestinian child deaths are the equivalent of 31,638 American child deaths. At this Palestinian death rate, the equivalent 31,638 Americans would be killed at the rate of 395 American children per month for seventy-eight months.

ISRAELI AND PALESTINIAN CHILD DEATHS IN UNITED STATES TERMS: SEPTEMBER 11, 2001

To further highlight the scale of these losses for Israelis and Palestinians, we can compare them to a seminal catastrophe for Americans, September 11, 2001.

The September 11, 2001, attack on the World Trade Center was a watershed event for Americans, shaking the sense of security and impunity that citizens of the world's sole superpower had taken for granted. In the attack, 2973 Americans died, all but nine over age eighteen.[14, 15] Given the sites of the attacks, adults had a greater probability than children did of being killed. However, Americans perceived the attacks as directed at the whole population, regardless of age. Accordingly, the death rate was computed based on 2000 census data for the total populations of the U.S., Israel and Palestine to yield the following equivalent number of "9/11s" for Israel and Palestine at the same time: 2973 American deaths on 9/11 (2973 divided by U.S. population in 2000, 282,338,631 = .000011) are the equivalent of 64 Israeli deaths (.000011 times Israeli population in 2000, 5,842,454) and 37 Palestinian deaths (.000011 times Palestinian population in 2000, 3,325,261).

Again, these equivalents are presented in terms of the *total* populations of Israel and Palestine. In keeping with the focus of this chapter on *child* deaths, these 9/11 deaths have been translated in terms of Israeli and Palestinian child deaths over the past 6.5 years, yielding the following, though they are still underestimations: For Israelis, 118 child deaths (September 29, 2000 to April 5, 2007) are the equivalent of *two* September 11 attacks over 6.5 years. For Palestinians, 930 child deaths (September 29, 2000 to April 5, 2007) are the equivalent of *twenty-five* September 11 attacks over 6.5 years.

When we consider the deaths of Israelis and Palestinians *of all ages* during the same period in terms of the 9/11 deaths, we find an even more striking comparison. According to statistics gathered by the Israeli human rights group, *B'Tselem*, during the past 6.5 years 1021 Israelis of all ages were killed by Palestinians and 4080 Palestinians of all ages were killed by Israelis, which translates into *sixteen September 11 attacks for Israelis* (9/11 death rate multiplied by the total Israeli population in 2000: .000011 times 5,842,454) and *one hundred ten September 11 attacks for Palestinians* (.000011 times 3,325,261) over the past 6.5 years.

DISCUSSION

Children in every society symbolize survival and innocence, the regeneration of persons and cultures–future life itself. Indeed, children are embodiments of past and future. They are symbols of peace (Greenbaum, 2006). For these reasons, although the killing of all civilians in war is immoral and illegal,[16] killing children is particularly reprehensible, deepening hatred among sworn enemies, and activating wishes for revenge.[17] This is especially true in anti-colonial and ethnic conflicts such as that between Israelis and Palestinians in which fear of annihilation is central to each people's narrative of the dispute and easily reinforced by corroborating rhetoric and behavior.

For example, when Palestinians kill Israeli children, deny the Nazi Holocaust, or publicly call for "death to the Jews," traumatic memories of and associations to the Holocaust are triggered among Jewish Israelis. Moreover, in the face of such acts, historical facts–that Europeans, not Palestinian Arabs, exterminated six million Jews or that Palestinian refugees have a human and legal right to return to their homes in Israel–become obscured or irrelevant to Israelis and to internationals who support Palestinian human rights.

Similarly, from the viewpoint of Palestinians, Israel's ongoing bombing of Palestinian children in Gaza and confiscation of their land in the West Bank (including East Jerusalem) for Jewish settlements, and denial of the Palestinian Nakba continue their historic trauma of dispossession and ethnic cleansing by Zionists in 1948 (Nakba) that has been documented by historians, including Jewish Israelis such as Pappe (2006) and Morris (1987, 2004).

Thus, the data presented herein provide an empirical window into the devastating loss that child deaths represent in the small societies of Israel and Palestine, one that significantly pushes Israelis and Palestinians back to their most primitive selves. This is especially apparent when their child casualties are considered in terms of a seminal tragedy of the more populous and larger territory of the United States–September 11, 2001: the equivalent of *two* 9/11s for Israelis and *twenty-five* 9/11s for Palestinians over 6.5 years.

Viewed in these terms, we might better understand the existential fury and retaliation that results from killing children in Israel and Palestine. Indeed, we need only remember that in response to the September 11 attacks, the U.S. government launched an invasion of Afghanistan and, recognizing the enormous symbolic power of 9/11 for Americans, appropriated it in justifying the invasion and ongoing war in Iraq. Indeed, even heretofore pacifist Americans were ready to bomb "the perps" for the 9/11 attacks.

Perhaps by considering the deaths of Israeli and Palestinian children in terms of the September 11 tragedy, Americans can begin to understand one source of the extreme hostility on both sides that helps to perpetuate the Israeli–Palestinian conflict. Moreover, given the significantly greater losses experienced by Palestinians, we might appreciate the desperation that motivates Palestinian suicide bombings, even while condemning the killing of civilians whether by states like Israel or those like Palestinians in national liberation struggles.[18]

In this regard, it is important to recall that the Palestinian young adults opposing Israeli occupation today spent their formative years during the first uprising.[19] For example, in describing the humiliation and despair Palestinians feel after decades of military occupation, Palestinian psychiatrist and director of the Gaza Community Mental Health Program, Doctor Eyad El-Sarraj (2001), recalls telling a *BBC* interviewer "that the amazing thing is not the occurrence of the suicide bombing, rather the rarity of them." Similarly, in a study of the dreams of West Bank Palestinian boys and girls, Palestinian-Israeli psychologist Shafiq Masalha (2003) found that these Palestinian dreamers felt no sense of security or protection, even in their homes or schools. Also, thirteen percent of those studied "see themselves as *shahids* (martyrs) in their dreams, many actively blowing themselves up in Israel. . . . Interaction with Israelis is characterized by physical confrontation and very little verbal confrontation. There is no positive encounter between the [two] sides in the dreams."

And with regard to suicide bombing, Masalha is quoted as saying, "I believe that the motives are the terrible lives that the children live daily. . . . This should be a warning not only to Israeli but also to Palestinian society [about] what they are doing to the next generation."[20]

CONCLUSION

This chapter compared the deaths of Israeli and Palestinian children in the first Intifada with those of the second, the *Al-Aqsa Intifada*, and translated these deaths into terms more "experience near"[21] to Americans: the September 11, 2001, terrorist attacks.

First, this chapter emphasizes that each child death is unequivocally tragic for Israelis and Palestinians. Moreover, it concludes that the killing of children in particular creates a distinctive emotional context in which the most intense primitive feelings, such as hostility, hatred, and revenge, are evoked within and between both peoples, which, in turn, leads to more killing of children and civilians by both sides. In sum, it perpetuates the conflict.

Second, these data also highlight the asymmetry that has defined the relationship between Palestinians and Israelis since 1948. Specifically, a review of child deaths consequent to the conflict reveals that a significantly greater number of Palestinian children than Israeli children have been killed since the start of the first uprising in 1987. Until the *Al-Aqsa Intifada*, the lives of Israeli children were virtually spared in the first uprising, whereas hundreds of unarmed Palestinian children were killed and injured by Israeli soldiers. In fact, between September 29, 2001 and now, *eight* times the number of Palestinian children have been killed compared to Israeli children. Like the *Radda Barnen* study of the first uprising, the present analysis suggests a continuing history of IDF aggression against Palestinian children in the context of their nonviolent resistance to an illegal military occupation.

This asymmetry in Palestinian and Israeli child deaths is important in understanding the perpetuation or resolution of the conflict. Among other things, this imbalance reflects the vastly disproportionate military and political power of the two peoples, particularly apparent in the Israeli response to resistance by a largely unarmed and severely impoverished people; the disproportionate availability to Palestinians and Israelis of relief services (doctors, hospitals, mental/physical rehabilitation services), material resources, and infrastructure (water, electricity, roads) when they are injured or killed; and the "facts on the ground" of the occupation itself, such as checkpoints, closures, curfews, which not only prevent the provision of relief and medical care to Palestinians but also contribute to their deaths. It also reflects the gross imbalance of vital political support by western nations and enforcement of international law, especially with regard to Israel by its leading ally, the United States.

Yet, it is this very asymmetry that points the way out: the consistent application and enforcement of international law, including holding accountable those–states as well as individuals–who kill civilians, especially children. As anthropologist Talal Asad (2007, p. 94) observes, "[M]assacres are not new. But there is something special about the fact that the West, having set up international law, then finds reasons why it cannot be followed in particular circumstances."

Indeed, the world at the start of the twenty-first century is one of unfairness, with growing gaps between rich and poor. It is unlikely that this asymmetry of resources, standard of living and political power is likely to be rectified any time soon. However, it is not unrealistic to expect that one basic requirement for nonviolent conflict resolution–equality before the law–can be achieved, which would also go a long way toward correcting the economic asymmetry. In fact, uniform adherence to international law provides the only source of hope for sustaining human fairness–in philosopher John Rawls' words, the "symmetry of everyone's relations to each other" (1971, p. 12)–among different peoples including Israelis and Palestinians.

In one sense, the deaths of all these innocent children, Israeli and Palestinian, can be likened to the "loss of innocence" that Americans felt after the September 11 attacks–the first foreign attack on the continental United States. Perhaps by reflecting on the violence inflicted on Israeli and Palestinian children in terms closer to home, Americans will be moved to pressure their government to restore the symmetry between Palestinians and Israelis that is essential for enduring peace. Concomitantly, international law prohibiting the killing of children must be uniformly enforced. Above all, the violence against children must stop.

NOTES

1. According to UNICEF, "An estimated 90 percent of global conflict-related

deaths since 1990 have been civilians, and 80 percent of these have been women and children" (from UNICEF (2006). *Child Protection Information Sheet: Protecting Children During Armed Conflict*, p. 7, referencing the work of O. Otunnu (2002). *Disarmament Forum.* 'Special Comment' on Children and Security, pp. 3–4. Geneva: United Nations Institute for Disarmament Research [On-line]. Available: http://www.unicef.org/protection/files/Child_Protection_Information_Sheets_(Booklet).pdf).

2. The *Radda Barnen* study period was from December 9, 1987 to December 7, 1989.

3. The "Green Line" refers to the border of Israel as established by 1949 armistice agreements ending the 1948 to 1949 war. It does not include the territory of the Palestinian West Bank (including East Jerusalem) and Gaza Strip that Israel has been occupying since the 1967 "Six Day War" with Egypt, Jordan and Syria. Thus, "within" the Green Line refers to Israel without those OPT.

4. The immediate cause of the uprising was Israeli Prime Minister Ehud Barak's authorization of a visit by former Defense Minister Ariel Sharon and about 1000 police to the Muslim holy site, Al-Aqsa Mosque, with the announced purpose of demonstrating Jewish sovereignty over the Mosque compound. The uprising broke out the next day, Friday, September 29, in response to the massive military presence surrounding the mosque on the Muslim day of prayers as thousands of Palestinians left the mosque, resulting in clashes with Israeli police that left 7 Palestinians dead and 200 wounded. *See* N. Chomsky (2000, November). Al-Aqsa intifada, *Znet* [On-line]. Retrieved August 31, 2007. Available: http://www.zmag.org/meastwatch/alaqsa.htm. However, this visit is regarded as lighting a match to the tinderbox of worsening social and economic conditions in the OPT following the Oslo Peace Accords, including closures, a doubling of the Jewish settler population, lack of freedom of movement, and frustrated Palestinian self-determination overall. *See*: A. Pacheco [2001]. Flouting convention: the Oslo Agreements, in R. Carey [Ed.] *The New Intifada* (pp. 181–206). London: Verso; S. Roy (2002, January). Why peace failed: An Oslo autopsy, *Current History.* pp. 8–16; S. Roy (2007). *Failing Peace*, London: Pluto Press; E. Said [2000, December 14]. *Palestinians Under Siege, London Review of Books* [On-line]. Retrieved August 31, 2007. Available: http://www.lrb.co.uk/v22/n24/print/said01_.html; G. Usher (2000, November 2–8). The intifada this time, Cairo: *Al-Ahram Weekly On-line*, Issue No. 506 [On-line]. Retrieved August 31, 2007. Available: http://weekly.ahram.org.eg/2000/506/re1.htm)

5. Remember These Children includes these groups: American Educational Trust (http://www.amedtrust.org); Americans for Middle East Understanding (http://www.amedtrust.org); The Parents Circle–Bereaved Families Forum (www.TheParentsCircle.com; http://www.013.net/hosting/undercon.html); The Israeli Committee Against House Demolitions (http://www.icahd.org/eng).

6. The *Radda Barnen* study defined a child as anyone under age sixteen. As that study was underway, the international legal definition of a child as under eighteen was established by adoption of the U.N. Convention on the Rights of the Child (UNCRC) on November 20, 1989, which entered into force on Septem-

ber 2, 1990. Under UNCRC (Part 1, Article 1), "a child means every human being below the age of eighteen years unless under the law applicable to the child, majority is attained earlier." Although Palestine is limited to U.N. Observer Status, Palestinian law complies with the UNCRC definition of a child as anyone under eighteen. Israel, as a U.N. member state, ratified UNCRC on November 2, 1991. However, Israel discriminates among children in the OPT by applying Israeli military law to Palestinians (Military order 132), which defines a child as someone under sixteen, while applying Israeli civil law to Jewish settlers in the OPT, which defines a child as younger than eighteen. This discrimination has been noted in the UNCRC response to Israel's initial report to the UNCRC monitor, the Committee On the Rights of the Child (CRC/C/8/Add.44 of 27 February 2002): "Concerns were also noted related to the following: in law, discrimination in the definition of the child with regard to Israeli children (e.g., persons under eighteen in the 1962 Guardianship and Legal Capacity Law, and the Youth [Trial, Punishment and Modes of Treatment] Law) and Palestinian children in the OPT (e.g., persons under 16 in Military Order no. 132);"

7. Data are a compilation of information from several government and human rights organization sources including: *B'Tselem*: the Israeli Information Center for Human Rights in the Occupied Territories; Israel Ministry of Foreign Affairs; Jerusalem Media and Communications Center; Addameer: Prisoner's Rights and Support Group; LAW: the Palestinian Society for the Protection of Human Rights and the Environment; Palestinian Center for Human Rights; and the Palestinian State Information Service.

8. The killing of civilians, by states or individuals, must be condemned. Still, Israeli settlements, illegally built on confiscated Palestinian land, represent a constant provocation and threat to Palestinian survival. Palestinian frustration is intensified by knowledge that the illegality of Israel's occupation-including attempts to alter the occupied territory such as settlement building, appropriation of resources-has been consistently recognized by the international community. *See* U.N. Security Council Resolutions 446, 452, 465; the Fourth Geneva Convention relative to the Protection of Civilian Persons in Time of War, August 12, 1949; Ruling by the International Court of Justice, "Legal Consequences of the Construction of a Wall in the Occupied Palestinian Territories," (July 9, 2004.) Also, while officially denying the illegality of the occupation and settlements, Israel's awareness of their illegality was recently publicized in an op-ed by Gershom Gorenberg in *The New York Times*: "The legal counsel of the Foreign Ministry, Theodor Meron, was asked [by then-Prime Minister Levi Eshkol] whether international law allowed settlement in the newly conquered land [1967]. In a memo marked 'Top Secret,' Mr. Meron wrote unequivocally, 'My conclusion is that civilian settlement in the administered territories contravenes the explicit provisions of the Fourth Geneva Convention.' In the detailed opinion that accompanied that note, Mr. Meron explained that the Convention–to which Israel was a signatory–forbade an occupying power from moving part of its population to occupied territory" (from G. Gorenberg,

"Israel's Tragedy Foretold," 2006, March 10, *The New York Times* [On-line]. Retrieved March 25, 2006. Available: http://www.nytimes.com/2006/03/10/opinion/10gorenberg.html).

9. Of the approximately 63 percent, 30.5 percent were killed by live or rubber-coated metal bullets; 11.3 percent by IDF shelling; 7 percent during IDF-targeted assassinations of others; 3.7 by tank or helicopter firing; 2.6 percent by IDF missile attacks; 2.6 percent at checkpoints because of denial of access to medical care; 2.5 percent by IDF bombs, land mines, house demolitions; 1.4 percent by settlers; and 1.2 by tear gas.

10. Of the 7.3 percent: 4.4 percent (N = 15) threw stones at checkpoints and armored personal carriers or tanks; and 2.9 percent (N = 10) were shot while engaging in armed and unarmed clashes or were shot because they had allegedly shot or stabbed a settler (N = 2).

11. In sum, the conflict is one that pits the self-determination of the native Arab population of historic Palestine against Zionist colonization of the same land for the creation of a Jewish state justified by centuries of European persecution and, to a lesser extent by biblical claims. The dispossession and ethnic cleansing of Palestinians that accompanied Israel's creation and the subsequent denial of the right of Palestinian refugees to return to their homes has, since 1948, evoked resistance from Palestinians in the Diaspora and hostility from Israel's Arab neighbors, and constant fear among Israel that it would be destroyed. Space does not permit a more lengthy account of the origin of the conflict. *See* N. Finkelstein (1995). *Image and Reality of the Israel-Palestine Conflict.* London: Verso; I. Pappe (2001). *The Making of the Arab-Israeli Conflict: 1947 to 1951.* London: I. B. Tauris; I. Pappe (2004). *The History of Modern Palestine: One Land,* Two Peoples. Cambridge: Cambridge University Press; and I. Pappe (2006). *The Ethnic Cleansing of Palestine.* Oxford: Oneworld Publications Limited.

12. Given that stillbirths can be attributed to many causes, I have excluded two Palestinian stillborns from the Remember These Children totals. (*See* N.T.N. Ngoc, M. Merialdi, H. Abel-Aleem, G. Carroli, M. Purwar, N. Zavaleta, L. Campodonico, M. Ali, G. Hofmeyr, M. Mathai, O. Lincetto, and J. Villar (2006, September). Causes of stillbirths and early neonatal deaths: data from 7993 pregnancies in six developing countries. *Bulletin of the World Health Organization, 84*(9), pp. 685–764; also available: http://www.who.int/bulletin/voumes/84/9/05-027300.pdf. *See also* R. Silver, M. Varner, U. Reddy, R. Goldenberg, H. Pinar, D. Conway, R. Bukowski, M. Carpenter, C. Hogue, M. Willinger, D. Dudley, G. Saade, and b. Stoll (2007, May). Work-up of stillbirth: A review of the evidence. *American Journal of Obstetrics and Gynecology, 196*(5), pp. 433–444; also available: http://pt.wkhealth.com/pt/re/ajog/fulltext.00000447-200705000-00005.htm. *See also* March of Dimes (November, 2005). Quick Reference and Factsheet: Stillbirth Retrieved June 6, 2007. Available: http://www.marchofdimes.com/professionals/14332_1198.asp

13. Source for census data for the United States, Israel, West Bank, and Gaza: "U.S. Census Bureau, International Data base, Midyear Population by Age and Sex, 2000 and 2007." Source for the Palestinian population of East Jerusalem for

2000: Jerusalem Institute for Israel Studies, Statistical Yearbook of Jerusalem, 2001 as reported by the Foundation for Middle East Peace, The Population of Jerusalem, 2000") [On-line]. Retrieved April 26, 2007. Available: http://www.fmep.org/settlement_info/stats_data/jerusalem/population_east_jerusalem_2000.html. Source for the Palestinian population of East Jerusalem for 2007: Jerusalem Institute for Israel Studies, as reported by N. Shragai (2007, February 21). Study: 57 percent of East Jerusalem residents are Arab. *Haaretz* [On-line]. Retrieved April 25, 2007. Available: http://www.haaretz.com/hasen/spages/828662.html

14. According to *Wikopedia Encyclopedia*, http://en.wikipedia.org/wiki/September_11,_2001_attacks#Fatalities and *CNN* [On-line]. Retrieved September 2, 2007. Available: http://www.cnn.com/2006/LAW/04/25/moussaoui.trial

15. There were 9 victims under age eighteen: 8 child passengers of two of the planes that crashed (AA77 and UA17) and a seventeen-year-old employee of Sandler O'Neill World Trade Center 382. Thus, of the 2973 who perished in the attacks, 2964 were eighteen or over. *See WorldNetDaily*, Littlest victims largely overlooked: untold story of the children slain by Sept. 11 terrorists [On-line]. Retrieved September 2, 2007. Available: http://www.worldnetdaily.com/news/article.asp?ARTICLE_ID=25771

16. *The Fourth Geneva Convention Relative to the Protection of Civilian Persons in Time of War*, was adopted August 12, 1949, and entered into force October 21, 1950. It is a cornerstone of international humanitarian law. *See* http://www.unhchr.ch/html/menu3/b/92.htm Israel ratified the convention in 1951. Palestinians have declared their adherence to the Conventions despite their ambiguous status. With regard to Palestine, according to International Humanitarian Law, International Committee of the Red Cross: "On 21 June 1989, the Swiss Federal Department of Foreign Affairs received a letter from the Permanent Observer of Palestine to the United Nations Office at Geneva informing the Swiss Federal Council 'that the Executive Committee of the Palestine Liberation Organization, entrusted with the functions of the Government of the State of Palestine by decision of the Palestine National Council, decided, on 4 May 1989, to adhere to the Four Geneva Conventions of 12 August 1949 and the two Protocols additional thereto.'" On 13 September 1989, the Swiss Federal Council informed the States that it was not in a position to decide whether the letter constituted an instrument of accession "due to the uncertainty within the international community as to the existence or non-existence of a State of Palestine." *See* http://www.icrc.org/ihl.nsf/WebSign?ReadForm&id=375&ps=P

17. For example, Avishai Margalit (2003) reports the case of a twenty-one-year-old bachelor, Mahmoud Ahmed Marmash, who blew himself up near Tel Aviv in May 2001: "On a videocassette recorded before he was sent on his mission, he said: 'I want to avenge the blood of the Palestinians, especially the blood of the women, of the elderly, and of the children, and in particular the blood of the baby girl Iman Hejjo, whose death shook me to the core."

18. It is important to note here that developments in international law allow resistance to military occupation, including, according to professor of international

law Richard Falk, "forcible resistance to forcible denial of self-determination," which the Israeli occupation and its settlements clearly represent to Palestinians as well as to the international community. (*See* R. Falk [2002, Winter]. Azmi Bishara, the right of resistance, and the Palestinian ordeal, *Journal of Palestine Studies, 31*, pp. 19–33. The argument made by some Palestinians that suicide bombing is a legitimate last resort for a people opposing occupation by the nuclear-powered, fourth-largest military in the world does not justify the killing of civilians, just as killing of civilians by the Israeli military in targeted assassinations or as "collateral damage" is not justified. According to Falk, these are violations of customary humanitarian law and the laws of war and considered terrorism whether state sponsored or by individuals in service of national liberation. *See also* R. Falk [2000, Winter], Beyond Oslo: The new uprising, international law and the Al-Aqsa Intifada," *Middle East Report, 217*, pp. 16–18. *See also* R. Falk and B. Weston, [1991], The relevance of international law to Palestinian rights in the West Bank and Gaza: In legal defense of the intifada." *Harvard Journal of International Law, 33*(1), No. 1, 129–157.)

19. Summing up the experience of children during the first uprising, psychiatrist Eyad El-Sarraj describes a community study of 1200 Gaza children aged seven to fifteen in "Peace and the Children of the Stone" E. El-Sarraj [1993, September]. *Challenge 4*(5) [Online]. Retrieved September 15, 2007. Available: http://www.gcmhp.net/eyad/stone.htm "The 'children of the stone' are not made of stone. They suffer pain and fear. The extent of their exposure to traumatic events is horrific even at the statistical level. According to a GCMHP survey of 2779 children, 92.5 percent were exposed to tear gas, 42 percent were beaten, 55 percent have witnessed beating, 4.5 percent have had their bones broken or other severe injured, 85 percent were exposed to night raids, and 19 percent were detained for short periods of time."

20. Quoted in Remember These Children: Introduction. [On-line]. Retrieved April 27, 2007. Available: http://www.rememberthesechildren.org/about.html

21. Psychoanalyst Heinz Kohut used this term to refer to an empathic way of relating to an individual patient, that is, from his or her viewpoint. Contrasted with "experience distant" statements, "experience near" observations by the analyst about a patient would be consistent with the way the patient him/herself might feel or define a situation (from H. Kohut [1971]. *The Analysis of the Self.* New York: International Universities Press).

REFERENCES

Alkhatib, A., Regan, J. & Barrett, D. (2007, August). The silent victims: Effects of war and terrorism on child development. *Psychiatric Annals, 37*(8), pp. 586–589.

Asad, T.(2007). *On suicide bombing.* New York: Columbia University Press.

Baker, A. M., & Kanan, H. M. (2003). The psychological impact of military violence on children as a function of distance from the traumatic event: The Palestinian case," *Intervention, Vol. 1,* (3), pp. 13–21.

B'Tselem (The Israeli Information Center for Human Rights in the Occupied Territories). Fatalities in the first Intifada. Retrieved April 9, 2007 [On-line]. Available: http://www.btse-lem.org/english/statistics/First_Intifada_Tables.asp

Dyregrov, A., Gjestad, R., & Raundalen, M. (2002). Children exposed to warfare: A longitudinal study. *Journal of Traumatic Stress, 15,* 59–68.

El-Sarraj, E. (2001, August 16). Why we have all become suicide bombers: Understanding Palestinian terror, *Middle East Realities.* Retrieved August 29, 2007. Available: http://www.middleeast.org/premium/read.cgi?category=Magazine&num=347&month=8&year=2001&function=text

Farsoun, S. & J. Landis (1990). The sociology of an uprising: The roots of the Intifada. In J. Nassar and R. Heacock, (Eds), *Intifada: Palestine at the Crossroads* (pp. 15–35). New York: Praeger.

Garbarino, J., Kostelny, K., & Dubrow, N. (1991). *No place to be a child: Growing up in a war zone.* New York: Lexington.

Goldson, E. (1993). War is not good for children. In L. Leavitt & N. Fox (Eds.), *The psychological effects of war and violence on children* (pp. 3–22). Hillsdale, NJ: Lawrence Erlbaum.

Graff, J. (1997). Targeting children: Rights versus realpolitik. In T. Kaptan (Ed.), *Philosophical perspectives on the Israeli-Palestinian conflict,* (pp. 157–184). New York: M. E. Sharpe, Inc.

Greenbaum, C. (2006), Prevention of violence to children in the Israeli-Palestinian conflict: A perspective from ecological systems theory, in C. W. Greenbaum, P. Veerman, N. Bacon-Shnoor (Eds.), *Protecting children during armed political conflict: A multidisciplinary perspective* (pp. 433–455). Oxford: Intersentia.

Leavitt, L., & Fox, N. (1993). *The psychological effects of war and violence on children.* Hillsdale, NJ: Lawrence Erlbaum.

Margalit, A. (2003, January 16). The suicide bombers, *New York Review of Books, 50*(1) [On-line]. Available: http://www.nybooks.com/articles/15979

Masalha, S. (1993). The effect of prewar conditions on the psychological reactions of Palestinian children to the Gulf War. In L. Leavitt & N. Fox (Eds.), *The psychological effects of war and violence on children* (pp. 131–142). Hillsdale, NJ: Lawrence Erlbaum.

Masalha, S. (2003). Children and violent conflict: Disturbing findings from a study of Palestinian children's dreams in the second Intifada. *Palestine-Israel Journal of Politics, Economics and Culture, 10*(1) pp. 62–70.

Morris, B. (1987). *The birth of the Palestinian refugee problem,* 1947–1949. Cambridge, MA: Cambridge University Press.

Morris, B. (2004). *The birth of the Palestinian refugee problem revisited.* Cambridge, MA: Cambridge University Press.

Nixon, A. (1990). The status of Palestinian children during the uprising in the Occupied Territories, Vol. 2. Stockholm, Sweden: *Radda Barrnen (Swedish Save the Children). Vol. 2.* pp. 225–293.

Pappe, I. (2006). *The ethnic cleansing of Palestine.* Oxford: Oneworld Publications.

Pickett, D. (2001, August 14). Jews here remain resolute Chicagoans mourn bombing victims, *Chicago Sun-Times* [On-line]. Retrieved August 31, 2007. Available: http://findarticles.com/p/articles/mi_qn4155/is_20010814/ai_n13921017

Rawls, J. (1971). *A theory of justice.* Cambridge, MA: Harvard University Press.

Chapter 12

PALESTINE: A NATION TRAUMATIZED

Jess Ghannam

INTRODUCTION

Middle East events from the Palestinian point of view are a chain of tragedies and traumatic losses. For example, the year 2008 will mark the sixtieth anniversary of the Palestinian *nakba* or catastrophe. In 1948, on the land where Palestinians had been living for centuries, about 800,000 indigenous Palestinians and more than 500 Palestinian villages were ethnically cleansed by paramilitary forces, thus creating the largest and oldest refugee problem in the world today. In 1967, when Israel began its occupation of the Gaza Strip and West Bank, Palestinians reported attempts to dispossess, dislocate, and displace an indigenous people from their homes, land and history. From the Palestinian point of view, the impact has been nothing short of catastrophic to the more than four million Palestinians living in Gaza and the West Bank, the more than five million Palestinians living in exile or as refugees, and the 1.2 million Palestinians living inside Israel. Every segment of Palestinian society has been affected and the economic, social, and health conditions for Palestinians have suffered.[1] In this chapter the focus of discussion will be on the medical and mental health conditions of Palestinians living under occupation in Gaza and the West Bank.

IS OCCUPATION HAZARDOUS TO HEALTH AND WELLNESS?

The Israeli occupation of Palestine, which is considered by many Palestinian and international organizations to be illegal, has had a devastating impact on every aspect of Palestinian existence. One of the most adversely affected areas has been the health-care sector. Palestinians—irrespective of age, gender, sex, or legal status—have experienced a steady decline and deterioration in their health and wellness. The public and private health-care infrastructure has also been devastated.

Many Palestinians believe that the intent of military occupation of Palestine is to dispossess, disconnect, and dislocate Palestinians from their land, their history, and themselves. They assume that the dismantling of Palestinian health and wellness is but one of the many systematic methods of control that the Israeli military use to colonize Palestine and to create conditions so that Palestinians will accept subjugation, colonization, and occupation. History reveals that Palestinians have rejected—and may continue to reject—occupation. Palestinian health and psychological wellness have, however, suffered tremendously.

INTERNATIONAL LAW AND HEALTH CARE

International law, specifically the Fourth Geneva Convention, explicitly states that an occupying army is responsible for the health and wellness of the inhabitants under occupation. Article 18 of the Fourth Geneva Convention states that occupiers have an obligation to protect health-care facilities from attack and to guarantee access of health-care to civilian inhabitants. (OHCHR- Office of the High Commissioner for Human Rights, 1949) It is well documented by the news media and International organizations that Israel has consistently violated international law and the Geneva Conventions with respect to every aspect of Palestinian health and health-care infrastructure. According to the Palestine Red Crescent Society (PRCS, 2002) and the Palestinian Health, Development, Infrastructure and Policy Institute (HDIP, 2002), nearly every Palestinian hospital and clinic in the West Bank, Gaza, and Jerusalem has been attacked—a clear breach of international law.

Denial of access to medical care is also prohibited under international law. Despite this, there are numerous reports from both Palestinian and Israeli human rights activists that Israel uses a complex system of closures, checkpoints, and military force that deprives Palestinian civilians of access to doctors, clinics, and hospitals. There are well over 500 armed, militarized checkpoints throughout the West Bank, and Gaza is completely sealed off. According to the Palestinian Ministry of Health (MOH, 2004). Since September 2000, 129 medically ill patients have died at Israeli checkpoints waiting to cross. This includes five women who died while giving birth at checkpoints. Some seventy Palestinian women have given birth while waiting at checkpoints on their way to local hospitals or clinics. Of the seventy births, about forty babies either died at the checkpoints from complications or were still-born. Since these statistics are from the MOH, they are likely to underrepresent the actual number of deaths. In addition, and what these statistics fail to capture, there are large numbers of medically ill Palestinians who die at home because of closures and checkpoints–either because they are too sick to travel or they refuse to be subjected to the humiliation of waiting at a checkpoint. For example, there are reports of hundreds of Palestinian cancer and dialysis patients who perish at home because they are too sick to travel (WHO report, 2003).

BARRIERS TO HEALTH CARE

Palestinians believe that the government of Israel is building an "apartheid wall" deep into Palestinian land in the West Bank. Hundreds of miles long, it separates Palestinians from their land, their families, and from each other. The International Court of Justice (ICJ) ruled in 2004 that the wall was illegal, and yet it continues to be built (ICJ, 2004; IMFA, 2005). Former President Jimmy Carter has also stated that the wall creates conditions of apartheid for Palestinians similar to those of apartheid South Africa (Carter, 2006). The health-care implications are devastating and according to a report by the HDIP Institute, the wall will have a direct impact on the health and wellness of more than 400,000 Palestinians (Barghouti, Jubran, Faqih, Nafe', Tawil, Awwad, & Khalili, 2004; Barghouti, Jubran, Awad, A1-Faqih, Nafe' & Khalili, 2005). Specifically, the HDIP report estimates that close to 40,000 Palestinians will not have access to any health-care services because of this illegal apartheid wall. More than 80,000 Palestinians (not including East Jerusalem) will not have access to any emergency care, general medicine, or specialized services including hospital services. Forty-one primary health-care clinics will become so isolated and cutoff from their respective communities that their ability to function will be significantly compromised.

Closure is yet another barrier that limits and damages health-care services in the West Bank, Gaza, and East Jerusalem. When the Israeli military institutes a policy of closure and curfew in Palestine, movement of people and goods is forbidden. Palestinian civilians are denied all freedom of movement, and all goods–including food and medicine–are restricted by the Israeli military and not allowed entry in the West Bank, Gaza, or East Jerusalem. Since the recent democratic elections in Palestine, the Israeli military instituted a severe form of closure in which medicines and health supplies have been either denied or restricted. International humanitarian aid has also been denied. This has caused catastrophic health conditions, especially in Gaza. According to reports of the General Union of Health Workers in Gaza, there is not a single complete functioning hospital or clinic in Gaza (Li & Lein, 2006; UNISPAL, 2007). Basic medicines and supplies have been denied entry into Gaza, as well as parts of the West Bank and East Jerusalem, causing massive degradation in the provision of health-care to Palestinian men, women, and children. There are extreme shortages of medicines, antibiotics, antiseptics, and other basic medical supplies. Basic foods are also being denied. For the first time in recorded history, Palestinian children are suffering from malnutrition and preventable childhood diseases. More than 80 percent of Palestinian children are now living below the international poverty line–less than $2 per day. Public health-care workers have also not been paid for more than six months because of the financial embargo. Calls and pleas from the international community–including the United Nations, the World Health Organization (WHO), Human Rights Watch, Amnesty International, and Doctors Without Borders/Médecins Sans Frontières (MSF)–for an end to these practices have been repeatedly ignored by the government of Israel. Reports of violations of international law and basic human rights are abundant.

HAZARDS TO HELPING PROFESSIONALS–CUTTING THE HEALING HANDS

The Fourth Geneva Convention explicitly states that civilian medical personnel must be protected from militarized aggression and allowed to provide medical aid to communities under occupation (OHCHR, 1949). Palestinian and international organizations reported that, as with all other obligations under international humanitarian law, the government of Israel has consistently violated the basic obligation to protect health-care professionals. Observers in the field reported that since September 2000 the Israeli military has intentionally targeted emergency medical personnel and ambulances (WHO & PRCS Media Release, 2003). Several Israeli soldiers have written letters to the government refusing to participate in this practice, further evidence that the targeting of Palestinian health-care professionals is explicitly sanctioned and encouraged by the Israeli government (Sfard, 2002). There have been almost 900 attacks on Palestinian RCS ambulances, resulting in the total destruction of twenty-eight ambulances. More than 200 emergency medical personnel have been shot and or injured resulting in twelve deaths. It is commonly understood that among the most hazardous jobs in Palestine are those in the health sector, especially emergency medical technicians. Many eye witnesses have reported that even if ambulances are not targeted, when they do arrive at trauma sites, the Israeli military will frequently prevent them from picking up and ministering to injured Palestinian civilians.

Hundreds of Palestinian civilians have bled to death because emergency medical technicians (EMT's) have been prevented from approaching and caring for injured Palestinians. These problems are exacerbated because ambulances, even when they have picked up an injured civilian, are stopped at checkpoints and prevented from quickly bringing the injured to hospitals and clinics (Palestinian Center for Human Rights-PCHR, 2002).

THE WORLD HEALTH ORGANIZATION ANNUAL REPORT

The WHO has been monitoring and evaluating the health status of Palestinians for decades, and their recent May 2006 annual report documents the progressive deterioration of health and health-care infrastructure for Palestinians (WHO Report, 2006). The report is very grim, and since its publication, the situation has worsened significantly. According to the WHO report, in 2005 the poverty and unemployment rate for Palestinians living in Gaza, the West Bank, and East Jerusalem was 43 percent and 22.5 percent, respectively. These numbers have effectively doubled since Israel and the United States imposed their economic blockade in 2006. For Palestinian refugees, especially those living in Gaza, the poverty and unemployment rates are above 80 percent now.

Some of the more significant findings of the WHO report include the following:

- Acute malnutrition has risen to almost 2 percent of the total population and is expected to rise.
- Stunting in Palestinian children under five years old has risen to almost 10 percent and is expected to rise in 2006.
- More than 25 percent of all children and more than 30 percent of all women of child-bearing age have iron-deficiency anemia. Almost 54 percent of children are on the verge of vitamin A deficiency.
- The main nontraumatic causes of death for Palestinians are cardiovascular diseases, cancer, diabetes, renal failure, and, for women, perinatal diseases.

Palestinians believe these worsening health conditions are a direct result of military occupation. The forced closures and curfews, the Israeli blockade of food and medicine, and the presence of the apartheid wall are well-documented by the news media. In other words, the progressive deterioration of health conditions for all Palestinians is being exacerbated by the occupation.

REFUGEE HEALTH–A CATASTROPHE

Officially, and according to the United Nations Relief and Works Agency (UNRWA) reports in 2006, there are more than twenty six refugee camps in the West Bank and Gaza with close to 1,700,000 total refugees (UNRWA, 2006). This number does not include the refugees living in camps in Lebanon, Syria, Jordan, Iraq, or beyond. For every health related index described before that details the worsening health conditions for Palestinians, the situation is far more deleterious for Palestinian refugees, wherever they live. Refugee health is significantly and appreciably worse on every single index of health-care and wellness–denial of care, denial of access, malnutrition, morbidity, mortality, acute malnutrition, and so on. Palestinian refugees suffer from some of the worse health conditions found anywhere in the world today. Unfortunately, neither the United Nations nor the international community has been able to alter these conditions, and if this trend continues, catastrophic increases in morbidity and mortality are expected for Palestinian refugees.

PSYCHOLOGICAL TRAUMA AND MENTAL HEALTH

Palestinians, especially Palestinian children, suffer from some of the highest rates of traumatic stress disorders in the world. According to the WHO report of 2006, more than 40 percent of the Palestinian population that was exposed to Israeli aggression had diagnoses of PTSD, depression, and anxiety disorders.

According to major studies done by the Gaza Community Mental Health Program GCMHP, more than 80 percent of Palestinian children living in Gaza have at least one symptom of PTSD. More than 34 percent of Palestinian children living in Gaza have witnessed the brutal beating of family or friends by the Israeli military and more than 24 percent have witnessed the shooting of a close friend. Among adults in Gaza exposed to Israeli violence and aggression, 62.3 percent witnessed friends or family being shot and more than 50 percent witnessed the Israeli military killing a friend or family member. Researchers have estimated that close to 70 percent of children in Gaza and the West Bank who have experienced Israeli aggression have diagnoses of PTSD. These results are among the highest rates of traumatic stress reported anywhere in the world (Thabet et al., 2007).

PTSD–TWO STUDIES WITH PALESTINIAN CHILDREN

The author and colleagues Salman Elbedour, Anthony Onwuegbuzie, Janine Whitcome, Fadel Abu Hein, Eyad Hallaq, Hassan Abu-Saad, and Qun Jiao, conducted two comprehensive projects evaluating the psychiatric status of Palestinian children, one group in Gaza, the other in Jenin in the West Bank.

Beginning in 1948 and intensifying since the start of the first Intifada in 1987, the international media have reported the continuous political trauma of Palestinians and their economic collapse, including bombings, targeted assassinations, home demolitions, land confiscation, and restrictive curfews. As in all war-like situations, it is the children, adolescents, and women of Palestine who take the brunt of psychological devastation and who are at high risk for developing serious social and psychological symptoms (Qouta, el-Sarraj, & Punamaki, 2001). According to the seminal work of the researchers at the GCMHP approximately 42 percent of Palestinian children and adolescents in the West Bank and the Gaza Strip have witnessed the death of a close family member, and 35 percent have witnessed violent clashes with the Israeli army (Qouta, el-Sarraj, & el-Masri, n.d.). Qouta, el-Sarraj, and el-Masri reported that the most common childhood diagnoses were PTSD, depression, and anxiety. Since that study was released, the psychological status of these children and adolescents has only worsened, and the violence by the Israeli military has expanded into full-scale warfare, including twenty-four-hour curfews, mass demolitions of homes, and prolonged military conflict. Since the beginning of the second Intifada on September 29, 2000, the Israeli army has killed more than 5000 Palestinians, including more than 1000 children (Amnesty International Press Release, 2003).

Children and adolescents of Palestinian refugee camps in Gaza and the West Bank have experienced not only political violence but also impoverished social conditions. The residents of these refugee camps have multiple risk factors: they are at the bottom of the socioeconomic ladder, with more than 70 percent living on less than $2.00 per day; they have a very high population density; their infrastructure is underdeveloped or destroyed; and they have limited access to medical care, and social and educational services (Thabet & Vostanis, 2000). These refugee camps are marginalized within the Palestinian society itself. Relative to adults, Palestinian refugee camps are characterized by alienation by and from the legal system, lack of cultural and social institutions, poor economic infrastructure, and a high proportion of children and adolescents (Fields, Elbedour & Abu Hein, 2002). Children and adolescents often account for most of refugee populations: 62.6 percent of the Gaza refugee population are below age eighteen (Thabet & Vostanis, 2000). The communities living in refugee camps in Gaza and the West Bank have become "invisible," both within the Palestinian community and outside their cultural groups. According to Fields and colleagues, religious institutions have become the nexus for developing other institutions—such as education and health care centers—under these difficult and isolating conditions (Fields et al., 2002).

Numerous independent researchers and studies have described the adverse traumatic consequences of occupation on the well-being of Palestinian children and adolescents (Garbarino & Kostelny, 1996; Qouta, Punamaki, & el-Sarraj, 2001; Thabet & Vostanis, 2000). Elbedour (1998) reported a PTSD rate ranging from 12 percent to 18 percent. Garbarino and Kostelny (1996) reported a similar rate of PTSD on the same population. More recently, in an investigation of the long-term effects of the first Intifada, Thabet and Vostanis (2000) reported an even higher level of prevalence of PTSD, with 41 percent of the sample showing moderate or severe symptoms.

In 1993, Elbedour, ten Bensel, and Bastien (1993) recognized the difficulties involved in assessing child development under wartime conditions and the limitations of studies that have relied on PTSD as a framework for judging individual posttrauma adjustment. This inquiry demonstrated that continuous exposure to wartime conditions does not habituate children to the political situation and that the effects of actual or perceived stress may radiate into different aspects of each child's developmental functioning. Based on the author's observations and work the traumatic effects of war and occupation on Palestinian children may last for generations.

Gaza Study

The author and colleagues decided to empirically evaluate the distress levels among Palestinian children living in Gaza. The participants for this study were 229 Palestinian adolescents (52.8% male) living in the Gaza Strip ranging in age from fifteen to nineteen years ($M = 17.13$, standard deviation [SD] $= 1.51$). These sample members belonged to families with an average of 4.12 members ($SD = 2.15$). We administered the following four measures: The Posttraumatic Stress Disorder Interview (PTSD-I); the Beck Depression Inventory–II (BDI–II); the Beck Anxiety Inventory (BAI); and the Coping Responses Inventory (CRI-Youth Form) (Beck & Steer, 1990; Watson, Juba, Manifold, Kucala, & Anderson, 1991; Moos, 1993; Beck, Steer & Brown, 1996). All scales were translated into Arabic.

Every child and adolescent in the study reported experiencing painful events that were directly associated with the Israeli occupation. In order of endorsement rate, the significant psychological traumatic events reported by the participants included the witnessing of (one) a friend being killed (48.5%), (two) a family member being killed (15.7%), (three) a home being demolished (7.9%), (four) a friend being injured through confrontation with Israeli soldiers (6.1%), (five) study participant being personally shot (4.4%), (six) a family member being shot (3.5%) (seven) firing of missiles (7.9%) (eight) physical injury to study participant (2.6%) and (nine) physical abuse of study participant involving kicking and punching by members of the Israeli army (1.8%). Approximately one-third (34.1%) of participants indicated that the painful event cited had directly involved them. Of those who indicated that the painful event cited had involved someone else, 31.0 percent reported that it had involved a friend, 16.6 percent a known society member, 11.8 percent a relative, 8.3 percent an immediate family member, and 6.1 percent a combination of family and friend.

Post-Traumatic Stress Syndrome

With respect to scores on the PTSD-I, using the fourth edition of the *Diagnostic and Statistical Manual of Mental Disorders* (DSM-IV) criteria, 68.9 percent of the sample members had developed PTSD (American Psychiatric Association, 1994). Interestingly, no statistically significant difference ($\pi^2 = 0.00$, p greater than 0.05) emerged between men (69.0%) and women (68.9%) with respect to the proportion diagnosed with PTSD. In addition, no statistically significant difference ($\pi^2[1] = 0.22$, $p > 0.05$) with regard to PTSD diagnosis emerged between participants who reported that their painful event directly involved them (67.6%) and those who reported that the event involved someone else (70.6%).

Depression

Using the *DSM-IV* criteria, the BDI scores revealed that 13.5 percent of the sample was classified as having serious depression, 26.5 percent as having moderate depression, 22.8 percent as having mild depression, and 37.2 percent as having minimal depression. Combining the first two percentages indicated that 40.0 percent of the participants reported moderate or severe levels of depression.

Jenin Study

Jenin is a small Palestinian village in the northern West Bank and on March 29, 2002, it was subjected to a full-scale assault by the Israeli army that continued for several days. By the time of the Israeli army withdrawal from the Jenin camp on April 18, 2002, fifty-two Palestinians–half of whom were Palestinian civilians–and twenty-three Israeli soldiers had been killed during the course of the incursion. In addition to the human toll, at least 150 residential buildings had been completely damaged or destroyed and approximately 450 families residing in the camp became homeless (General Assembly resolution ES-10/10, 2002).

One month after this assault, our research group had the opportunity to go to Jenin and evaluate the psychiatric status of this village using instruments that had been previously score validated. In this chapter, we offer our preliminary descriptive findings of the psychiatric effects on children and adolescents of acute traumatic assault in a warlike environment. The present investigation has particular significance because several organizations, such as Human Rights Watch, have attempted to reconstruct what occurred during the incursion (*Human Rights News*, 2002). However, these limited investigations have exclusively focused on those who died or who were physically injured. Moreover, little or no data have been collected on civilians in close proximity to this violent incursion who did not necessarily receive any physical injuries. In particular, the psychological effects of the military assault on children living in Jenin, to date, have not been studied. In this respect, the present investigation is unique. Indeed, we believe that the present study represents the first empirical psychological investigation conducted in Jenin since this incursion.

Participants and Procedure

The researchers received permission to conduct the study from the education office in the city of Ramallah in the West Bank. A social worker (with a master's degree) who worked in a community mental health center in the city of Jenin was recruited to collect the data (i.e., she served as a research assistant). This center provides mental health services and psychotherapy to traumatized individuals and families in that region. The research assistant demonstrated thorough background knowledge in the area of assessment of psychopathology issues and was experienced in collecting data.

The research assistant obtained permission from the principals of the two schools that served the children of the Jenin refugee camp on the condition that the study would maintain the highest standards of confidentiality and privacy. With the assistance of the principals, she was able to identify 200 children who reside in the Jenin refugee camp. The research assistant visited the families of these children and provided them with a description of the purpose of the study and information about possible risk and confidentiality. Those families who agreed to allow their children to participate in the study were requested to sign an informed consent form. Out of the 200 families that were approached, 114 (57%) agreed to participate.

The research assistant invited five participants at a time to the community mental health center to complete the battery of instruments. Working in small groups allowed the research assistant to answer questions or to help participants who might have difficulty reading some concepts and items on any of the surveys. Collecting the data in the center also allowed any children who experienced emotional trauma triggered by responding to the survey items to receive psychotherapy services. The children were informed that their participation in the investigation was completely voluntary and anonymous, and they could withdraw from the study at any time. Also, they were informed that no identifying information would be collected, thereby making their responses completely anonymous. Participants did not receive any incentive for their participation, other than the opportunity to tell their stories.

A slight majority of the 114 participants were male (58.3%). The ages of the sample members ranged from nine to eighteen years ($M = 13.88$, SD = 2.03). Nearly two-thirds (63.2%) of the sample were in elementary or middle school, with the remainder attending high school.

These adolescents were administered the following three measures: PTSD-I questionnaire, the BDI–II, and the BAI (Beck & Steer, 1990; Watson, Juba, Manifold, Kucala, & Anderson, 1991; Beck, Steer & Brown, 1996). All scales were translated into Arabic. Several steps were taken to promote the validity and cultural appropriateness of instruments. All these measures, which were originally written in English, were translated into Arabic by a social worker and psychologist faculty (with doctoral degrees) from Ben-Gurion University in the Negev. A clinical psychologist (with a doctoral degree) from Birzeit University in the West Bank, who was bilingual in both English and Arabic, translated the Arabic versions into English using standard back-translation techniques. Any discrepancies in translation were resolved to the satisfaction of both sets of translators, thereby maintaining the meaning and cultural appropriateness of the items. Finally, a small pilot study ($n = 7$) was conducted to maximize the content-related validity of the instruments.

Preliminary Findings

Every participant in the sample reported experiencing painful events that were directly associated with the occupation and military assault on Jenin. Specifically, the events reported by the participants, in order of endorsement rate, included the witnessing of: (1) Palestinians being killed by Israeli soldiers (38.6%); (2) incursion of the Jenin camp (18.4%); (3) confrontation with the Israeli army (13.2%); (4) shells being fired during the incursion (5.3%); (5) firing of missiles during the incursion (7.9%); (6) physical injury of civilians (2.6%); and (7) physical injury by Israeli soldiers (1.8%). Most participants indicated that the painful event cited had directly involved them.

Post-Traumatic Stress Syndrome

With respect to scores on the PTSD-I, 64.9 percent of the sample members had developed PTSD. Interestingly, no statistically significant difference ($x^2 = 0.85$, p greater than .05) emerged between men (61.9%) and women (70.7%) with respect to the proportion demonstrating PTSD symptomology. Similarly, no statistically significant difference ($x^2 = 2.76$, $p > .05$) emerged between elementary and middle school participants (60.9%) and high school participants (76.2%) with regard to PTSD symptoms.

Depression

The BDI scores revealed that 24.1 percent of the sample were classified as having serious depression, 17.6 percent as having moderate depression, 30.6 percent as having mild depression, and 27.8 percent as having minimal depression. Combining these percentages indicated that 41.7 percent of the participants reported moderate or severe levels of depression.

Discussion of Results–Gaza, Jenin, and an Ominous Future

The present study indicates that a significant proportion of Palestinian children and adolescents living in the Gaza Strip and the West Bank city of Jenin are experiencing psychological distress as a result of the violence associated with the second Intifada. Approximately two-thirds of the sample members in both Gaza and Jenin are classified as having developed PTSD (68.9% in Gaza; 64.9% in Jenin). For the civilian population of the Gaza Strip, this proportion is larger than that reported by Qouta, Punamaki, et al. (2001). The PTSD rate of 69.0 percent for boys and 68.9 percent for girls in the current inquiry also is much greater than the corresponding proportions of 3.7 percent for boys and 6.3 percent for girls reported by Kilpatrick et al. (2003) using a household probability sample of 4023 adolescents age twelve to seventeen.

In the United States, PTSD has been found to have lifetime prevalence rates between 7.8 percent (Kessler, Sonnega, Bromet, Hughes, & Nelson, 1995) and 12.3 percent (Resnick, Kilpatrick, Dansky, Saunders, & Best, 1993) among adults, who, because of their older status, should have had more opportunity to experience this disorder. Although it seems inappropriate to make comparisons with normative data obtained in a different country without first validating the measure on the sample of interest, such general comparisons highlight the global context and significance of these data. As such, the present prevalence rates among Palestinian children and adolescents are extremely disturbing, especially bearing in mind the fact that PTSD has been found to lead to negative outcomes, including depression and suicidal behavior (Grunebaum, Malone, & Mann, 2003), as well as increasing the likelihood of developing additional psychiatric conditions in absence of receiving treatment. Seemingly in correlation with this, nearly one half of the Palestinian participants in both Gaza and Jenin (40.0% and 41.9%, respectively) were classified as reporting moderate or severe levels of depression. This proportion is much greater than the rate for major depressive symptoms of 7.4 percent for boys and 13.9 percent for girls in the United States, as reported by Kilpatrick et al. in 2003. However, similar to the U.S. proportion, women in Jenin reported higher levels of depression than did men. Thus, depression among Palestinian children and adolescents in Jenin has a gender context. In Gaza, no statistically significant difference between genders was reported in regard to depression.

The results of the anxiety scale demonstrate that Palestinian adolescents are predominantly occupied with an intense experience of uncertainty and anxiety. Disturbingly, all sample participants in Gaza and two-thirds of sample participants in Jenin (100.0% and 67.0%, respectively) reported moderate or severe levels of anxiety.

Findings from the coping scale also paint a disturbing picture. Specifically, between 28.8 percent (cognitive avoidance) and 69.9 percent (logical analysis) of the sample members reported undesirable coping responses. These results suggest that a significant proportion of adolescents in Gaza do not have the necessary coping resources to deal with problems and stressors. Unfortunately, poor coping responses have been found to predict an array of negative outcomes such as alcohol and drug use, conduct disorder, and behavior problems (Moos, 1993).

Another crucial finding relates to the complication that arises from an abundance of stressors and distressing circumstances in adolescents' lives. The canonical discriminant analysis revealed that adolescents diagnosed with PTSD living in Gaza tended to be those who reported the highest levels of depression, anxiety, and positive reappraisal coping and the lowest levels of seeking guidance and support coping. Seeking alternative rewards served as a suppressor variable. Thus, adolescents in the Gaza Strip are experiencing extremely high rates of psychological maladjustment, with one mental disorder (e.g., anxiety, depression) increasing the likelihood of the adolescent's experiencing another mental problem (e.g., PTSD).

Common themes that pervade the responses of the participants in both Gaza and Jenin are the multiple losses they have endured, including personal, family, and community losses. Home destruction and death or injury of family members and close friends are prevalent traumatic events they have experienced during this Intifada. For example, approximately one half (48.5%) of the participants in Gaza reported the death of a family member, and 15.7 percent and 7.91 percent witnessed the demolition of homes and the injury of a friend, respectively. Also, approximately one-third (34.1%) of participants indicated that the painful event cited had directly involved them. Of those who indicated that the painful event cited had involved someone else, 31.0 percent reported that it had involved a friend, 16.6 percent a known society member, 11.8 percent a relative, 8.3 percent an immediate family member, and 6.1 percent a combination of family and friend. The findings of the present study suggest that adolescents experience significant levels of psychological distress as a result of the high frequency of anxiety, depression, and preoccupation with the traumatic situation. Studies by Garbarino, Kostelny, and Dubrow offer support for these findings (1991a, b). Specifically, these researchers found that the accumulation of traumatic experiences is increasingly becoming a core feature of their lives, rather than an isolated incident of trauma. The present results also are consistent with Goenjian (2000), who found that political violence increases the risk of individuals developing severe and chronic PTSD reactions associated with chronic anxiety and depressive reactions.

Comparing the present results with those examining the rate of PTSD among Palestinian children and adolescents in Gaza during the first Intifada (1987–1993) (Elbedour, 1998) demonstrates that the psychological damage inflicted by the violence of the past three years is substantially more chronic, interfering substantially with individuals' adaptive functioning. According to Elbedour (1998), between 12 and 18 percent of Palestinian youth were found clinically to meet the criteria for PTSD during the first Intifada. Using the Child Behavior Checklist (Achenbach, 1991), Garbarino and Kostelny (1996) explored this topic and found similar estimates of psychological distress among the Palestinian children. The present figures, as indicated earlier, are disturbing given the fact that PTSD significantly increases the risk of comorbidity and the development of a host of disturbance including anxiety, depression, and drug dependence (Pfefferbaum, 1997). Even more disturbingly, at the time of writing (i.e., since the collection of the current data), the situation in both Gaza and Jenin has worsened, with the occurrence of events that have led to the breakdown of the "Roadmap to Peace" (*BBC News World Edition*, 2003). Thus, it is likely that the present estimates of the prevalence of PTSD, depression, and anxiety represent a lower bound.

Both the findings of the study in Gaza and the preliminary results of the study in Jenin suggest that Palestinian children and adolescents living in these areas experience some of the highest levels of PTSD, depression, and anxiety in the world today. The paucity of mental health resources available for these children also will portend a future of emotional and psychiatric devastation that is very troubling.

As such, although trauma victims seek psychological assistance, it is more important that they receive social justice (Summerfield, 1995). In Gaza, which has a population density of 2,150 people per kilometer (Thabet & Vostanis, 2000), 70 percent of the 860,000 inhabitants are still labeled refugees (Yahya, 1991), and more than 50 percent still live in "permanently temporary" shanty towns, which are "places where people exist rather than live" (McDowall, 1989, p. 20). In Jenin, the partially rebuilt camp has been completely enclosed by the "apartheid wall" and endures frequent incursions, curfews, and closures at the discretion of the Israeli army. In such a disintegrated climate it is difficult to receive the social, community, and interpersonal support needed to cope with or protect against the anxieties and worries of an uncontrollable environment (Elliot, 2002). Schools that typically function as a secure base, for example, are unprepared to deal with large-scale crises. These realities are relevant factors that may precipitate or intensify the severity of their traumatic exposure and thus predict deficits in their sense of safety, power, and protection.

These results provide compelling evidence that the violence must be stopped if Palestinian youth are to recover psychologically. Indeed, without such systematic efforts of permanently resolving the conflict and implementing mental health and social and cultural interventions, continued political violence, coupled with the aversive impoverished socio economic conditions, are potent risk factors that will serve to continue these horrific scenarios rather than lead to a just and peaceful resolution.

SOME CLINICAL REFLECTIONS: TRAUMA OR RESILIENCE?

The results of the Jenin and Gaza studies and of the wealth of other work done in Palestine may very well portend a very bleak future for Palestinians, especially Palestinian children. With about 66 percent of Palestinian children in Jenin and Gaza experiencing PTSD and PTSD-like conditions, the magnitude of distress that this community is confronting is staggering. There is, however, another possible interpretation of these results. If 66 percent of these children have PTSD, what is it about the remaining 34 percent of children who do not have PTSD?

Many Palestinian children are exposed to multiple and chronic traumatic experiences, yet, it may be said that it is only 66 percent of these children who develop these conditions and that 34 percent of the sample did not develop PTSD. What about these children? What is it about these children that they are protected from developing PTSD? Despite the context of extensive trauma, many Palestinian children do not develop PTSD and in fact continue to function in school, in relationships, and at home with their families. Perhaps our research and work should also address how it can be possible to function within such a traumatic and impoverished environment. I would suggest that the concept of resilience could be another promising research strategy. Many possible hypotheses could account for the arguably profound resilient nature of these children (and many adults for that matter). Possible explanatory constructs include the nature and structure of extended family life in Palestine. This is certainly consistent with observations of how Palestinian families exhibit an amazing capacity for loving and tender feelings, even in the midst of occupation and warlike conditions. Perhaps a kind of psychological antibody is developed and some children are inoculated psychologically before traumatic exposure. The possibility of coping with trauma in the context of a supportive and loving extended family certainly offers a very different context than for those families that are fragmented and disenfranchised. The fact that many Palestinians do not develop PTSD when they are exposed to multiple traumas, chronic trauma, and transgenerational trauma is a remarkable phenomenon that is worthy of further investigation and a testament to the resilience of the Palestinian community. This may offer a glimmer of hope so necessary to create a future of freedom, peace, justice, and self-determination for Palestine.

ACKNOWLEDGMENTS

I would like to thank my colleagues Salman Elbedour, Anthony Onwuegbuzie, Janine Whitcome, Fadel Abu Hein, Eyad Hallaq, Hassan Abu-Saad, and Qun Jiao for their hard work and commitment to making these studies a reality under very difficult circumstances and for their input and direction on this chapter. I would also like to thank Dr. Jamshid Marvasti for his guidance. Finally, I would like to thank Cathryn Haeffele for her support and final editorial input, without which this chapter would not have been completed.

NOTE

1. For Palestinians and people from the Arab World, there have been several defining events in Middle East: the dispossession in 1948 of some 800,000 Palestinians (the creation of the State of Israel); the 1967 Six-Day War with the Israeli annexation of East Jerusalem, the West Bank, and Gaza; the first Palestinian Intifada (1987–1993); the second "Al-Aqsa" Intifada (2000–present); the failure of the Oslo Peace Accords and the subsequent attempts to bring peace to the region, and the invasion and "defeat" of the Israeli Army in Lebanon in 2006.

REFERENCES

Achenbach, T. M. (1991). *Manual for the child behavior checklist/4-18 and 1991 profile.* Burlington, VT: University of Vermont, Department of Psychiatry.

American Psychiatric Association. (1994). *Diagnostic and statistical manual of mental disorders,* 4th ed. (DSM-IV). Washington, DC: APA Publication.

Amnesty International Press Release. (2003, September 29). *Israel/occupied territories: No one is safe–the spiral of killings and destruction must stop* [On-line]. Retrieved November 21, 2003. Available: http://web.amnesty.org/library/Index/ENGMDE150882003?open&of=ENG-PSE

Barghouti, M., Jubran, J., Faqih, R., Nafe', A., Tawil, H., Awwad, K., & Khalili, S. (2004) "Health and segregation: The impact of the Israeli Separation Wall on access to health care services." *HDIP Report* [On-line]. Retrieved September 15, 2007. Available: http://www.hdippg/

Barghouti, M., Jubran, J., Awad, N., Al-Faqih, R., Nafe', A., & Khalili, S. (2005). "Health and segregation II: The impact of the Israeli Wall on access to health care services." *HDIP Report* [On-line]. Retrieved September 15, 2007. Available: http://www.hdip.org/

BBC News World Edition. (2003, November 19). UN endorses Mid-East roadmap [On-line]. Retrieved November 21, 2003. Available: http://news.bbc.co.uk/2/hi/middle_east/3283949.stm

Beck, A. T., & Steer, R. A. (1990). *Beck anxiety inventory manual.* San Antonio, TX: Psychological Corporation.

Beck, A. T., Steer, R. A., & Brown, G. K. (1996). *Beck depression inventory-second edition.* San Antonio, TX: Psychological Corporation.

Carter, J. (2006). *Palestine peace not apartheid.* New York: Simon & Schuster.

Elbedour, S. (1998). Youth in crisis: The well-being of Middle-Eastern youth and adolescents during war and peace. *Journal of Youth & Adolescence, 45*(4), pp. 57–65.

Elbedour, S., ten Bensel, R., & Bastien, D. (1993). Ecological integrated model of children and adolescents of war: Individual and social psychology. *Child Abuse and Neglect, 17,* pp. 805–819.

Elliott, T. L. (2002). Children and trauma: An overview of reactions, mediating factors, and practical interventions that can be implemented. In C. E. Stout (Ed.), *The psychology of terrorism* (Vol. 2, pp. 49–73). Westport, CT: Praeger Publishers.

Fields, R., Elbedour S., & Abu Hein, F. (2002). The Palestinian suicide bomber. In. C. E. Stout (Ed.), *The psychology of terrorism: Clinical aspects and responses* (Vol. 2, pp. 193–223). Westport, CT: Praeger Publishers.

Garbarino, J., & Kostelny, K. (1996). The effects of political violence on Palestinian children and adolescents' behavior problems: A risk accumulation model. *Child Development, 67,* pp. 33–45.

Garbarino, J., Kostelny, K., & Dubrow, N. (1991a). *No place to be a child: Growing up in a war zone.* Lexington, MA: D. C. Heath.

Garbarino, J., Kostenly, K., & Dubrow, N. (1991b). What children and adolescents can tell us about living in danger. *American Psychologist, 46,* pp. 376–383.

Goenjian, A. K. (2000). Prospective study of posttraumatic stress, anxiety, and depressive reactions after earthquake and political violence. *American Journal of Psychiatry, 157,* pp. 911–916.

Grunebaum, M. F., Malone, K. M., & Mann, J. J. (2003). Association of comorbid post-traumatic stress disorder and major depression with greater risk for suicidal behavior. *American Journal of Psychiatry, 160,* pp. 580–582.

Human Rights News (2002, May). "Jenin: IDF military operations." *Human Rights Watch Publications.* Vol. 14, No. 3 (E) [On-line]. Retrieved September 15, 2007. Available: http://hrw.org/reports/2002/israel3/

International Court of Justice (2004, July 9). "Legal consequences of the construction of a wall in the occupied Palestinian territory." *General List. No. 131.* (Archived in the Hague and the United Nations.)

Israeli Ministry of Foreign Affairs (2005, July 10). "Cabinet Communique 10 Jul 2005." *Jerusalem* [On-line]. Retrieved September 15, 2007. Available: http://www.israelmfa.gov.iI/MFA/Government/ Communigues/2005/ Cabinet±Commu iii qne+ I 0-Jul-2005 .htrn

Kessler, R. C., Sonnega, A., Bromet, E., Hughes, M., & Nelson, C. B. (1995). Post-traumatic stress disorder in the national co-morbidity survey. *Archives of General Psychiatry, 52,* pp. 1048–1060.

Kilpatrick, D. G., Ruggiero, K. J., Acierno, R., Saunders, B. E., Resnick, H. S., & Best, C. L. (2003). Violence and risk of PTSD, major depression, substance abuse/dependence, and comorbidity: Results from the National Survey of Adolescents. *Journal of Consulting and Clinical Psychology, 71,* pp. 692–700.

Li, D. & Lein, Y., translated by Ashkar, A. & Eran, 5. (2006, September) "Israel's bombing of the Gaza power plant and its effects." *B'Tselem Status Report* [On-line]. Retrieved September 15, 2007. Available: www.btselem.orgfDownload/200609 Act of Vengeance Eng.doc

McDowall, D. (1989). A profile of the population of the West-bank and Gaza strip. *Journal of Refugee Studies, 2*(1), pp. 20–25.

Moos, R. H. (1993). *Coping responses inventory-youth form professional manual.* Odessa, FL: Psychological Assessment Resources.

Office of the High Commissioner for Human Rights (1949, August 12). "4th Geneva Convention, Article 18." Geneva convention relative to the protection of civilian persons in time of war. Adopted on August 12th, 1949. Entry into force October 21st, 1950 [On-line]. Retrieved September 15, 2007. Available: http://www.unhchr.ch/htrnl/menu3/b/92.htm

Palestinian Red Crescent Society (2002). "Operating under siege: January 2001-December 2002." *Al Beireh.* [On-line]. Retrieved September 15, 2007. Available: http://www.palestine rcs.org/

Palestinian Health, Development, Infrastructure and Policy Institute (2002). "Developing against the odds: Annual report." *Ramallah* [On-line]. Retrieved September 15, 2007. Available: http://wwwhdip.org/publications/Anual%20Report.pdf

Palestinian Center for Human Rights (2002, September). Report on Israeli attacks against Palestinian medical personnel. *Gaza* [On-line]. Retrieved September 15, 2007. Available: http://www.pchrgaza.org/files/Reports/Englishlpdf medical/mcdical%20report%202 .pd I

Palestinian Ministry of Health (2004, August). "Health status in Palestine." The Annual Report 2004. *Gaza* [On-line]. Retrieved September 15, 2007. Available: http://www.rnoh.gov.ps/index.asp?deptid5&pranchi&=59&action=details&serial=727

Pfefferbaum, B. (1997). Post-traumatic stress disorder in children: A review of the past 10 years. *Journal of the American Academy of Child and Adolescent Psychiatry, 36,* pp. 1503–1511.

Qouta, S., el-Sarraj, E., & el-Masri, M. (n.d.). *An epidemiological study in the prevalence of stress related psychiatric disorders among Palestinians in the Gaza Strip.* Retrieved November 18, 2003. Available: http://www.gcmhp.net/NewResearch/Epidemiological.html

Qouta, S., el-Sarraj, E., & Punamaki, R. L. (2001). Mental flexibility as resiliency factor among children and adolescents exposed to political violence. *International Journal of Psychology, 36*(1), pp. 1–7.

Qouta, S., Punamaki, R. L., & el-Sarraj, E. (2001). The impact of the peace treaty on psychological well-being: A follow-up study of Palestinian children and adolescents. *Child Abuse & Neglect, 19*(10), pp. 1197–1208.

Resnick, H. S., Kilpatrick, D. G., Dansky, B. S., Saunders, B. E., & Best, C. L. (1993). Prevalence of civilian trauma and post-traumatic stress disorder in a representative national sample of women. *Journal of Consulting and Clinical Psychology, 61*, pp. 984–991.

Sfard, M. (2002, May 19). "Why Israel's 'seruvniks' say enough is enough." *The Observer: Woridview Extra* [On-line]. Retrieved September 15, 2007. Available: http://www.guardian.co .uklisracl/comrnent/0,,7 1 8335 ,00.html

Summerfield, D. (1995). Addressing human response to war and atrocity: Major challenges in research and practices and the limitations of Western psychiatric models. In R. J. Kleber; C. R. Figley, & B. P. R. Gersons (Eds.), *Beyond trauma: Cultural and societal dynamics.* New York: Plenum Press.

Thabet, A., Abu Tawahina, A., el-Sarraj, E. & Vostanis, P. (2007, August 8). "Exposure to war trauma and PTSD among parents and children in the Gaza strip." *European Child and Adolescent Psychiatry* [On-line]. Retrieved September 15, 2007. Available: http://www.gcmhp.net/

Thabet, A. & Vostanis, P. (2000). Post-traumatic stress disorder reactions in children and adolescents of war: A longitudinal study. *Child Abuse & Neglect, 24*(2), pp. 291–298.

United Nations General Assembly Resolution ES-b/b. (2002, May 7). Treaty Series. Vol. 75 No. 973. 17th Plenary Meeting. [On-line]. Retrieved September 15, 2007. Available: http://domino.un.org/UNTSPAL.NSF/361eea1cc0830l c485256cf60060695 9/72da83ff10657 c998 5256hc2005b8d23 !OpenDocument

United Nations Relief & Works Agency. (2006, December). "Palestinian refugee statistical profile figures." *Public information Office* [On-line]. Retrieved September 15, 2007. Available: http://www.un.org/mirwpblications/pdf/ui 1-dec06.pdf

Watson, C. O., Juba, M. P., Manifold, V., Kucala, T., & Anderson, P. E. D. (1991). The PTSD interview: Rationale, description, reliability, and concurrent validity of a DSM-III-based technique. *Journal of Clinical Psychology, 47*, pp. 179–188.

World Health Organization. (2003, May 17). Report: "Health conditions of, and assistance to, the Arab population in the occupied Arab territories, including Palestine." *Fifty-Sixth World Health Assembly* [On-line]. Retrieved September 15, 2007. Available: http://domino.un.org/UNISPAL.NSF/8dl6a89359b63d6785256c8b00574cc0/857500d3b7641c798525723d006f 8956!OpenDocument

World Health Organization. (2006, May 22). Report: "Health conditions in the occupied Palestinian territory, including east Jerusalem, and in the occupied Syrian Golan: Progress Report." *Fifty-Ninth World Health Assembly.* A59/1NF.DOC./3. Agenda Item 13 [On-line]. Retrieved September 15, 2007. Available: http://ftp.who .ingh/ehwhaJpdf files/WHA5 9/ A5 91D3 -en.pdf

World Health Organization and the Palestine Red Crescent Society. (2003, March 15). Media Release: "International, Israeli, Palestinian health workers call on Israeli Government to guarantee health workers protection" *Jerusalem* [On-line]. Retrieved September 15, 2007. Available: http://dominoun.on!/UNJSPAI .NSF/fd 807e4666 I e36898525 70d00069e9 I 8/8hcb 1764a 1 d33c27 8525 6cecOO5 cb 1 3a! OpenDocument

Yahya, A. (1991). The role of the refugee camps. In J. R. Nassar, & R. Heacock (Eds.) *Intifada: Palestine at the Crossroads* (pp. 91–106). New York: Praeger.

Chapter 13

TRAUMA OF TERRORISM: PHARMACOTHERAPY IN ACUTE TRAUMA AND PTSD

Jamshid A. Marvasti and Kenneth M. Cunningham

INTRODUCTION

There is a growing interest in the use of pharmacotherapy to treat symptoms associated with post-traumatic stress disorder [PTSD]. This interest stems, in part, from advances in neuroimaging research demonstrating that specific neurobiological processes play a role in the development and ongoing manifestation of PTSD. Also, the heterogeneity of PTSD symptoms and higher rates of comorbidities among individuals with PTSD has generated interest in the use of medications that have demonstrated efficacy in reducing symptoms associated with other psychiatric disorders. There has also been a wider range of pharmacological agents available to clinical practitioners, that has stimulated research and advances in clinical practice. Now, there is an abundance of evidence demonstrating that a wide range of pharmacological agents can ameliorate the core symptoms of PTSD and other comorbidities.

PTSD is a prevalent and disabling condition that is associated with significant impairments across the biological, psychological and social dimensions of human behavior. The American Psychiatric Association (APA) (2000) defines PTSD as the development of certain characteristic symptoms following a psychologically distressing event that is outside the range of normal human experience. According to the *DSM-IV-TR* (APA, 2004) there are two fundamental criteria for a diagnosis of PTSD. The first involves witnessing, experiencing, or otherwise being confronted with an event that involves actual or possible death, grave injury or threat to physical integrity. Second, a patient's response to the event must involve severe helplessness, fear, and horror and with children disorganized or agitated behavior.

Although anyone who is exposed to an overwhelming trauma is at risk for PTSD, many people will never go on to develop the disorder. The severity of the traumatic experience, length of exposure, and the age of exposure can influence the onset, severity, and duration of PTSD. According to McFarlane, Yehuda, and Clark (2002) the manifestation of PTSD is also a result of the way an individual processes information about traumatic memories. When people are exposed to traumatic experiences, their efforts to cope are influenced by the interaction of certain cognitive and neurobiological processes. Cultural ideology, community support and a few other variables influence whether someone will develop PTSD. Understanding a culture's ideology can elucidate how a nation's citizens respond to war or terror. For example, the Nazi SS doctors (who committed atrocities during the Holocaust) did not experience any PTSD, as compared with some Vietnam veterans who have suffered tremendously in this regard (Hough, 2004). It has been implied that the behavior of the Nazi doctors was integrated into their ideology. Stuart Twemlow (Hough 2004) has agreed that this large group identification by these Nazi doctors gave them "protection" against experiencing their traumatic actions. These German SS doctors believed they were hurting "bad" people, people who had caused Germany to lose WWI and were dangerous to humanity. Conversely, Vietnam veterans felt betrayed by their military superiors and government leaders in this "unpopular" and "unnecessary" war. Some veterans have felt that they hurt "innocent" people in Vietnam. It is the difference between perceptions that may influence the development of PTSD. This can be seen in the label given to these two wars: the Vietnam War was titled an "Ambivalent War" where WWII was considered a "Holy War" for Germans.

DIAGNOSIS OF PTSD

The symptoms associated with PTSD are typically conceptualized into two main categories, primary and secondary symptoms. The primary symptoms associated with PTSD, as explained by Korn & Leeds (2002), fall into three categories: (1) intrusive or reexperiencing symptoms; (2) avoidance and numbing symptoms, and (3) physiological hyperarousal. Often, the primary symptoms of PTSD lead to secondary symptoms that are often more enduring and include excessive sensitivity to stress and significant impairments in social, familial, and occupational functioning. Secondary symptoms of PTSD are often diagnosed as comorbid conditions and disorders, which can complicate the treatment process. According to Kessler, Sonnega, Bromet, Hughes and Nelson (1995), more than 80 percent of individuals who have a diagnosis of PTSD, could also meet criteria for at least one other Axis I or Axis II *DSM-IV-TR* diagnosis, such as major depressive disorder, borderline personality disorder, and substance-related disorders. In general, symptoms of PTSD could be summarized as:

1. Intrusive symptoms include recurrent manifestations of the traumatic event without any conscious desire to recall them. Flashbacks and nightmares may be present and during the flashbacks the victim may dissociate from the present surroundings. Nightmares and night terrors are intrusive manifestations of traumatic memories that have not been integrated into the consciousness.
2. Compulsive reexposure refers to the tendency of individuals who have been diagnosed with PTSD to place themselves in situations that are reminiscent of some aspect of the original trauma.
3. Reenactment of trauma occurs through risk-taking behavior and is a variation of compulsive reexposure to trauma.
4. Revictimization is also seen in victims of PTSD, especially those of sexual and physical abuse.
5. Avoidance and numbing behaviors develop as a defense reaction against the traumatic and painful emotions and become maladaptive coping skills. At times, traumatized patients are unable to modulate the arousal state and consequently may split off the memory and dissociate.
6. Attention disorder, distractibility, and stimulus discrimination are functions that are regulated in the brain by the limbic system. Neurohormonal changes that occur in the limbic system following exposure to a traumatic event make it difficult for the victim to attend to affective stimuli that are appropriate to the present situation without being overcome by excessive sensory input (van Der Kolk, Mcfarlane, & Weisseth, 1996).
7. Changes in personal identity and defense mechanisms are common effects of traumatic experiences. Dissociative states and dissociative identity disorder are also associated with complex PTSD.

COMPLEX PTSD

Sometimes labeled as disorders of extreme stress, not otherwise specified, complex PTSD presents a challenge to clinical practitioners. For many individuals with PTSD, the long-term effects of childhood abuse and trauma set into motion a wide range of somatic, affective, behavioral, and interpersonal problems that are often diagnosed as comorbid disorders. Prominent PTSD researchers and clinical practitioners have proposed that these other problems do not constitute comorbid diagnoses but are complex adaptations to chronic developmental trauma. It is important to consider the possibility that comorbid disorders are manifestations of adaptive efforts to cope with extensive patterns of abuse and neglect throughout childhood development. Children are particularly susceptible to the impact of neurobiological stress responses, particularly if the exposure to traumatic stress has been pervasive throughout their development. Therefore, patients with complicated clinical presentations may require interventions that go beyond those designed for the core symptoms of PTSD.

Complex PTSD has been conceptualized into seven symptom clusters: (1) impairment in mood regulation; (2) self-destructive activity (e.g. self-mutilation, substance abuse, bulimia); (3) somatization disorders; (4) dissociation and amnesia; (5) alterations of identity and sense of self; (6) attachment disorder and pathological object relationships; (7) possible development of self-defeating personality traits.

INCIDENCE OF PTSD

Historically, PTSD has a lifetime prevalence in the range of 7 to 12 percent, with women being more than twice as likely as men to suffer from this condition (Kessler et al., 1995). Rape has been identified as the most common traumatic event among both men and women. Other events associated with the development of PTSD include combat exposure, childhood maltreatment (physical, sexual, and emotional), and natural or human made disasters (Resnick, Kilpatrick, Dansky, Saunders, & Best, 1993). Women are more likely to encounter traumatic events such as a sexual molestation and sexual abuse, whereas men are more likely to be exposed to physical violence, accidents, and combat experience. Not only are women twice as likely to develop PTSD but also their symptoms are more likely to persist than are symptoms among men (Kessler et al., 1995). Conversely, recent studies of U.S. veterans of war in Iraq and Afghanistan suggest that men and women may be equally susceptible to PTSD symptoms.

GENDER DIFFERENCES IN REACTION TO TRAUMA

There are differences in the ways men and women react to traumatic stress. Perry, Pollard, Blakely, Bakar and Vigilante (1995) reviewed literature pertaining to anthropological and Darwinian models of neurobiological adaptation to traumatic stress as a way of explaining these gender differences. According to these authors (Perry et al., 1995), when primitive tribes or clans would go to war, the victorious tribe would slaughter the adult males of the defeated tribe and take the women and children into bondage as their own property and slaves. Women and children were more likely to survive and eventually become incorporated into the new tribe if they dissociated or responded with numbness and compliance. Conversely, if the men of the tribe were to "freeze" as a defense mechanism during battle, this would most likely result in death and be a detriment to the survival of the species (Perry et al., 1995). From this perspective, differences in the way men and women react to traumatic stress evolved from the pursuit of survival of the species. In 1993, the Bureau of Alcohol, Tobacco and Firearms (BATF) conducted a military-style raid of the Branch Davidian Complex in Waco, Texas, that lasted 51 days and ultimately ended with the death of eighty Davidians, twenty of whom were children. Perry and colleagues (1995) conducted a study of children who were released from the Branch Davidian Complex and had post-traumatic behaviors. Whereas male children tended to demonstrate aggression, antisocial behavior, and anger, young girls exhibited symptoms of anxiety, panic attacks and sleep disturbances. Researchers (Perry et al., 1995) speculated that male children tend to have an "external locus of control," that is characterized by displacing the symptoms of trauma on others, blaming others, exhibiting acting-out behavior, and aggression as a result of their trauma. Conversely, female children followed an "internal locus of control" and generally blamed themselves for their own victimization and develop guilt feelings.

ADDICTED TRAUMA VICTIMS (ATV)

Addictive spectrum disorders appear as the most common, and treatment refractory, comorbidities associated with PTSD. We developed the concept of "addicted trauma victim" (ATV) to refer to either: (1) a victim of trauma who uses illicit drugs or alcohol or misuses prescriptions drugs to alleviate their psychic pain or physical suffering; or (2) a substance abuser who has a past history of trauma and childhood maltreatment.

Epidemiological research suggests that between 30 and 60 percent of patients who seek treatment for substance abuse disorders also have a diagnosis of PTSD. Many people with substance abuse disorders have a history of trauma that is generally hidden or masked by the problems associated with and secondary to the substance abuse. These patients often describe their alcohol or substance abuse as a form of self-medication or abuse substances in an attempt to feel normal rather than to get high or euphoric. After many years of treating people with a history of PTSD and a co-occurring substance disorders, it became apparent that this population had a higher risk for treatment dropout when compared to their nonaddicted counterparts (Marvasti & Pinto, 2004). The reason for this appears to be twofold. First, therapists are more likely to emphasize the remission of addictive behaviors over the treatment of trauma and childhood abuse. Second, patients with PTSD and a co-occurring substance-related disorder are frequently denied access to treatment programs that address trauma-related symptoms until the substance disorder is in remission. Because this population seemed particularly susceptible to a higher percentage of treatment failures, dropouts, and relapses, we suggested a coordinated dual treatment program that would simultaneously address the substance abuse and trauma symptoms.

RATIONALE FOR THE USE OF PHARMACOTHERAPY WITH PTSD

The use of pharmacotherapy to treat symptoms associated with combat-related stress dates back to the Civil War, when veterans were given bromides, opium, chloral, and brandy (Davidson, 1997). At that time, the symptoms associated with combat stress were termed "soldier's heart" or "irritable heart" because Civil War veterans would often present with complaints of chest pain, rapid or irregular heartbeat, and dizziness. During the WWI the trauma of trench warfare led to different descriptions, such as "shell shock" and "battle fatigue." Throughout WWII barbiturates, insulin, stimulant medications, and ether were used to ameliorate combat-related stress reactions in veterans.

After WWII, there was a wider recognition of trauma-related stress reactions in civilian populations that were similar to those experienced by combat veterans. Advances in medicine also provided physicians with a wider range of pharmaceutical agents to address stress reactions. Gradually, the use of benzodiazepines to manage symptoms of insomnia and anxiety or low-dose antidepressants for symptoms of depression became accepted as effective forms of pharmacotherapy.

For many years, the most widely used treatments for PTSD consisted of CBT; however, in some instances prolonged exposure to cognitive restructuring for treatment of complex PTSD, was found to exacerbate the symptoms rather than to alleviate them (van der Kolk, 2001). Some studies (Perlstein, 2004) began to suggest that when the two forms of therapies were compared with one another pharmacotherapy may surpass the use of CBT in the treatment of PTSD. In most instances, it is preferable to combine the pharmacotherapy with the various CBT approaches (Marvasti, 2004 as cited in Finn, 2004).

Advances in neuroimaging research (Bremner & Vermetten, 2004; Bremner et al., 2003; Shin, Rauch, & Pitman, 2006) have shown how chronic stress and trauma can create neurobiological changes in specific regions of the brain. A substantial body of evidence has demonstrated that traumatic events can result in deficits in neurotransmitters, disrupted brain pathways, and unprocessed sensory motor memory. Stress and trauma may also block or slow down the development of neurons in the brain, a phenomenon known as neurogenesis (McFarlane, Yehuda, & Clark, 2002). Research suggests that pharmacotherapy can impact these neurobiological processes and not only reduce core symptoms of PTSD but also symptoms associated with comorbidities and other functional deficits (Hamner et al., 2003; Petrakis et al., 2006; Sherman, 2006).

PATHOPHYSIOLOGY OF PTSD

To a large extent, our understanding of the pathophysiology of PTSD stems from the autonomic nervous system and its role in balancing the regulation of our basic survival drives. The autonomic nervous system utilizes two neurotransmitters, epinephrine and norepinephrine, to prepare us when we perceive threat or danger. The hypothalamus, thalamus, and cerebral cortex are the regions of the brain responsible for activating the autonomic nervous system and regulating our stress reactions. Specifically, the thalamus is the region of the brain responsible for transmitting sensory input of any perceived threat to both the hypothalamus and the cerebral cortex. The cerebral cortex is thought to play a role in the experience of fear, and the hypothalamus is considered responsible for activating the autonomic nervous system, which increases adrenalin and blood flow to the brain and muscular system. The increase in blood flow and adrenalin sets into motion the "fight or flight response," causing increased heart rate and dilated pupils, and increases blood flow to areas of the body that will prepare us to respond to the perceived threat.

This basic understanding of the autonomic nervous system was elaborated on by numerous researchers, who proposed that the limbic system also played a role in our bodies' reactions to stress. The limbic system refers to the innermost and primitive structures of the brain including the thalamus and hypothalamus and also the amygdala, hippocampus, pituitary gland, and the nucleus accumbens [NAc], sometimes referred to as the dopamine pathway. Advances in research methodology throughout the 1970s increased our understanding of how the various brain structures are interconnected and function to mediate emotion, perceptions, and behavior. The limbic system is responsible for our fundamental responses to perceived threat. Research now demonstrates that the medial prefrontal cortex, hippocampus, and amygdala play important roles in our perceptions and experience of anxiety.

Current advances in neuroimaging research (Shin, Rauch, & Pitman, 2006) have suggested that the amygdala, medial prefrontal cortex, and hippocampus may be involved in the pathophysiology of PTSD. Neuroimaging studies (Nutt & Malizia, 2004; Shin et al., 2005) have used various forms of symptom provocation to elucidate the neural mechanisms underlying the manifestation of PTSD. For example, Shin and colleagues (2005) found that the amygdala has a heightened responsivity during symptomatic states and during the processing of trauma unrelated affective information. When we perceive a threat, the secretion of adrenocorticotropin from the pituitary gland stimulates the release of glucocorticoids from the adrenal gland. When people are exposed to traumatic events, particularly chronic exposure, the release of these elements can become the norm rather than the exception, which subsequently results in the oversecretion of glucocorticoids. High levels of glucocorticoids, and other stress hormones, have been associated with decreased hippocampal volume and impairments in learning and memory (Ozlewski & Varrasse, 2005).

IMPACT OF STRESS AND TRAUMA ON THE BRAIN

Chronic high levels of the stress hormone, cortisol, may induce a decrease in brain-derived neurotropic factor. It is speculated that this deficit, plus the decrease in neurogenesis and cell repair, may contribute to the chronicity of PTSD symptoms in victims. It is also speculated that this neurotropic factor may protect serotonin and dopamine neurons against assault. Some researchers hypothesize that antidepressant medication, such as selective serontonin reuptake inhibitors (SSRIs) or physical exercise may reactivate gene-expression of this factor that in turn can decrease the level of the PTSD symptoms (Korn & Leeds, 2002; Ozlewski & Varrasse, 2005).

Neurocirculatory Model

The prefrontal cortex has the task of tending to current environmental cues and inhibiting irrelevant stimulation capable of distracting sensory input. This section of the brain plays an important role in the regulation of emotion, attention, and conditioned fear (Rauch, Shin & Wright, 2003). When sensory information is received by the brain, the amygdala assigns meaning to this information by connecting and integrating memory images with the associated emotional experiences. The amygdala also participates in fear conditioning. When the amygdala becomes hyperresponsive to stimulation perceived as a threat or danger, it facilitates fear conditioning and results in symptoms of hyperarousal. There are indications that CBT may have an impact in the regulation of the amygdala response by providing new but different perceptual experiences and eventually helping to integrate and process traumatic memories (Cahill, Rauch, & Hembree, 2003). Hippocampus atrophy may also reduce regions of the brain that are responsible for identifying safe contexts and may cause specific memory problems (Ozlewski & Varrasse, 2005).

Dysregulation of Neurotransmitters

Clinically, low levels of serotonin are seen in patients with PTSD. Serotonin is one of the neurotransmitters produced by the brain that modulate pain, cognition, aggression, motor coordination, and sleep and wake cycles. It also has an impact on appetite, sexuality and libido, stress, and memory. Increases in serotonin regulate mood and impulsivity. For example, when the amygdala is stimulated by serotonin, mood stabilizes and control over impulsivity is regained. Therefore, when low levels of serotonin are prolonged it may lead to symptoms such as increased impulsivity, increased anxiety, irritability, aggression, rumination, and suicidality. Serotonin is also associated with the stabilization of glucocorticoid production through the hypothalamic pituitary adrenal axis (HPA axis) (Preston, 2003). Low levels of serotonin may lead to excessive levels of corticosteroids, which subsequently interfere with memory processes and learning capacity among patients with PTSD (Wong, 2002).

Dopamine is another neurotransmitter that is inhibitory and may affect attention, emotion, learning, and motor function. Its function in stress response is to direct the attention and concentration to the perceived threat or danger. Dopamine is also known to be a precursor to norepinephrine. When dopamine levels increase in the brain, symptoms such as impaired attention, motor deficit, apathy, anhedonia, and depression appear. However, increased levels of dopamine are also responsible for restlessness, agitation, and psychotic disorders (Stahl, 2003).

Gamma-aminobutyric acid (GABA) is also one of the most prevalent inhibitory neurotransmitters. It has an impact on feeling emotions and moods and its task is possibly to decrease neuronal excitability (Antai-Otong, 2000).

Norepinephrine is another neurotransmitter that can play a role in the manifestation of PTSD. The primary behavioral effect of norepinephrine is to increase vigilance and attentiveness to the environment. It can also increase an individual's responsiveness to other excitatory neurotransmitters. According to Preston (2003) numerous animal studies have found that high levels of stress can cause an increase in the secretion of norepinephrine. It is speculated that the flashbacks and nightmares associated with PTSD may be caused by hyperactivity of norepinephrine receptors in the prefrontal cortex of the brain (Preston, 2003).

Endorphins are endogenous opioids that are released in the brain under physiological stress. Excessive amounts of the endogenous opioids cause analgesia, which protects animals and human beings against pain while they initiate the defensive mechanisms to fight the danger. It is known that endorphins and norepinephrine interfere with explicit memory, which may cause a feeling of dissociation during the threat response (Preston, 2003).

PHARMACOTHERAPY AGENTS AVAILABLE FOR PTSD

PTSD is considered a biphasic disorder involving heterogeneous neurotransmitters and a wide range of symptom manifestation. Although SSRIs are generally considered the first line of short-term and long-term treatment of PTSD, research suggests that non-SSRI antidepressants, neuroleptics, antiepileptics, and adrenergeric receptor modulators are also effective pharmacological agents (Davis, Frazier, Williford, & Newell, 2006; Sherman, 2006). Positive symptoms of PTSD such as hyperarousal, reexperiencing of trauma, and intrusive thoughts may be more sensitive to medication than are the negative symptoms of PTSD, such as withdrawal, numbness, and avoidance (Forster, Schoenfield & Marmar, 1995). Patients with a diagnosis of PTSD also often have comorbid disorders that present a complex clinical picture. According to Jose Canive (cited in Sherman, 2006), a leading PTSD researcher and clinician, beginning with symptoms that are most troubling to the patient will facilitate a positive therapeutic relationship and compliance with the treatment process.

Clinical practitioners will often begin treatment by choosing a medication that will target comorbid disorders, such as depression and anxiety, because these symptoms are typically more troubling to the patient than the core PTSD symptoms. For example, if someone with PTSD also has comorbidity of attention deficit hyperactivity disorder (ADHD), enuresis or major depressive disorder then a medication such as imipramine may be the treatment of choice because it would be effective in treating PTSD as well as the comorbid disorders. Patients with PTSD and comorbidities of depression, social phobia, and panic disorders, may respond to one of the SSRIs such as sertraline because of the effectiveness of this medication in treating social phobia, anxiety, and panic attacks. Victims of PTSD who have been diagnosed with obsessive compulsive disorder (OCD) may also respond to an SSRI medication because it has demonstrated efficacy in the treatment of both disorders. There have been some proposed treatment protocols that provide some guidelines for sequencing pharmacological interventions; however, choosing the appropriate medication for treatment of PTSD is both a science and an art.

What follows is a list of the wide range of pharmacological agents used in the treatment of PTSD: SSRI and serotonin norepinephrine reuptake inhibitors (SNRIs) antidepressants (fluoxetine and venlafaxine), serotonin agonist and antagonist (buspirone and cyproheptadine), tricyclic antidepressants (TCAs) (imipramine), monoamine oxidase inhibitors (phenelzine), antiepileptics and mood stabilizers (divalproex and lithium carbonate), anxiolytics (benzodiazepines), beta-adrenergic blocking agents (propranolol), alpha-adrenergic agonist-antagonist (clonidine), opioid antagonists (naltrexone), and antipsychotics (risperidone).

SSRI Antidepressants

Among all the SSRIs, sertraline, paroxetine, and fluoxetine have received the most attention in the research literature. In a systematic review of research articles pertaining to the use of pharmacotherapy of PTSD, Ipser, Seedat & Stein (2006) found evidence to support the use of SSRIs as a first-line agent in the treatment of PTSD. In theory, SSRIs change the noradrenergic and serotonergic systems of the brain that are involved in activating states of arousal in the mind. The effectiveness of these medications may also be related to the potency of serotonin over norepinephrine reuptake blockade (Crockett & Davidson, 2002). Research suggests that PTSD symptoms such as impulse control, sleep disorders, and repetitive response to intrusive recollections and traumatic memories are considered to be disorders of five hydroxy tryptophan (5-HTP) which may also explain the efficacy of SSRIs. Animal studies have revealed that serotonin type 2 (5-HT2) receptor pathways are mediators of conditioned avoidance, resilience to stress and the process of learned helplessness (Krystal, 1990). Essentially, SSRIs inhibit the reuptake of serotonin in the synapse, which causes a downregulation of receptors, such as 5-HT2, while influencing other neurotransmitters such as dopamine and norepinephrine.

Many physicians are using SSRIs medication to prevent the transformation of acute stress disorder into PTSD. For example, Pollack is investigating the efficacy of escitalopram with patients who have recently been exposed to a traumatic event and have developed an acute stress syndrome (as cited in Kilgore, 2005). Although the evidence is still preliminary, he reported that when escitalopram was administered within a few weeks of the trauma, his patients were less likely to develop symptoms of PTSD. Although the possible mechanism of action of the SSRI in these cases is not clear, the hope is that the drug will help stop the cycle of increased arousal and anxiety that may be predisposed to full-blown PTSD (Pollack, as cited in Kilgore, 2005).

Robert, Hamner, Ulmer, Lorberbaum & Durkalski, (2006) conducted a 12-week, prospective, open-label trial of escitalopram to assess its efficacy, safety, and tolerability in the treatment of PTSD among military veterans. Researchers initiated treatment with 10 mg of escitalopram daily for four weeks and increased the dose to 20 mg daily for the remainder of the study (Robert et al., 2006). Although the findings from this research suggest that escitalopram can be effective and is well-tolerated among patients with combat-related PTSD, there is a need for larger, randomized controlled trials among individuals with combat and noncombat-related PTSD.

Sertraline has demonstrated efficacy in the short-term and long-term treatment of PTSD, regardless of the nature of the trauma or the age of trauma occurrence. One study (Stein, van der Kolk, Austin, Fayyad, & Clary, 2006) compared the effects of sertraline among adult patients with different index traumas and found this medication to be significantly more effective than placebo was regardless of whether patients had experienced interpersonal trauma or childhood abuse. Rothbaum and colleagues (2006) conducted a study to compare the benefit of augmenting sertraline with prolonged exposure (PE) therapy with the results from using sertraline alone. Among all the CBT approaches, PE is considered one of the more effective psychotherapeutic interventions among patients with PTSD. The sample consisted of 65 men and women outpatients with chronic PTSD. All participants initially received ten weeks of sertraline alone and were then randomly assigned to five additional weeks of sertraline alone (n = 31) or sertraline plus ten sessions of twice-weekly PE (n = 34) (Rothbaum et al., 2006). Although the patients who received sertraline alone reported a significant reduction is PTSD symptoms after ten weeks, no further reduction in symptoms was reported after an additional five weeks. Those who received a combination of sertraline and PE did report a further reduction in their symptoms after five additional weeks.

Paroxetine is also effective in the short-term and long-term treatment of PTSD and is indicated for all three major symptom clusters of PTSD: reexperiencing, avoidance and emotional numbing, and hyperarousal.

SSRI Discontinuation Syndrome

Abrupt discontinuation of this medication may result in SSRI withdrawal syndrome. The discontinuation syndrome has several characteristics, such as flulike symptoms, insomnia, nausea, imbalance, sensory disturbance, and hyperarousal symptoms such as agitation and anxiety. Because this syndrome is often misdiagnosed as a return of depression or anxiety, we developed the mnemonic "Hangman" to improve accurate detection of SSRI discontinuation:

H= headache
A= anxiety
N= nausea
G= gait instability
M= malaise
A= asthenia (fatigue)
N= numbness

Side Effects of SSRI

Although SSRIs are generally considered safe medication there are numerous side effects that need to be assessed on an ongoing basis. These side effects can range from something as simple as excessive yawning during the daytime (Beale & Murphree, 2000) to serotonin syndrome and upper intestinal bleeding, which requires immediate medical attention.

Serotonin syndrome can be a life-threatening complication that is marked by changes in cognition, behavior, autonomic nervous system function, and neuromuscular activity. Often this syndrome is precipitated by the concurrent use of two or more medications that increase serotonin neurotransmission in the brain; however, incidents of the syndrome have been linked to single drug exposure. Serotonin syndrome is typically treated by discontinuation of pharmacotherapy but in some instances may require treatment with an anti-serotonergic medication, such as cyproheptadine (Martin, 1996).

Reviewing psychopharmacology literature (including the *Physician's Desk Reference* [*PDR*]) reveals that SSRIs may predispose people to bleeding disorders by blocking the uptake of serotonin into platelets. Nocturnal bruxism (grinding of the teeth) is another potential side effect of SSRIs; the headaches associated with bruxism need to be differentiated from migraine or nonmigraine headaches, because these conditions can also be exacerbated by SSRI medication. Many people will be unaware of grinding their teeth during sleep and may present with complaints of a morning headache. Fluoxetine has been associated with decreased rapid eye movement (REM) sleep, increased dreaming, nightmares, and sexual dreams and obsession. Other potential sleep disturbances include myoclonus (periodic leg movements during sleep) and restless legs syndrome (RLS). There is some potential for sexual dysfunctions, including anorgasmia, the retardation of ejaculation, and a lack of sexual desire. However, since genital anesthesia is a side effect of

SSRIs, these medications have also been used to reduce obsession with the sexuality in the treatment of sexual offenders and paraphilias. Citalopram may be contraindicated for these populations, because it has been associated with spontaneous orgasms, yawning, and clitoral priapism. Amotivational syndrome and apathy have been reported as potential side effects of SSRIs. These side effects may surface after several months of treatment and may frequently be misdiagnosed as recurrence of initial depression. Because amotivational syndrome is often dose oriented, increasing the dose may exacerbate these symptoms. According to Popper (1998), apathy and amotivational syndrome may also be misdiagnosed as marijuana-induced amotivational syndrome if the patient was also using cannabis for self-medication.

SUICIDALITY AS A SIDE EFFECT OF ANTIDEPRESSANTS IN CHILDREN AND ADOLESCENTS

In 2004, the Food and Drug Administration (FDA) issued a public health advisory to warn the general public that the use of the newer SSRIs such as fluoxetine, sertraline, and paroxetine, had been associated with increased depression and suicidal thoughts and behavior. Prompted by research (Simon, 2006) suggesting that antidepressant use increased suicidal risk among children and adolescents, in 2005 the FDA extended this public health advisory to include all antidepressant medications. According to Simon (2006), among 10,000 children and adolescents taking antidepressant medication for depression, approximately six will die by suicide during the next 6 months and another thirty will be hospitalized after a serious suicidal attempt. For adults, the corresponding numbers are four suicide deaths and ten hospitalizations for suicide attempts. Of those 10,000 children and adolescents, approximately 3000 will stop taking their medication within few weeks, 4000 will never return for a second follow-up visit and approximately 6000 will not recover from depression during the next six months (p. 2723).

Despite the obvious concern about these statistics, Simon (2006) suggests that there is still a fair amount of uncertainty regarding the validity of these findings. Simon (2006) reported that larger observational studies actually found a decrease in suicidal risk among patients who began taking antidepressant medication. In addition, another study assessed the relationship between adolescent suicide rates and rates of antidepressant prescription medication and found that communities with larger rates of antidepressants use have, on average, lower rates of suicide (Gibbons, Hur, Bhaumik, & Mann, 2006).

In response to the growing uncertainty about the suicidal risk associated with SSRIs, the FDA reanalyzed all episodes of suicidal behavior in pediatric trials of antidepressant medication. Results from this meta-analysis determined that the risk of suicidal ideation, suicidal behavior and suicide attempts was approximately twice as high among pediatric patients taking newer antidepressant medication than it was for those on placebo (Hammad, Laughren, & Racoosin, 2006). According to Simon (2006) the FDA's meta-analysis suggests that among drugs there is a wide degree of variation in the level of suicidal risk, and newer antidepressants may be specifically associated with violent suicide attempts, rather than with suicide in general.

Despite these findings, the FDA did not advise against the use of antidepressants but rather made several recommendations for the use of these medications with children. First, fluoxetine is the only drug approved by the FDA for treatment of depression in pediatric populations and should be the first line of treatment. Second, physicians prescribing other antidepressants should inform parents that all other antidepressant medications are off label and are not yet approved by the FDA for treatment of depression in children. Third, suicide attempts, regardless of whether they are associated with antidepressant medication or not, are generally unpredictable. In this regard, all patients and family should be warned about sudden suicidal ideation that may develop and that agitation and restlessness may be early signs of the danger. Fourth, regular follow-up is strongly recommended and is essential to identify any development of suicidality.

OTHER USEFUL MEDICATIONS

Patients who have been diagnosed with PTSD often present with comorbidities or symptoms that are only partially responsive to pharmacotherapy with SSRIs. When patients have little to no response to an SSRI, clinicians should consider an adjunctive antidepressant medication, rather than discontinuing the initial medication. According to the research literature, there are several medications that are effective in reducing the core symptoms of PTSD and, in some instances, simultaneously target symptoms associated with comorbidities. For example, adding bupropion not only can augment the therapeutic response to an SSRI, but also can reduce problems with sexual dysfunction that are associated with SSRI medication. Dr. Hamner (as cited in Sherman, 2006) suggested that buspirone at a dosage of 30 to 40 mg a day not only can reduce symptoms of anxiety but also can potentiate SSRI antidepressants. Cyproheptadine can be effective in preventing nightmares in children at dosage of 4 mg just before bedtime (Marvasti, 2004; Marvasti & Dripchak, 2004). However, the combination of cyproheptadine with an antihistamine can have a serotonin antagonist effect.

Serotonin Norepinephrine Reuptake Inhibitors (SNRIs)

Davidson, Rothbaum, and Tucker (2006) conducted a six-month, double-blind, placebo controlled trial among 329 adult outpatients with a primary diagnosis of PTSD to determine the efficacy of venlafaxine extended release (ER), a SNRI. Researchers concluded that when compared with the placebo group, the treatment group improved significantly on cluster symptoms, such as reexperiencing, avoidance, and numbing but not for hyperarousal. Also, the remission rate among the venlafaxine ER group was higher than placebo, and the medication was well-tolerated over the course of the study (Davidson, Rothbaum, & Tucker, 2006).

Tricyclic Antidepressants

There are relatively few controlled studies (Davidson, Kudler, & Smith, 1990; Kosten, Frank, Dan, McDougle, & Giller, 1991) investigating the effectiveness of TCAs in reducing symptoms associated with PTSD. TCAs were among the first antidepressant medications used to treat comorbid symptoms of anxiety; however, the use of other anxiolytics, such as benzodiazepines, became more commonplace due to their ability to immediately diffuse symptoms of panic and acute anxiety. Still, after several weeks of treatment, it appears that TCA efficacy is comparable with that of benzodiazepines. Symptoms such as tension, apprehension, and worry are more responsive to antidepressants; however, somatic symptoms associated with anxiety disorders are responding better to benzodiazepines.

Side Effects

The cardiac and anticholinergic effects associated with these medications are limiting the use of this medication. Other side effects associated with TCAs, include orthostatic hypotension, sedation, weight gain, and cardiotoxicity.

Monoamine Oxidase Inhibitors

Although monoamine oxidase inhibitors (MAOIs) were initially used to promote abreaction among Vietnam veterans with combat-related PTSD, a few small controlled trials found that these medications were also effective in reducing symptoms associated with comorbid disorders such as depression and anxiety (Hogben & Cornfield, 1981; Kosten et al., 1991; Shestatzsky, Greenburg, & Lerer, 1988). There has been a lack of large placebo-controlled trials investigating the efficacy of MAOIs with PTSD, because the dietetic restrictions and risk of hypertensive crises associated with this class of medications has decreased interest in their use as first-line agents with PTSD and other psychiatric disorders. According to Davidson et al. (2006), MAOIs should not be considered as a first-line treatment for PTSD; however, it may be useful as an adjunctive therapy among patients who have a minimal response to SSRIs after four to six weeks of treatment.

Mood Stabilizers and Antiepileptics

Several studies have provided support for the use of antiepileptics and mood-stabilizing medications in the treatment of PTSD (Berlant, 2004; Lipper, Davidson, & Grady, 1986; Petty, Davis, & Nugent, 2002). According to these researchers, mood stabilizers and antiepileptics are effective in reducing aggressive symptom clusters that are not well-described in the diagnostic criteria for PTSD but are very common and particularly destructive in occupational and other social settings. Topiramate, hydantoin and carbamazepine have also been shown to reduce symptoms of mood instability, impulsivity and severe agitation (Berlant, 2004; Lipper et al., 1986).

Valproate is a mood stabilizer indicated in the treatment of bipolar disorder and for symptoms of irritability, aggression, and impulsive behavior. These symptoms are associated with a range of other psychiatric disorders, including PTSD (Forster et al. 1995). Research investigating the effectiveness of valproate with PTSD has primarily been conducted among combat veterans, because they are more likely to report symptoms of impulsivity, irritability, and severe reexperiencing of combat related trauma (Fesler, 1991; Petty et al. 2002). Fesler (1991) conducted a study to determine the effectiveness of adjunctive valproate among sixteen Vietnam combat veterans with moderate to severe hyperarousal and reexperiencing symptoms. A-mong the fourteen participants included in the final analysis, half the patients reported a significant reduction in the core symptoms of PTSD and nine participants also reported significant improvement in the duration and quality of their sleep. Eleven out of the fourteen also reported a significant reduction in hyperarousal symptoms, and none of the participants reported any serious or long-term side effects (Fesler, 1991).

Hydantoin is an antiepileptic medication indicated for the treatment of epilepsy; however, it is believed that this medication acts by modulation of glutamatergic transmission. As noted previously, research has suggested that symptoms of PTSD are the result of alteration of glutamatergic transmission with subsequent neurological toxicity. Bremner et al. (2005) found that hydantoin influenced memory, cognition, and brain structure among individuals with a diagnosis of PTSD. Participants treated with hydantoin demonstrated a significant increase in right brain volume when compared with those who received placebo. Because the increase in hippocampal volume was correlated with a reduction in symptom severity, Bremner et al. (2005) concluded that hydantoin not only has a positive effect on cognition and brain structure of individuals with PTSD but also may reduce symptom manifestation.

In regard to adding mood stabilizers for patients who respond partially to SSRIs, Davidson et al. (2005) suggested augmentation with valproic acid or lamictal especially for patients with symptoms of impulsivity and aggression.

Side Effects

Side effects of valproate include dizziness, drowsiness, hair loss and thinning, nausea, tremor, weight gain, hyperammonemia, thrombocytopenia, vomiting, hepatotoxicity, and pancreatitis.

Anxiolytics

Benzodiazepines have been used to treat symptoms of anxiety for many years. Research suggests that these medications can also reduce acute somatic symptoms associated with anxiety. Although benzodiazepines are generally not indicated for long-term treatment of anxiety disorders or PTSD, they are perhaps the most effective therapy for the acute relief of anxiety and anxiety-driven somatic complaints. According to Dr. Jose Canive benzodiazepines should not be considered as a first choice (as cited in Sherman, 2006); however, in some instances these medications can be used cautiously to manage symptoms of panic in patients without a substance-abuse history. In addition, older veterans with a poor tolerance for SSRIs, in particular prefer to take benzodiazepines. When prescribed intermittently along with other medications, short-acting benzodiazepines, such as lorazepam are most effective.

Side Effects

Common side effects of benzodiazepines include drowsiness, ataxia, behavioral problems, hyperactivity, hypersalivation, seizure exacerbation, and psychosis. Elderly patients and individuals with an organic brain syndrome may be particularly at risk for such side effects as sedation and cognitive impairment. Children may be susceptible to behavioral activation. Withdrawal symptoms and rebound anxiety are also important considerations when discontinuing this medication. Also, blood dyscrasias and hepatic dysfunction are two possible idiosyncratic side effects associated with the use of clonazepam.

Beta-Adrenergic Blocking Agents

There is a growing interest in the use of beta-adrenergic blocking agents for the prevention and treatment of PTSD. Propranolol has long been used to treat symptoms of anxiety, especially for public-speaking anxiety, performance anxiety, fear of flying, and other phobias and is the only beta-blocker that can cross the brain barrier. Clinical researchers have also hypothesized that blocking beta-adrenergic receptors might tone down consolidation of emotional memories. One recent study among emergency room patients who have experienced a traumatic event, found that those patients who experienced tachycardia were more likely to develop symptoms of PTSD (Pitman & Delhanty, 2005). Charney (2002) found that the use of beta-blockers among individuals with PTSD reduced the consolidation of their fear memories and augmented psychotherapy. One study found that propranolol significantly impairs the memory of an emotionally arousing story, but did not affect the memory of an emotionally neutral story (Cahill as cited in Kilgore, 2005). These findings support the long-standing assumption that memories associated with emotionally charged experiences become over-consolidated as a result of the activation of the beta-adrenergic stress hormone systems, particularly in the amygdala. Clinical researchers have proposed that blocking the beta-adrenergic receptors, would prevent the over-consolidation of traumatic memories and ultimately reduce the manifestation of PTSD symptoms.

Pitman and Delahanty (2005) report the use of propranolol with emergency rooms patients who were exposed to trauma within six hours of the traumatic event.

Side Effects

Beta-adrenergic blockers may be contraindicated for patients who have asthma or a heart block. Hypotension, bradycardia, and increase in asthmatic attacks and dizziness may be some of the side effects.

Alpha-Adrenergics

Friedman (2006) suggests that antiadrenergics can reduce symptoms of hyperarousal, insomnia, and reexperiencing symptoms. There is some preliminary support for the use of alpha1-adrenergic antagonist medications, such as prazosin for symptoms of insomnia and sleep disorders with prominent nightmares.

Clonidine is an alpha-blocker that is indicated for treatment of cardiovascular conditions, such as high blood pressure. Khoshnu (2006) referred to a study from the Yale University PTSD Unit that provided evidence to support the use of clonidine within three days of the traumatic event for the duration of seven to nine days.

According to Raskind and colleagues (2003), prazosin was effective in treating PTSD symptoms such as nightmares and other symptoms in combat veterans.

At this time, the evidence supporting the use of clonidine should be considered preliminary because there is a need for large, randomized placebo-controlled studies.

Side Effects

Hypotension, syncope, and change in heart rate are cited as potential side effects.

Opioid Agonists

Petrakis and colleagues (2006) conducted a twelve-week medication study to assess the effects of disulfiram and naltrexone on alcohol use outcomes and on psychiatric symptoms among veterans with co-occurring PTSD. Participants were randomly assigned to four groups: (1) naltrexone alone; (2) placebo alone; (3) disulfiram and naltrexone; and (4) disulfiram and placebo. Patients with a diagnosis of PTSD reported improvement in outcome measures of alcohol use and overall psychiatric symptoms.

Atypical Antipsychotic Medications

There have been several studies supporting the use of atypical antipsychotic medications as an adjunctive therapy with PTSD. Many of the clinical trials of atypical antipsychotic medications have been conducted among veterans with combat-related trauma.

In a randomized double-blind, placebo-controlled trial, Hamner et al. (2003) found that risperidone is effective for treating comorbid psychotic symptoms among patients with PTSD. Lambert (2006) conducted a study to determine the effects of aripiprazole (Abilify) in the management of PTSD in returning global war on terrorism veterans. They found that aripiprazole was well-tolerated and was effective in the management of sleep disorders, nightmares and agitated behavior during sleep and was also helpful in decreasing hyperarousal. Because one research participant experienced a paradoxical excitation response to the medication, they suggested that this medication should be studied further in conjunction with other medication and therapy intervention.

There is also evidence supporting the use of adjunctive quetiapine among patients with noncombat-related PTSD. Ahearn, Mussey, Johnson, Krohn, and Krahn (2006) evaluated the effectiveness of quetiapine among patients with PTSD who were already on a stable dose of an SSRI but continued to experience PTSD symptoms. Research participants had a mix of combat-related and noncombat-related PTSD and were on a stable dose of an SSRI for at least six weeks at the onset of the study. After eight weeks of receiving a moderate dose of quetiapine, research participants reported an overall improvement in PTSD symptoms (Ahearn et al., 2006).

Hamner (as cited by Sherman, 2006) recommends the use of atypical antipsychotic medications as a third or fourth line of treatment for patients who have been refractory to adequate trials of other medications. Patients with persistent symptoms of hyperarousal, aggressiveness, mood swings or those with pronounced dissociative symptoms would be considered candidates for one of the atypical antipsychotic medications. Hamner argues that one-third to one half the customary dosage for schizophrenia or acute bipolar disorder are usually effective when treating patients with PTSD. However, when patients are clearly demonstrating symptoms of psychosis, he recommended a dose that will go as high as tolerated by the patient (Sherman, 2006).

Side Effects

The side effects associated with the atypical antipsychotic medications include weight gain, metabolic syndrome, hyperlipidemia, hyperprolactinemia, obesity, increased blood sugar, tremor, muscle spasms, muscle rigidity, tardive dyskinesia, and rare complications such as agranulocytosis and neuroleptic malignant syndrome.

ALGORITHM OF TREATMENT FOR PTSD

Davidson et al. (2005) proposed an algorithm of treatment for PTSD, which is considered one of the initial efforts to develop a protocol for managing symptoms of PTSD. Because the first-line pharmacological intervention is an SSRI, they suggest the use of paroxetine, sertraline, or fluoxetine. The starting dose for fluoxetine can be as low as 10 mg, sertraline 25 mg, and paroxetine 10 mg starting doses per day. Although other drugs in the category of SSRIs, such as citalopram, fluvoxamine, and escitalopram may be beneficial, they lack evidence of controlled trial success. According to Davidson et al. (2005) most studies have demonstrated that SSRIs reduced depressive symptoms between weeks two and four; however, one study noted significant improvement in anger-irritability after a one-week trial of sertraline.

Davidson et al. (2005) suggested that insomnia or nightmares may be treated with prazosin, trazodone, escitalopram or TCAs in a low dose. However, if after further response, that means less than 25 percent rate improvement, and if core PTSD symptoms still exist after a four- to six-week period of an adequate dose of an SSRI, one may switch to a different SSRI, SNRI, mirtazapine, TCA, or prazosin. They explain that an alternative is to augment the same medication with another pharmacological agent.

If the patient does not respond to a maximum dose of SSRIs and the symptoms persist after six to twelve weeks, another alternative is to introduce a second treatment while maintaining the initial medication as prescribed. The next medication that would be added would be determined based on the presence or absence of specific symptoms or comorbidity. For example, one needs to see if there is sleep disturbance, bipolar spectrum symptoms, psychotic symptoms, and substance-abuse problems, or there is the presence or absence of specific symptoms, comorbidity, including the specific evidence of core PTSD symptoms (intrusion, avoidance, numbing, hyperarousal). For example, those who demonstrate excessive arousal, hyperactivity, and possibly dissociation may benefit from the addition of an antiadrenergic agent. Those exhibiting aggression, impulsively, and labile behavior might benefit from adding an anticonvulsant agent or mood stabilizer medication. Patients with fear, paranoia, hypervigilance and psychotic-like symptoms may benefit from atypical antipsychotic medications.

PHARMACOTHERAPY AND PREVENTION OF PTSD

There is a growing interest in the use of prophylaxis to prevent the onset of PTSD. Because the excessive release of corticotrophin-releasing factor and other stress hormones has been associated with the consolidation of traumatic memories, clinical researchers have hypothesized that various pharmacological agents can disrupt the memory consolidation process and potentially prevent the onset of PTSD. More specifically, the alpha2 adrenergic agonists, opioids, or beta-adrenergic antagonists, such as propranolol, are thought to prevent the release of presynaptic norepinephrine, which would inhibit the consolidation of traumatic memories and fear conditioning (Kilgore, 2005). The hallmark of PTSD is the uncontrollable arousal state that is mediated by adrenergic dysregulation. Marmar (as cited by MacReady, 2002) suggested that adrenergic blockers given in the first hours after the incident can reduce terror and the arousal state, and interrupt the neuronal imprinting that leads to long-term symptoms. When the patient is seen within the first few days of the traumatic event, Marmar also recommended the use of a mood stabilizer as an adjunctive pharmacotherapy to further reduce memory consolidation and to prevent sensitization to cues that may trigger the original trauma in the mind of the patient.

Several studies have found evidence to support the use of propranolol to prevent the onset of PTSD (Pitman et al., 2002; Vaiva et al., 2003; Zatzick et al., 2005). Pitman et al. (2002) investigated the effect of propranolol in preventing the release of stress hormones following exposure to a traumatic event. Participants for the study included a random sample of forty-one emergency department patients who were largely exposed to motor vehicle accidents. Within six hours of the traumatic event, eighteen of the forty-one patients received 40 mg four times a day over the course of ten days. The remaining participants agreed to take part in the study but wanted treatment as usual. At one month after the traumatic event, the PTSD rate was 30 percent in the placebo group and 18 percent in the propranolol group. At three months, the psychophysiological testing results suggested that propranolol had an impact on limiting the onset of PTSD among the treatment group. Saxe and colleagues (2006) performed an observational study of the relationship between the amount of morphine given to severely burned children and children with PTSD symptoms. They found that children who received higher doses of morphine had a greater reduction in PTSD symptoms over a six-month stay in the hospital. However, an alternative explanation of this finding is that the analgesic quality of morphine decreases the intensity of repeated traumatic memories of the events such as painful dressing changes that a burn victim goes through (Saxe et al., 2006).

Schelling and colleagues found that an exogenously administered dose of cortisol can reduce the likelihood for the onset of PTSD in cardiac patients. Cardiac patients who received cortisone before and after operations reported significantly fewer PTSD symptoms than comparison patients (Schelling et al., 2004).

One study (Debiec, 2004 as cited by Kilgore, 2005) hypothesized that propranolol may partly disrupt "reconsolidation of fear memories" via the amygdala's making the memory significantly weaker. The notion of reconsolidation still is considered a controversial issue among the professionals. It is not clear what exactly happens to traumatic memories after they are reawakened and whether attempts to block this reconsolidation process actually block memory restorage or make memories harder to retrieve. There are also ethical questions as Doctor Karim Nader reported. He maintained that "therapeutic forgetting," a phrase that has helped fuel some of the ethical debates, is misleading from this point of view. He suggested that memory erasure is not what they are aiming for. With reactivation of memory, the mechanisms mediating the intensity of the memory will also undergo reconsolidation, and that is what he and other researchers are targeting. He suggested that we are trying to affect the intensity of the memory, to turn down the volume (Nader as cited in Kilgore, 2005).

In a related study (Vaiva et al., 2003), a group of eleven emergency room trauma victims were treated with a propranolol immediately following a traumatic event and compared with eight patients who refused propranolol but agreed to participate in the study. Although the treatment participants were not randomly selected, researchers indicated that the two groups did not differ on "demographics, exposure characteristics, and physical injury severity and peritraumatic emotional responses" (Vaiva et al., 2003, p. 947). The first dose was administered within two to twenty hours after the traumatic event and thereafter the participants received 40 mg of propranolol three times a day for seven days. Outcome measures included the measure of heart rate at day seven and an assessment of PTSD symptoms and diagnosis at a two-month follow-up interview. Although this study was nonrandomized, results from this study found that patients who refused propranolol scored higher on levels of PTSD symptoms and were more likely to receive a diagnosis of PTSD (Vaiva et al., 2003).

SUMMARY

In this chapter we have explained the utilization of medication for the treatment of PTSD; trauma may change the biochemical and anatomic structure of the brain and possibly can be treated with biochemical material. However, we would like to insist that treatment of trauma is multifaceted, and pharmacotherapy is only one aspect needed for overall treatment. It should always be combined with psychotherapy and milieu therapy.

In addition to the use of pharmacotherapy and other evidence-based interventions, there is a need to identify protective factors and develop strategies to prevent the onset of PTSD. According to Friedman (2006) one of the most important protective factors for returning global war on terror veterans may be the social support they receive from friends, family, and society. Because of the political polarization among U.S. citizens during the Vietnam War, many returning veterans became targets for those who disagreed with the war. As Friedman has pointed out, "hopefully it [our nation] has become sophisticated enough at this time not to confuse our feelings about the war with our feelings about the Warriors."

REFERENCES

Ahearn, E. P., Mussey, M., Johnson, C., Krohn, A., & Krahn, D. (2006). Quetiapine as an adjunctive treatment for post-traumatic stress disorder: An 8-week open-label study.

International Journal of Clinical Psychopharmacology, 21(1), pp. 29–33.

American Psychiatric Association. (2000). *Diagnostic and statistical manual of mental disorders* (4th ed., Text Rev). Washington, D.C.: Author.

Antai-Otong, D. (2000). The neurobiology of anxiety disorders: Implications for psychiatric nursing practice. *Issues in Mental Health Nursing, 21*(1), pp. 71–89.

Beale, M. D., & Murphree, T. (2000). Excessive yawning and SSRI therapy. *International Journal of Neuropsychopharmacology, 3*(3), pp. 275–276.

Berlant, J. (2004). Prospective open label study of add-on and monotherapy of topiramate in civilians with chronic nonhallucinatory post-traumatic stress disorder. *BioMedCentral Psychiatry, 4*, p. 24.

Bremner, J. D., Mletzko, T., Welter, S., Quinn, S., Williams, C., Brummer, M., Siddiq, S., Reed, L., Heim, C. M., Nemeroff, C. B. (2005, March). Effects of phenytoin on memory, cognition and brain structure In post-traumatic stress disorder: A pilot study. *Journal Psychopharmacology, 19*(2), pp. 159–165.

Bremner, J. D., & Vermetten, E. (2004). Neuroanatomical changes associated with pharmacotherapy in post-traumatic stress disorder. *Annals of New York Academies of Science, 1032*, pp. 154–157.

Bremner, J. D., Vythilingam, M., Adil, J., Khan, S., Nazeer, A. & Afzal, N. (2003). Cortisol response to a cognitive stress challenge in posttraumatic stress disorder (PTSD) related to childhood abuse. *Psychoneuroendocrinology, 28*(6), pp. 733–750.

Cahill, S. P., Rauch, S. A., & Hembree, E. A. (2003). Effect of cognitive-behavioral treatments for PTSD on anger. *Journal of Cognitive Psychotherapy, 17*(2), pp. 113–131.

Charney, D. S. (2002). Update on treatment of anxiety disorders. *The Journal of Clinical Psychiatry CNS Discourses, 2*(1), pp. 1–4.

Crockett, B. A., & Davidson, J. R. (2002). Pharamcotherapy for post-traumatic stress disorder. In D. J. Stein & E. Hollander (Eds.), *Textbook of anxiety disorder.* Washington, D.C.: American Psychiatric Publishing.

Davidson, J. R. (1997). Biological therapies for post-traumatic stress disorder: An overview. *Journal of Clinical Psychiatry 58*, pp. 29–32.

Davidson, J. R., Bernik, M., Connor, K. M., Friedman, M.J., Jobson, K. O.,Kim, Y., Lecrobier, Y., Ma, H., Njerga, F., Stein, D. J. & Zohar, J. (2005). A new treatment algorithm for post-traumatic stress disorder. *Psychiatric Annals, 35*(11), pp. 887–898.

Davidson, J., Kudler, H., & Smith, R. (1990). Treatment of post-traumatic stress disorder with amitriptyline and placebo. *Archives of General Psychiatry, 47*, 2, pp. 59–266.

Davidson, J. R., Rothbaum, B. O., & Tucker, P. (2006). Venlafaxine extended release in post-traumatic stress disorder: A 6-month randomized controlled trial. *Journal of Clinical Psychopharmacology, 26*(3), pp. 256–267.

Davis, L. L., Frazier, E. C., Williford, R. B., & Newell, J. M. (2006). Long-term pharmacotherapy for post-traumatic stress disorder. *CNS Drugs, 20*(6), pp. 465–476.

Fesler, F. A. (1991). Valproate in combat-related post-traumatic stress disorder. *Journal of Clinical Psychiatry, 52*(9), pp. 361–364.

Finn, R. (2004, September) Medication useful as adjunct to psychotherapy in PTSD. *Clinical Psychiatry News, 32*(9), p. 48.

Forster, P. L., Schoenfeld, F. B., & Marmar, C. R. (1995). Lithium for irritability in post-traumatic stress disorder. *Journal of Traumatic Stress, 8*(1), pp. 143–149.

Friedman, M.J.(2006, January). New approaches help heal combat-related PTSD. *NeuroPsychiatry Reviews. 7*(1) p. 18.

Gibbons, R. D., Hur, K., Bhaumik, D. K., &Mann, J. J. (2006). The relationship between antidepressant prescription rates and rate of early adolescent suicide. *American Journal of Psychiatry, 163*, pp. 1898–1904.

Hammad, T. A., Laughren, T., & Racoosin, J. (2006). Suicidality in pediatric patients treated with antidepressant drugs. *Archives of General Psychiatry, 63*, pp. 332–339.

Hamner, M. B., Faldowski, R. A., Ulmer, H. G., Frueh, B. C., Huber, M. G., & Arana, G. W. (2003). Adjunctive risperidone treatment in post-traumatic stress disorder: A preliminary controlled trial of effects on comorbid psychotic symptoms. *International Journal of Clinical Psychopharmacology, 18*(1), pp. 1–8.

Hogben, G. L., & Cornfield, R. B. (1981). Treatment of traumatic war neurosis with phenelzine. *Archives of General Psychiatry, 38*(4), pp. 440–445.

Hough, G. (2004). Does psychoanalysis have anything to offer an understanding of terrorism? *Journal of American Psychoanalysis Association, 52*(3), pp. 813–828.

Ipser, J., Seedat, S.,& Stein, D. J. (2006, October). Pharmacotherapy for post-traumatic stress disorder–A systematic review and meta-analysis. *South Africa Medical Journal, 96*(10), pp. 1088–1096.

Kessler, R. C., Sonnega, A., Bromet, E., Hughes, M., & Nelson, C. B. (1995). Post-traumatic stress disorder in the national comorbidity survey. *Archives of General Psychiatry, 52*(12), pp. 1048–1060.

Kilgore, C. (2005). Propranolol, other drugs eyed to block PTSD: Idea is that blocking B-adrenergic receptors might tone down consolidation of emotional memories. *Clinical Psychiatry News, 33*, 67 [On-line]. Retrieved December 21, 2006. Available: www.clinical psychiatry.com/article/PIIS0270664405703015/fulltext

Khoshnu, E. (2006). Clonodine for treatment of PTSD. *Clinical Psychiatry News, 34*(10), p. 22.

Korn, D. L., & Leeds, A. M. (2002). Preliminary evidence of efficacy for EMDR resource development and installation in the stabilization phase of treatment of complex post-traumatic stress disorder. *Journal of Clinical Psychology, 58*(12), pp. 1465–1487.

Kosten, T. R., Frank, J. B., Dan, E., McDougle, C. J., & Giller, E. L. (1991). Pharmacotherapy for post-traumatic stress disorder using phenalzine and imipramine. *Journal of Nervous Mental Disorders, 179*, pp. 366–370.

Krystal, H. (1990) Animal models for post-traumatic stress disorder. In Giller E. L. (Ed.). *Biological assessment and treatment of post-traumatic stress disorder.* (pp. 3-26). Washington, D.C.: American Psychiatric Press.

Lambert, M. T. (2006). Aripiprazole in the management of post-traumatic stress disorder symptoms in global war on terrorism veterans. *International Journal of Clinical Psychopharmacology, 21*(3), pp. 185–187.

Lipper, S., Davidson, J. R., & Grady, T. A. (1986). Preliminary study of carbamazepine in post-traumatic stres disorder. *Psychosomatics, 27*, 849–854.

MacReady, N. (2002, February) Adrenergic blockers shortly after trauma can block PTSD. *Clinical Psychiatry News, 30*(2), p. 9.

Martin, T. G. (1996). Serotonin syndrome. *Annals of Emergency Medicine, 28*(5), pp. 520–526.

Marvasti, J. A. (2004, March). Terror, trauma and therapies for victims. Paper presented at the American College of Forensic Psychiatry, 22nd Annual Symposium in Forensic Psychiatry, San Francisco, CA.

Marvasti, J. A. & Dripchak, V. L. (2004). The impact of terrorism, terror and trauma on children: Implications for treatment. *Journal of Forensic Psychiatry, 25*, pp. 19–38.

Marvasti, J. A., & Pinto, C. (2004). The concept of addicted trauma victims (ATV): Treatment for dual diagnosis of substance abuse and child abuse. In J. A. Marvasti (Ed.), *Psychiatric treatment of victims and survivors of sexual trauma* (pp. 51–72). Springfield, IL: Charles C Thomas, Publisher.

McFarlane, A. C., Yehuda, R.,& Clark, C. R. (2002). Biologic models of traumatic memories and post-traumatic stress disorder: The role of neural networks. *Psychiatric Clinics of North America, 25*(2), pp. 253–270.

Nutt, D. J., & Malizia, A. L. (2004). Structural and functional brain changes in post-traumatic stress disorder. *Journal of Clinical Psychiatry, 64*, pp. 11–17.

Ozlewski, T., & Varrasse, J. F. (2005). The neurobiology of PTSD: Implications for nurses. *Journal of Psychosocial Nursing, 43*(6), pp. 41–47.

Perlstein, S. (2004). For comorbid PTSD, drug tx may surpass CBT. *Clinical Psychiatry News, 32*(3), p. 42.

Perry, B. D., Pollard, R. A., Blakely, T. L., Baker, W. L., & Vigilante, D. (1995). Childhood trauma, the neurobiology of adaptation, and "use" dependent development of the brain: How "states" become "traits." *Infant Mental Health Journal, 16*(4), pp. 271–291.

Petrakis, I. L., Poling, J., Levinson, C., Nich, C., Carroll, K., Ralevski, E. & Roonsaville, B. (2006). Naltrexone and disulfiram in patients with alcohol dependence and comorbid post-traumatic stress disorder. *Biological Psychiatry, 60*(7), pp. 777–783.

Petty, F., Davis, L., & Nugent, A. L. (2002). Valporate therapy for chronic combat induced post-traumatic stress disorder. *Journal of Clinical Psychopharmacology, 22*(1), pp. 100–101.

Pitman, R. K., & Delhanty, D. L. (2005). Reevaluating the association between emergency department heart rate and the development of post-traumatic stress disorder: A public health approach. *Biological Psychiatry, 10*(2), pp. 99–106.

Pitman, R. K., Sanders, K. M., Zusman, R. M., Healy, A. R., Cheema, F., Lasko, N. B., Cahill, L. & Orr, S. P. (2002). Pilot study of secondary prevention of post-traumatic stress disorder with propranolol. *Biological Psychiatry, 51*, pp. 189–192.

Popper, C. W. (1998) Management of SSRI-induced apathy in a child with OCD. In *Masters in Psychiatry* (pp. 4–11). Greenwich, CT: Chiggott Connection.

Preston, J. (2003, September). *The neurobiology of anxiety, depression, and traumatic stress.* Handout presented at J & K Seminars, Lancaster, PA.

Raskind, M. A., Peskind, E. R., Kanter, E. D., Petrie, E. C., Radant, A., Thompson, C. E., Dobie, D. J., Hoff, D., Rein, R. J., Straits-Troster, K., Thomas, R. G. & McFall, M. M. (2003). Reduction of nightmares and other PTSD symptoms in combat veterans by prazosin: A placebo-controlled study. *American Journal of Psychiatry, 160*(2), pp. 371–373.

Rauch, S. L., Shin, L. M., & Wright, C. I. (2003). Neuroimaging studies of amygdale function in anxiety disorders. *Annals of the New York Academy of Science, 985*, pp. 389–410.

Resnick, H. R., Kilpatrick, D. G., Dansky, B. S., Saunders, B. E., & Best, C. L. (1993). Prevalence of civilian trauma and post-traumatic stress disorder in a representative national sample of women. *Journal of Consulting and Clinical Psychology, 61*, pp. 984–991.

Robert, S., Hamner, M. B., Ulmer, H. G., Lorberbaum, J. P., & Durkalski, V. L. (2006). Open label trial of escitalopram in the treatment of post-traumatic stress disorder. *Journal of Clinical Psychiatry, 67*(10), pp. 1522–1526.

Rothbaum, B. O., Cahill, S. P., Foa, E. B., Davidson, J. R., Compton, J., Connor, K. M., Astin, M. C. & Hahn, C. G. (2006). Augmentation of sertraline with prolonged exposure in the treatment of post-traumatic stress disorder. *Journal of Traumatic Stress, 19*(5), pp. 625–638.

Saxe, G., Geary, M., Bedard, K., Bosquet, M., Miller, A., Koenen, K., Stoddard, F., & Moulton, S. (2006). Separation anxiety as a mediator between acute morphine administration and PTSD symptoms in injured children. *Annals New York Academy of Sciences, 1071*, pp. 41–45.

Schelling, G., Kilger, E., Roozendaal, B., de Quervain, D. J., Briegel, J., Dagge, A., Rothenhausler, H. B., Krauseneck, T., Nollert, G. & Kapfhammer, H. P. (2004). Stress doses of hydrocortisone, traumatic memories, and symptoms of post-traumatic stress disorder in patients after cardiac surgery: A randomized study. *Biological Psychiatry, 55*, pp. 627–633.

Sherman, C. (2006). Antidepressants often just a first step in PTSD: Following intial SSRIs, adrenergic anatagonists, anticonvulsants, atypical antipsychotics often used [Electronic

Version]. *Clinical Psychiatry News* [On-line], *34*, 25. Retrieved December 21, 2006. Available: www.clinicalpsychiatrynews.com/article/PIIS0270664406713315/fulltext

Shestatzsky, M., Greenburg, D., & Lerer, B. (1988). A controlled trial of phenalzine in post-traumatic stress disorder. *Psychiatric Research, 24*, pp. 149–155.

Shin, L. M., Rauch, S. L., & Pitman, R. K. (2006). Amygdala, medial prefrontal cortex, and hippocampal function in PTSD. Annals New York Academy of Sciences, 1071,pp. 67-79.

Shin, L. M., Wright, C. I., Cannistraro, P. A., Wedig, M. M., McMullin, K., Martis, B., Macklin, M. L., Lasko, N. B., Cavanaugh, S. R., Krangel, T. S., Orr, S. P., Pitman, R. K., Whalen, P .J. & Rauch, S. L.. (2005). A functional magnetic resonance imaging study of amygdala and medial prefrontal cortex responses to overtly presented fearful faces in post-traumatic stress disorder. *Archives of General Psychiatry, 62*, pp. 273–281.

Simon, G. E. (2006). The antidepressant quandry - considering suicide risk when treating adolescent depression. *New England Journal of Medicine, 355*(26), pp. 2722–2723.

Stahl, S. M. (2003). Deconstructing psychiatric disorders, part 2: An emerging, neurobiologically based therapeutic strategy for the modern psychopharmacologist. *Journal of Clinical Psychiatry, 64*(10), pp. 1145–1146.

Stein, D. J., van der Kolk, B. A., Austin, C., Fayyad, R., & Clary, C. (2006). Efficacy of sertraline in post-traumatic stress disorder secondary to interpersonal trauma or childhood abuse. *Annals of Clinical Psychiatry, 18*(4), pp. 243–249.

Vaiva, G., Ducrocq, F., Jezequel, K., Benoit, A., Lestavel, P., Brunet, A. & Marmar, C. R. (2003). Immediate treatment with propranolol decreases post-traumatic stress disorder. *Biological Psychiatry, 54*(9), pp. 947–949.

van der Kolk, B. (2001). The psychobiology and psychopharmacology of PTSD. *Human Psychopharmacology: Clinical and Experimental, 16* ,pp. S49–S64.

van der Kolk, B. A., McFarlane, A. C.,& Weisaeth, L. (1996). *Traumatic stress. The effects of overwhelming experience on mind, body, and society.* New York: The Guilford Press.

Wong, C. M. (2002). Post-traumatic stress disorder: Advances in psychoneuroimmunology. In R. Yehuda (Ed.) Recent advances in the study of biological alterations in post-traumatic stress disorder. *The Psychiatric Clinics of North America, 25*(2), pp. 369–384.

Zatzick, D. F., Russo, J., Pitman, R. K., Rivara, F., Jurkovich, G., & Roy-Bryne, P. (2005). Reevaluating the association between emergency department heart rate and the development of post-traumatic stress disorder: A public health approach. *Biological Psychiatry, 57*(1), pp. 91–95.

Chapter 14

FEMALE SUICIDE WARRIORS/BOMBERS

Jamshid A. Marvasti and Susan Plese

We are proud that our women . . . are present and active, side by side with the men, often more active than men, in all scenes including cultural, economic, and military areas. They strive, sometimes more effectively than the men. . . . Women who are capable of fighting take military training. . . . Those women who are unable to fight in the war fronts serve behind the front lines with such ardor and courage that makes the hearts of their men tremble. . . .

Ruhollah Khomaini[1]

You are my army of roses that will crush Israeli tanks.
Y. Arafat (addressing 1000 Palestinian women in 2002)

INTRODUCTION

In western society, it is often difficult to conceive of women as warriors and killers. Although women have fought in wars with and alongside men since before the time of Christ, a woman acting alone, as in the case of a murderer or serial killer, or a woman acting alone as a suicide bomber is hard for some to fathom. In fact, male killers far outnumber women, and modern American women, at least, are still restricted by the military on the battlefield.

Before beginning our discussion of the female suicide bomber/warrior/martyr, we would like to draw the reader's attention to terminology. The word martyr has been used frequently by various cultures to refer to someone who has died for a cause. Yet there is a greater depth to this word that must be examined through the lenses of various cultures. Language always indicates a cultural perception. For example, the word martyr in Arabic and Persian language is shahid (male) and shahida (female), which mean witness, "in the sense of one who is a witness to the Truth of God"(Hussain, 2004). Both his or her life and death bear witness to the truth. He or she is the heart of history. Furthermore, "shahid means 'present'. . . . They are for ever alive, present, witnesses, and observers" (Shariati, n.d.). In current Middle Eastern culture, martyrdom is active: The martyr kills herself as well as the perceived enemy for a cause; in western culture, martyrs are put to death because of a cause for which they have been fighting. They are sentenced to death by those who think that by destroying the sources of malcontent, they also destroy revolutionary ideas they fear. To put it simply, the main difference is that in the East martyrs become such because of how they died; in the West, martyrs are so named because of how they lived. In the Middle East, one's country is referred to as the "motherland," with all its connotations of birth and nurture. In European countries, one's country is normally called "father-land," with its connotations of protector, hunter, breeder, and economic provider.

HISTORY OF FEMALE WARRIORS

Lothene Experimental Archaeology (n.d.) has provided an historical perspective on female warriors through the ages. According to Lothene, women have served as warriors as far back as 1300 B.C. with the Hittites, whose likenesses, in full war regalia, appear on fortress walls. During the Viking and Saxon periods, women served both as pirates and as warriors. An ancient sacred poem of India, written between 3500 and 1800 B.C., tells the story of Queen Vishpla of India, who lost her leg in battle, was fitted with an iron prosthesis, and returned to the field. Queen Aahhotop I of Egypt led armies against Thebes from circa 1570 to 1546 B.C. Several sources refer to women giving birth on the battlefield and to women fighting in late pregnancy using specially fitted armor (Lothene, n.d.).

Women sometimes led armies against their own husbands, as did Catherine the Great against Czar Peter of Russia. Isabelle of England, wife of Edward II, also took up arms against her husband and fled to Scotland. When Edward III ascended the throne, she led a troop of noblewomen in the ensuing war. The king finally sentenced her to a convent to prevent any more of her conquests. His own Queen, Phillipa of Hainault (mid 1300s), led 12,000 soldiers against a Scots invasion and captured their king, David Bruce (Lothene, n.d.).

Early Christian martyrs were executed, often by being thrown into public amphitheaters with wild animals as sport, because they would not renounce their religion. Joan of Arc, perhaps the most famous of Christian martyrs, was burned at the stake in the fifteen century at age nineteen, after a trial alleging heresy and witchcraft. Dressed as a man, she led her troops into the battle of Orleans, undertaken to give the south of France back to its rightful king during the French and English Hundred Years War. She claimed to hear the voices of saints and angels that told her it was the will of God for Charles VII to inherit the throne and be coronated at Reims Cathedral, which he was.

During the English Civil War, women often defended their homes–their castles–against siege. Lady Brilliana Harley held Brampton Castle for seven weeks; Lady Mary Bankes defended Corfe Castle. Lady Lude defended her Scotish home and fired the first shot of the Jacobite attack (Lothene, n.d.). It was not unusual for women in later times to dress as men in order to serve in the military. Some were not found out until after their deaths. King Charles banned women from wearing men's clothing during the English Civil War, but the practice continued.

Gertrudis Bocanegra led an army of women in 1810, during the Mexican War of Independence; Lakshmi Bai of India led an uprising against British attempts to take her home. It is estimated that 750 women disguised themselves as men in order to fight in the American Civil War (Lothene, n.d.).

Throughout recorded history women have fought to protect their homes and their lands and to quell uprisings. Most often they were upper class, the wives or daughters of rulers. In some cases they fought alongside their husbands; in others, against them, at least once in revenge for a broken betrothal. They used the same weapons as men; it is interesting that women often had to disguise themselves as men in order to fight alongside them. With the fairly recent appearance of female suicide warriors/bombers, however, a woman's gender actually works for her because she is less suspect than a man; what's more, she does not battle with traditional weapons as her earlier sisters did. Instead, her own body, strapped with explosives, is her weapon; the battlefield has no boundaries, no front lines. She kills not just enemy troops but civilians as well, the inevitable "collateral damage" of war. From her point of view, however, she is still fighting for the same things as women did centuries ago: her home, her dignity, and her country.

THE ISSUE OF CULTURE AND GENDER

Traditionally, the female role, both in the East and West, has been to give birth and to nurture. Western culture has promoted the status of women in business and industry and has largely accepted her independence and decision making but has not succeeded in erasing her gender as "destiny." Since the sexual revolution in the 1960s, when women were first liberated by the pill that allowed them decisions over childbearing, literature has discussed women's role as homemaker and mother versus that of "working" career mother or simply single career woman without children.

There are indications that Middle Eastern women, however, have had few of the freedoms their western sisters embrace. In fact, the biblical concept of the wife as property, defined by her ability to produce—a young barren woman deemed useless and a burden to her family—and even the murder of a female family member to restore a family's honor after a sexual transgression are still factors in parts of the Middle East. It is impossible, then, to separate the effects of gender from those of culture when discussing the motivation of shahida in the East. Possibly, it is not the female gender in and of itself but rather the cultural role and status placed on women that can have an impact on her motivations. In a patriarchal society, men rule the community; therefore a man cannot become marginalized because of his gender. Women, however, can become marginalized solely because of their gender. Certain writers have connected being marginalized, or the threat of it, as a motivating factor for female suicide bombers.

Various writers have claimed the female suicide bombers' reasons and motivations were personal (*see* "Why Would Women Do This?"). Although these reasons may have been personal, their "person" is created within a certain culturally gender-specific society. The notion of "personal," then, is not a simple concept. If these women were not women in that specific culture, they would not have some of the personal issues that may have motivated them. However, the external factor of occupation and invasion appears to be the most common variable among all suicide bombers, male and female, rather than any specific personal element.

WHY WOULD WOMEN DO THIS?

When beginning a discussion on suicide warriors' motivations it is important to note Durkheim's idea that the motivation for suicide appears to be related to "a force common in their environments" (Durkheim, 1897) rather than an individual's personal experience. Durkheim has written that the inclination to commit suicide has its source in the moral constitution of groups within a society: "Suicide must be related to social concomitants." He has suggested that collective social forces are more significant determinants for suicide than individual personal factors. However, a review of the literature reveals that several writers have ignored the environment of female suicide bombers, and have focused only on personal issues of these warriors. When they have focused on the suicide bombers' external environments, they have looked only at gender inequality and cultural attitudes toward women as common circumstances motivating a potential female suicide bomber. Interestingly, the importance of what has happened to this community by an outside perceived enemy is minimized. For example, various authors have noted that all of the societies in which women have participated in suicide bombing are patriarchal (Beyler, 2003, as cited in Skaine, 2006). Schweitzer (2006) has reported that "Female suicide bombers appear almost exclusively in societies that are heavily traditionalist and conservative, where women lack equal rights and their status in society is much lower than that of their male counterparts."[2] What Schweitzer and others have failed to note, however, is that the societies in which female suicide bombers appear are also communities under invasion or occupation by a foreign army. Possibly the most repressive culture for women in the Middle East may be Saudi Arabia, yet no female suicide bombers have been seen there. One wonders if this is because they are not under military occupation and invasion and have not been exposed to death, destruction, and humiliation from a foreign force.

We have suggested that communities that are devastated by military invasions, occupation, daily violence, poverty, humiliation, perceived injustice, interruption of electricity, and basic services will be preoccupied by survival rather than gender inequality. In these cultures, the enemy at this time is not the men of the society; the enemy is the occupier and invader. As Skaine has noted, "Individuals who associate female bombers with motivations of gender oppression will find oppression is not borne by one gender but is born of despair and hopelessness" (2006, p. 38).

LITERATURE REVIEW: PERSONAL REASONS

It is necessary to study the work of writers who have focused primarily on female suicide bombers' personal circumstances in order to understand how and why their motivations have been misconstrued. Some authors have completely ignored what is occurring in the women's external environment and instead have focused on personal issues such as divorce, infertility, family dishonor, or illicit affairs.

Tzoreff presents several examples. Hanadi Garedat, a twenty-seven-year-old unmarried lawyer, carried out an attack on Jaifa in 2003 (2006). Tzoreff has stated that her status as an educated, independent woman was not recognized by the patriarchy, and some attribute her involvement to hopelessness in her future as a spinster. Yet Tzoreff does not refer to the other side of her story. Garedat's brother and cousin were shot and killed by Israeli special forces while sitting in front of their home in Jenin (Toolis, 2003). Garedat had been buying presents for her brother's marriage at the time he was killed. She rushed home and began screaming and hugging his body at the hospital morgue (Toolis, 2003). Her mother relayed how after her brother's death, Garedat would wake up screaming in the middle of the night (a possible symptom of PTSD). She was depressed and unable to get out of bed. Furthermore, Garedat's life had already been deeply affected by the occupation. Jenin is full of military checkpoints that impede travel, making even a visit to the hospital difficult or impossible (Toolis, 2003). It would be a mistake to ignore these facts as motivational. Garedat was given the title of the "bride of Haifa" to honor her marriage to the soil of her homeland, a significant recognition usually reserved only for men (Toolis, 2003). Tzoreff suggests that "marriage" to her homeland was a substitute for a husband she never had (2006). This statement blatantly ignores the assertion from her mother that Garedat was independent and actually refused to get married because she wanted to continue her studies (Toolis, 2003).

Another writer, Barbara Victor, has also tended to focus on personal motivations for female suicide bombers (Kimmerling, 2003). Although she does acknowledge that these women become bombers to assuage the suffering of their nation, she also calls them "troubled" women, some of whom are attempting to purify their honor and that of their family (Victor, 2003). Tzoreff's claims are similar. Wafa Idris, for example, was divorced after years of being unable to produce offspring. Tzoreff suggests that, after returning to her parent's house as an economic burden, the only way to recover her honor was to become a shahida for her nation. Tzoreff, however, does cite Palestinian sources who state that she was also motivated by the death of her former husband and brother by Israeli military (2006).

Tzoreff has maintained that after being seduced by suicide recruiters, some women (regardless of whether they became pregnant) choose suicide bombing to recover both their own honor and that of their families, knowing that the status of their families would also be upgraded (2006). According to Tzoreff, Aayat al Ahras, age eighteen, and Andleeb Takatka, age twenty-one, both students, chose suicide bombings in March and April 2002 for this reason. "Although through their behavior they had defiled their families' honor, which could only lead to social death, both—by self sacrifice through suicide—escaped the humiliating deaths they would otherwise have suffered" (2006).[3] Although it is acknowledged that bringing honor to one's family may be of vital importance to certain peoples, we maintain that there are deeper motivations behind becoming a suicide bomber.

Tzoreff (2006) suggested that Rim Riashi, a married mother, may also have attempted to regain her own honor. Despite the fact that she had witnessed the deaths of family members and was living under occupation, Tzoreff concluded that she became a suicide bomber after gossip unearthed her relationship with a lover.

Tzoreff also writes of Faiza'Amal Juma'a (with a nickname of Ahmad), another woman who did not fit into social norms. She was apparently exploited by recruiters because she was a "manly-woman"–transsexual, thirty-five, and unmarried. Tzoreff felt that Ahmad recognized her own predicament and was unable to resign herself to her God-given female sexuality when she asked, "Who will want to marry someone like me?" Tzoreff concluded that "the only way for Faiza Ahmad to redress her sin of refusing [her role] was by death as a shahida." However, this explanation loses it credibility when one acknowledges that there are transsexuals in various other countries, such as Iran, Indonesia, and Kuwait, that are mostly Muslim, traditional, and unaccepting of alternative sexuality, yet there are no female suicide bombers there. We think that such a supposition, in the face of death and military occupation, is far too simplistic and possibly a distortion of what really is happening in nations with suicide bombers. If a woman is exposed to gossip about her sexual activities, why should she kill Israelis? Killing is frequently accompanied by hate. Yet why should these women hate Israelis? These writers do not explore this aspect of the subject. How would Tzoreff and others explain the suicide bombing by a respected Palestinian grandmother, Fatima al-Najar? *The New York Times* reported that she was a member of Hamas which "had threatened to resume suicide bombing in response to the Israeli shelling of houses in Beit Hamum. The shelling killed nineteen people, most of them women and children, as they slept," (Erlanger, 2006). Al-Najar commited the first suicide bombing claimed by Hamas in over two years. She had no transsexuality, no barrenness, and no sexual affairs. Afterwards her daughter reported that this venerable matriarch was willing to sacrifice her life because one of her grandsons was killed and another disabled by Israeli troops.

Several of the messages left by female suicide bombers are very clearly related to protecting the Palestinian people. One example is a statement from the videotape of Ayat Al-Akhras: "I am going to fight instead of sleeping Arab armies who are watching Palestinian girls fighting alone. . . . It is an Intifada until victory'" (Pedahzur, 2005, p. 140). Yet even when the motivation is taken from the lips of the bomber herself, some of those who relay their stories have returned the focus to personal motivations. After Al-Akhras's death, it was rumored that she was pregnant by her fiancé before they were married. Even after acknowledging her words, Pedahzur stated that Al-Akhras's actions were probably due to her fear of future social sanctions from her family and that she "probably preferred to end her life for a noble cause"(2005, p. 140). What Pedahzur has failed to acknowledge is that if someone finds herself in an unbearable personal situation, she may choose suicide. Yet there must be some other issue if that person also becomes homicidal, killing other people (perceived enemies) in the process of her own death.

One wonders if writers' political ideology, religion, nationality and affiliation have an impact on conclusions they draw from their study of female suicide bombers' motivations. An article edited by an Israeli writer and published through Tel Aviv University includes writings regarding female suicide bombers in various parts of the world (Schweitzer, 2006). Motivations for Palestinian female suicide bombers are connected with a desire to change their gender status, to promote feminist ideas, and to resolve personal issues of honor and family,yet motivations of Chechen female suicide bombers surprisingly are attributed to nationalistic goals. In Arab and Iranian literature, however, one reads that Palestinians also are becoming suicide bombers for the struggle of their nation's freedom. In their literature, they assert that the rage and desire for revenge they feel after witnessing the deaths of their friends and family members is a significant reason for choosing to commit this violent act.

MEDIA COVERAGE

The western news media often tend to look for personal or emotional reasons for women suicide bombers' actions rather than the sociological reasons that drive male bombers. As Patkin has said, "Media coverage, especially in the West, appears to actively search for alternate explanations behind women's participation in terror in a way that does not seem paralleled in the coverage of male suicide bombers, whose official ideological explanations appear to be taken at face value" (Patkin, 2004). In an effort to understand a woman's motive, however, her personal background and marital status are probed for clues such as divorce, barrenness or infidelity. Her nationalism is largely dismissed. In general, the media does not examine a male bomber's personal life or emotional state in this same way when searching for a rationale for this violent act. We would question the media's assumption that eastern women can not think or act independently, apart from male or hormonal influences and cultural dictates.

One case shows how the media may choose information based on ingrained suppositions. In the case of Hanadi Garedat, a lawyer mentioned previously, the western news media implied that she became a shahida because she was unmarried and childless. That interpretation ignores the complexity of Middle Eastern culture. If a woman in this culture wanted to attend college for a professional degree, she would most likely have to refuse a husband; if she did not, she would likely have several children in succession and could not pursue her vocation. In fact, she may have chosen a career not because of childlessness but because she chose not to marry and have children in order to pursue a career. In western societies women can often have both (given compromises, of course) but many eastern women do not have that option.

Another female suicide bomber proved to be an anomaly for the media. Reem Salih al-Rayasha was only twenty one when she became a "martyr" (Patkin, 2004). She was a wife and mother of two children. It has been reported that she loved her children very much, yet to her, motherhood could not compare to being able to use herself as a weapon against enemy. Her strongest desire was to be a martyr for her people and God. In her own words, "I decided to be a martyr for the sake of my people. I am convinced God will help and take care of my children" (Patkin, 2004). Several media reports did not focus on her sentiments, however. Instead they suggested that she committed this act to make up for an affair she had been having with a married man (Patkin, 2004).

Despite evidence of the contrary, "perceptions of women's motivations for terrorism continue to be colored by the notion that women are emotional and irrational, perhaps even driven by hormonal balances; rarely have their actions been interpreted as intelligent, rational decisions" (Patkin, 2004).

FOREIGN INVASION

We find it important to note that many women in the Middle East have personal histories that cause cultural marginalization: specifically, lack of a husband, divorce, or inability to conceive. Most of these women do not choose to be suicide bombers, however. On the other hand, some female suicide bombers who have children and husbands still choose the path of a shahida. A Palestinian grandmother, for example, who was highly respected by her children and grandchildren, chose to become a suicide bomber because she believed she needed to contribute to her country's freedom from invasion. What is common about all of the female suicide bombers, however, is exposure to violence, injustice, trauma, losses, and invasion by a perceived enemy. When an entire nation or tribe is being attacked and victimized, gender equality and marginalization are not the main issues. Survival is the issue. One cannot compare an eastern war-torn community to a peaceful western country. If one examines what happened to America right after 9/11, one could see that Americans were focused on their collective national grief, not gender or economic and social inequity between male and female.

Others have written from a perspective that challenges the power of personal issues in creating suicide bombers. For example, Pape has stated that "what cuts across . . . various personal situations is the common motive to end the threat of a foreign occupation. . . . Suicide terrorism in Iraq is driven not by religion but by a clear strategic objective: To prevent the establishment of a government under the control of the United States" (Pape, 2005). We would say that a female suicide bomber's objective may be similar to that of a man. In Patkin's words, the activism of a female suicide bomber is not prompted merely by broken marriage, barrenness, depression, poverty, grief, psychological trauma, or assurance of preserving her family's honor by her death. Too many case studies have indicated otherwise (Patkin, 2004). One need only look at what women go through under military occupation and invasion to see how critical a factor this could be in motivating them to commit violence. Certainly they have a great deal to lose when occupying forces invade their homes, assault a father in the front of his family, terrorize their children, and take control over their movements. Some Iraqi, Chechen, and Palestinian women live with that reality.

CASE HISTORIES

A twenty-eight-year-old divorcée, Wafa Idris, is believed to be the first female Palestinian suicide bomber. Her husband divorced her after she miscarried a child and remained infertile. She was a medic and had witnessed many atrocities. It has been reported that she loved children and was particularly distressed by their suffering and deaths. She blew herself up in Jerusalem in 2002, killing an elderly man (Davis, 2003). Doctor Abdel Sadeq, head of the Department of Psychiatry at Cairo University, related the tragedy of her story: "from Mary's womb issued a child who eliminated oppression, while from the body of Wafa Idris came shrapnel that eliminated despair and aroused hope." Davis (2003) felt that this woman probably took her cue from nineteen-year-old Loula Abboud, one of the early female suicide bombers. Loula became an activist after the destruction of her home by the Israelis. She said that her motivation and commitment were similar to her mother's activism as a Communist in her youth. Instead of marching to protest, she was using a weapon to fight. She appeared to have not only a strong religious connection but also an awareness of her impact on the community. Her only regret was the potential impact that her death would have on her mother, even though "she will know that I died and killed for her" (Davis, 2005, p. 81).

As indicated by the previous example, violence, invasion of one's homeland, and humiliation are powerful motivations for human beings to act. The effect of war-time loss and the power of rage may be underestimated. The "black widows" of Chechnya serve as another example. More than thirty Chechen women have served as suicide bombers since 1999. Their motive is to assist fellow Chechens to establish an independent Muslim state in the Russian-occupied territory of Chechnya (Murphy, 2005). In fact, the women are called black widows because many of them have lost husbands, brothers, and fathers in the 1994 to 1996 war with Russia. "Others have been traumatized by the Russian military, which routinely kidnaps and tortures Chechen civilians and destroys their homes" (Murphy, 2005). Abu Walid, a Saudi national who joined the Chechen rebels, said in an interview for Al Jazeera television network that the black widows have been threatened in their homes. "Their honor and everything has been threatened. They do not accept being humiliated and living under occupation. They say that they want to serve the cause of almighty God and avenge the death of their husbands and persecuted people" (Murphy, 2005). Murphy has noted that Chechen rebels say that "the Russians are ignoring the deep domestic rage that motivates suicide attack." However, several writers who have focused on Chechen widows' being a burden to society and their families, have suggested that this is enough of a motivation for becoming suicide bombers.

One could also listen to the mother of two Chechen suicide bombers to confirm that rage, anger, and humiliation were the main motivations for her daughters. Lyuba Ganiyev, mother of ten children, with only four surviving, said that two of her daughters were detained for three days and beaten by Russians. They came home saying that they could not live after such shame. Shortly afterward, in September 2002, they died, while unused explosives were still strapped to their torsos, at the Dubrova Theatre siege (Murphy, 2005).

SAFETY AND SECURITY BEFORE GENDER EQUALITY

In reviewing the literature, there are indications that some authors have implied that the priorities of peaceful, affluent western countries could be the same as those of war-torn Middle Eastern cultures fighting occupation. Schweitzer (2006), as one example, has written that female activists have had little influence in the power of patriarchal organizations they support. They have no voice in planning or choice of target or timing. Instead, they may be used as inexpensive pawns requiring little or no training. In other words, the woman's participation is simply "a form of employment in the male-dominated domain of suicide bombing" (Schweitzer 2006). Any feminist agenda is applied after the fact, Schweitzer has stated, "to redeem—or even to glorify—the aberration of a female suicide bomber." What's more, he has written that bombers have not been able to advance any social agenda. We would suggest that all suicide bombers recruited for this task, regardless of gender, are treated like pawns. They are all soldiers under the command of a higher officer. Tzoreff has also quoted from a university professor who stated that "the national struggle has only a meager chance to succeed unless the social structure is promoted. . . . For how can a person whose society oppresses him defend it and his country? . . . Family sorrow upon the birth of a girl affects the life of that girl as she grows up and becomes a woman–a woman constrained by dictates of attire and social behavior whenever she leaves her home: studies, work, social life, reading of books, finding a husband–she may not, she can not, initiate anything. And a nation half of whose population is shackled–how will it become liberated" (Tzoreff, 2006).[4] Yet, we believe that by focusing on these inequalities, these authors are missing the larger picture: These are a people at war. In Iraq for example, in the past five years, more than half a million civilians have been killed. How can anyone have a chance of becoming "liberated" from anything under these circumstances? Therefore, we are surprised by the perplexity expressed by Raphael Israeli, a professor at a Hebrew University, "While self-immolating young women are glorified posthumously, there seems to be no change in the fortunes of the living women" (Skaine, 2006, p. 168). Beyler, another writer, has noted that any equity women gain in war does not extend to women in peacetime (Skaine, 2006). We suggest that it is impossible to know if this equity would extend to female suicide bombers, because their lives end before peace arrives. What is clear, however, is that people are continuing to misunderstand the immediate needs of the culture of a suicide bomber and wrongly focus on the struggle of a gender equality.

Furthermore, we maintain that countries at peace cannot be compared to those at war. For example, in Iraq, both men and women are concerned with the protection of their children and family (since no place is safe). In a community experiencing war or invasion, everyone regardless of gender is affected. It would be unusual for a woman to focus her attention on gender equality and discrimination in employment when her primary issue is survival. One Palestinian woman who held her dead child in her arms during an interview said that the West could learn something from the East in regard to gender equality. "You American women talk constantly of equality. Well, you can take a lesson from us Palestinian women. We die in equal numbers to the men" (Skaine, 2006, p. 33). Standish (2006) has also written that the lack of security is why female suicide bombers exist. "Female suicide bombing in Chechnya and Palestine is a result of long-term conflict and human insecurity . . . as order and the social structure of life breakdown during violent conflict, factions acquire populations loyalties by providing services and resources" (Standish, 2006).

THE EFFECT OF "HIERARCHY OF NEEDS"

In the Middle East, two concepts of liberation coexist: One is liberation from an outside occupying army (a situation western women do not face); the other is liberation from restraints placed on a person, or an entire gender, by one's own culture. If one's country is under occupation, defeating the enemy (occupier) will come to the forefront as a priority. Other issues such as gender inequality and social class disparity will fall to the wayside during a war. People of a country will unite under their one commonality, their nation or tribe. In a time of peace, however, people are able to focus on their individual differences and examine the specific structure of their society and its "oppressive" rules. This human need to prioritize has been examined and largely codified in the work of Abraham Maslow, a mid-twentieth-century psychologist, who identified the hierarchy of needs, beginning with the most basic need to survive. Theoretically, one cannot address a higher need, such as love or esteem, until more primitive needs such as food, water, physical safety, and security have been satisfied. So it is that a starving person or one in terror of death by an occupying army cannot concentrate on clothing or cultural restrictions. Once people do not need to focus on the next meal, they will be more inclined to look at gender inequalities and how to overcome them.

ACCEPTANCE OF VOLUNTEER FEMALE SUICIDE BOMBERS

We have explored possible motivations for women to become suicide bombers. These elements are what encourage them to look for an organization to join. These organizations have increasingly come to accept women as suicide bombers because they have been a success. Literature has revealed that women have been "successful" suicide bombers precisely because they are women. Female suicide bombers are desirable for a number of reasons. Zedalis (2004) has identified four rationales for why women are accepted as suicide bombers:

1. The stereotype of women as nonviolent makes them less suspicious and gives them easier access to populated areas that almost guarantees multiple casualties. Frequently they use western dress or appear to be pregnant, or both. Guards may be hesitant to search them, and the element of surprise and shock value work in favor of their ultimate success.
2. The use of women adds to the total number of combatants, and the chance of a high death count with one action is increased.

3. Women suicide bombers tend to attract more media attention, which serves as both a recruitment tool and high-visibility publicity. When they attack, the media pounce, looking for a rationale based on long-held and somewhat simplistic views of gender. Women garner far more attention than men do who carry out similar bombings, and attention to the cause is what fuels an increase in martyrs.

4. Women provide the "psychological factor." Zedalis notes that in the Israeli-Palestinian conflict, they are designed to embarrass the Israeli government (Zedalis, 2004). Other writers have noted that a male warrior's masculinity also may be threatened by a female bomber.

Other authors offer additional rationales: Middle Eastern cultural norms may dictate that women's bodies are not to be seen by males who are not related to them. In the absence of female guards, a male soldier is unlikely to search a woman in the same manner he would a man. Some women hide explosives under their clothing, pretending to be pregnant. "Soldiers don't want to shoot their mother or their wife. There's this ingrained sexism that they're going to hesitate a second before killing a woman" (Skaine, 2006).

CONCLUSION

As we have mentioned previously, suicide bombing breeds more suicide bombers. Identification with the "hero" or "martyr" is a well-known psychological phenomenon for young people in these communities. Research has also indicated that it is becoming more common for women to take on this role. As Reuter has commented, "An eight-year-old may calmly sit at the dinner table and announce her intention to become a shahida" (Reuter, as cited by Patkin, 2004). A twelve-year-old may express her desire to follow her brother "in honor of Wafa Idris, who proved that women can do as much as men" (Victor, 2003). Furthermore, it is Clara Beyler who offers a disturbing insight. "For the generations of post-suicide bombers, one problem caused by these women is that [girls] have a new kind of heroes to look up to: suicide bombers. They take them as role models and want to grow up to die" (Beyler as cited by Skaine, 2006) It is clear from events occurring in the Middle East that the existence of female suicide bombers should offer a sober warning to all.

The information in this chapter confirms the results of the research of others, which indicates that there is no one overriding motivation or profile for female suicide bombers. Moreover, not enough information is available to make generalizations. However, the most common variable evident among all the suicide bombers is the military occupation and invasion of their land or holy places. Although some literature continues to focus only on personal motivations of female suicide bombings, it is evident that motivations for women are not unlike those for men, despite gender differences that researchers and western media, especially, would ascribe to them. As Kruger has noted, "The notion that women are motivated to participate in terrorist activities for different reasons than men is largely a result of gender-biased expectations of women's roles in violent organizations. If we assume women are motivated by gender-specific reasons, we will fail to recognize women as legitimate rational actors in violent organizations" (Skaine, 2006, p. 171).

We believe that nationalism and the urge to fight against occupation touches the hearts of both men and women, as does cultural humiliation, personal history of loss, death of friends and family, desperation and rage. In every culture there is a minority that believes that violence (suicide and homicide) is appropriate redress and use it as their coping mechanism.

NOTES

1. The complete Message of Imam Khomeini can be found in "The Last Message: The Political and divine will of his holiness." Available: http://www.irna.com. occasion.ertehal/english/will/1mnew1.htm
2. There are a multitude of "traditional, conservative" societies without female suicide bombers, for example, Saudi Arabia, Iran, Indonesia, Pakistan, and so on.
3. In other cultures, such as in the Congo, however, women are pulling together to reject this type of dishonoring. Although this country also has traditionally rejected women who have been raped, local women's groups, connecting with other international organizations, have created mediation and public awareness programs to encourage the embracing of these women. Certain cultures are performing "purifying" rites to assist in reintegrating these women with their families and society. It is encouraging to see other cultures embracing women who have gone through this ordeal (from Z. Salbi [2006, Winter]. Women on the other side of war. *Amnesty International,* pp. 12–15).
4. However, what Tzoreff seems not to have considered is that there are also guidelines for males in these countries in regard to clothing, attire, and social behavior.

REFERENCES

Beyler, C. (2003, February 12). Messengers of death, female suicide bombers [On-line]. Retrieved June 21, 2007. Available: www.ict.org.il/articles/articledet.cfm?articleid=470 Cited in R. Skaine, (2006). *Female suicide bombers.* London: McFarland & Company, Inc.

Davis, J. M. (2005). Do they kill for their mothers? In Y. Danieli, D. Brom, & J. Sills (Eds.),

The trauma of terrorism: Sharing knowledge and shared care, an international handbook (pp. 79–82). New York: The Haworth Maltreatment and Trauma Press.

Davis, J. M. (2003). *Martyrs: Innocence, vengeance, and despair in the Middle East.* New York: Palgrave Macmillan.

Durkheim, E. (1987). *Suicide,* New York: The Free Press. (original work published 1897.)

Erlanger, S. (2006, November 23). Grandmother carries out Gaza suicide bombing. *The New York Times* [On-line]. Retrieved October 24, 2007. Available: www.nytimes.com/2006/11/23/world/middleeast/24mideastcnd

Hussain, I. (2004, February 22). *On Martyrdom* [On-line]. Retrieved May 28, 2007. Available: http://www.islamfrominside.com/Pages/Articles/On%20Martyrdom.html

Kimmerling, B. (2003, December 15). Sacred rage. *The Nation, 277*(20), pp. 23–30.

Lothene Experimental Archaeology (n.d.). A short history of women soldiers [On-line]. Retrieved April 18, 2007. Available: www.Lothene.org/press19.html

Murphy, K. (2005). Chechen women are increasingly recruited to become suicide bombers. In L. S. Friedman (Ed.), *What motivates suicide bombers?* (pp. 77–83), New York: Greenhaven Press.

Pape, R. A. (2005). *Dying to win.* New York: Random House Trade Paperbacks.

Patkin, T. T. (2004). Explosive baggage: Female Palestinian suicide bombers and the rhetoric of emotion. *Women and Language, 27*(2), pp. 79–99.

Pedahzur, A. (2005). *Suicide terrorism.* Malden, MA: Polity Press.

Reuter, C. (2004). My life is a weapon: Modern history of suicide bombing. Princeton, NJ: Princeton University Press. Cited in T. T. Patkin (2004). Explosive baggage: Female Palestinian suicide bombers and the rhetoric of emotion. *Women and Language, 27*(2).

Schweitzer, Y. (2006, August). *Female suicide bombers: Dying for equality?* N. 84, Tel Aviv: Jaffee Center for Strategic Studies, Tel Aviv University.

Shariati, A. (n.d.) An excerpt from *Jihad and Shahadat* [On-line]. Retrieved June 28, 2007. Available: http://www.al-islam.org/beliefs/philosophy/shahadat.html

Skaine, R. (2006). *Female suicide bombers.* London: McFarland & Company, Inc.

Standish, K. (2006, November). Human security and gender: Female suicide bombers in Palestine and Chechnya. *Peace & Conflict Review* [On-line]. Retrieved April 23, 2007. Available: http://www.review.upeace.org/article

Toolis, K. (2003, October 12). The revenger's tragedy: Why women turn to suicide bombing. *Guardian* [On-line]. Retrieved May 12, 2007. Available: http://www.guardian.co.uk

Tzoreff, M. (2006, August). The Palestinian shahida: National patriotism, Islamic feminism, or social crisis. In Y. Schweitzer (Ed.), *Female suicide bombers: Dying for equality?* N. 84, Tel Aviv: Jaffee Center for Strategic Studies, Tel Aviv University. pp. 13–23.

Victor, B. (2003). *Army of roses: Inside the world of Palestinian women suicide bombers* [On-line]. Retrieved May 6, 2006. Available: http://www.ipcs.org/newDisplayReview.jsp

Zedalis, D. D. (2004, June). *Female suicide bombers.* Carlisle, PA: Strategic Studies Institute.

Chapter 15

UNDERSTANDING THE MOTHERS OF SUICIDE BOMBERS AND MARTYRS

Jamshid A. Marvasti and Claire C. Olivier

In the dark of the moonless night,
And a storm between us and shore,
Do these oblivious people know,
What we are up against anymore?
Hafez (an Iranian poet of the 14th century)[1]

The Land is a mother that never dies.

Maori proverb

INTRODUCTION

Joyce Davis (2005) wrote an article regarding Palestinian suicide bombers entitled, "Do they kill for their mothers?" We have explored this possibility through reviewing the Middle East cultural and political literature. Palestinians have referred to their occupied country as their "motherland." Their poets have described the beauty of their "motherland," a craving to return to their "mother," and a need for nurturing from their mother. They have often referenced olive trees that grew plentifully from their motherland. Palestinians have been waiting for years, now decades, for the reunion of this mother and child. So are suicide bombers doing this for their "mother"? Possibly this is one explanation for their actions: if their occupied home represents their mother in a symbolic way, they are sacrificing their lives to rejoin her. In addition to their motherland, they also refer to their biological mothers in songs.[2] One such example can be heard in the songs and slogans chanted

285

about martyrdom by Palestinian children as they parade in the streets:

> *Oh mother, my religion has called me to Jihad and self-sacrifice*
> *Oh mother, I am working toward immortality; I will never retreat*
> *Oh mother, don't cry over me if I am shot down, laid out on the ground*
> *For death is my path; martyrdom, my desire.*
>
> (Oliver & Steinberg, 2005, p. 60)

Davis (2005) has related how the "men who send them out to die and kill" have said that they do not have to actively recruit Palestinian boys to become martyrs. These men reported that youth are eager to learn how to fire guns and throw grenades. The boys want to be picked for suicide operations. As Davis has commented, suicide recruiters feel that the main motivation for this enthusiasm seems to be the boys' mothers. "They do it for the women who they see crying every time an Israeli tank destroys a home." They want to lessen the pain of the "black shawled women" as they crumble to the ground beside their sons' bloodied bodies wrapped in white shrouds (p. 79). The rage that these mothers feel for the memories of their dead sons and now daughters permeates the family members (p. 79). If one son gets killed it may encourage the other siblings to seek revenge. It seems to be a vicious cycle for a family to be a caught in: to attempt to lessen the pain of a grieving mother by avenging a brother's death and fighting for freedom while now leaving the mother with another child to grieve over.

The mother and child relationship and bond is one of the strongest attachments for the human being, and it may be shocking when the mother appears to give up her "protective measures" toward her child and directs him or her towards death. In ancient history, there is an old war story about a young adolescent going to war who asked his mother what he should do during the battle because his hand and his sword were too short to reach the enemy. Reportedly his mother advised him "to take one step forward toward them."[3]

Doctor Sarraj, a prominent psychiatrist living in Gaza, has commented on this "maternal instinct" issue. He has reported that during recent Palestinian demonstrations and battles of Lebanon the press has accused Palestinian mothers of pushing their children into "the line of fire" and then crying over their deaths.[4] Questions have been raised over the maternal feelings that these Palestinian women have for their children. Do these children want to live? Are these children hoodlums who provoke the soldiers into killing them? These questions ignore the fact that Palestinians are defending their land and their dignity (Sarraj, 2000). These questions also provoke questions of racial philosophy. A prejudicial line of thinking is that if Palestinian women have no feelings for their children, then Palestinian women are not really human and therefore not even equal to animals because animals care for their young in times of danger. A similar line of thought was expressed by white South Africans of blacks, European colonizers of Native Americans, German Nazis of Jews, and Australians of aborigines (Sarraj, 2000).

TYPOLOGY OF MOTHERS:
A CULTURAL CONTEXT FOR PUBLIC VERSUS PRIVATE
RESPONSES

Western news media sources may give the impression that there are two types of "mothers of martyrs": those who are prowar (who encouraged and sent their children to become suicide bombers) and those who are propeace (who are against any kind of violence). We would suggest that this approach is inaccurately simple and ignores cultural components, which when reviewed offer a more comprehensive understanding. A mother's external expressions may be full of strength, nationalism, and support for resistance, yet one must not assume that this is all she feels in her heart. Inside, she may also be deeply grieving, for she has still lost a son or daughter. Whether one supports their children's actions or not, we argue that an important point often overlooked by the media is that these women are in a unique situation they would not have chosen for themselves. Many of the world's mothers do not even have to consider "choosing" what they will support: the life of their child or the life of their nation. Even that description is too black and white because if these women's children do not fight against their enemy, one may wonder if their nation will ever be free from an occupation that has already led to the deaths of so many of their children. These mothers may be wondering if there is a tipping point, if after a certain number of suicide attacks, something will change, and the enemy will leave.

Although some mothers may publicly appear to be possesing pride, and honor, regarding the actions of their child for their nation's cause, it is necessary to look at the culture surrounding these women. As Doctor Sarraj has explained, "in this tribal society we have two sets of language-one for the public, which is a language of steadfastness . . . a language of being proud . . . even of dying." He continues that this is different from what is going on inside: "underneath of course we're human beings and we suffer. Sometimes even the expression of grief for the martyr . . . is something that people are even ashamed of" (Hanna, 2001).

It is with this understanding that we review the Middle Eastern history and culture, which may give us some insight into the Palestinian women who are "mothers of martyrs," and mothers of children who chose to become suicide bombers. September 2000 began the Al-Aqsa Intifada, the second uprising of its kind for Palestine after the first one in 1987 (Habiballah, 2004). During this time of conflict with Israel Defense Forces (IDF), many people lost their lives, especially Palestinian youth who participated in this confrontation by throwing stones at Israeli soldiers. According to the Human Rights Monitoring Group, a Palestinian organization, in the first 3.5 years of the second Intifada more than 2800 Palestinians have been killed, 426 of whom were children and teens (Hale, 2004). This is in comparison to the 870 Is-raelis who were killed, 92 of which were children under eighteen (Hale, 2004). An informal study of 151 Palestinian mothers was also conducted. Of these mothers, 73 had children who were killed during the conflict between Pale-stine and Israel, and the other 78 had children who had been imprisoned. The mothers of children who had died suffered greatly from depression and sadness; many of them also experienced physical problems (i.e., digestive problems) that could be traced to the trauma they had experienced (Hale, 2004).

Nahed Habiballah, a New York University graduate student from Jerusa-lem, interviewed sixteen "mothers of martyrs" from the West Bank between July and September of 2001 and the summer of 2002 (Habiballah, 2004). In her findings it was made clear that these mothers cared deeply for "their mar-tyred" sons, and although they tried, it was difficult to prevent their sons from going to confrontation areas where the IDF was located. Children grow up seeing the effects of their occupied land and their "oppressors." Yet these mothers were also caught between two extremes of protecting their children and supporting their quest for freedom from occupation. As one of the moth-ers interviewed stated, "Who else will defend our land if it is not our young men, but on the other hand, even though they are considered martyrs, it is still hard to lose a son" (Habiballah, 2004). Martyrdom has become inte-grated into Palestinian culture over the past twenty years. Mothers of martyrs are expected to be examples of strength for their community, especially since martyrs are expected to be celebrated not mourned; at the same time they struggle for an outlet to really grieve as mothers (Habiballah, 2004). Davis (2005) has relayed the story of Douad, a mother in Ramallah who spoke of her thirteen-year-old son, Muhammad. This "affectionate, responsible, intel-ligent Boy Scout" was killed by Israeli troops in the neighborhood street. She stated that as a mother she will always weep for him and never forget him or the other boys that Israelis have killed. Neither will she let her family forget the land that they have lost or the struggle that they have endured since 1948. Her investment in keeping these memories alive is shown in the fol-lowing quote, "every time it calms down, we make sure the fire comes on again because we insist upon results" (Davis, 2005, p. 80). It would be inter-esting to know if she realizes that Israeli mothers also weep for their innocent children who have been killed in suicide bombings.

In the beginning of the Islamic Revolution in Iran (1980), one of the authors of this chapter (JAM) witnessed the assassination of a government official and his young son in the streets of Tehran. This government official had spent years in jail during the previous regime. The author watched as the official's wife (and mother of the son) and daughter arrived screaming and crying. The bodies of the deceased were covered with bloody blankets. Occasionally the blanket would slightly slip off their bodies, revealing their feet. When this happened the mother would scream and cry. Her daughter would hold her, telling her not to cry because it would bring joy to the enemy. The mother would then immediately stop crying and would shout nationalistic slogans like other people around them. However, at times when she could see the bodies of her son and her husband, she again would cry, and the daughter would remind her not to make the enemy happy. Occasionally, the daughter herself would cry but then pull herself together and chant revolutionary slogans. This sad experience illustrated how in public, families may not mourn because they feel it is a sign of weakness and suffering and would show that the enemy could affect them.

One needs to look at Middle East culture to better understand families' reactions. When young people die or are killed, it is traditional for the family to decrease its pain by pretending that they are going to the wedding of the deceased, rather than to a funeral. This is because a child's wedding is such a momentous occasion, so a child dying before his or her wedding adds further sadness to the tragedy. In regard to martyrs, however there may be a second reference to a "wedding," because there is also a spiritual wedding to their "real" loved one, their God. This was the response of a Palestinian family when the son killed himself and others in April 1994 as revenge for the massacre of Muslim worshipers by an Israeli extremist (Hassan, 2001). The bomber's family celebrated his martyrdom as if preparing for a wedding. Guests came to the house to offer congratulations; treats were served that the martyr had specified in his will. Despite celebrations, there is grief as well. Another mother of a suicide bomber from the Gaza Strip, when asked how she would have responded if she had known what her son would do, stated, "I would have taken a cleaver, cut open my heart, and stuffed him deep inside. Then I would have sewn it up tight to keep him safe" (Hassan, 2001).

INTERVIEWS

Nahed Habiballah (2004), through her interviews with sixteen mothers of martyrs in the West Bank, found that there were common themes shared by these mothers.

These mothers felt outrage at accusations that they sent their children to die and feel that blame should be on Israel. Palestinian parents are the victims.

They have had to face being unable to protect their children. Danger is everywhere and can result in the death of a child as he or she walks home from school (Habiballah, 2004). This fear has been validated through reports that found that in the first two years of the second Intifada, 245 Palestinian students were killed and 2610 students were wounded going to or coming from school (Khouri, 2006).

These women face a dilemma of being patriotic and raising their children to fight against the occupation but having the cost be the lives of their children. As Habiballah has pointed out, these children are aware of what is happening politically from an early age and can therefore experience hatred for the Israel occupation early in their lives (Habiballah, 2004).

They turn to religion for comfort and consolation after having lost one of their children. Women give their martyred son the image of being a bridegroom entering heaven, offering him to God who is waiting for him.

In addition these mothers of martyrs experienced societal pressure to be strong and not grieve for their sons. Yet they idealized their martyred son, and knew the details of their son's death, including the way he was shot, and how the bullet affected his body. These mothers, however, can differ in how they express their sorrow and how much of a role religion played in their life, which therefore affected how they responded to their children's deaths (Habiballah, 2004).

Habiballah (2004) has found that religion is what can offer some comfort to these women. Women who are religious may believe that this is what God has chosen for their child and now they are with God in heaven. Religion can help the pain that comes from wondering if a son has died in vain or if his death helped his country. There also may be comfort in believing this act was part of a religious obligation. Umm Nidal, the mother of a suicide bomber/martyr, was interviewed by *Al-Sharq Al-Awsat*, a London-based Arabic language daily paper. During this talk, she was asked how the idea of becoming a martyr had entered her son's soul. In her response she stated, "Jihad is a [religious] commandment imposed upon us. We must instill this idea in our son's souls. . . . What we see every day—massacres, destruction, bombing [of] homes—strengthened, in the souls of my sons . . . the love of Jihad and martyrdom'" (IslamReview.com).

Nidal went on to describe how the happiness of this world is incomplete; eternal happiness is available in the next world, through martyrdom. She was happy her son had achieved this happiness: "my son was not destroyed, he is not dead; he is living a happier life than I. Had my thoughts been limited to this world, I would not sacrifice Muhammad." In reviewing her statements, it seems that in her mind, she was encouraging him out of love, believing true happiness would be through martyrdom. She was giving to him as all mothers hope to give, what they believe to be the best for their children. It is also clear that the impact of living under occupation had possibly strengthened her convictions, because she commented on the destruction and violence she sees every day. In addition, she was not encouraging her son to do something she herself would not do. As she has stated, "I encouraged all my sons to die a martyr's death, and I wish this even for myself" (IslamReview.com).

In her interviews with the mothers, Habiballah was able to glean their attitudes toward Israel, the occupation, and the death of their children in resisting the occupation. One woman described how her husband had begged their son not to leave the house because there had been an increasing number of confrontations between Palestinian youths and Israeli soldiers, but he did go out and was shot. He had to be transferred to a hospital in Jordan, and his mother had trouble getting through the borders. At first his father was not even allowed through. His mother did not want him to die, yet she stated it was in his blood to fight for his country. His mother also felt that if he was going to die, it should have been in a bigger way that would have killed more enemies, like suicide bombing. This mother stated that if she had the chance to become a suicide bomber she would.

Another mother interviewed stated she did not know her son would go to throw rocks at the Israeli soldiers, but she could understand why he did this. As she stated, "The Intifada should go on or the blood of our children will go to waste. . . . Israelis have complete control over our lives" (Habiballah, 2004). When asked if she supported peace with Israel she responded, "Not this kind of peace, they took all of our land and they want to give us half of it now, not even a half, maybe a quarter and they refuse to give us Jerusalem and this is the problem. If they really wanted peace they would have never entered Al-Aqsa mosque, it is not theirs." (Habiballah, 2004).

Her home is surrounded by checkpoints and each time there is a fight, the Israeli soldiers fire from both sides. Her house has been demolished by bullets. Since the death of her son, her husband who used to work on the Israeli side, does not work. He cannot consider working with them. For this mother as well, her faith in God and knowing her son is with God, gives her strength (Habiballah, 2004).

Although there may be commonalities among these mothers, each may have her own view as to whether violence is the way to continue this fight. Davis has relayed the story of the mother of a twenty-two-year-old deceased suicide bomber (Davis, 2005). This mother commented that her son was very religious and obsessed with the afterlife. Yet she felt that he did not hate the Israelis, because their family had had Israeli friends while he was growing up and he also worked with them. Even though she loved him dearly and will always treasure his memory, she also feels that what he did was bad. "We do not support it when the Israeli kill our people, so we cannot support it when their innocent people are killed by us, we just cannot condone that kind of martyrdom" (Davis, 2005, p. 80).

ARE THESE MOTHERS DIFFERENT FROM "US"?

There has been criticism of Palestinian mothers by Israel and "western" media sources, who have suggested that these women have "sacrificed" their children to win support and save their homeland or embarrass Israel (Habiballah, 2004). One may wonder if these mothers are unlike the mothers around the world whose sons and daughters are fighting for their country. American mothers lost more than 50,000 sons and daughters in the Vietnam War. Although there were antiwar protests by the general population, there were not large demonstrations by the mothers telling the government to stop taking their sons to their deaths nor have there been in regard to the war in the Middle East. Was it doubted that these mothers loved their children tremendously?[5] One may wonder then, are these mothers so different from Palestinian mothers? All mothers can be caught between their personal feelings and roles as mothers and their support for the survival of their nation.

If one has not lived in a culture of war, it may be easier to create a distinction between "us" and "them." As Evans (1999) has commented, "The accusation of fanaticism is the easiest way to explain the existence of martyrs and their supportive mothers-as long as they are supporting a cause different from one's own." She continues that this type of dismissal has existed as long as there have been martyrs. In fact, one of the first recorded tales of a mother of martyrs occurred during Maccabean Revolt in 167 B.C. when a Maccabean mother had seven sons who were martyred (Evans, 1999).[6] In using these accusations, people may use terminology to distinguish themselves from these "fanatical" mothers, such as "we" would never do that "we" would never encourage our children to "die for the cause." Yet one may wonder if a person would be as certain of these convictions living in a war zone or occupied territory. Erlanger (2005) has reported on one Palestinian mother, Marian Ghaben, who lost three sons all at once. Her children, who were playing in a strawberry field, were blown apart by an Israel tank shell aimed at militants. Six children from Ghaben's extended family also died in this explosion. This mother stated that her family had nothing to do with politics; her family never threw stones at the Israelis. Yet she had to gather the scattered remains of her children from the field where the bombing occurred. Ghaben angrily commented, "This is a massacre. I ask those with hearts, not only Arabs but those who still have hearts and a conscience, if this happened in Israel everyone would condemn it! . . . But what about us? I collected the parts of my children. And if someone gives me a gun, I'll kill [Ariel] Sharon. . . . Put the explosive here! [pointing to her waist] I'll go to the tank and explode myself. . . . I wanted peace. I wanted to go vote. I want to protect my other children" (Erlanger, 2005).

Maybe if "we" experienced what these mothers experience, then the line between "us" and "them" would become blurry and Palestinian mothers would be seen for what they are: mothers who are like mothers everywhere, caught in a uniquely horrifying situation.

There is another element to consider that Ghaben has perhaps unknowingly alluded to in her comment about wanting to protect her other children. It still remains a mystery as to how these mothers can protect their children from harm. As Hale (2004) has noted, "In a conflict where children are at constant peril of becoming accidental victims of violence or sucked into dangerous activism, Palestinian mothers face obstacles and dilemmas few in the Western world can envision." Wasfiya Idris is the mother of Wafa, the first female suicide bomber who blew herself up in 2002. Idris has commented, " It's almost impossible to be a good mother under the circumstances we live in. We have no control over anything" (Hale, 2004).[7] Can one fault a mother for supporting a fight that may lead to the death of a child but may save other children from dying? The situation in Palestine, Iraq, and even within the Israeli community varies greatly from other countries that send their soldiers "off" to war. These citizens are fighting the violence that is right outside (and sometimes inside) their homes, restaurants, schools and even bus stations.

CONCLUSION

From the literature we have seen that mothers living in a war zone or occupied territory face challenges not experienced by many other mothers, even those whose children become soldiers. Although it may be a quick answer to suggest fanaticism as the explanation for the reactions of the mothers of suicide bombers and martyrs, we have illustrated that a deeper investigation reveals more complex circumstances and factors. It may be easy to condemn another for an action that seems inconceivable, yet we suggest these actions are only inconceivable because they are misunderstood. These actions and behaviors must be seen within their cultural context; they are only a piece of a much larger picture. We end with an excerpt from a poem written from the perspective of a female Palestinian suicide bomber, to her mother entitled, "Yumma" [mother]. This poem sheds light on her motivations and feelings about the potential impacts of her actions. The poet states that she does not wish any one else to have to go through the same suffering;

yet, is she referring also to the suffering of Israeli children and families?

> *Yumma don't be scared for me,*
> *I am here for our land to be free. . . .*
> *Be happy I left an impact in hearts and minds like those of words engraved*
> *in stone. . . .*
> *Yumma, my memory and our peoples' resistance will live on forever,*
> *All this suffering we have been through I do not wish on another. . .*
> *Yumma, tell my son that I did not abandon him, never!*
> *I did it for his freedom and our people's right to be able to live free, forever!*
> *. . .*

Neda Khalil (2004)

NOTES

1. Shams al-Din Muhammad Hafez-e Shirazi (also known as Hafez) was a Persian poet and mystic of the 1300s. His lyrical poems, which are referred to as gazals, are famous for their beauty and ability to illustrate Sufi themes of love and mysticism.

2. *The Washington Times* reported that a Syrian singer and his musical band were detained by the FBI terrorism task force during a recent flight to Los Angeles. This singer has written a song about the "glorification" of suicide bombers to liberate Palestine. Their song title would be translated in English language as "mother of a martyr." The song explains the story of a mother who mourned the death of her son until she recognized that "he died for a good cause and he should be glorified for what he did." The newspaper reported that the song opens with the voice of a mother crying over her son; the son has said good-bye through friends and family and left with the weapon in one palm and his heart in the other hand. He went to fight to free "Palestine and South Lebanon" (from A. Hudson [2004, July 29]. Syrian music star sings praise of suicide bombers. *Washington Times* [On-line]. Retrieved January 7, 2007. Available: www.washingtontimes.com).

3. In the Middle East there is an old tale about a mother monkey and her child. The story tells how they were placed in a room with a metal floor that gradually was being heated and burned the body of both monkeys. Eventually, the mother monkey placed her child on the floor and sat on it to prevent her own burning. There are also examples of the other extreme in terms of maternal instinct. A mother cat, in addition to caring for her own litter, adopted a pug puppy who was unable to be fed by its mother. The puppy shares the mother cat's milk with the other kittens in addition to being bathed and fed by the mother cat (from www.pittsburghlive.com/x/dailycourier/s_446072.html).

4. In a study involving albino rats, it was discovered there was an inverse correlation between the size of the litter and maternal behavior: meaning the smaller the litter size, the higher the maternal instinct (from www.psychosomatic

medicine.org/cgi/content/abstract/20/3/215). One potential explanation stated that a high level of maternal instinct for a large litter may result in overtaxing the mother, leaving her unable to protect the majority of her young. It is not being suggested that Palestinian mothers are sacrificing their children for their own survival, but it is interesting to note that suicide bombers themselves may be sacrificing themselves for the greater community.

5. During the First Gulf War there were radio broadcasts during which family members in the United States would send messages to their children fighting abroad, telling them how they missed them and hoped they were safe. In addition, some families told their sons and daughters "Don't be a Hero," and "We need you here."

6. Part of the importance of the Maccabee story is due to the fact that these Maccabee martyrs have been revered by both Jewish and Christian traditions (from J. Obermann [1931]. The sepulcher of the Maccabean martyrs. *Journal of Biblical literature.* Vol. 50. Cited in S. Evans, [1999]. Mothers of Martyrs: A Palestinian Institution with Judaeo-Islamic Roots. *Journal of Psychology and Judaism, 23*(2), pp. 67–83 [On-line]. Retrieved March 1, 2007. Available: http://www.ingentaconnect.com). Hale (2004) has also illustrated how the Maccabee mother exhibited behaviors very similar to those of modern Palestinian mothers of martyrs.

7. It is important to note that although mothers around the world have felt the pain of losing a child who goes to fight a war, there is a difference when the war is actually on your homeland, all around you. With the exclusion of Pearl Harbor, the United States for example, has not seen war on its soil for many years. This is very different from the conflict in the Middle East. In the United States many mothers can offer some kind of protection to their children. Palestinian or Iraqi mothers, however, are faced with danger for their children whether they are fighting or just going to school. Mothers from western countries whose children become soldiers are in a different situation than mothers in the Middle East. Western mothers know their children will be trained, and given proper weapons and protective gear. Palestinian women know their children, if they are involved in this conflict, are throwing rocks at tanks and armed soldiers with guns.

REFERENCES

Davis, J. M. (2005). Do they kill for their mothers? In Y. Danieli, D. Brom, & J. Sills (Eds.), *The trauma of terrorism: Sharing knowledge and shared care, an international handbook* (pp. 79–82). New York: The Haworth Maltreatment and Trauma Press.

Erlanger, S. (2005, January 10). Arab mother grieves for sons slain by tank. *The New York Times.*

Evans, S. (1999, Summer). Mothers of martyrs: A Palestinian Institution with Judaeo-Islamic roots. *Journal of Psychology and Judaism, 23*(20), pp. 67–83.

Habiballah, N. (2004) Interviews with mothers of martyrs of the Aqsa Intifada. *Arab Studies Quarterly, 25*(1), 15+.

Hale, E. (2004). For Palestinian moms, some painful choices. *USA Today* [On-line]. Retrieved June 18, 2007. Available: www.usatoday.com/news/world/2004-03-30-palestinian-moms_x.htm

Hanna, M. (2001, August 9). Suicide bombers win public honor; parents grieve in private. *Cnn.com* [On-line]. Retrieved March 21, 2007. Available: http://archives.cnn.com/2001/WORLD/meast/08/09/hanna.focus

Hassan, N. (2001, November). An arsenal of believers: Talking to the "human bombs." *The New Yorker Fact* [On-line]. Retrieved March 2, 2007. Available: http://www.newyorker.com/fact/content/?011119fa_FACT1

IslamReview.com. (2002, June 5). An interview with the mother of a suicide bomber. Retrieved June 21, 2007. Available: www.islamreview.com/articles/interview.htm

Khalil, N. (2004). *Yumma (mother).* Retrieved on June 18, 2007. Available: www.google.com: "Neda Khalil" Yumma

Khouri, R. (2006) Ehud Olmert's Profound Ethics and Deep Lies [On-line]. Retrieved September 20, 2007. Available: www.ramikhouri.com

Oliver, A. M., & Steinberg, P. (2005). *The road to Martyrs' Square: A journey into the world of the suicide bomber.* New York: Oxford, University Press.

Sarraj, E. (2000, November). Children in the line of fire. *Le Monde diplomatique* [On-line]. Retrieved September 30, 2006. Available: http://mondediplo.com/2000/11/08mideastchild?var_recherche=palestinian%20children

Shergald (2007, February 27). Mind of the palestinian suicide bomber [On-line]. Retrieved April 20, 2007. Available: http://www.myleftwing.com/showDiary.do?diaryId=14547

Chapter 16

NEUROBIOPSYCHOSOCIAL ASPECTS OF VIOLENCE

Gagan Dhaliwal

INTRODUCTION

As we have seen in the previous chapters, violence is a part of human civilization. Military war by definition is inextricably linked with violence. In this sense, one can understand why soldiers are "violent." Yet what about "civilians?" Where does their violence come from? What are the biopsychosocial aspects of violence? In this chapter we endeavor to delineate risk factors predisposing individuals to aggression and violence with a focus on biological, social, psychological and medical aspects. Although many of the studies presented have been conducted in the United States, the conclusions are relevant to much of the world's population. What follows is an attempt to understand the intricate complexities of violence in human beings.

DEFINITIONS

Before we get into the causes of violence, two terms require defining and differentiation: violence and aggression. Violence is a general term to describe actions, usually deliberate, that cause or are intended to cause injury to people, animals, or nonliving objects. Violence and its associated factors are complex and multidimensional. Furthermore, violence has a heterogeneous quality because a combination of risk factors increases an individual's violence potential instead of one specific cause.

Aggression is not the same as violence; an aggressive person may not necessarily be violent. Aggression is a behavior characterized by verbal or physical attacks, yet it may be either appropriate and self-protective or destructive and violent. Aggression can be further divided into two subtypes: impulsive-reactive-hostile-affective subtype and controlled-proactive-instrumental-predatory subtype (Vitiello & Stoff, 1997).

Disinhibition and affective instability accompany impulsive types of aggression that are often explosive, uncontrolled, accompanied by anger or fear, characterized by high levels of arousal, and, at times, even self-directed. For example, John gets angry and hits others when someone makes fun of him at school. He cannot handle insults well, becomes angry and frustrated easily, and often gets into trouble for getting into fights.

Nonimpulsive (controlled) aggression, on the other hand, is less likely to present with affective instability. This type of aggressive behavior is goal specific, and evidence of low heart rate and skin conductance indicating low autonomic arousal supports this. For example, Jim does not get angry often but will remember when someone insults him. He calmly plans out how he will retaliate in order to harm the other person who slighted him. He uses a weapon when he realizes the other person is stronger and waits for the right opportunity to harm him or her.

ORIGINS OF VIOLENCE

Although there is no single gene responsible for violence, about 44 to 72 percent of aggressive behavior is attributed to genetic predisposition (Slutske, 2000). The other major factor that contributes to the violent expression of aggression is environment.

Parents can develop violence in their children either through genetic inheritance, demonstrations of parental aggression, or as happens in most cases, a combination of the two. Multiple studies have measured correlations between parental practices and the way their children mature and concluded that biological and social factors interact jointly to generate violent children, adolescents, and adults (Lyons et al., 1995).

NEUROBIOLOGY OF HUMAN VIOLENCE

Experimental laboratory models of aggression in rodents and other animals support the involvement of brain serotonergic (5-HT) neurotransmissions, particularly 5-HT1A receptors in violent episodes, to explain the neurological path of human violence (Collins, Davis, & Cherek, 1996; Huber, Smith, Delago, Isaksson, & Krvitz, 1997; Mehlman et al., 1995; Reisner,

Mann, Stanley, Huang, & Houpt, 1996).

The hypothalamus and limbic systems are parts of the brain closely linked to emotions and aggression. The orbital prefrontal cortex modulates limbic and hypothalamic activity, and therefore its lesions result in increased aggression. The serotonin system modulates activity of the prefrontal cortex and anterior cingulate cortex. Low serotonin levels increase aggressive behavior by elevating dopamine transmission, thereby increasing vulnerability to impulsivity and noradrenergic function (Cleare & Bond, 1997; Lidberg, Tuck, Asberg, Scalia-Tomba, & Bertilsson, 1985; Maclean, 1990).

GABA, a primary inhibitory neurotransmitter, is known to prevent aggression. However, another amino acid, glutamate, increases hostility and violent responses. Similarly, nicotinic receptors reduce aggressive responses; muscaranic receptors increase it. The interaction among these various receptors and neurotransmitters is immensely complicated and hard to simplify.

Impulsivity or impulsive response to provocation increases violence potential. Nucleus accumbens, orbitofrontal regions, and the amygdala are the three main areas of the brain involved with impulsivity. The brainstem and diencephalons are the excitatory parts of brain, responsible for impulse-mediating capacity; the higher suboptimal and cortical areas modulate or inhibit the impulsive aggression. Any factors that increase the activity or reactivity of the brainstem (e.g., chronic traumatic stress, testosterone, dysregulated serotonin, or norepinephrine systems) or decrease the moderating capacity of the limbic or cortical areas (e.g., neglect in childhood) will increase an individual's aggressivity, impulsivity, and capacity to display violence (Perry, 1997, 2001).

PHYSIOLOGIC PATHWAYS TO VIOLENCE

Raine, Stoddard, Bihrle, and Buchsbaum (1998) studied physiological markers to determine if there were identifiable physiological pathways that allowed subjects to commit murder. They compared positron emission tomography (PET) after F-fluorodeoxyglucose tracer injection on forty-one people tried for murder and forty-one controls matched for age and gender but found no significant differences. However, when they separated alleged murderers who had experienced childhood abuse and neglect from alleged murderers who suffered no childhood abuse and neglect, they found significant differences in prefrontal glucose uptake. These findings suggest that there may be two pathways that contribute to one's committing murder: one involving brain physiology and the other pointing to societal and family influences.

IMPACT OF AGE ON VIOLENCE

As we age, we become less impulsive, less reactive and more thoughtful. Our brain has grown and organized itself from the inside-out and the bottom-up fashion. More complex areas have developed to control and modulate the more reactive, primitive functioning, lower parts of the brain (Coffee & Brumback, 1998). This reduction in impulsivity and reaction also leads to a decrease in physical violent expression.

RISK FACTORS FOR VIOLENCE

Guns are easily available in the United States. As Pfeiffer has suggested, poverty and easy access to weapons can lead to violent incidents, especially when poor children are unable to see ways to improve their social position (Pfeiffer, 1998). Kathleen Heide identified fifteen risk factors that contributed to adolescents who commit homicide. She divided these factors into social features and personality characteristics. The social features are child abuse, child neglect, absence of positive male role models; as well as societal factors such as, crisis in leadership, lack of heroes and witnessing violence; and resource availability, such as access to guns, involvement in alcohol and drugs, poverty, and lack of resources. The personality characteristics are low self-esteem, inability to deal with strong negative feelings, boredom and nothing to do, poor judgment, prejudice and hatred, and a sense of little or nothing left to lose (Heide, 1997, 1999).

IMPACT OF PSYCHIC TRAUMA ON VIOLENCE

Emotional trauma influences the pattern, intensity, and nature of sensory perceptual and affective experience of events during childhood (Perry, 1994; Perry et al., 1995). Exposure to violence activates a set of threat responses in the child's developing brain that alter the developing brain (Lauder, 1988; McAllister, Katz & Lo, 1999) and may manifest as changes in emotional, behavioral, and cognitive functioning.

Children vary in their individual responses to threats. The specific changes in neurodevelopment and functioning that occur will depend on the child's response to the threat, the specific nature of the violent experience(s), and a host of factors associated with children, their family and community (Perry & Azad, 1999).

POVERTY AND VIOLENCE

Children and adolescents growing in poverty, exposed to drug-related altercations and parental crime, are more violent than those growing up without these risk factors, as reported by the Office of Juvenile Justice and Delinquency Prevention (1998).

Poverty plays a significant role in creating violence. America has the highest rate of child poverty as compared to seventeen other industrialized countries. Unfortunately, poverty reduces parental involvement and supervision, therefore increasing defiant and delinquent behaviors (*Trop v. Dulles*, 1958; Ruttenberg, 1994).

In addition, impoverished adults are more likely to suffer from depression or substance abuse (Garbarino, 1999), which impairs their ability to parent properly. Combining poverty with earlier exposure to violence tends to push children and adolescents into violent crimes (Patterson, 1943).

In addition to exposure to violence, children's exposure to their parents' marital problems increases the risk of future domestic violence (Rosner, Wiederlight, Rosner, & Wieczorek, 1979). Thirty-three out of forty-five juvenile killers came from divorced family homes (Petti & Davidman, 1981). Clinical research reveals that children raised by single parents in poorer communities are at higher risk of dropping out of school, using drugs, and becoming delinquent than are those raised either in two-parent homes or by single parents with better economic resources.

IMPACT OF MEDIA VIOLENCE

In WWII, war was something fought "elsewhere." America's knowledge about what was "really happening" was sparse. Now, it is not only the soldiers who can see the horrors of war, but also anyone with a television or computer can experience the visual details of violence occurring around the world. An average child spends more than three hours a day watching television. The contents of television, videogames, music, and films have become increasingly violent (Donnerstein, Slaby, & Eron, 1995). Violent wrestling shows are some of the most popular programs on television. Huston and colleagues (1992) have estimated that the average eighteen-year-old will have viewed 200,000 acts of violence on television. Although it continues to be strongly contested, some say that even with solid emotional, behavioral, cognitive, and social anchors provided by a healthy home and community, this pervasive media violence can increase aggression and antisocial behavior (Lewis, Mallouh, & Webb, 1989; Myers et al., 1995). This process is accompanied by an increasing sense that the world is more dangerous than it is

(Gerbner, 1992) and desensitizes children to future violence (Perry & Azad, 1999).

PSYCHIATRIC ASPECTS OF VIOLENCE

Does mental illness make humans more violent? There are still arguments in the research literature as to whether the evidence supports this perception. There are substantial differences in the methods used in studies of the risk for violence in people with mental illness, resulting in a large variability in their estimates of risk (Gillies & O'Brien, 2006).

Substance abuse was the risk factor most commonly associated with an increase in the risk of violent behavior in mentally ill individuals. However, men suffering from schizophrenia with different histories of violence were assessed with neuropsychological testing (Naudts & Hodgins, 2006). The testing revealed that schizophrenics (with a stable pattern of antisocial and aggressive behavior since childhood) performed better on neuropsychological tests tapping specific executive functions but poorer on orbitofrontal functions when compared to schizophrenics with no history of violence. Violent schizophrenics showed fewer soft neurological signs. They displayed larger reductions in volume of the amygdala, more structural abnormalities of the orbitofrontal system, more abnormalities of white matter in the amygdalaorbitofrontal system, and smaller reductions in volumes of the hippocampus when compared to nonviolent individuals (Naudts & Hodgins, 2006).

Some individuals become violent with consumption of drugs or alcohol, or both, due to the lesser likelihood that they will follow conventional rules for social interaction (Ruttenberg, 1994). The financial burden of supporting a drug or alcohol habit may also necessitate the use of violence in the individual's life. Many adolescents who kill had previously used drugs and alcohol. Twenty-four (36%) of seventy-two homicidal juveniles studied regularly used alcohol; twenty-nine (40%) subjects in this group regularly or heavily used drugs (Office of Juvenile Justice and Delinquency Prevention, 1998). Similarly, Straus found that two-thirds of the twelve homicidal juveniles he studied had histories of substance abuse (Straus, 1974).

Certain psychiatric disorders should be considered while evaluating violent individuals, especially psychoses, substance abuse, conduct disorder, intermittent explosive disorder, and neurological disorders involving the frontal and temporal lobes. Myers and associates found that 97 percent of juvenile murderers had a *DSM-III-R* psychopathology. Their psychiatric diagnoses consisted of ADHD, conduct disorders, separation anxiety disorders, and phobias. These adolescents also exhibited family and school dysfunction, including histories of child abuse, exposure to prior violence, history of past arrests, and promiscuous sexual behavior (Myers et al., 1995).

Malmquist concluded that juvenile murderers are an inadequately treated, emotionally and behaviorally disturbed population with profound social problems. Suicidal ideation, drug use, child abuse, parental alcoholism, and mental illness significantly stood out as common characteristics of youth who kill (Malmquist, 1990). A number of published studies support a strong correlation between having a history of child abuse and juvenile violence (Duncan & Duncan, 1971; Malmquist, 1971).

Individuals with certain personality disorders, especially those with antisocial and paranoid types, are more predisposed to violence. Personality disorders are characterized by inflexible, maladaptive patterns of perceiving, relating to, and thinking about the environment and oneself. These patterns include antisocial, paranoid, avoidant, and dependent personality traits. The risk of violence may be understood in terms of four fundamental personality dimensions: (1) impulse control; (2) affect regulation; (3) narcissism; and (4) paranoid cognitive personality style.

Low impulse control and affect regulation increase the risk for violence across disorders, especially for primary and comorbid substance abuse disorders. Research has revealed that a paranoid cognitive personality style and narcissistic injury increases the risk for violence in persons with schizophrenia spectrum disorders and individuals with personality disorders (Nestor, 2002).

MEDICAL ASPECTS OF VIOLENCE

Medical disorders can present with violence or aggression. The major diagnoses that this is seen in are epilepsy, hypoxia, electrolyte disturbances, hepatic disorders, renal disease, systemic infections, hypoglycemia, hyperthyroidism, and heavy metal poisoning.

A possible relationship between epilepsy and violence has been debated for more than a century and "epilepsy defense" has been used in many criminal cases. There is no greater prevalence of epilepsy in persons convicted of violent crimes than in other prisoners matched as controls. There is no evidence that violence is more common among epileptics than among nonepileptics, and no evidence that violence is more common in patients with temporal lobe epilepsy than in those with other types of epilepsy. Ictal violence is rare, and when it does occur it usually takes the form of "resistive violence," as in the result of physical restraint at the end of a seizure while the patient is still confused. Violence early in a seizure is extremely rare, stereotyped, and never supported by consecutive series of purposeful movements

(Treiman, 1986).

While considering the previous medical causes of violence, one should rule out the presence of delirium. Medical literature indicates that hypoxia, electrolyte disturbances, hepatic disorders, renal disease, systemic infections, hypoglycemia, hyperthyroidism, and heavy metal poisoning can present as a neuropsychiatric syndrome known as delirium. Delirium is a complex neuropsychiatric syndrome with an acute onset and fluctuating course and is commonly found in many medical settings. It occurs with higher frequency in elderly people and in those with preexisting cognitive impairment or dementia. The core disturbance involves an acute generalized impairment of cognitive function that affects orientation, attention, memory, and planning and organizational skills. The treatment involves identifying the underlying medical disorder precipitating delirium, providing support, orientation, and psychotropic medications (Meagher, 2001).

CONCLUSION

Violence and its associated factors are complex and multidimensional. Some individuals may suffer from a mental illness that increases their violence potential, especially if these individuals also suffer from substance abuse. However, mental illness does not necessarily create a violent attitude. Other factors that may increase the risk of violence include growing up in poverty, exposure to family or neighborhood violence, and certain medical conditions. Violence in human beings is heterogeneous in nature because no single factor or gene can cause or explain violence. Each and every individual develops a different violence potential based on genetic and environmental influences. Therefore each individual's violence potential should be considered from all biological and environmental factors.

REFERENCES

Cleare, A. J., & Bond, A. J. (1997). Does central serotonergic function correlate inversely with aggression? A study using d-fenfluramine in healthy subjects. *Psychiatry Res, 69*, pp. 89–95.

Coffee, C. E., & Brumback, R. A. (1998). *Textbook of pediatric neuropsychiatry.* Washington, D.C.: American Psychiatric Press, Inc.

Collins, D., Davis, C., & Cherek, D. (1996). Tryptophan depletion and aggressive responding in healthy males. *Psychopharmacology, 126*, pp. 97–103.

Donnerstein, E. Slaby, R. & Eron, L. (1995). The mass media and youth aggression. In L. Eron, J. Gentry, & P. Schlegel (Eds.), *Reason to hope: A psychosocial perspective on violence and youth.* Washington, D.C.: American Psychological Association.

Duncan, J. W. & Duncan, G. M. (1971). Murder in the family: A study of some homicidal adolescents, *American Journal of Psychiatry, 127,* p. 1498.

Garbarino, J. (1999). *Lost boys: Why our sons turn violent and how we can save them.* New York: The Free Press.

Gerbner, G. (1992). Society's storyteller: How television creates the myths by which we live. *Media & Values, 59,* pp. 8–9.

Gillies, D., & O'Brien, L. (2006, May). Interpersonal violence and mental illness: a literature review. *Contemporary Nurse, 21*(2), pp. 277–286.

Heide, K. M. (1997, Spring). Juvenile homicide in America: How can we stop the killing? *Behavioral Sciences and Law, 15*(2), pp. 203–220.

Heide, K. M. (1999). *Young killers: The challenge of juvenile homicide.* Thousand Oaks, CA: Sage.

Huber, R., Smith, K., Delago, A. Isaksson, K., & Krvitz, E. (1997). Serotonin and aggressive motivation in crustaceans: Altering the decision to retreat. *Proceedings of the National Academy of Sciences, 94,* pp. 5939–5942.

Huston, A. C., Donnerstein, E., Fairchild, H., Ferhlach, N. & Katz, P. (1992). *Big world, small screen: The role of television in American society.* Lincoln, NE: University of Nebraska Press.

Lauder, J. M. (1988). Neurotransmitters as morphogens. *Progress in Brain Research, 73,* pp. 365–388.

Lewis, D. O., Mallouh, C., & Webb, V. (1989). Child abuse, delinquency, and violent criminality. In D. Chiccetti & V. Carlson (Eds.), *Child maltreatment: Theory and research on the causes and consequences of child abuse and neglect.* Cambridge, MA: Cambridge University Press.

Lidberg, L., Tuck, J., Asberg, M., Scalia-Tomba, G., & Bertilsson, L. (1985). Homicide, suicide and CSF 5-HIAA. *Acta Psychiatrica Scandinavica, 71,* pp. 230–236.

Lyons, M. J., True, W. R., Eisen, S. A., Goldberg, J., Meyer, J. M., Faranone, S. V., Eaver, L. J., & Tsuang, M. T. (1995). Differential heritability of adult and juvenile antisocial traits. *Archives of General Psychiatry, 52*(11), pp. 906–915.

Maclean, P.D. (1990). *The triune brain in evolution: Role in paleocerebral functions.* New York: Plenum Press.

Malmquist, C. (1971). Premonitory signs of homicidal aggression in juveniles. *American Journal of Psychiatry, 128*(4), pp. 93–97.

Malmquist, C. (1990). Depression in homicidal adolescents. *Bulletin American Academy Psychiatry Law, 18*(1), pp. 23–36

McAllister, A. K., Katz, L. C., & Lo, D. C. (1999). Neurotrophins and synaptic plasticity. *Annual Review of Neuroscience, 22,* pp. 295–318.

Meagher, D. J. (2001). Delirium: Optimising management. *British Medical Journal, 322,* pp. 144–149.

Mehlman, P., Higley, J., Faucher, I., Lily, A. A., Tauh, D. M., & Vickes, J. H. (1995). Low CSF-HIAA concentrations and severe aggression and impaired impulse control in nonhuman primates. *American Journal of Psychiatry, 151,* pp. 1485–1491.

Myers, W. C., Scott, K., Burgess, A. W., & Burgen, A. G. (1995). Psychopathology, biopsychosocial factors, crime characteristics and classification of 25 homicidal youths. *Journal of the American Academy of Child and Adolescent Psychiatry, 34*(11), pp. 1483–1489.

Naudts, K., & Hodgins, S. (2006). Neurobiological correlates of violent behavior among persons with schizophrenia. *Schizophrenia Bulletin, 32*(3), pp. 562–572.

Nestor, P.G. (2002). Mental disorder and violence: Personality dimensions and clinical features, *American Journal of Psychiatry 159,* pp. 1973–1978.

Office of Juvenile Justice and Delinquency Prevention. (1998). *Serious and violent juvenile offenders.* Washington, D.C.: U.S. Department of Justice, Office of Juvenile Justice and Delinquency Prevention.

Patterson, G. R. (1943). Psychiatric study of juveniles involved in homicide. *American Journal of Orthopsychiatry, 13,* pp. 125–139.

Perry, B. D. (1994). Neurobiological sequelae of childhood trauma: Post-traumatic stress disorders in children. In M. Murberg (Ed.), *Catecholamines in post-traumatic stress disorder: Emerging concepts* (pp. 253–276). Washington, D.C.: American Psychiatric Press.

Perry, B. D. (1997). Incubated in terror: Neuro developmental factors in the cycle of violence. In J. Osofsky (Ed.) *Children, youth and violence: The search for solutions.* (pp. 124–148). New York: Guilford Press.

Perry, B. D. (2001). The neurodevelopmental impact of violence in childhood. In D. Schetky & E. Benedek (Eds.), *Textbook of child and adolescent forensic psychiatry.* (pp. 221–238). Washington, D.C.: American Psychiatric Press, Inc.

Perry, B. D., & Azad, I. (1999). Post-traumatic stress disorders in children and adolescents. *Current Opinion in Pediatrics, 11*, pp. 121–132.

Perry, B. D., Pollard, R. A., Baker, W. L., Sturger, C., Vigilante, D., & Blakely, T. L. (1995). Continuous heart rate monitoring in maltreated children. *Annual Meeting of the American Academy of Child and Adolescent Psychiatry, New Research.*

Petti, T. A., & Davidman, L. (1981). Homicidal school-age children: Cognitive style and demographic features. *Child Psychiatry & Human Development, 12*, pp. 82–85.

Pfeiffer, C. (1998). Juvenile crime and violence in Europe. *Crime & Justice, 23*(255), pp. 257–258.

Raine, A., Stoddard, J., Bihrle, S., & Buchsbaum, M. (1998). Prefrontal glucose deficits in murderers lacking psychosocial deprivation. *Neuropsychiatry Neuropsychol Behav Neuro, 11*(1), pp. 1–7.

Reisner, I., Mann, J., Stanley, M., Huang, Y., & Houpt, K. (1996). Comparison of cerebrospinal fluid monoamine metabolite levels in dominant-aggressive and non-aggressive dogs. *Brain Research, 714*, pp. 57–64.

Rosner, R., Wiederlight, M., Rosner, M.B., & Wieczorek, R. R. (1979). Adolescents accused of murder and manslaughter: A five-year descriptive study. *Bulletin of the American Academy of Psychiatry & Law, 4*, pp. 342–351.

Ruttenberg, H. (1994). The limited promise of public health methodologies to prevent youth violence, *Yale Law Journal, 103*, pp. 1885–1896.

Slutske, W.S. (2000). The genetics of antisocial behavior. *Current Psychiatry Rep, 3*(2), pp. 158–162.

Straus, M. (1974). Cultural and organizational influences on violence between family members. In R. Prince & D. Barried (Eds.), *Configurations: Biological and cultural factors in sexuality and family life.* Washington, D.C.: Health.

Treiman, D. M. (1986). Epilepsy and violence: Medical and legal issues. *Epilepsia, 27* (Suppl) 2, pp. S77–S104.

Trop v. Dulles (1958), 356 U.S. 86, 101.

Vitiello, B., & Stoff, D. M. (1997). Subtypes of aggression and their relevance to child psychiatry. *Journal of American Academy of Child Adolescent Psychiatry, 36*(3), pp. 307–315.

Chapter 17

HISTORY OF WAR CRIMES, MARTYRDOM, AND SUICIDE BOMBERS/WARRIORS

Jamshid A. Marvasti and Valerie L. Dripchak

What a vast difference there is between the barbarism that precedes culture and the barbarism that follows it.

Christian Friedrich Hebbel (1813–1869)

To observe the past is to take warning for the future.

Lope de Vega

INTRODUCTION

People who are now known as terrorists were once called "incendiaries" because they started fires or set off incendiary devices. The first person identified in this way was a seventeenth-century Scottish nationalist, John Painter. The term "terrorist" was initially used in 1795 to describe the actions of the Jacobean revolutionaries. Throughout this "reign of terror" the Jacobeans were rumored to have coined this term to describe their method of forcing opponents' compliance by arrest or torture. During the nineteenth century in Russia, Alexander II was assassinated by an anarchist or Narodnik (Populist), who now would be labeled a terrorist (*Wikipedia Encyclopedia*: Terrorism).

In this chapter, we present the literature that explores the political violence relating to modern-day terrorism. There is also a historical review of such topics as war crimes, martyrdom, and suicide warriors because they illustrate similarities in spite of different positions or points of view.

HISTORICAL DEFINITIONS OF WAR CRIME

The terror of the unseen is what the science of history hides, turning a disaster into an epic.

Philip Roth

History is usually written by the victors in wars. Losers of war cannot bring charges against the victors or identify the war crimes against them because they are without any power or authority to do so. The main concept within a "war crime" is that individuals can be held responsible for their actions as soldiers or actions as a group or a nation. Although prisoners of war and combatants may not be punished for acts they committed during fighting (unless the other side punished its own soldiers for those same acts as well) mistreatment of civilians or soldiers, crimes against humanity, and genocide fall under the category of war crimes.

There have been attempts to control wartime behavior for thousands of years. Although it was generally accepted that war atrocities were part of "the nature of the beast," the beast was war itself. The First Geneva Convention "laws of war" were signed in 1864 and were modified several times (1899, 1907, 1925, and 1929) before WW II (Trombly, 2003). After WW II, the massacre of Jewish civilians by the Nazi army and the mistreatment of civilians and prisoners of war by the Japanese army prompted the Allied Forces (the victors) to prosecute those who perpetrated these crimes. The Nuremberg Trials ended with the execution of twelve Nazi leaders, and in 1948, seven Japanese commanders were hanged following a similar process (Kafala, 2003). Even though Emperor Hirohito was not put on trial by the Allied Forces, it is conceivable that if the Japanese had been the victors, the American commanders and the U.S. president would have been charged with war crimes because of the deliberate killing of civilians in Hiroshima and Nagasaki.

Although war crimes have been adjudicated at The Hague International Court in modern times, there are individual governments who act on their own. An example of this action was the kidnap, trial, and subsequent hanging of Adolf Eichmann by Israel in 1960. In 2005 to 2006, the Italian Justice System and the German Court System charged CIA agents with the kidnapping and abduction of their citizens, transferring them to Egypt and Afghanistan for coercive interrogation (Abadi, 2007; *Il Giornale*, 2007; *Time*, 2007). Apparently, these actions were part of the "War on Terrorism."

The law on war crimes continues to evolve with the accepted current consensus from the Fourth Geneva Convention: "Willful killing, torture or inhuman treatment, causing great suffering or serious injury to body or health, unlawful transfer or confinement of person or property not justified by military necessity and carried out wantonly" (Kafala, 2003). The most recent attempt to define "laws of war" was in 2003 when the Rome Treaty established an International Criminal Court. Although 90 countries have ratified this treaty, the United States refused to sign it as the U.S. was concerned that the court could be used for "politically motivated prosecutions" of Americans (Kafala, 2003).

War crimes continue to be committed today, with some nations or groups going unchallenged. Alain Gresh (2006), in Le Monde Diplomatique; explained that Article 54 of the Geneva Convention states that starving civilians as a method of warfare is prohibited. This same Article also forbids the following: "to attack, destroy, remove or render useless objects that are indispensable to the survival of the civilian population." Gresh suggested that this Article be applied to the Israeli army's offensive incursion into the occupied territories and that their actions be considered war crimes because they blockaded the civilian population. Likewise, the bombing of Gaza's power station, which resulted in the loss of electricity for 750,000 Palestinians during the intense summer heat, also should be considered war crimes within the scope of this document (Gresh, 2006).

Rob de Wijk (2003) explored war crimes committed by the Dutch army in fighting insurgents in Indonesia in a strategy of search-and-destroy missions. He explained that the Dutch army's counterinsurgent operations could be perceived as war crimes because they did not discriminate between combatants and civilians. The Dutch burned down entire villages in order to eliminate warrior bases. Similarly past U.S. Secretary of Defense, Donald Rumsfeld, argued that force is needed "to drain the swamp they live in" (Knowlton, 2001, p. 6).

The concept of war crimes continues to be tested within international law. The trials of Yugoslav President Milosevic and Saddam Hussein are the current examples of victors trying losers. Saddam was hanged and Milosevic was sent to prison because they were found guilty of war crimes.

HISTORICAL DEFINITION OF MARTYRDOM IN ISLAM

Martyr is the heart of history.
Doctor Ali Shariati (Iranian sociologist)[1]

The cause, not the death, makes martyrs.
Napoleon I

Islam has a branch that is called Shia. Most Shia live in Iran, Southern Lebanon, and Iraq. Martyrdom is an important tenet of this branch. Their hero is Imam Hussein, the grandson of Mohammed the Prophet. He and seventy-two of his comrades were surrounded at the city of Karbala in Iraq by an enemy of several thousand, and all were killed. This event became the most significant case of Islamic martyrdom for the Shia. The night before the final battle, Imam Hussein told his comrades that they had a choice of surrender or fighting to the death. He had decided to fight yet asked his men if they wished to leave the camp in the middle of the night to avoid this certain death. None of his men chose to defect, and the next day they all became martyrs. Imam Hussein is called "King of," "Lord of," and "Master of Martyrs" (Shams al-Din, 1985).

This event created a milestone in Islamic religion, and the Shia recognize the anniversary of his death every year. This annual commemoration for Imam Hussein is called Ashura. In the month of the anniversary, millions of Shia Moslems gather in groups to honor him. They beat their chests, they hit their backs with chains, and they cry or yell slogans about martyrdom and Imam Hussein. Slogans such as "everyday is Ashura" and "every land is Karbala" are well-known in the Shia population. The identification with this image of Imam Hussein, "the Ultimate Martyr," and the 72 other martyrs are pure motivation for self-sacrifice. The highest honor in Shia society is to be a martyr such as Imam Hussein (Shams al-Din, 1985).

The significance of Ashura was illustrated by the Shah Abbas, an Iranian monarch who lived 500 years ago. He arranged for his wars to begin on the anniversary of the death of Imam Hussein and the seventy-two martyrs. During the memorial gathering, the soldiers became excited, beating their chests and crying for the martyrs. While they were captivated and energized like this, Shah Abbas would order the attack on the enemy.

HISTORY OF SUICIDE WARRIORS

Suicide Attackers in Ancient Times

According to anthropologist Scott Atran (2003b), suicide terrorist attacks may be traced back to two thousand years ago with the revolt of the Jews against the Roman rule in Judea. At that time the Jewish sects of Zealots and Sicarii wanted to revive Jewish public sentiment against Jewish collaborators; against the Greeks, who had settled in and desecrated the sacred soil of Israel; and against the Romans, who ruled Judea. These Jewish sects initially began their uprising in their youth by throwing stones; the Roman soldiers responded by using wooden staves (instead of swords) to control the crowds (Atran, 2003b). In looking at modern times, one may see some surprising similarities. Today, it is the Palestinians who are throwing stones at the Israelis; and Israeli forces may use plastic bullets (in addition to real ones) to disperse them. As Atran has noted, historically, Jewish sects' attacks intensified with the use of "suicide dagger attacks" in public forums, hoping to force Rome to increase their brutal reactions. Their intention was to gain support from the general Jewish population for the uprising by inciting more violence. Thus, these first suicide attacks would serve to unite the Jewish population to support the rebellion. Although the revolt ended in 73 A.D. this example of suicide activism inspired more uprisings in future generations (Atran, 2003b).

Around the same time, a Moslem activist group in Iran assassinated their enemies by killing them with knives in "close quarters." The leaders of this group reportedly gave these killers hashish to help inspire them for their assignment, during which they would definitely be killed (therefore a kind of suicide). The modern word, assassin, is derived from this word hashish (*Wikipedia Encyclopedia*: Suicide Bombing).

The period of the Crusades is another time in recorded history that people intentionally died so that the enemy also endured loss of lives. During this time, the Knights Templar destroyed one of their own ships (killing 140 Christians) in order to kill ten times as many Muslims (*Wikipedia Encyclopedia*: Suicide Bombing).

There are some indications that suicide attacks and self-sacrifice were also evident in American military history. At the Alamo in Texas, certain American soldiers voluntarily stayed despite the clearly overwhelming force of Mexican soldiers. In South Carolina, African American Union Army soldiers carried out a suicide attack against a Confederate prison (Answer.com).

Suicide Warriors in the First Part of the Twentieth Century

During WWII, the Japanese kamikaze repeatedly used fully fueled fighter planes to crash into ships and buildings that contained U.S. military personnel. This destruction was significant as well as alarming and eventually became one of the main reasons that American leaders supported the use of the atomic bomb in the Pacific Theater. In just one series of these attacks, the 1945 Battle of Okinawa, approximately 2,000 kamikaze attackers rammed their planes into more than 300 ships, killing 4,900 sailors and wounding more than 4,800 additional people (Axel, 2002).

During the Vietnam War, the U.S. military documented a number of incidents in which deaths were caused by Vietnamese children who had explosives strapped to their bodies. After these "suicide warriors" mingled socially with the American soldiers, their explosives were detonated. The frequency of these incidents continues to be debated, but these suicide attacks were cited by the military to condone the use of deadly force against Vietnamese children (*Wikipedia Encyclopedia*: Military Use of Children).

Modern-Day Suicide Activism

According to Atran (2003a, b), there have been more acts of suicide terrorism in the twentieth and twenty-first centuries than in all the past centuries combined, primarily due to the development of explosives. Suicide terrorism tends to be used by those groups who are less powerful against parties who are materially stronger. This occurs particularly when less-expensive fighting methods do not bring the type of impact against the enemy.

Generally, the news media and literature support that terrorism and suicide attacks are the weapons of a weaker party that is fighting a more organized and stronger government. Chomsky (2001) challenged this theory and declared that "terrorism is not the weapon of the weak, but the weapon of those who are against us," whoever "us" happens to be. He suggested that it is primarily a weapon of the strong because the strong control the doctrinal systems of the populace. Therefore, their terror methods do not count as terrorism but are classified as counterterrorism.

Many partisan groups have existed in Europe during the past two decades. The Italian Red Brigade, French Direct Action, German Red Army Faction, Provisional IRA, and the independent Basques in Spain have all used tactics that could identify them as terrorist organizations in the eyes of the beholders.

Middle East Warriors

The first recorded contemporary suicide attack occurred in 1980 in Iran during the Iran-Iraq War. Hossein Fahmideh, a thirteen-year-old Iranian boy, detonated himself as he jumped underneath an Iraqi tank. The results were the disabling of the tank, which stopped the Iraqi tank division's advance and his own death (*Wikipedia Encyclopedia*: Hossein Fahmideh). In *My Life Is a Weapon*, Reuter (2002) describes the genesis of the modern "culture of death" by referring to the "human bomb" and suicide warriors. During the eight years of the Iran-Iraq war, the Iranian army had "Suicide Battalions." These warriors were inspired by the Imam Hussein martyrdom in Karbala in 680, A.D. They raced in "human wave attacks" into the Iraqi military lines and were blown up as they ran across minefields. This tactic of martyrdom (self-sacrifice), as explained by Reuter (2002), was exported to Lebanon's Shias and from there spread to non-Shia Muslim groups and followers of other religions (e.g., Hinduism).

The historical literature (Schweitzer, 2000; Atran, 2003b) reveals that another contemporary suicide terrorist attack occurred in December 1981, with the destruction of the Iraqi embassy in Beirut. Twenty-seven people were killed and more than 100 injured in this attack. After the assassination of Lebanese President Basher Gemayel in September 1982, suicide bombing became institutionalized as a popular political weapon in the Middle East. In 1983, a small group known as Hezbollah directed a series of suicide attacks against western targets in their own land. The first of these attacks was aimed against the American embassy in Beirut (April), followed by attacks on the U.S. Marines headquarters and the French Multinational Force (October), who were stationed in Lebanon. The last two simultaneous attacks resulted in 300 deaths and dozens of serious injuries. By 1985, the effect of these attacks led Israel to yield most of the territory gained during their 1982 invasion and occupation of Lebanon. The Hezbollah suicide attacks at that time also led to the withdrawal of western forces as well as the U.N. Peace Keeping forces from Lebanon. The outcome of these suicide missions served to bring a small and little known political group to international attention.

According to Schweitzer (2000), suicide terrorism in Israel and Palestine began in 1992. The attacks were initiated by Hamas, the Hezbollah-trained members of the Islamic Resistance movement, and the Palestine Islamic Jihad (PIJ), whose main goal is to force the Israeli Army to leave their OP (Occupied Palestine). Other suicide activist groups include the Egyptian Islamic Jihad and the Gama's al-Islamiya, who each carried out one attack in 1995. The Gama's al-Islamiya attacked a police station in Rijake as a retaliatory act to the disappearance of one of its group leaders and his eventual extradition to Egypt. The Jihad Group used two suicide bombers to destroy the Egyptian embassy in Pakistan, killing fifteen people and wounding more than thirty. It is noteworthy that both groups avoided using suicide activities on Egyptian soil because they did not want to alienate their constituency in Egypt. That country is also known to have a more efficient, but brutal, security forces as compared to other countries.

Liberation Tigers of Tamil Eelam (LTTE)

The LTTE is a secular group of men and women whose mission was to secede from the Sri Lankan government and establish an independent Tamil state. The LTTE has been known for its fierce and well-trained fighters, who are dedicated to their cause and pioneered the use of suicide bombing vests (Balasingham, 2003). The *BBC News* (2000) cited them as responsible for more suicide attacks than any other group in history. According to Mansdorf (2003), the Tigers are given cyanide pills to avoid being captured alive and disclosing military information. Morgan (2001) described the suicide bomber as "a mind like steel but a heart like petals of a flower."

Al-Qaeda Terrorists

The more recent networking of militant groups from North Africa, the Arabian Peninsula, and Central and Southeast Asia through Al-Qaeda stemmed from the Soviet-Afghan War (1979–1989). According to Atran (2003b), the United States provided financial and technical backing to enable these groups to unify their doctrines, training and methods (including suicide attacks). Al-Qaeda, led by Osama bin Laden, has been responsible for some of the most deadly attacks in modern times. In August 1998 simultaneous suicide attacks against the American embassies in Nairobi and in Dar-e-Sallaam resulted in 300 deaths and 5000 wounded (Schweitzer, 2000). On September 11, 2001, this group was accused of the attacks against the Twin Towers in New York and the Pentagon in Washington, D.C. These September 11, 2001, attacks in the United States are considered to be the most "historical event" that they have perpetrated. As Chomsky (2001, 2002) explains, this event was especially significant because the directions of the guns changed; now going toward the United States. For the first time since 1814 (the burning of Washington, D.C. by the British), the national territory of the United States was attacked by foreigners.

Iranian Suicide Bomber/Warrior

At the time of the Shah's dictatorship there were no reported suicide attacks against the regime, but there were incidents that when the partisans were surrounded by police, they used their last bullet on themselves and committed suicide rather than surrender to the enemy. After the Islamic revolution, several suicide attacks were made by oppositional groups (e.g., Mojahedin Khalgh), which resulted in the death of a warrior and his target. On September 28, 1981, Hashemi Nejad, one of the high-level clergymen, was assassinated at the end of his teaching session in the city of Mashhad.[2] Shahid Sadoughi was killed in the same manner by a suicide bomber who had a grenade in his pants and was able to get close to this high-ranking clergyman from the city of Yazd.[3]

History of Jewish Terrorism

According to historical literature, it was a liability in 1936 to support the Jewish people's request for a homeland. Because Great Britain needed the Arab oil supplies, the British agreed to limit Jewish emigration to Palestine. Following WWII, Jewish extremist groups, like the Irgun and the Stern gang, developed strategies that were similar to today's militant Palestinians in order to reestablish Israel as their nation. Some of their actions included the blowing up of the King David Hotel in Jerusalem in July, 1946, leaving ninety-one people dead. Another action led to the assassination of Lord Moyne, a British foreign office minister, and Count Bernadotte, a U.N. mediator, as well as a number of the Swedish royal family in 1948. It was further noted that some of the future Israeli prime ministers, namely Menachem Begin and Yitzhak Shamir, were members of these militant groups (*Wikipedia Encyclopedia*: Jewish terrorists).

CONCLUSION

The history of political violence and suicide activity against powerful enemies dates back to ancient times. What is different, in the present time, is the extent of the lethality of the weapons and the speed of conveying the information to the world. Also, the extent of distortion, disinformation, justification, war propaganda, and double standards has increased substantially due to the possible presence of the global news media and information technology. Religion has always been exploited by warriors to legitimize their violence or persuade their comrades to fight for their goals. Since history is written mostly by the victor, "history" no longer may be considered the "judge" and "fact finder." At times differentiating between "terrorist" and "freedom fighter" is difficult, and Mohammad and Ali's hero and martyr become George's and Tony's terrorist and fascist. As Arthur Schlesinger, Jr. pointed out, "historians are prisoners of their own experiences" (2007). We all bring to the historical accounts the biases of our culture, our age, and our personalities. Therefore, the quest to achieve objectivity may only be an illusive goal.

NOTES

1. Doctor Ali Shariati was an Iranian sociologist who wrote some of the most progressive books about Islam. In his books he attempted to present a clear and authentic picture of Islam. He felt that if the new generations could have a more truthful understanding of Islam, social change would be more successful. Shariati received his doctorate in sociology in 1964 from the Sorbonne University. When he returned to Iran, he was arrested at the border by the Shah Regime and accused of participating in hostile political activity while studying in France. He was released in 1965 and began teaching and lecturing. Later he underwent a second prison term under harsh conditions for eighteen months. However, he was released after popular pressure and international protest against the Iranian regime. He remained under surveillance by the Iranian security police (SAVAK). He eventually went to England and within a short period of time died unexpectedly. There are rumors that he was possibly

murdered by his enemies (for more information please see: www.shariati.com/bio.html).

2. Abdul-Karim Hashemi Nejad was a prominent Islamic clergyman and is considered to be one of the great Shia scholars of his time. After the establishment of the Iranian Islamic revolution he became one of the religious leaders in Khorasan Providence, Iran. In 1981, he was attacked by a grenade while teaching in a classroom. He is considered a martyr, and there has been a university named in his honor.

3. Mohammad Sadoughi was a prominent clergyman in the Yazd providence in Iran. He was deeply involved in the Iranian Islamic revolution of 1979. He was assassinated by a suicide bomber who carried a grenade in his pants and detonated it while hugging Sadoughi. Sadoughi is considered to be a martyr and a university has been named in his honor.

REFERENCES

Abadi, C. (2007, Spring). Disappeared but not silenced. *Amnesty International, 23*, p. 12–15.

Answer.com Suicide attack, history [On-line]. Retrieved November 29, 2006. Available: http://www.answers.com/topic/suicide-attack

Atran, S. (2003a). Genesis of suicide terrorism. *Science, 299*, pp. 1534–1539.

Atran, S. (2003b). Genesis and future of suicide terrorism [On-line]. Retrieved December 12, 2006. Available: http://www.interdisciplines.org/terrorism/papers/1

Axel, A. (2002). *Kamikaze*. New York: Longman.

Balasingham, A. (2003). *The will to freedom- An inside of Tamil resistance*. Mitcham, England: Fairmax Publishing, LTD.

BBC News (2000, May 2). Tamil tigers: A fearsome force [On-line]. Retrieved on August 25, 2006. Available: http://news.bbc.co.uk/1/hi/world/south_asia/526407.stm

Chomsky, N. (2001, October). The new war against terror. *Chomsky.Info* [On-line]. Retrieved on February 12, 2007. Available: www.chomsky.info/talks/20011018.htm

Chomsky, N. (2002). *911*. New York: Seven Stories Press.

Chomsky, N., & Achcar, G. (2007). *Perilous power: The Middle East and U.S. foreign policy*. Boulder, CO: Paradigm Publishers.

Il Giornale (2007, Gennaio 30) America Oggi. Abu Omar, le accuse di Pollari: "Mi sento un capro espiatorio," p. 12

de Wijk, R. (2003). The limits of military power. In T. J. Lennon (Ed.), *The battle for hearts and minds* (pp. 3–28).Cambridge, MA: MIT Press.

Gresh, A. (2006, June). Israel's offensive against peace: War crimes. *Le Monde diplomatique* [On-line]. Retrieved February 7, 2007. Available: http://mondediplo.com/2006/06/19palestine?var_recherche=palestinian%20children

Kafala, T. (2003, July). What is a war crime? *BBC News* [On-line]. Viewpoints, 496, Retrieved August 23, 2006. Available: http://news.bbc.co.uk

Knowlton, B. (2001, September 19). But Rumsfeld says arrest of rebel might not avert retaliation by America: Afghan clerics weigh handover of bin Laden. *International Herald Tribune*, p. 6.

Mansdorf, I. J. (2003, April 15). The psychological framework of suicide terrorism. *Jerusalem Letter/Viewpoints*, 496 [On-line]. Retrieved September 10, 2006. Available: www.jcpa.org/jl/vp496.htm

Morgan, J. (2001, September 19). Fanatical, but not insane. *Baltimore Sun*, p. 2a.

Reuter, C. (2002). *My life is a weapon: A modern history of suicide bombing.* Princeton, NJ: Princeton University Press.

Schlesinger, A. M. (2007, January 17). History remains the best antidote to the temptations of military might. *Manchester Journal Inquirer*, p. 19.

Schweitzer Y. (2000, February 21). *Suicide terrorism: Development & characteristics.* Presentation at the International Conference on Countering Suicide Terrorism, Herzeliya, Israel.

Shams al-Din, S. M. M. (1985). *The rising of Al Husayn: Its impact on the consciousness of Muslim society.* Boston, MA: Routledge & Kegan Paul.

Time Magazine (2007, March 5). Europe Raps the CIA, p. 18.

Trombly, M. (2003). A brief history of the laws of war. *Society of Professional Journalists* [On-line]. Retrieved March 1, 2007. Available: http://www.globalissuesgroup.com/geneva/history.html

Wikipedia Encyclopedia: Terrorism [On-line]. Retrieved May 15, 2006. Available: http://en.wikipedia.org/wiki/Terrorism

Wikipedia Encyclopedia: Suicide bombing [On-line]. Retrieved December 5, 2005. Available: http://en.wikipedia.org/wiki/Suicide_bombing

Wikipedia Encyclopedia: Military use of children [On-line]. Retrieved December 5, 2005. Available: http://en.wikipedia.org/wiki/Military_use_of_children

Wikipedia Encyclopedia: Jewish terrorists [On-line]. Retrieved December 5, 2005. Available: http://en.wikipedia.org/wiki/jewishterrorists

Wikipedia Encyclopedia: Hossein Fahmideh [On-line]. Retrieved December 5, 2005. Available: http://en.wikipedia.org/wiki/Hossein_Fahmideh

INDEX

319

256–257, 264, 292, 311
Vietnam Syndrome, xiv, 16, 189–190
Vigilante, D., 244, 267, 306
Violence
    Definition of, 297
    Impact of age on, 300
    Impact of media, 301
    Impact of psychic trauma on, 300
    Medical aspects of, 303
    Neurobiology of human, 298
    Origins of, 298
    Physiologic pathways to, 299
    Poverty and, 301
    Psychiatric aspects of, 302
    Risk factors for, 300
Vitiello, B., 298, 306
Volkan, V., 15, 18–19, 27, 33–35, 38, 45, 49,
        56, 58–59, 114, 120, 187, 189, 192,
        205
Von Drehle, D., 106, 120
Vostanis, P., 228–229, 236, 240
Vythilingam, M., 265

W

Wagner, A. W., 71, 77
War (*see also* Violence)
    Cause of, 15
    Freud's statement regarding, 16
    Theories of, 15–16
War Crimes
    Geneva Conventions, xx–xxi, 308–309
    Hague International Conference, 308
    "Laws of War," 308–309
Washington Post, 54, 104, 111, 120, 191, 205
Waters, R., 125, 135
Watson, C. O., 229, 232, 240
Webb, V., 301, 305
Wedig, M. M., 268
Weisaeth, L., 268
Weise, D., 205
Welter, S., 265
West Bank, 13, 27, 49, 50, 53–54, 74, 107,

109, 150, 174, 181–182, 193–194,
205, 207, 213–214, 216, 218, 220,
222–228, 230–233, 237, 288–289
Whalen, P. J., 268
Wheels of Justice, 137, 165, 173
Wieczorek, R. R., 301, 306
Wiederlight, M., 301, 306
Williams, M. E., 56–57, 59, 76, 119, 135, 165,
        179–180, 182
Williams, C., 265
Williford, R. B., 250, 265
Wilson, S., 37, 54, 59
Wilson, Woodrow, 197–198, 204–205
Wong, C. M., 249, 268
Woodward, B., 193, 205
Woody, W., 35, 57
World Health Organization, 218, 225–226,
        240
World War I, 45, 48–49, 125, 156–157, 179,
        190, 192, 194, 197–198, 242, 246
World War II, 11, 40, 44, 49, 58, 93, 125, 139,
        153, 157, 179, 186, 190, 242, 246,
        301, 311, 314
Wright, C. I., 248, 267, 268

Y

Yahya, A., 236, 240
Yazd (Iran), 314, 316
Yehuda, R., 62, 68, 77, 242, 247, 266, 268

Z

Zacharia Zubeidi, 38
Zatzick, D. F., 263, 268
Zedalis, D. D., 281–282, 284
Zinn, H., 142, 145, 155–157, 159, 165–166,
        169, 183
Zionists, 4, 36, 91, 213
Zohar, J., 265
Zoroya, G., 18, 27, 74
Zusman, R. M., 267

ABOUT THE EDITOR

Jamshid A. Marvasti, M.D. is an adult and child psychiatrist practicing at Manchester Memorial Hospital in Manchester, Connecticut for the last thirty years. He is the author of a number of articles and chapters of books on the subject of psychic trauma and psychotherapy. In 2000, he edited *Child Suffering in the World: Child Maltreatment by Parents, Cultures and Governments in Different Countries and Cultures.* He is the principal author and editor of two books: *Psychiatric Treatment of Victims and Survivors of Sexual Trauma* and *Psychiatric Treatment of Sexual Offenders* both published in 2004 by Charles C Thomas, Publishers. Doctor Marvasti was previously an Associate Clinical Professor of Psychiatry at the University of Connecticut.

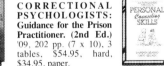
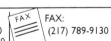

Due Date	Date Ret...	www...
JUL 0 8 2010	JUL 0 6 2010	
OCT 2 5 2012	OCT 2 5 2012	
ImarU10/SS	MAR 1 6	

www.library.humber.ca